In this volume, and on the cover, you'll meet a character who looks exactly like Chitoge. Also, in the *Nisekoi* video game* that will hit shelves right around when this volume comes out, there's a character who's identical to Chitoge. We didn't coordinate the two on purpose—the world is full of mysterious coincidences!

*Currently only available in Japan

Naoshi Komi

NAOSHI KOMI was born in Kochi Prefecture, Japan, on March 28, 1986. His first serialized work in *Weekly Shonen Jump* was the series *Double Arts*. His current series, *Nisekoi*, is serialized in *Weekly Shonen Jump*.

NISEKOI:
False Love
VOLUME 16
SHONEN JUMP Manga Edition

Story and Art by
NAOSHI KOMI

Translation ✐ Camellia Nieh
Touch-Up Art & Lettering ✐ Stephen Dutro
Design ✐ Fawn Lau
Shonen Jump Series Editor ✐ John Bae
Graphic Novel Editor ✐ Amy Yu

NISEKOI © 2011 by Naoshi Komi
All rights reserved.
First published in Japan in 2011
by SHUEISHA Inc., Tokyo.
English translation rights arranged
by SHUEISHA Inc.

The stories, characters and incidents mentioned
in this publication are entirely fictional.

Printed in the U.S.A.

Published by VIZ Media, LLC
P.O. Box 77010
San Francisco, CA 94107

10 9 8 7 6 5 4 3 2 1
First printing, July 2016

www.shonenjump.com

www.viz.com

NISEKOI

False Love

vol. 16: Look-Alike

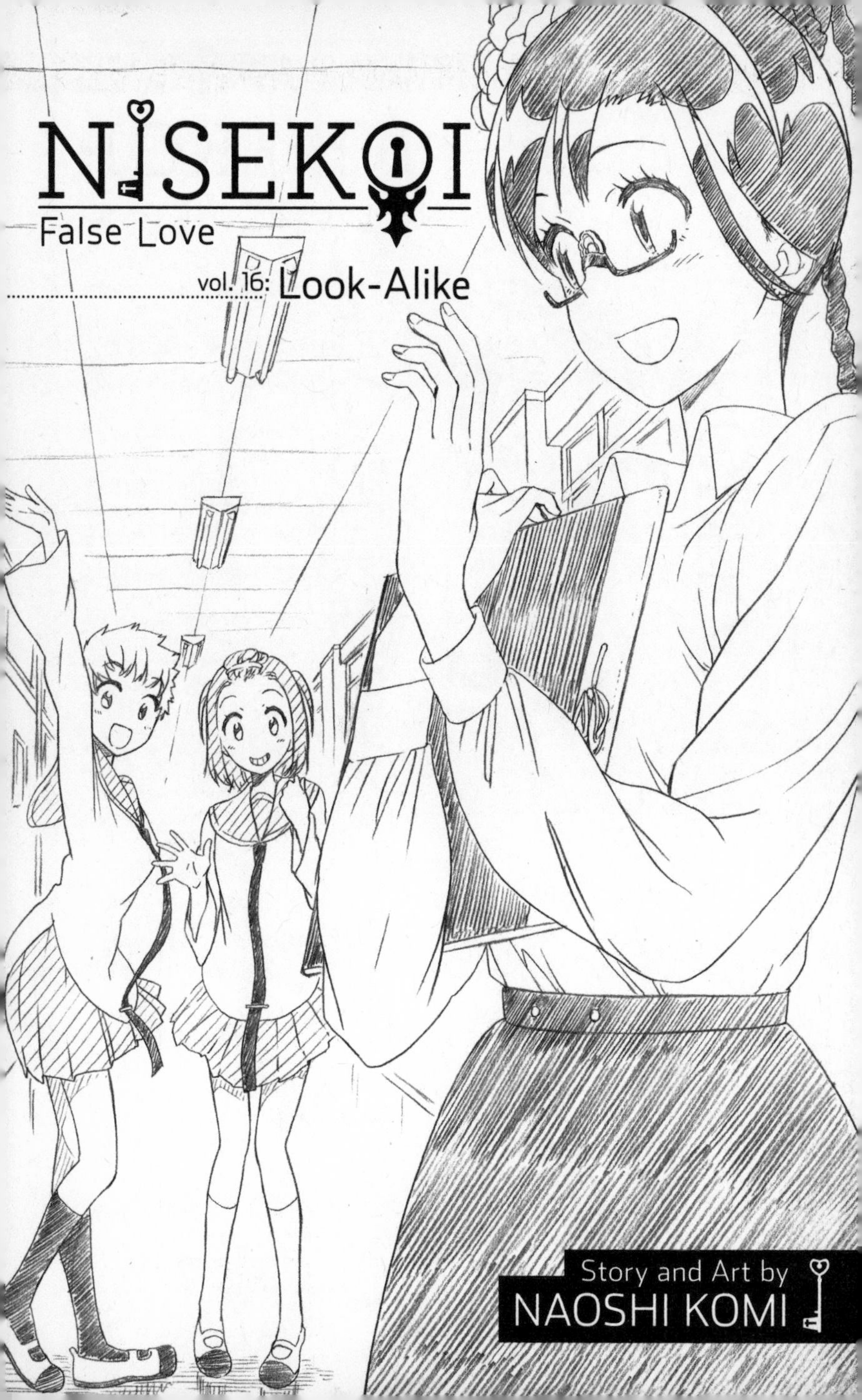

Story and Art by
NAOSHI KOMI

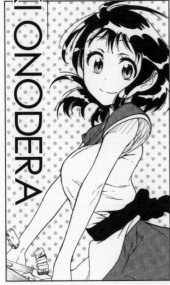

CHITOGE KIRISAKI

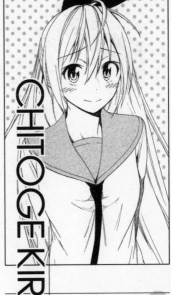

A half-Japanese bombshell with stellar athletic abilities. Short-tempered and violent. Comes from a family of gangsters.

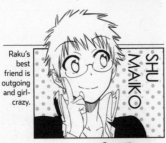

RAKU ICHIJO

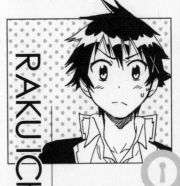

A normal teen whose family happens to be yakuza. Cherishes a pendant given to him by a girl he met ten years ago.

KOSAKI ONODERA

A girl Raku has a crush on. Beautiful and sweet, Kosaki has no shortage of admirers. She's a terrible cook but makes food that *looks* amazing.

SHU MAIKO

Raku's best friend is outgoing and girl-crazy.

RURI MIYAMOTO

Kosaki's best gal pal. Comes off as aloof, but is actually a devoted and highly intuitive friend.

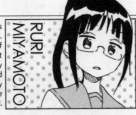

MARIKA TACHIBANA

Daughter of the chief of police, Marika is Raku's fiancée, according to an agreement made by their fathers—an agreement Marika takes very seriously! Also has a key and remembers making a promise with Raku ten years ago.

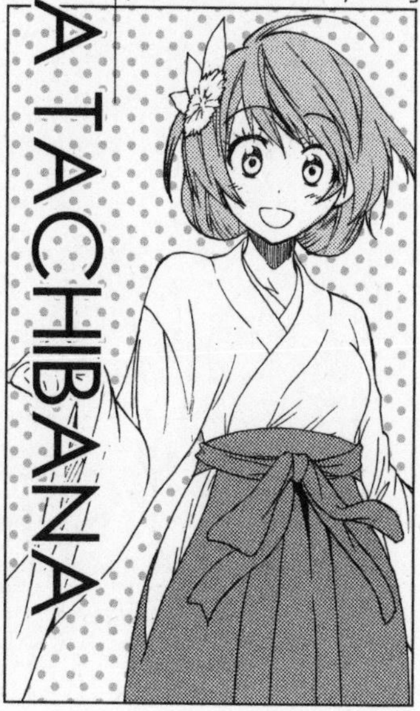

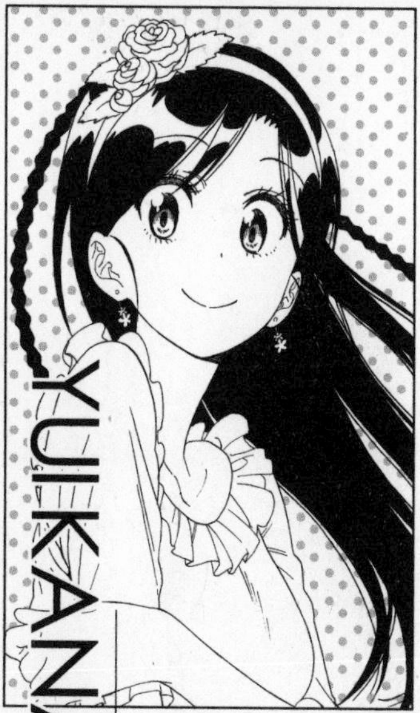

YUI KANAKURA

A childhood friend of Raku's, Yui is the head of a Chinese mafia gang and the homeroom teacher of Raku's class at his school. She is currently staying at Raku's house and also has a special key linked to some kind of promise...

CHARACTERS & STORY

Ten years ago, Raku Ichijo made a promise with a girl he loved that they would get married when they met again...and he still treasures the pendant she gave him to seal their pledge.

Thanks to his family's circumstances, Raku has to pretend he's dating Chitoge Kirisaki, the daughter of a rival gangster. Despite their constant spats, Raku and Chitoge manage to fool everyone. Chitoge also has a token from her first love ten years ago—an old key. Meanwhile, Raku's crush, Kosaki, also has a key, as does Marika, the girl Raku's father has arranged for him to marry. Now, Raku's childhood friend Yui has been hired as their homeroom teacher. It turns out that she, too, has a key connected to a special promise. Where will all their hearts lead them?!

SEISHIRO TSUGUMI

Trained as an assassin in order to protect Chitoge, Tsugumi is often mistaken for a boy.

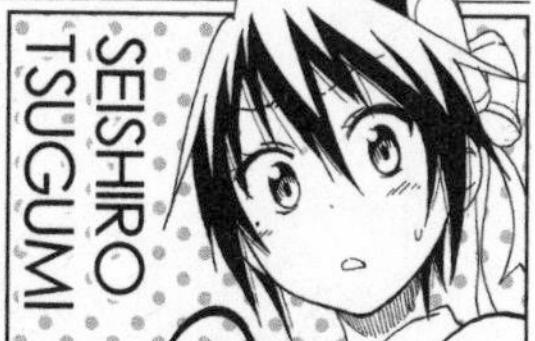

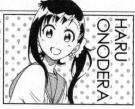

HARU ONODERA

Kosaki's adoring younger sister. Has a low opinion of Raku.

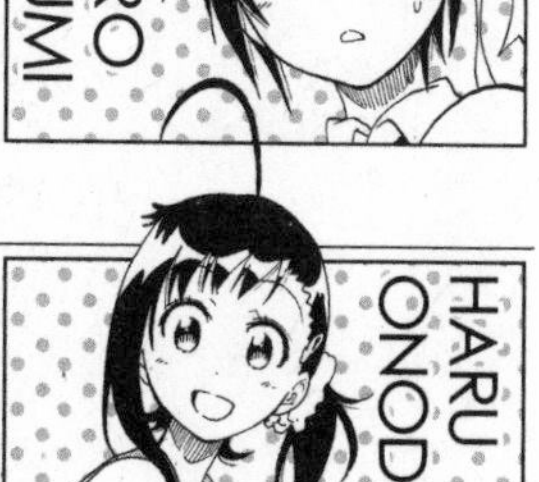

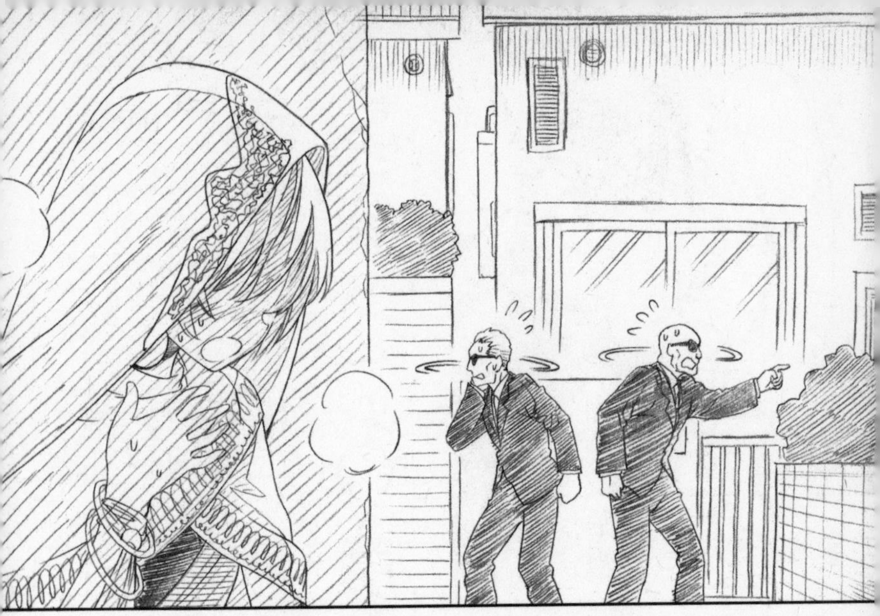

NISEKOI

False Love

vol. 16: Look-Alike

TABLE OF CONTENTS

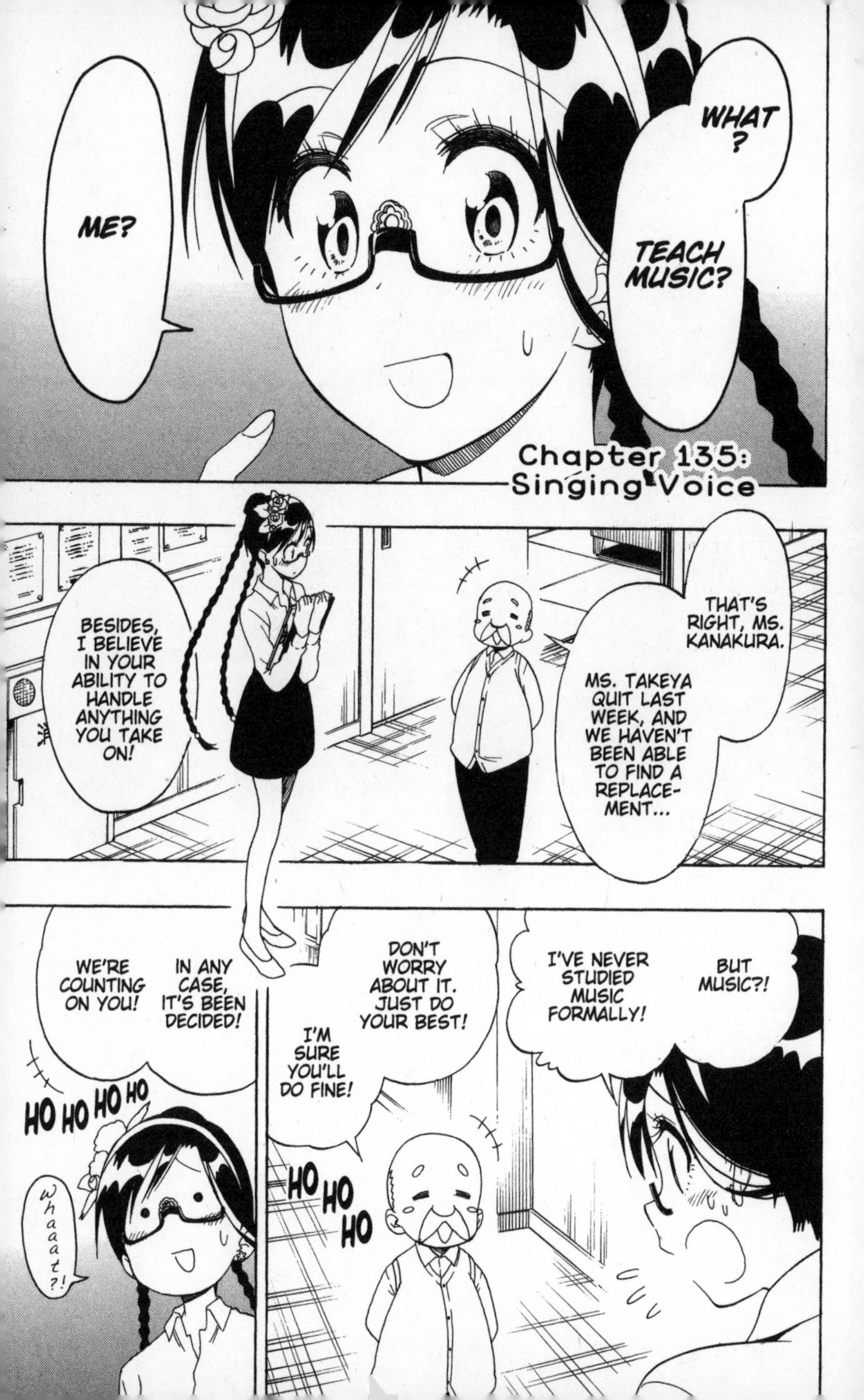
WHAT? TEACH MUSIC?
ME?
Chapter 135: Singing Voice
THAT'S RIGHT, MS. KANAKURA.
MS. TAKEYA QUIT LAST WEEK, AND WE HAVEN'T BEEN ABLE TO FIND A REPLACEMENT...
BESIDES, I BELIEVE IN YOUR ABILITY TO HANDLE ANYTHING YOU TAKE ON!
BUT MUSIC?!
I'VE NEVER STUDIED MUSIC FORMALLY!
DON'T WORRY ABOUT IT. JUST DO YOUR BEST!
I'M SURE YOU'LL DO FINE!
HO HO HO
IN ANY CASE, IT'S BEEN DECIDED!
WE'RE COUNTING ON YOU!
HO HO HO HO
Whaaaat?!

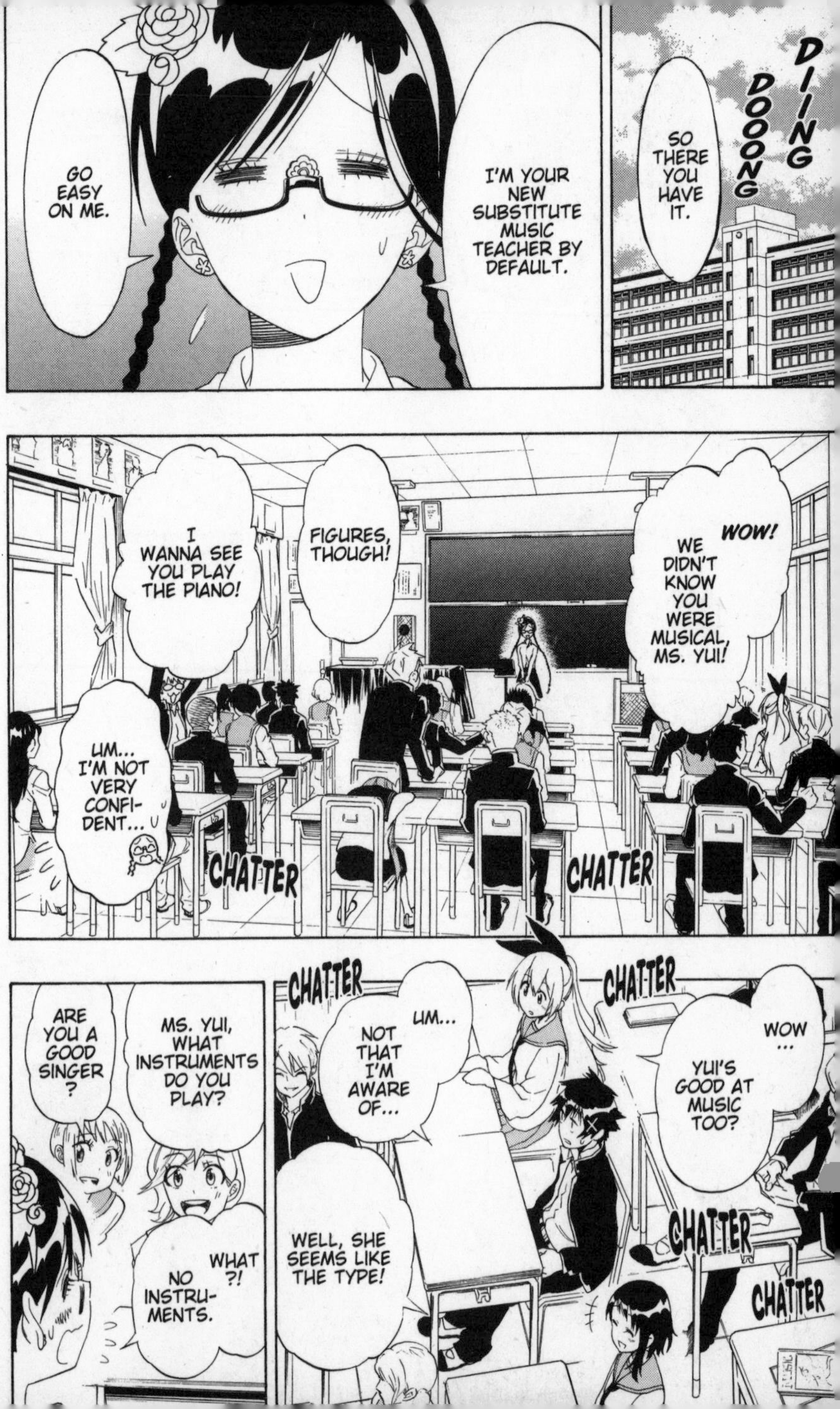
DIING
DOOONG
SO THERE YOU HAVE IT.
I'M YOUR NEW SUBSTITUTE MUSIC TEACHER BY DEFAULT.
GO EASY ON ME.
WOW!
WE DIDN'T KNOW YOU WERE MUSICAL, MS. YUI!
FIGURES, THOUGH!
I WANNA SEE YOU PLAY THE PIANO!
UM... I'M NOT VERY CONFIDENT...
CHATTER
CHATTER
CHATTER
CHATTER
WOW...
YUI'S GOOD AT MUSIC TOO?
UM...
NOT THAT I'M AWARE OF...
WELL, SHE SEEMS LIKE THE TYPE!
CHATTER
CHATTER
MS. YUI, WHAT INSTRUMENTS DO YOU PLAY?
ARE YOU A GOOD SINGER?
WHAT?!
NO INSTRUMENTS.

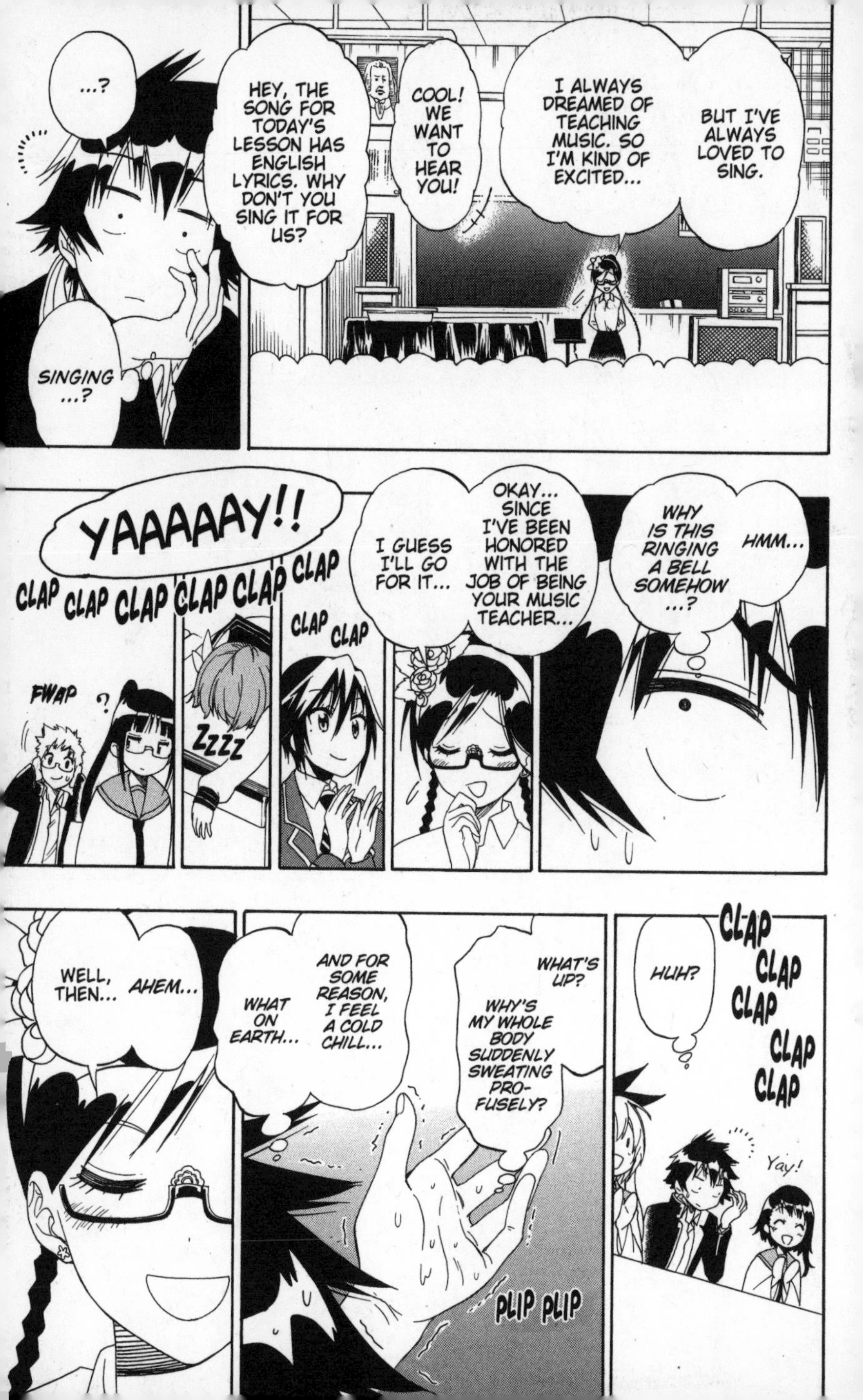
BUT I'VE ALWAYS LOVED TO SING.
I ALWAYS DREAMED OF TEACHING MUSIC. SO I'M KIND OF EXCITED...
COOL! WE WANT TO HEAR YOU!
HEY, THE SONG FOR TODAY'S LESSON HAS ENGLISH LYRICS. WHY DON'T YOU SING IT FOR US?
...?
SINGING...?
HMM...
WHY IS THIS RINGING A BELL SOMEHOW...?
OKAY... SINCE I'VE BEEN HONORED WITH THE JOB OF BEING YOUR MUSIC TEACHER...
I GUESS I'LL GO FOR IT...
CLAP CLAP
CLAP CLAP CLAP CLAP CLAP CLAP
YAAAAAY!!
ZZZZ
FWAP
CLAP CLAP CLAP CLAP CLAP
HUH?
Yay!
WHAT'S UP?
WHY'S MY WHOLE BODY SUDDENLY SWEATING PRO-FUSELY?
AND FOR SOME REASON, I FEEL A COLD CHILL...
WHAT ON EARTH...
PLIP PLIP
AHEM...
WELL, THEN...

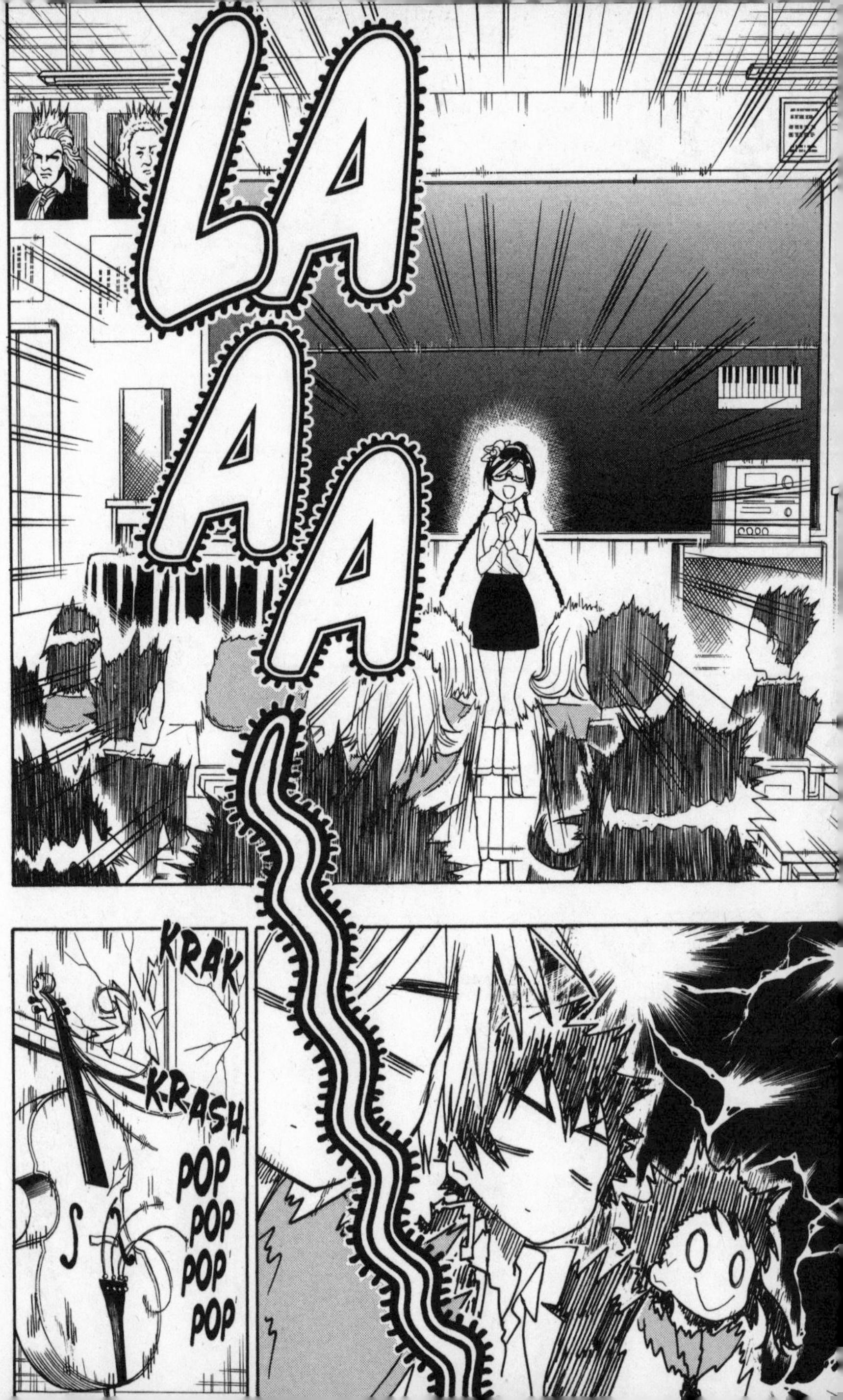
LA
A
A
KRAK
KRASH
POP
POP
POP
POP

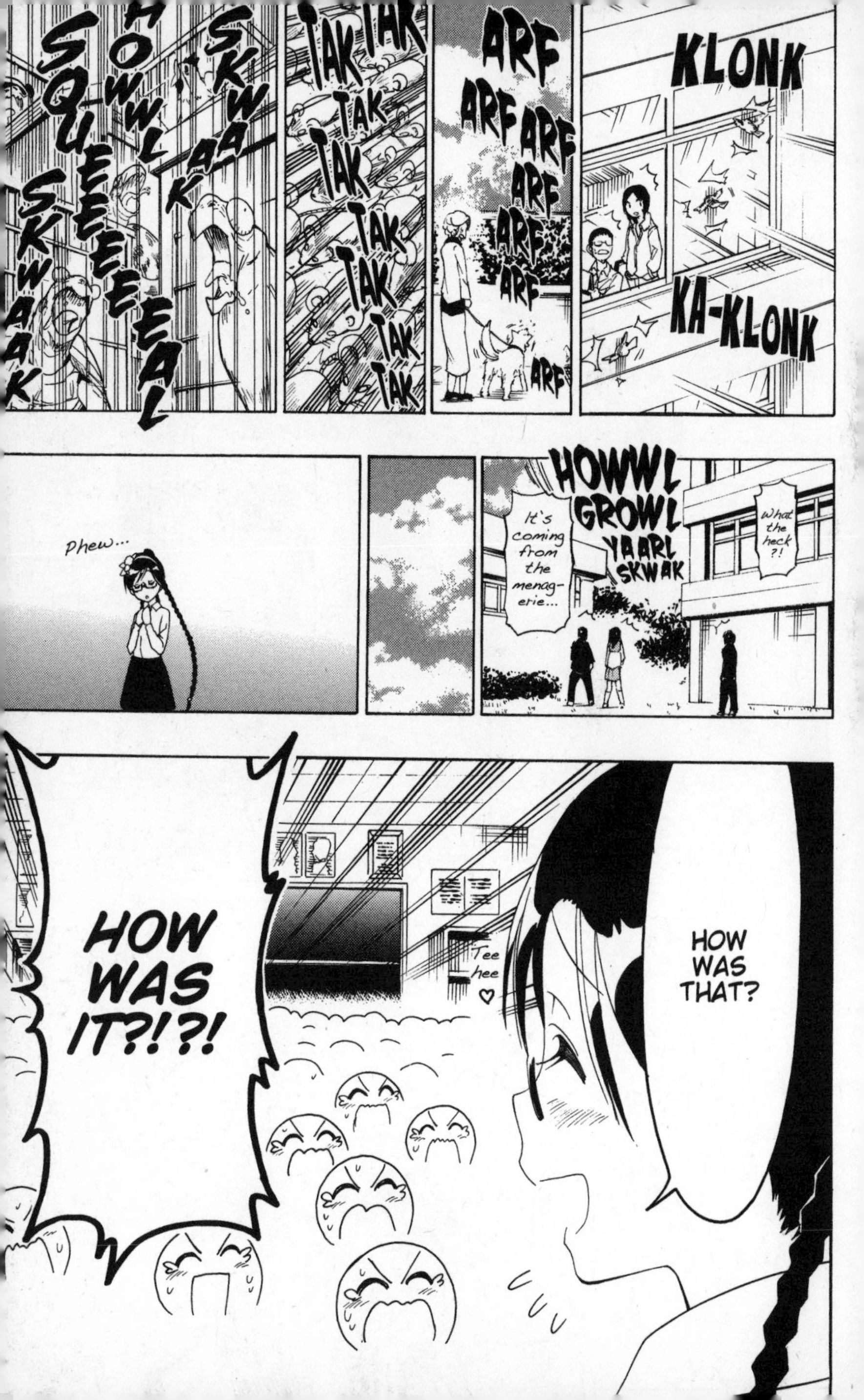
KLONK
KA-KLONK
ARF ARF ARF ARF ARF ARF
ARF
TAK TAK TAK TAK TAK TAK TAK TAK
SKWAAK
HOWWL
SQUEEEEEEAL
SKWAAK
HOWWL GROWL YAARL SKWAK
What the heck?!
It's coming from the menagerie...
Phew...
HOW WAS THAT?
Tee hee ♡
HOW WAS IT?!?!

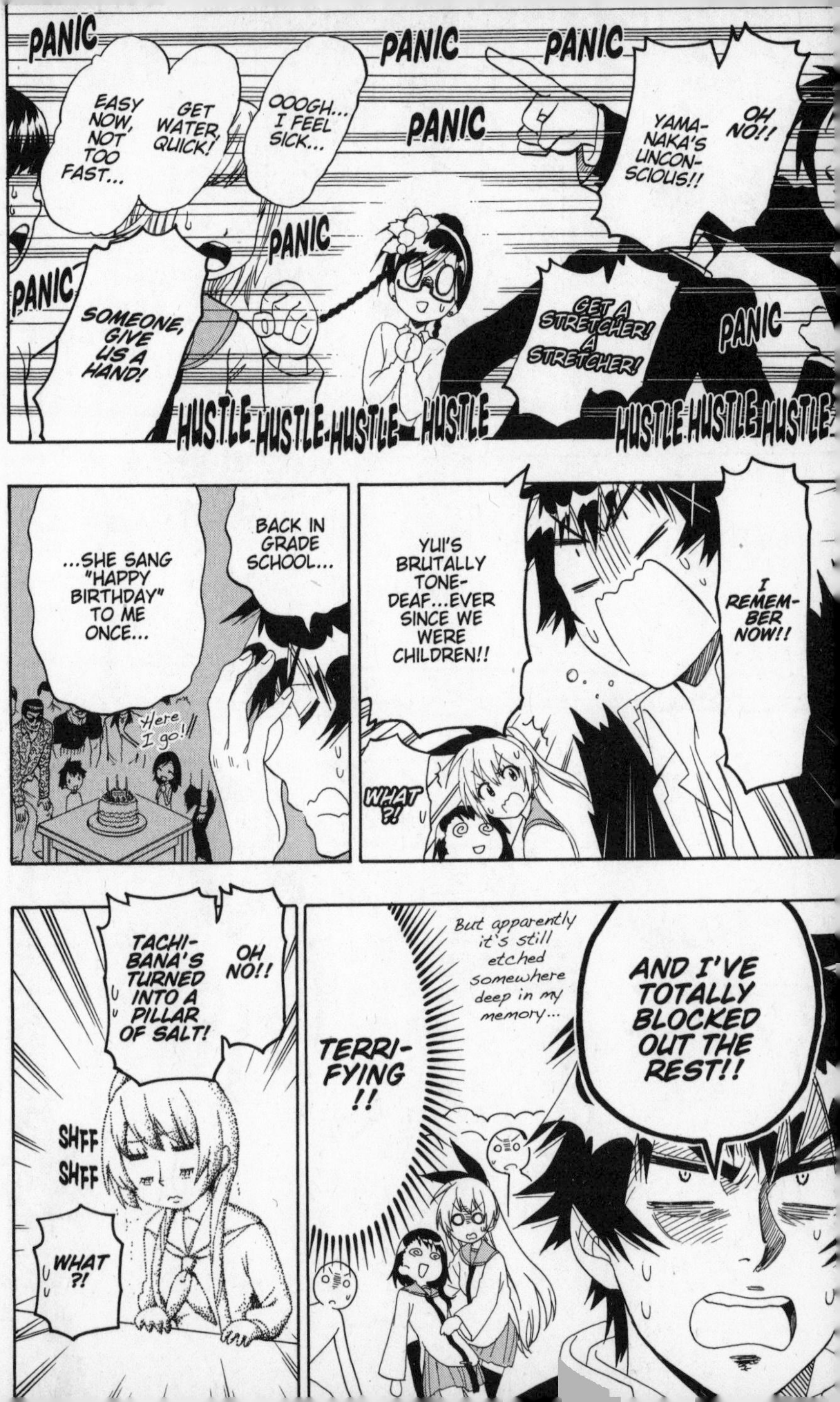
PANIC
PANIC
OH NO!! YAMANAKA'S UNCONSCIOUS!!
PANIC
GET A STRETCHER! A STRETCHER!
PANIC
OOOGH... I FEEL SICK...
GET WATER, QUICK!
EASY NOW, NOT TOO FAST...
PANIC
PANIC
PANIC
SOMEONE, GIVE US A HAND!
HUSTLE HUSTLE HUSTLE
HUSTLE HUSTLE HUSTLE HUSTLE
I REMEMBER NOW!!
YUI'S BRUTALLY TONE-DEAF...EVER SINCE WE WERE CHILDREN!!
WHAT ?!
BACK IN GRADE SCHOOL...
...SHE SANG "HAPPY BIRTHDAY" TO ME ONCE...
Here I go!!
AND I'VE TOTALLY BLOCKED OUT THE REST!!
But apparently it's still etched somewhere deep in my memory...
TERRIFYING!!
OH NO!! TACHIBANA'S TURNED INTO A PILLAR OF SALT!
SHFF SHFF
WHAT ?!

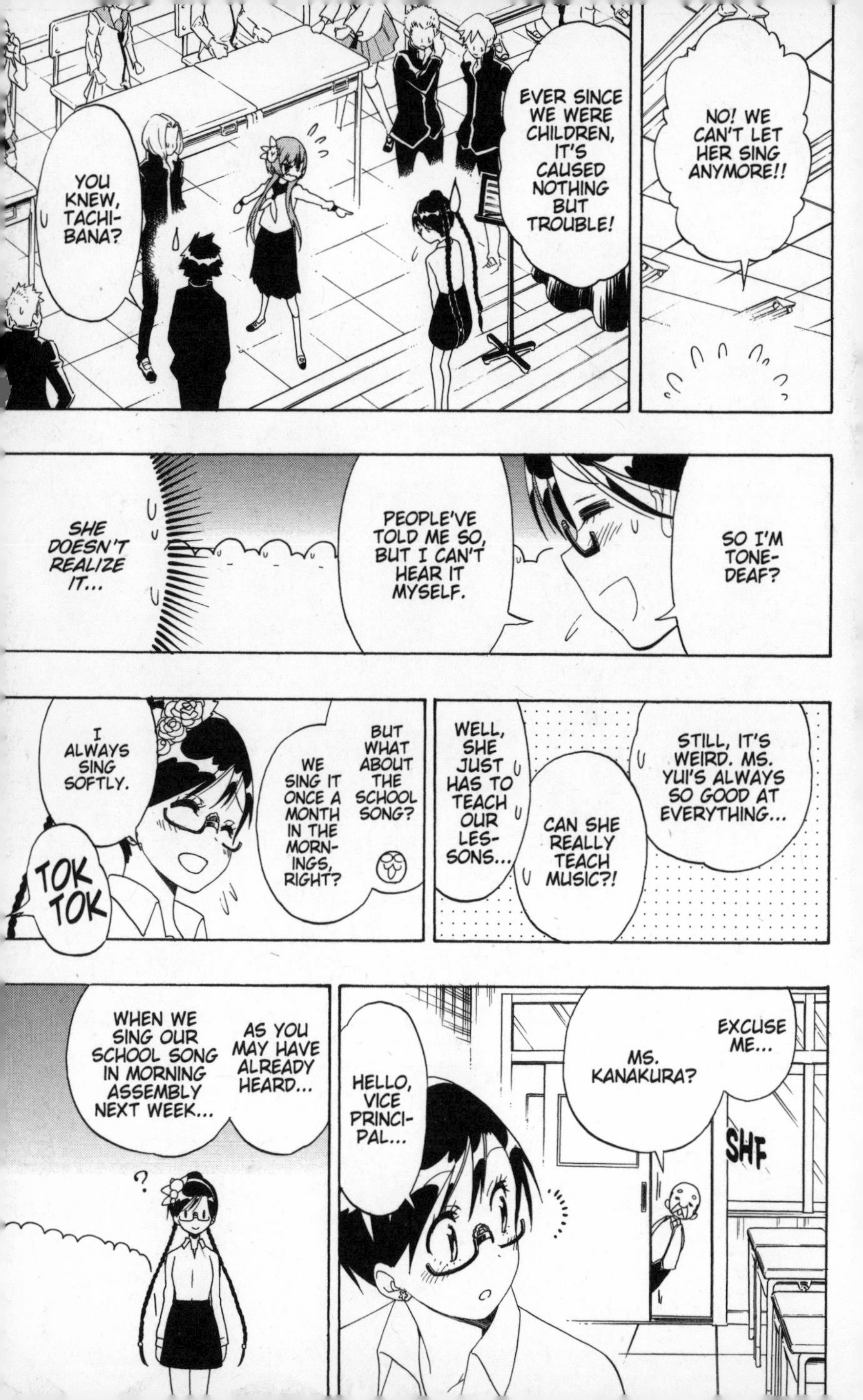
NO! WE CAN'T LET HER SING ANYMORE!!
EVER SINCE WE WERE CHILDREN, IT'S CAUSED NOTHING BUT TROUBLE!
YOU KNEW, TACHIBANA?
SO I'M TONE-DEAF?
PEOPLE'VE TOLD ME SO, BUT I CAN'T HEAR IT MYSELF.
SHE DOESN'T REALIZE IT...
STILL, IT'S WEIRD. MS. YUI'S ALWAYS SO GOOD AT EVERYTHING...
CAN SHE REALLY TEACH MUSIC?!
WELL, SHE JUST HAS TO TEACH OUR LESSONS...
BUT WHAT ABOUT THE SCHOOL SONG?
WE SING IT ONCE A MONTH IN THE MORNINGS, RIGHT?
I ALWAYS SING SOFTLY.
TOK TOK
EXCUSE ME...
MS. KANAKURA?
SHF
HELLO, VICE PRINCIPAL...
AS YOU MAY HAVE ALREADY HEARD...
WHEN WE SING OUR SCHOOL SONG IN MORNING ASSEMBLY NEXT WEEK...

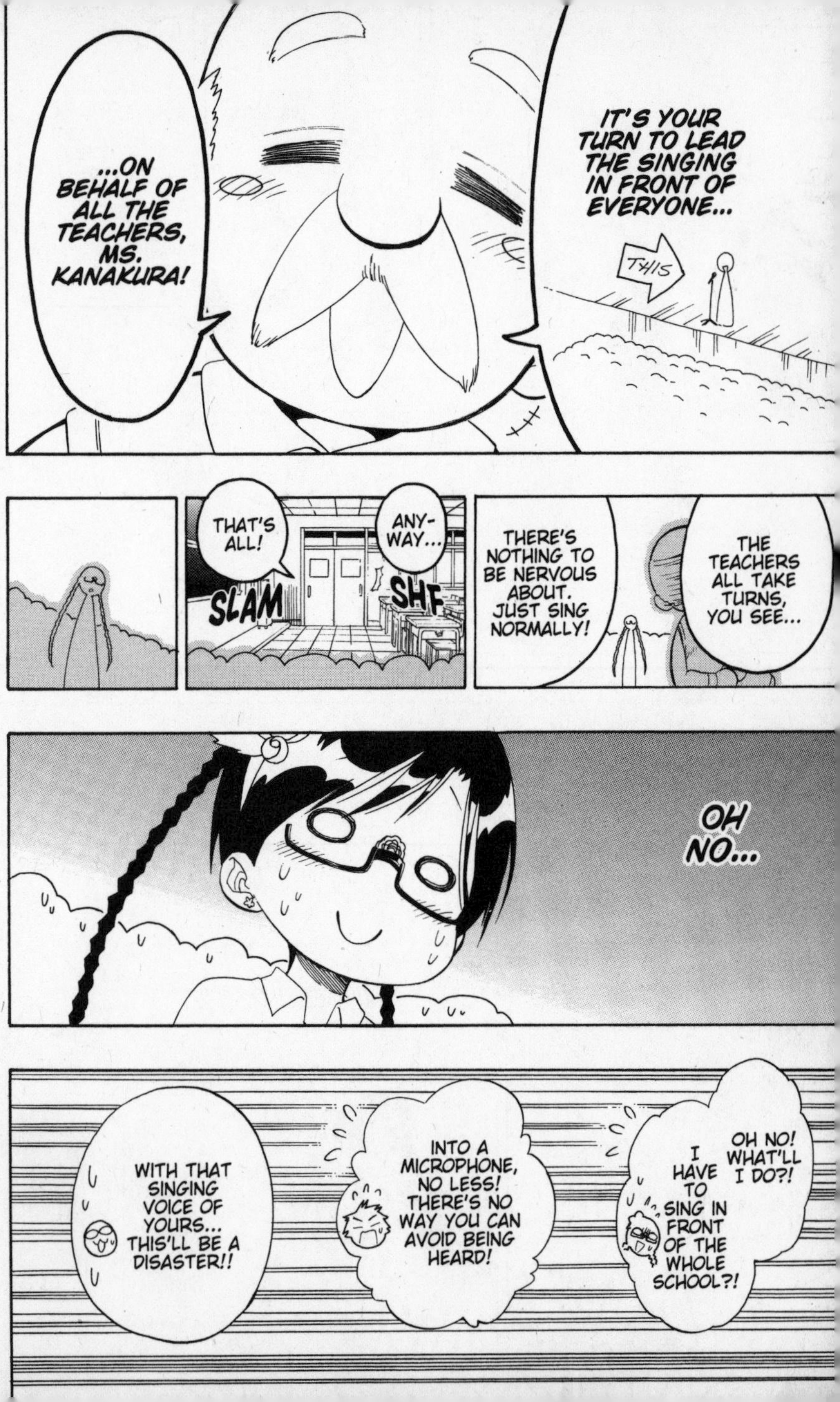
IT'S YOUR TURN TO LEAD THE SINGING IN FRONT OF EVERYONE...
THIS
...ON BEHALF OF ALL THE TEACHERS, MS. KANAKURA!
THE TEACHERS ALL TAKE TURNS, YOU SEE...
THERE'S NOTHING TO BE NERVOUS ABOUT. JUST SING NORMALLY!
ANY-WAY...
SHF
THAT'S ALL!
SLAM
OH NO...
OH NO! WHAT'LL I DO?!
I HAVE TO SING IN FRONT OF THE WHOLE SCHOOL?!
INTO A MICROPHONE, NO LESS! THERE'S NO WAY YOU CAN AVOID BEING HEARD!
WITH THAT SINGING VOICE OF YOURS... THIS'LL BE A DISASTER!!

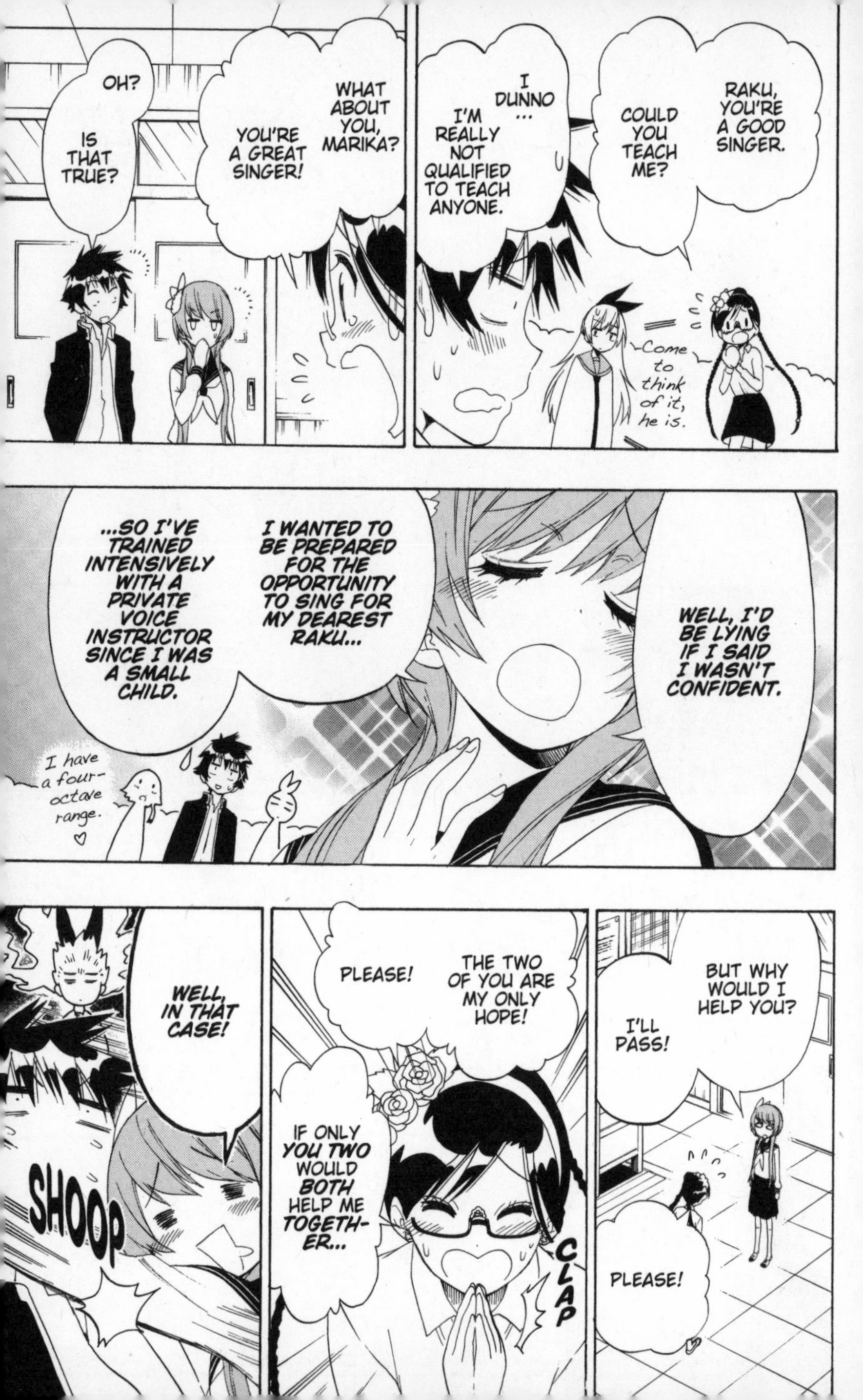
RAKU, YOU'RE A GOOD SINGER.
COULD YOU TEACH ME?
Come to think of it, he is.
I DUNNO...
I'M REALLY NOT QUALIFIED TO TEACH ANYONE.
WHAT ABOUT YOU, MARIKA?
YOU'RE A GREAT SINGER!
OH?
IS THAT TRUE?
WELL, I'D BE LYING IF I SAID I WASN'T CONFIDENT.
I WANTED TO BE PREPARED FOR THE OPPORTUNITY TO SING FOR MY DEAREST RAKU...
...SO I'VE TRAINED INTENSIVELY WITH A PRIVATE VOICE INSTRUCTOR SINCE I WAS A SMALL CHILD.
I have a four-octave range. ♡
BUT WHY WOULD I HELP YOU?
I'LL PASS!
PLEASE!
THE TWO OF YOU ARE MY ONLY HOPE!
PLEASE!
IF ONLY *YOU TWO* WOULD *BOTH* HELP ME *TOGETHER*...
CLAP
WELL, IN THAT CASE!
SHOOP

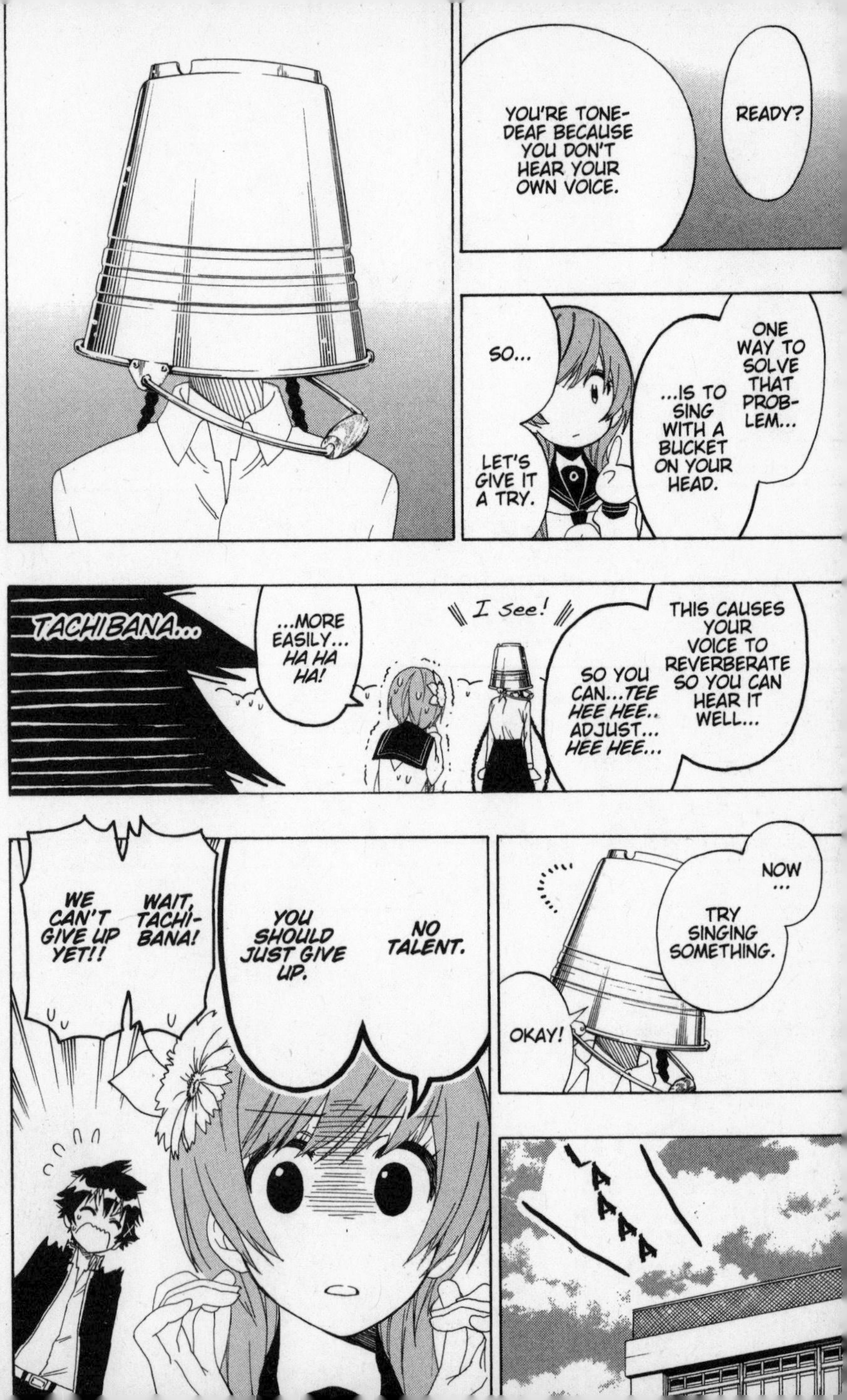
READY?
YOU'RE TONE-DEAF BECAUSE YOU DON'T HEAR YOUR OWN VOICE.
ONE WAY TO SOLVE THAT PROB-LEM...
...IS TO SING WITH A BUCKET ON YOUR HEAD.
SO...
LET'S GIVE IT A TRY.
THIS CAUSES YOUR VOICE TO REVERBERATE SO YOU CAN HEAR IT WELL...
SO YOU CAN...TEE HEE HEE.. ADJUST... HEE HEE...
I see!
...MORE EASILY... HA HA HA!
TACHIBANA...
NOW ...
TRY SINGING SOMETHING.
OKAY!
LAAAA
NO TALENT.
YOU SHOULD JUST GIVE UP.
WAIT, TACHI-BANA!
WE CAN'T GIVE UP YET!!

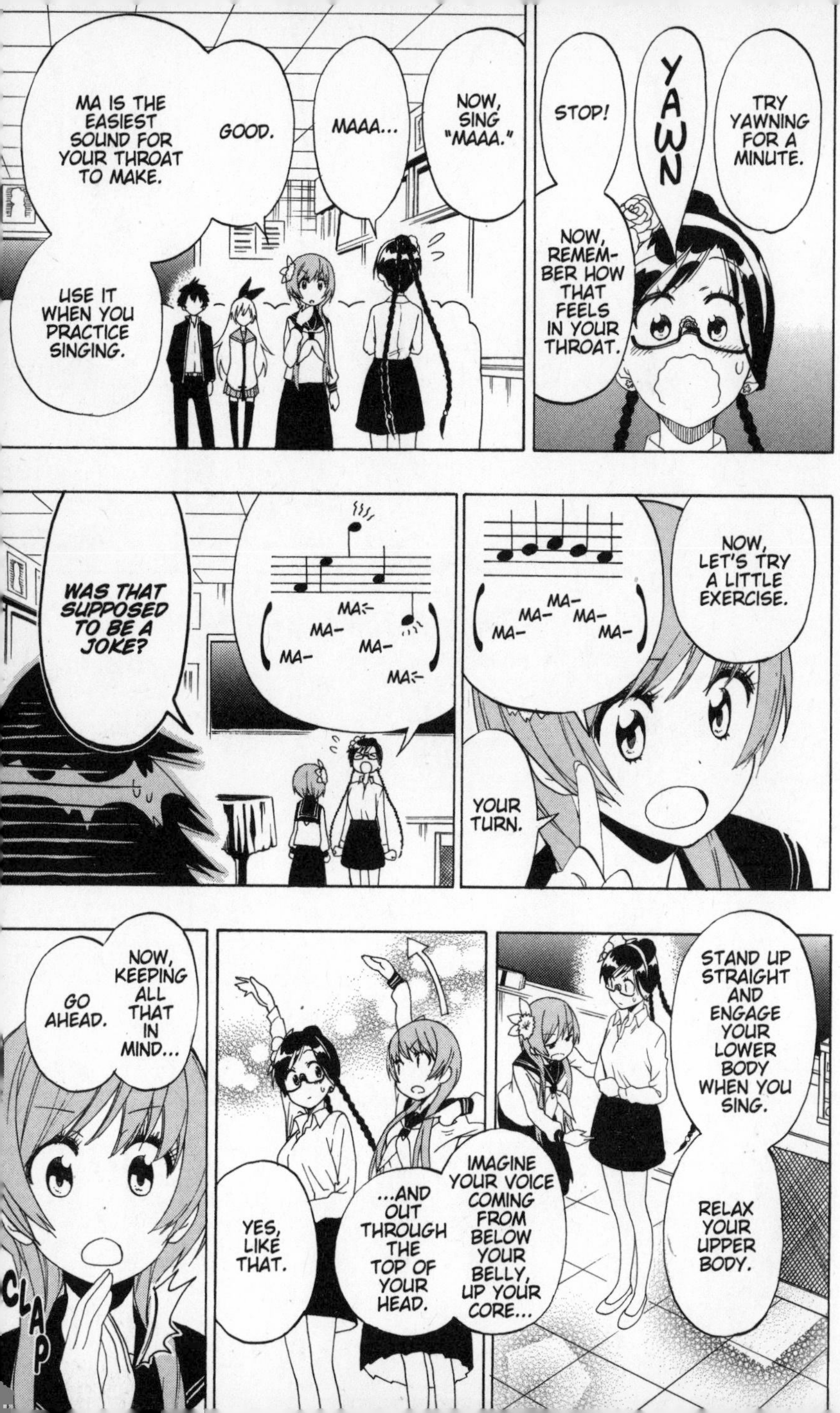
TRY YAWNING FOR A MINUTE.
YAWN
STOP!
NOW, REMEMBER HOW THAT FEELS IN YOUR THROAT.
NOW, SING "MAAA."
MAAA...
GOOD.
MA IS THE EASIEST SOUND FOR YOUR THROAT TO MAKE.
USE IT WHEN YOU PRACTICE SINGING.
NOW, LET'S TRY A LITTLE EXERCISE.
MA- MA- MA- MA- MA-
YOUR TURN.
MA- MA- MA- MA- MA- MA-
WAS THAT SUPPOSED TO BE A JOKE?
STAND UP STRAIGHT AND ENGAGE YOUR LOWER BODY WHEN YOU SING.
RELAX YOUR UPPER BODY.
IMAGINE YOUR VOICE COMING FROM BELOW YOUR BELLY, UP YOUR CORE...
...AND OUT THROUGH THE TOP OF YOUR HEAD.
YES, LIKE THAT.
NOW, KEEPING ALL THAT IN MIND...
GO AHEAD.
CLAP

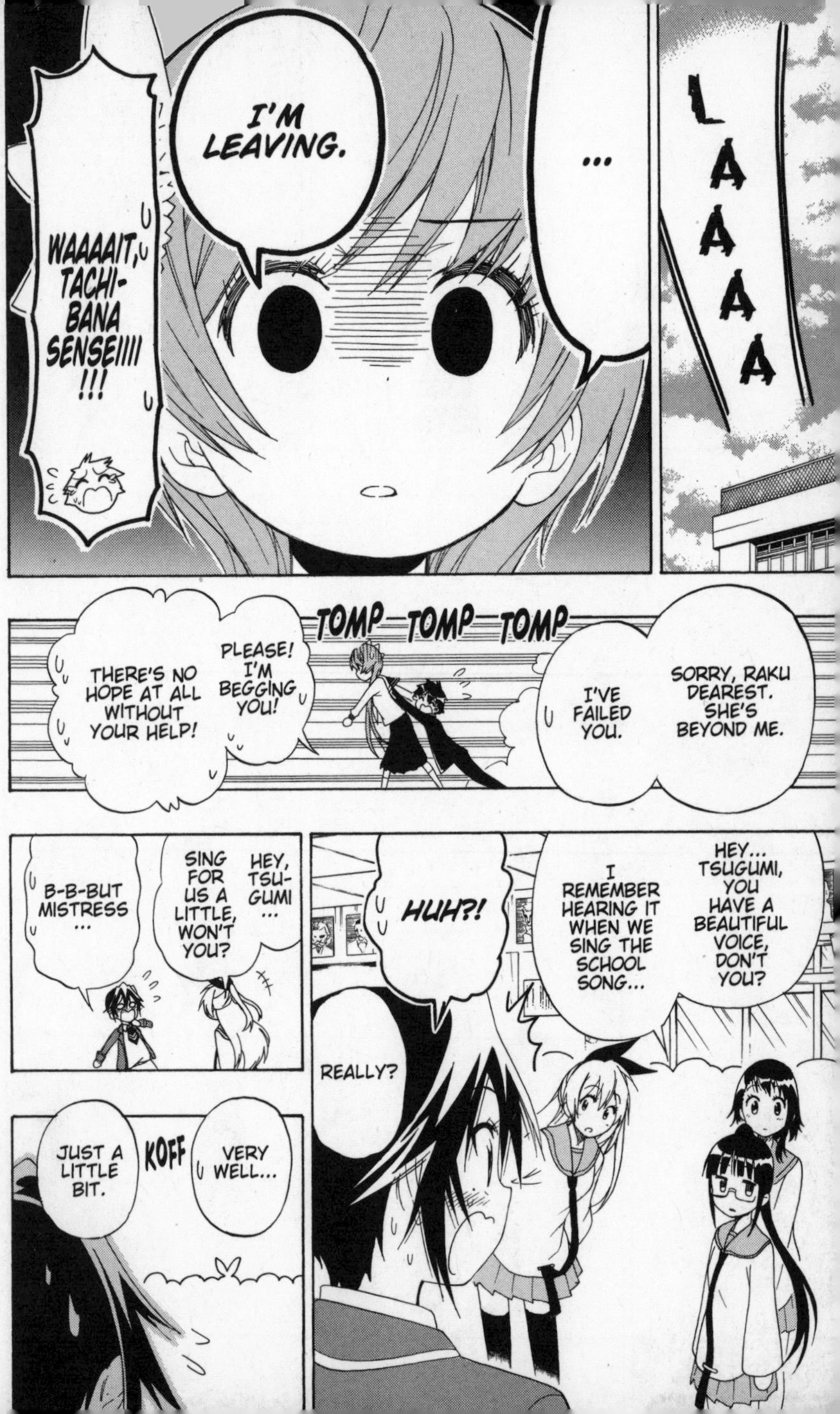
LAAAA
...
I'M LEAVING.
WAAAAIT, TACHI-BANA SENSEI!!!!!!
SORRY, RAKU DEAREST. SHE'S BEYOND ME.
I'VE FAILED YOU.
TOMP TOMP TOMP
PLEASE! I'M BEGGING YOU!
THERE'S NO HOPE AT ALL WITHOUT YOUR HELP!
HEY... TSUGUMI, YOU HAVE A BEAUTIFUL VOICE, DON'T YOU?
I REMEMBER HEARING IT WHEN WE SING THE SCHOOL SONG...
HUH?!
REALLY?
HEY, TSU-GUMI...
SING FOR US A LITTLE, WON'T YOU?
B-B-BUT MISTRESS...
VERY WELL...
KOFF
JUST A LITTLE BIT.

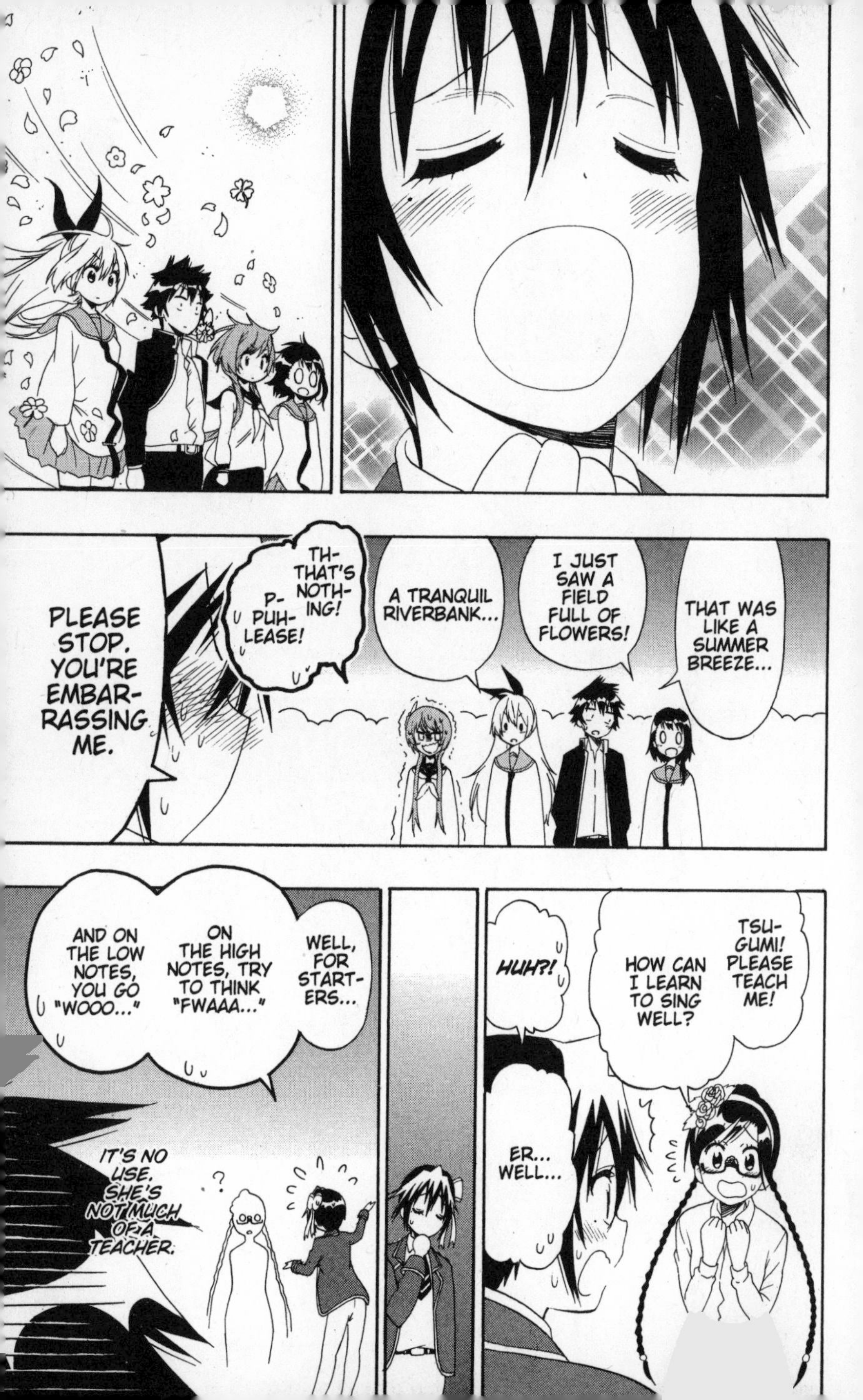
THAT WAS LIKE A SUMMER BREEZE...
I JUST SAW A FIELD FULL OF FLOWERS!
A TRANQUIL RIVERBANK...
TH- THAT'S NOTHING! P- PUH-LEASE!
PLEASE STOP. YOU'RE EMBARRASSING ME.
TSUGUMI! PLEASE TEACH ME!
HOW CAN I LEARN TO SING WELL?
HUH?!
ER... WELL...
WELL, FOR STARTERS...
ON THE HIGH NOTES, TRY TO THINK "FWAAA..."
AND ON THE LOW NOTES, YOU GO "WOOO..."
IT'S NO USE. SHE'S NOT MUCH OF A TEACHER.

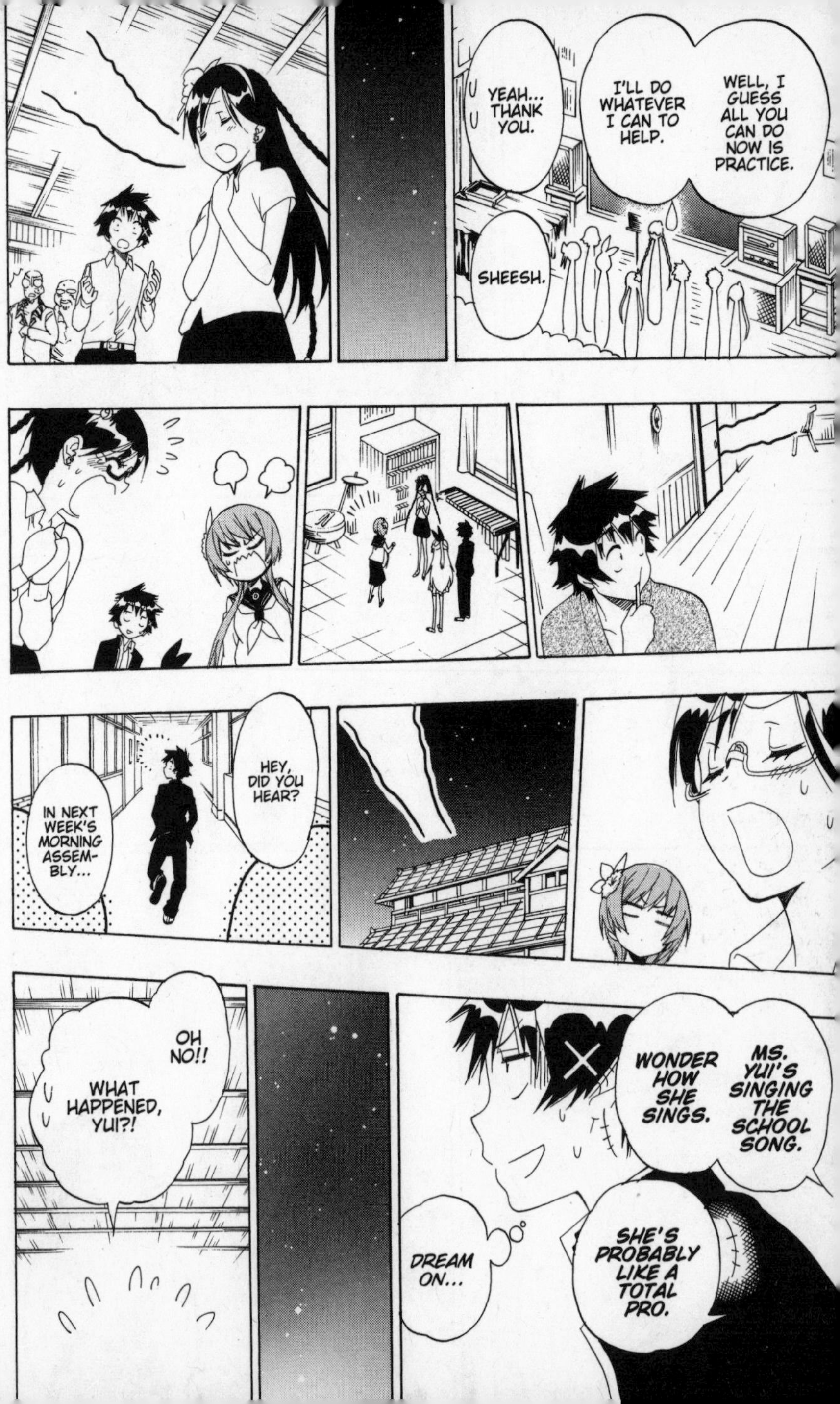
WELL, I GUESS ALL YOU CAN DO NOW IS PRACTICE.
I'LL DO WHATEVER I CAN TO HELP.
YEAH... THANK YOU.
SHEESH.
HEY, DID YOU HEAR?
IN NEXT WEEK'S MORNING ASSEM-BLY...
MS. YUI'S SINGING THE SCHOOL SONG.
WONDER HOW SHE SINGS.
SHE'S PROBABLY LIKE A TOTAL PRO.
DREAM ON...
OH NO!!
WHAT HAPPENED, YUI?!

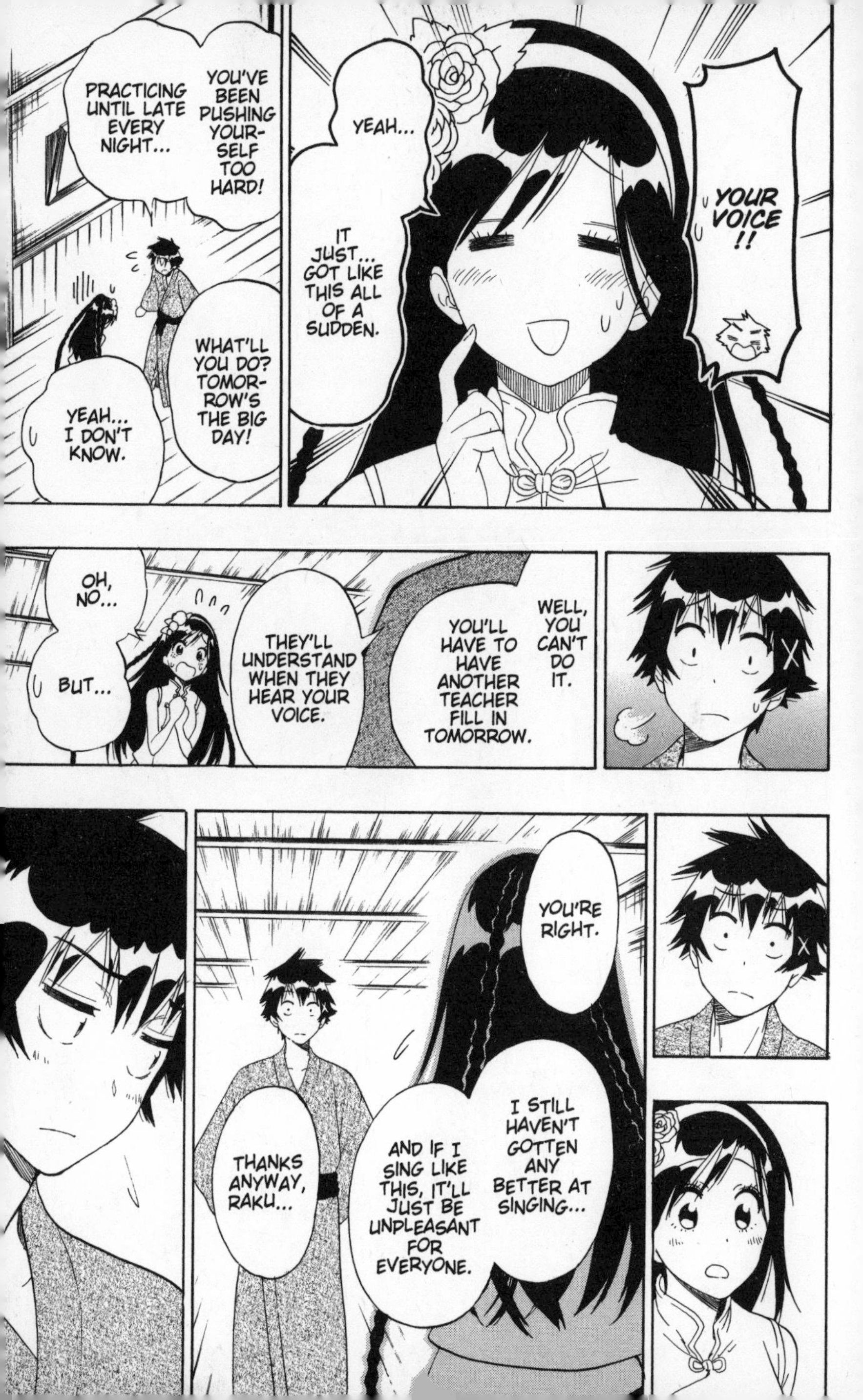
YOUR VOICE!!
YEAH...
IT JUST... GOT LIKE THIS ALL OF A SUDDEN.
YOU'VE BEEN PUSHING YOUR-SELF TOO HARD!
PRACTICING UNTIL LATE EVERY NIGHT...
WHAT'LL YOU DO? TOMOR-ROW'S THE BIG DAY!
YEAH... I DON'T KNOW.
WELL, YOU CAN'T DO IT.
YOU'LL HAVE TO HAVE ANOTHER TEACHER FILL IN TOMORROW.
THEY'LL UNDERSTAND WHEN THEY HEAR YOUR VOICE.
OH, NO...
BUT...
YOU'RE RIGHT.
I STILL HAVEN'T GOTTEN ANY BETTER AT SINGING...
AND IF I SING LIKE THIS, IT'LL JUST BE UNPLEASANT FOR EVERYONE.
THANKS ANYWAY, RAKU...

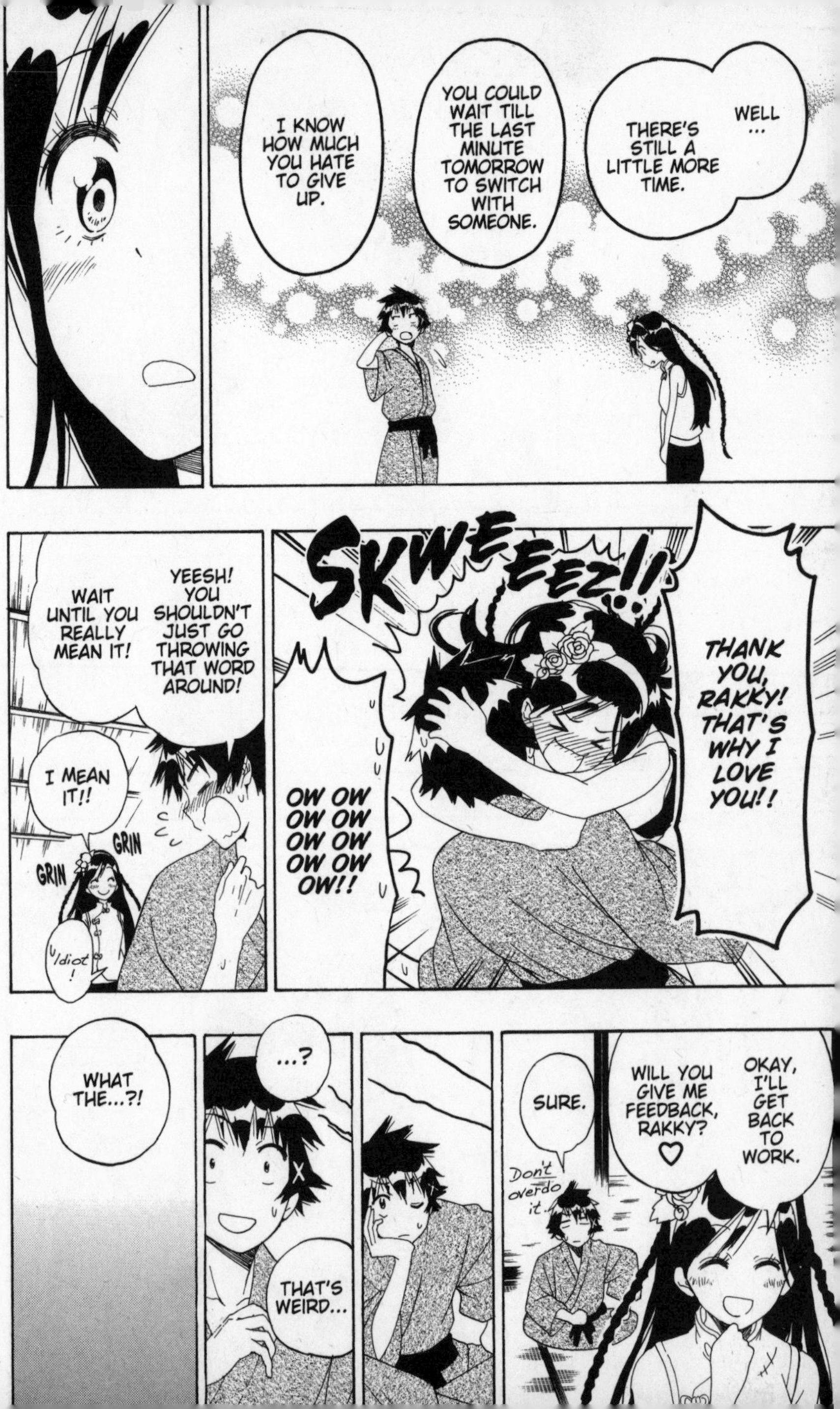
WELL ...
THERE'S STILL A LITTLE MORE TIME.
YOU COULD WAIT TILL THE LAST MINUTE TOMORROW TO SWITCH WITH SOMEONE.
I KNOW HOW MUCH YOU HATE TO GIVE UP.
SKWEEEZ!!
THANK YOU, RAKKY! THAT'S WHY I LOVE YOU!!
OW OW OW OW OW OW OW OW OW!!
YEESH! YOU SHOULDN'T JUST GO THROWING THAT WORD AROUND!
WAIT UNTIL YOU REALLY MEAN IT!
I MEAN IT!!
GRIN
GRIN
Idiot!
OKAY, I'LL GET BACK TO WORK.
WILL YOU GIVE ME FEEDBACK, RAKKY? ♡
SURE.
Don't overdo it.
...?
THAT'S WEIRD...
WHAT THE...?!

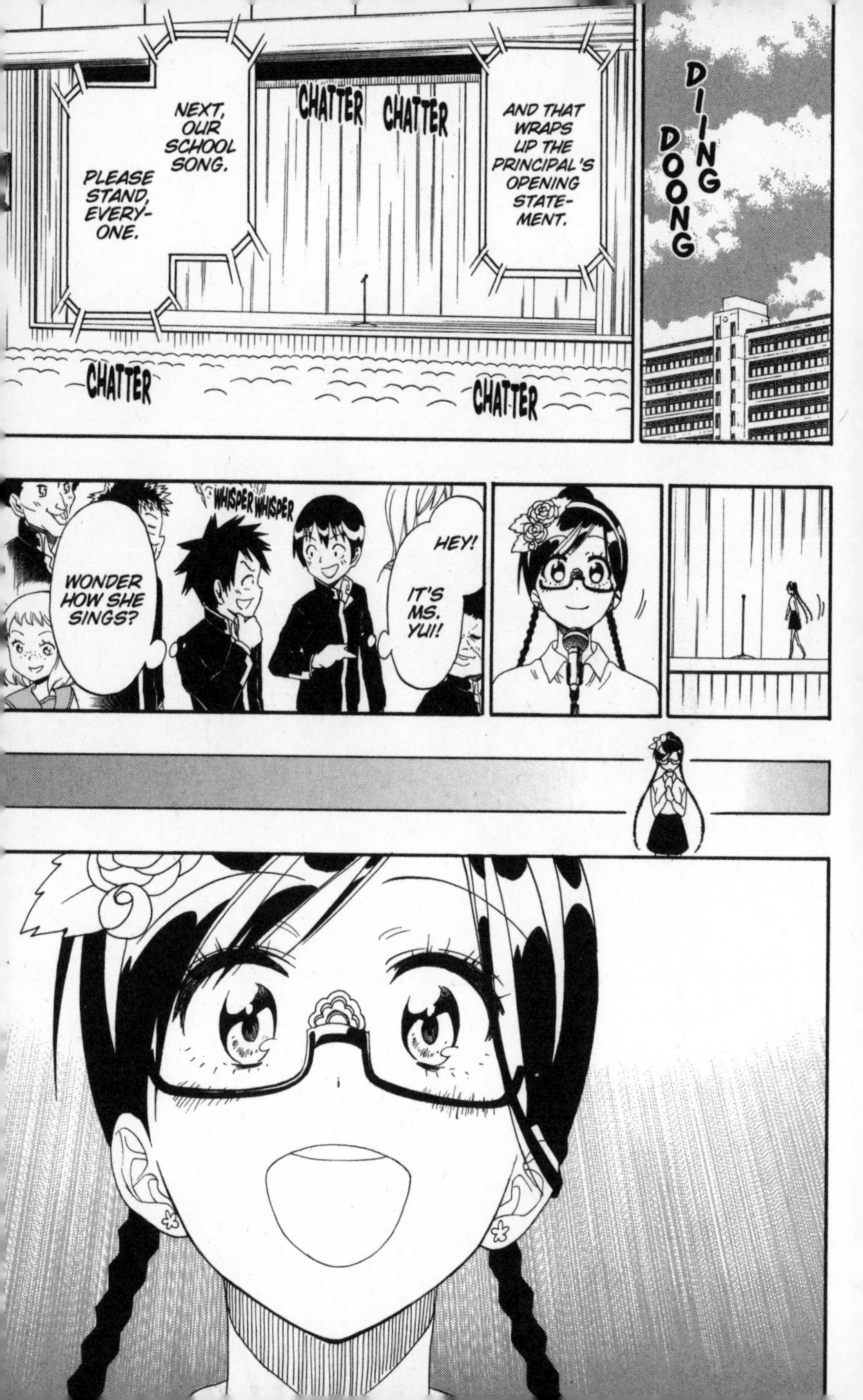
DIIING
DOONG
AND THAT WRAPS UP THE PRINCIPAL'S OPENING STATEMENT.
CHATTER
CHATTER
NEXT, OUR SCHOOL SONG.
PLEASE STAND, EVERY-ONE.
CHATTER
CHATTER
HEY!
IT'S MS. YUI!
WHISPER WHISPER
WONDER HOW SHE SINGS?

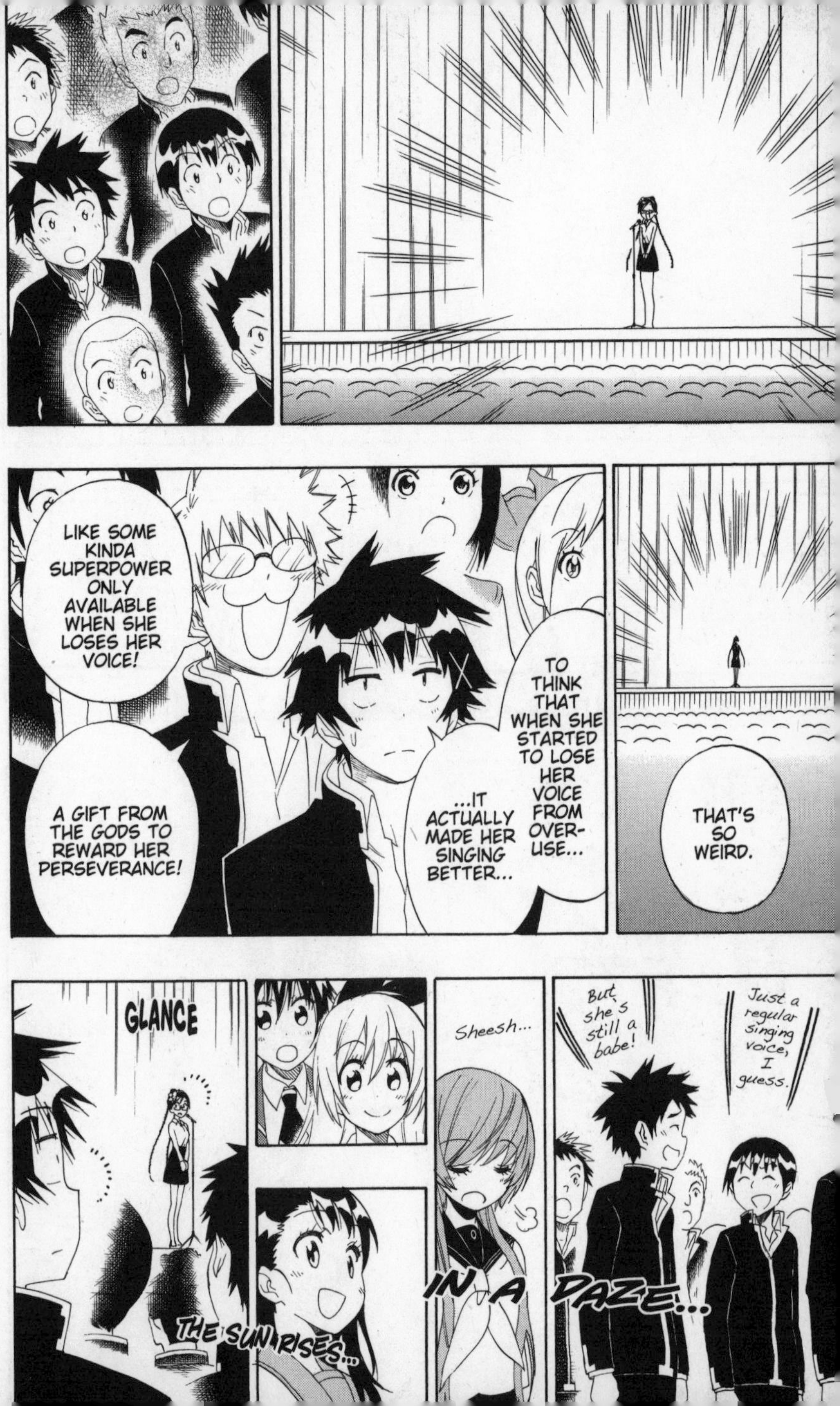
THAT'S SO WEIRD.
TO THINK THAT WHEN SHE STARTED TO LOSE HER VOICE FROM OVER-USE...
...IT ACTUALLY MADE HER SINGING BETTER...
LIKE SOME KINDA SUPERPOWER ONLY AVAILABLE WHEN SHE LOSES HER VOICE!
A GIFT FROM THE GODS TO REWARD HER PERSEVERANCE!
Just a regular singing voice, I guess.
But, she's still a babe!
Sheesh...
IN A DAZE...
THE SUN RISES...
GLANCE

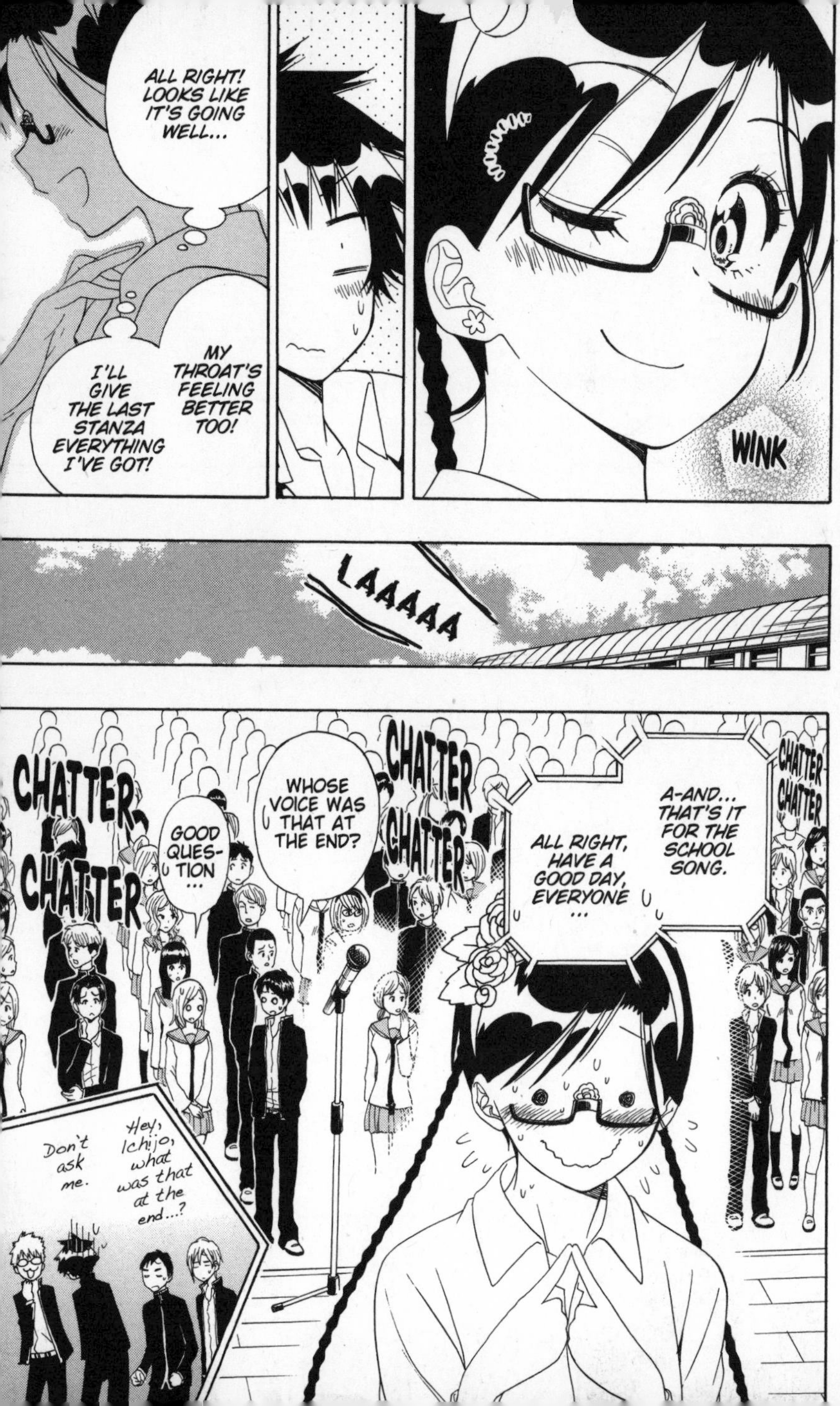
WINK
ALL RIGHT! LOOKS LIKE IT'S GOING WELL...
MY THROAT'S FEELING BETTER TOO!
I'LL GIVE THE LAST STANZA EVERYTHING I'VE GOT!
LAAAAAA
CHATTER CHATTER
A-AND... THAT'S IT FOR THE SCHOOL SONG.
ALL RIGHT, HAVE A GOOD DAY, EVERYONE...
CHATTER CHATTER
WHOSE VOICE WAS THAT AT THE END?
GOOD QUESTION...
CHATTER CHATTER
Hey, Ichijo, what was that at the end...?
Don't ask me.

Bonyari High School Song

The faint gray light shines
   through the clouds

Illuminating our beautiful town

At the crest of Mount Bonyari

In a daze, the sun rises

Bonyari, Bonyari, oh, Bonyari High!

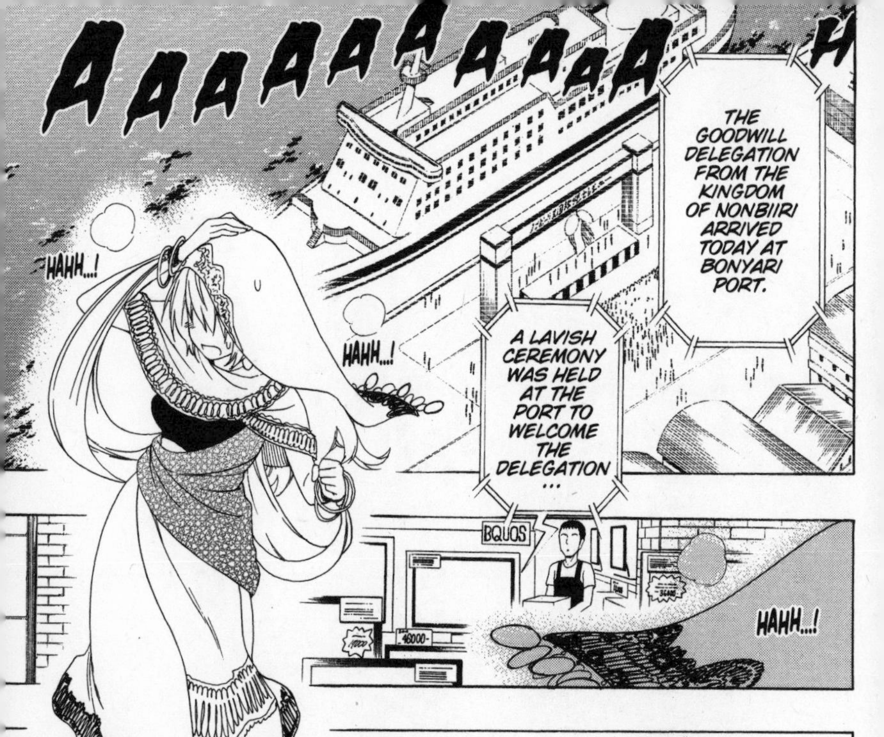
AAAAAAAAAAH
THE GOODWILL DELEGATION FROM THE KINGDOM OF NONBIIRI ARRIVED TODAY AT BONYARI PORT.
A LAVISH CEREMONY WAS HELD AT THE PORT TO WELCOME THE DELEGATION...
HAHH...!
HAHH...!
BQUOS
HAHH...!

Chapter 136: Look-Alike

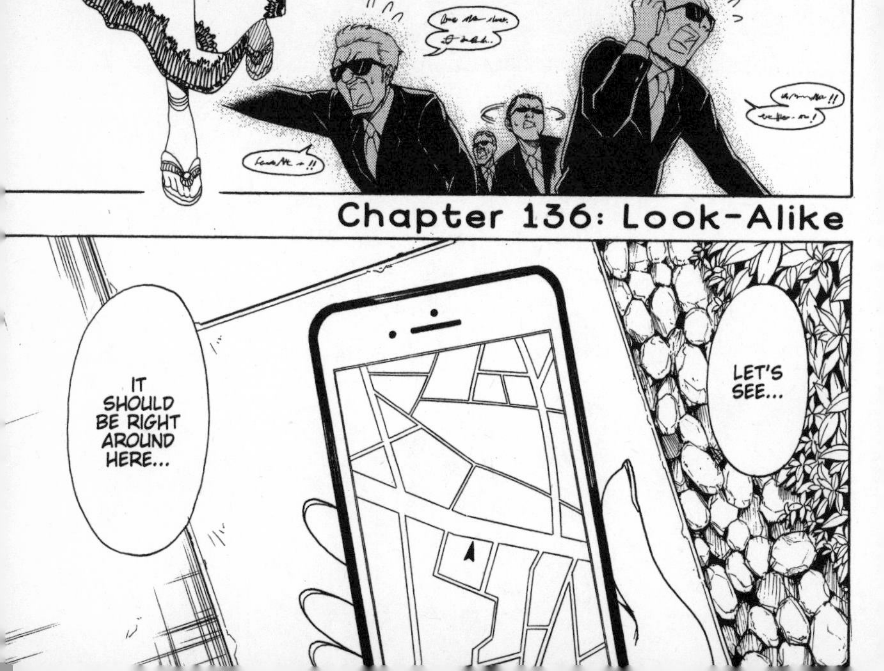
LET'S SEE...
IT SHOULD BE RIGHT AROUND HERE...

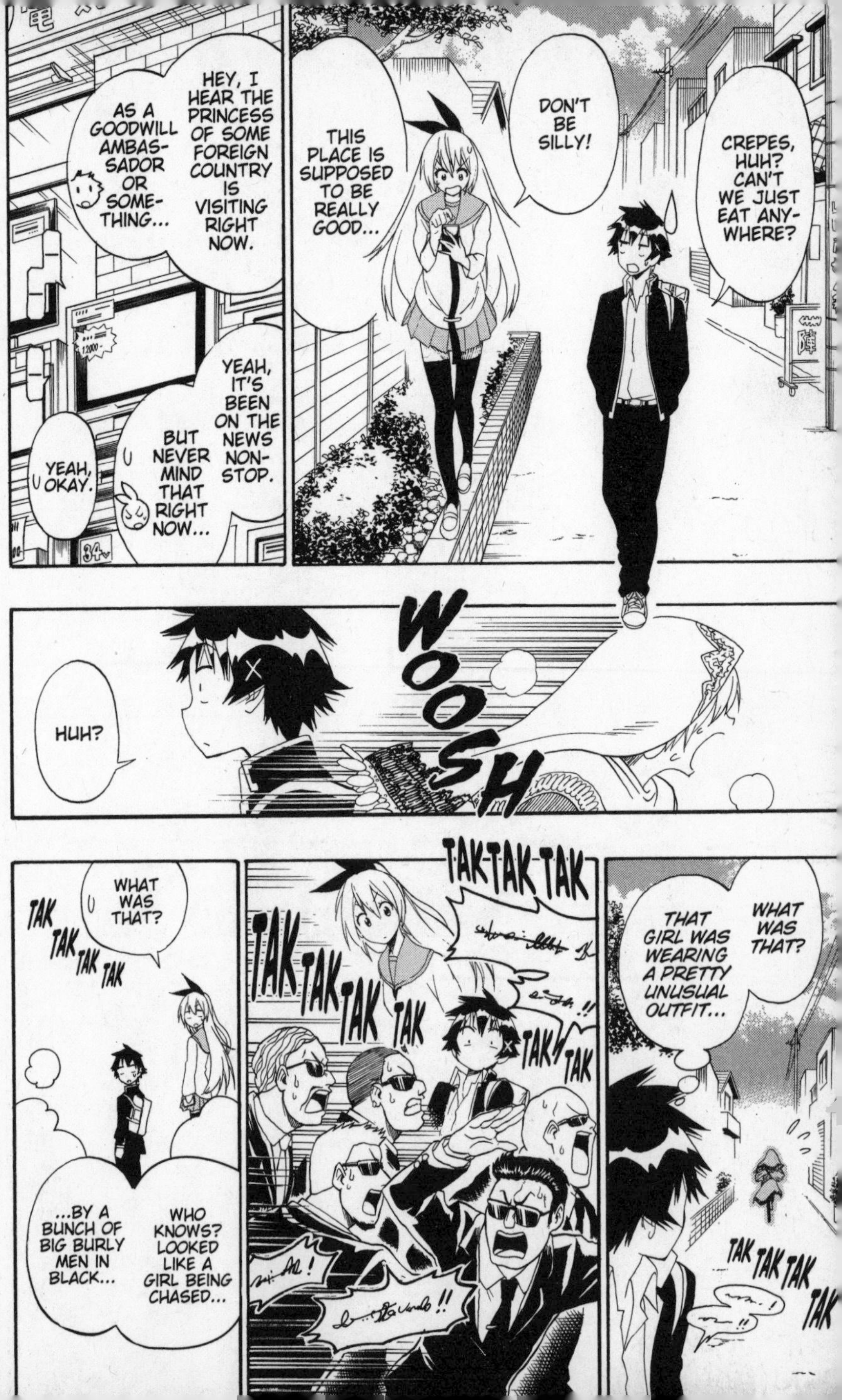
CREPES, HUH? CAN'T WE JUST EAT ANY-WHERE?
DON'T BE SILLY!
THIS PLACE IS SUPPOSED TO BE REALLY GOOD...
HEY, I HEAR THE PRINCESS OF SOME FOREIGN COUNTRY IS VISITING RIGHT NOW.
AS A GOODWILL AMBAS-SADOR OR SOME-THING...
YEAH, IT'S BEEN ON THE NEWS NON-STOP.
BUT NEVER MIND THAT RIGHT NOW...
YEAH, OKAY.
WOOSH
HUH?
WHAT WAS THAT?
THAT GIRL WAS WEARING A PRETTY UNUSUAL OUTFIT...
TAK TAK TAK TAK
TAK-TAK-TAK
TAK TAK TAK TAK
TAK TAK
WHAT WAS THAT?
TAK TAK TAK TAK
WHO KNOWS? LOOKED LIKE A GIRL BEING CHASED...
...BY A BUNCH OF BIG BURLY MEN IN BLACK...

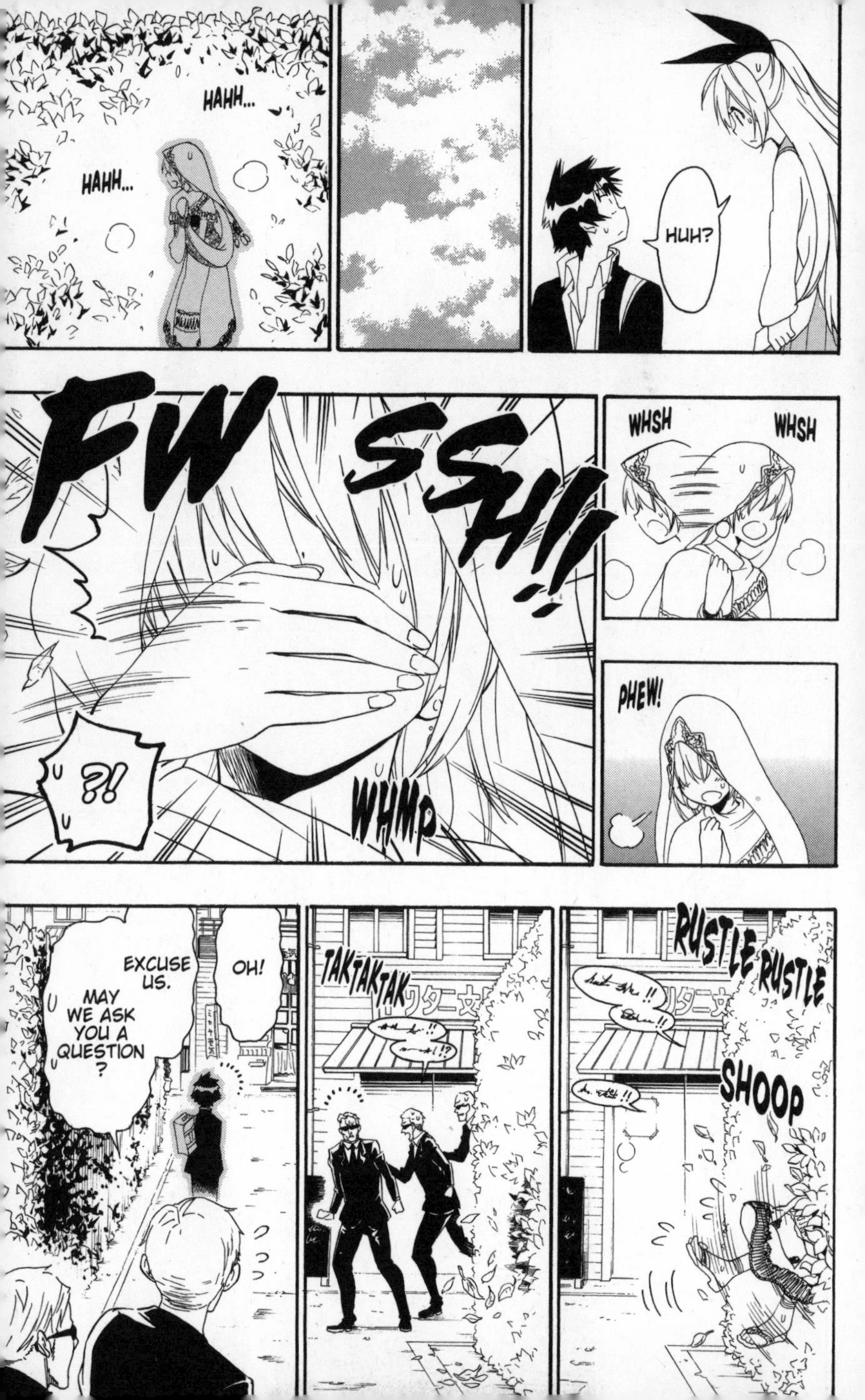
HUH?
HAHH...
HAHH...
WHSH
WHSH
PHEW!
FWSSH!!
?!
WHMP
RUSTLE RUSTLE
SHOOP
TAKTAKTAK
OH!
EXCUSE US. MAY WE ASK YOU A QUESTION?

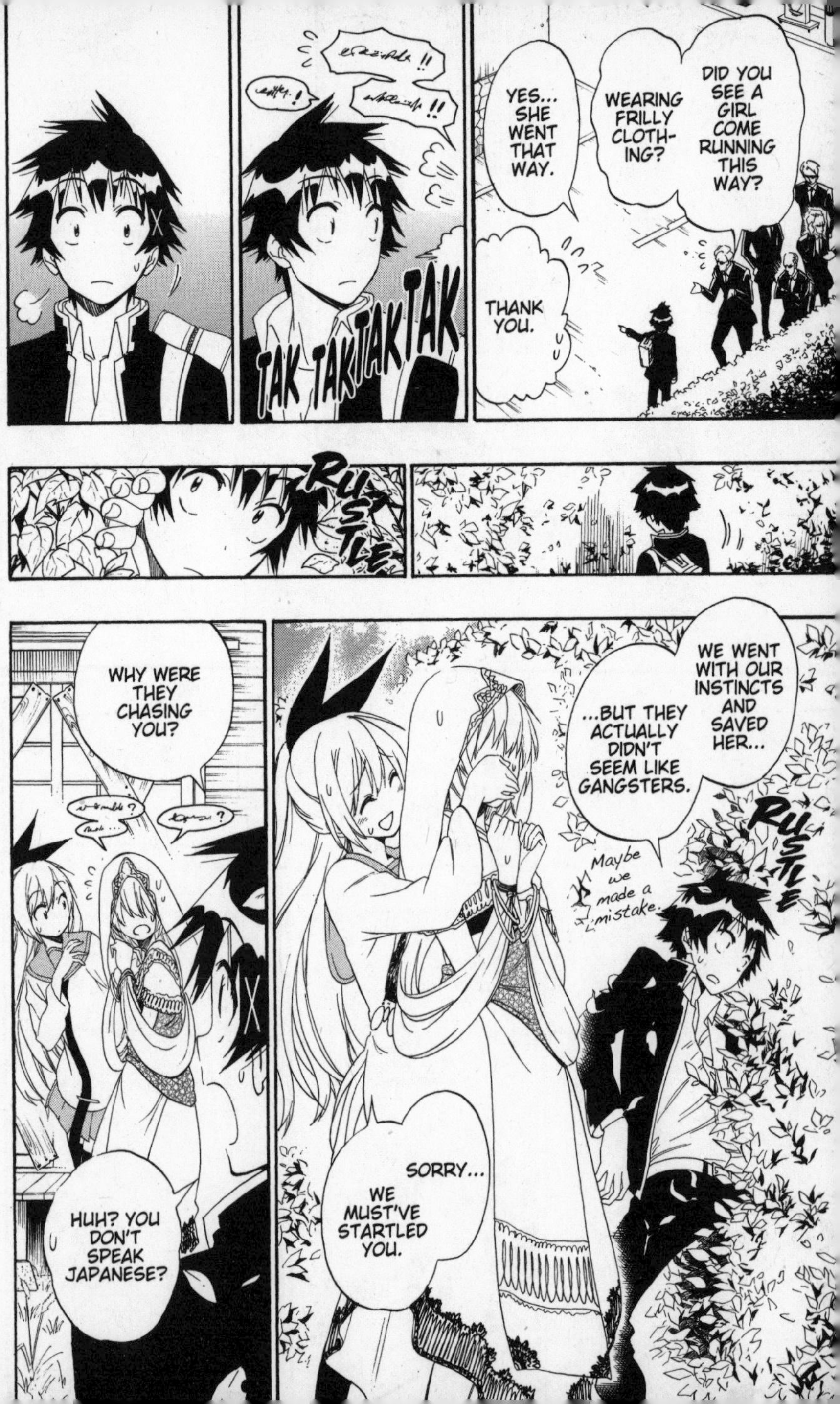
DID YOU SEE A GIRL COME RUNNING THIS WAY?
WEARING FRILLY CLOTH-ING?
YES... SHE WENT THAT WAY.
THANK YOU.
TAK TAK TAK TAK
RUSTLE
WE WENT WITH OUR INSTINCTS AND SAVED HER...
...BUT THEY ACTUALLY DIDN'T SEEM LIKE GANGSTERS.
Maybe we made a mistake.
RUSTLE
SORRY...
WE MUST'VE STARTLED YOU.
WHY WERE THEY CHASING YOU?
HUH? YOU DON'T SPEAK JAPANESE?

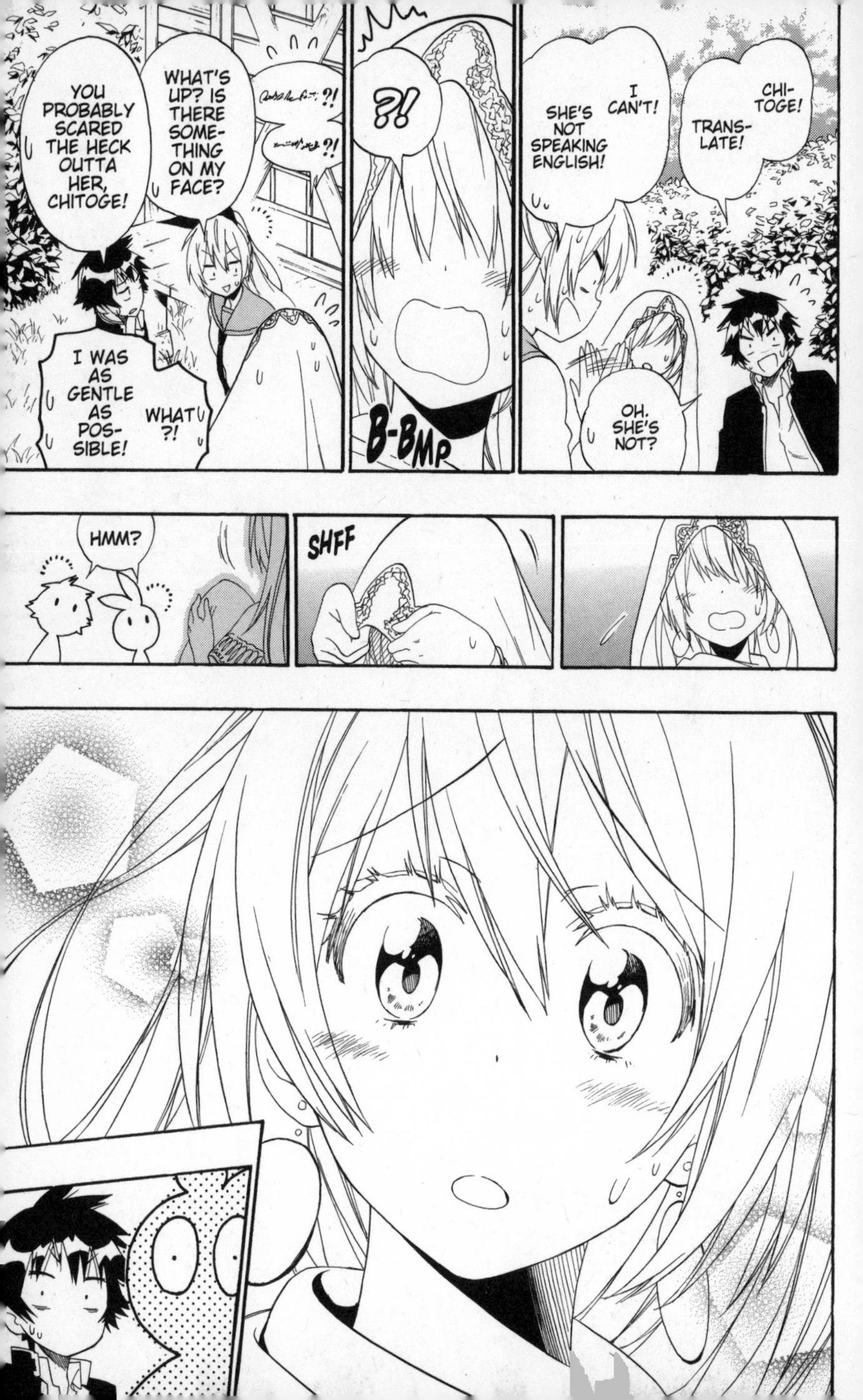
CHI-TOGE! TRANSLATE!
I CAN'T! SHE'S NOT SPEAKING ENGLISH!
OH. SHE'S NOT?
?!
B-BMP
WHAT'S UP? IS THERE SOME-THING ON MY FACE?
YOU PROBABLY SCARED THE HECK OUTTA HER, CHITOGE!
WHAT?!
I WAS AS GENTLE AS POS-SIBLE!
SHFF
HMM?

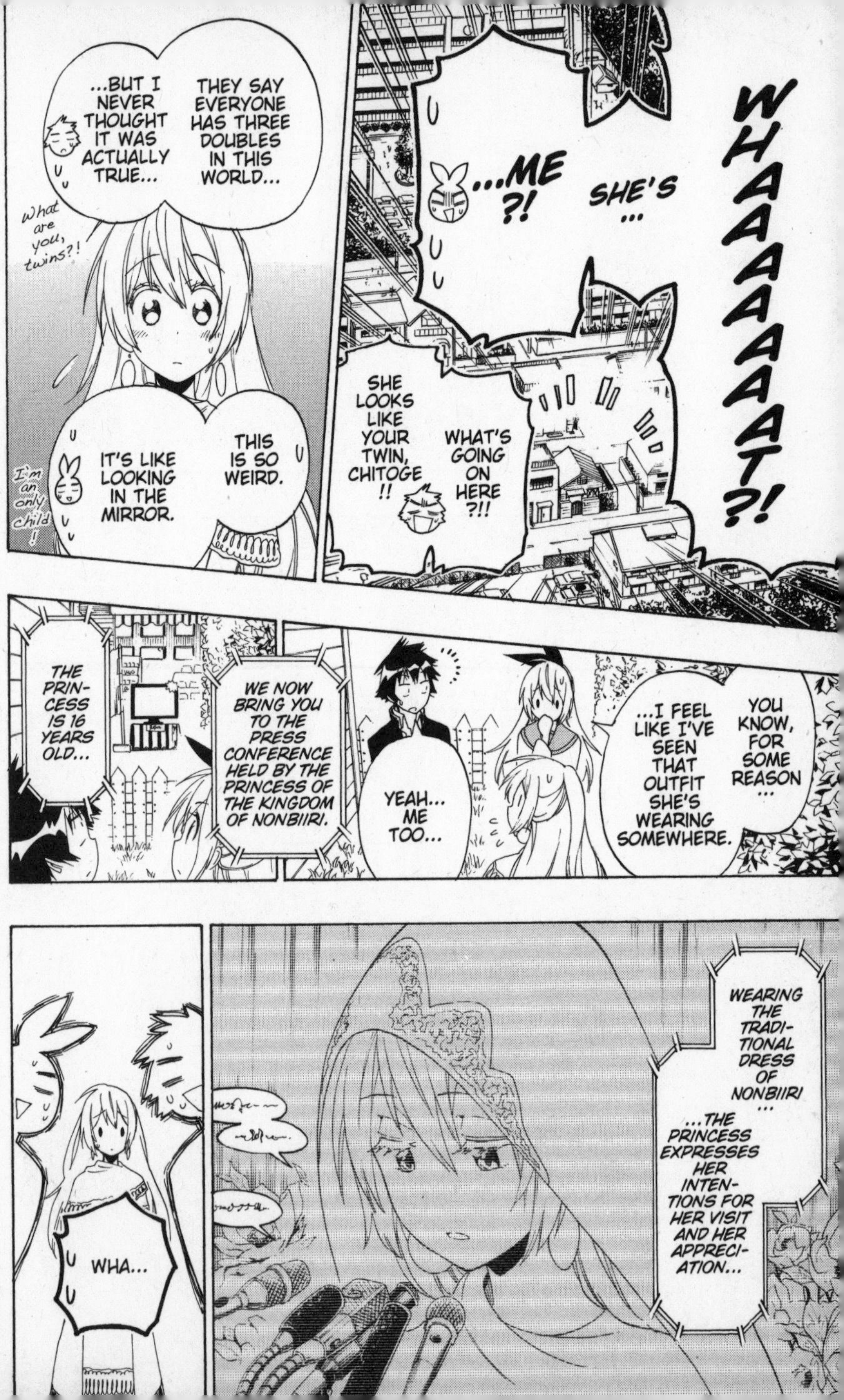
WHAAAAAAAT?!
SHE'S ...
...ME ?!
WHAT'S GOING ON HERE ?!!
SHE LOOKS LIKE YOUR TWIN, CHITOGE !!
THEY SAY EVERYONE HAS THREE DOUBLES IN THIS WORLD...
...BUT I NEVER THOUGHT IT WAS ACTUALLY TRUE...
What are you, twins?!
THIS IS SO WEIRD.
IT'S LIKE LOOKING IN THE MIRROR.
I'm an only child!
YOU KNOW, FOR SOME REASON ...
...I FEEL LIKE I'VE SEEN THAT OUTFIT SHE'S WEARING SOMEWHERE.
YEAH... ME TOO...
WE NOW BRING YOU TO THE PRESS CONFERENCE HELD BY THE PRINCESS OF THE KINGDOM OF NONBIIRI.
THE PRINCESS IS 16 YEARS OLD...
WEARING THE TRADITIONAL DRESS OF NONBIIRI ...
...THE PRINCESS EXPRESSES HER INTENTIONS FOR HER VISIT AND HER APPRECIATION...
WHA...

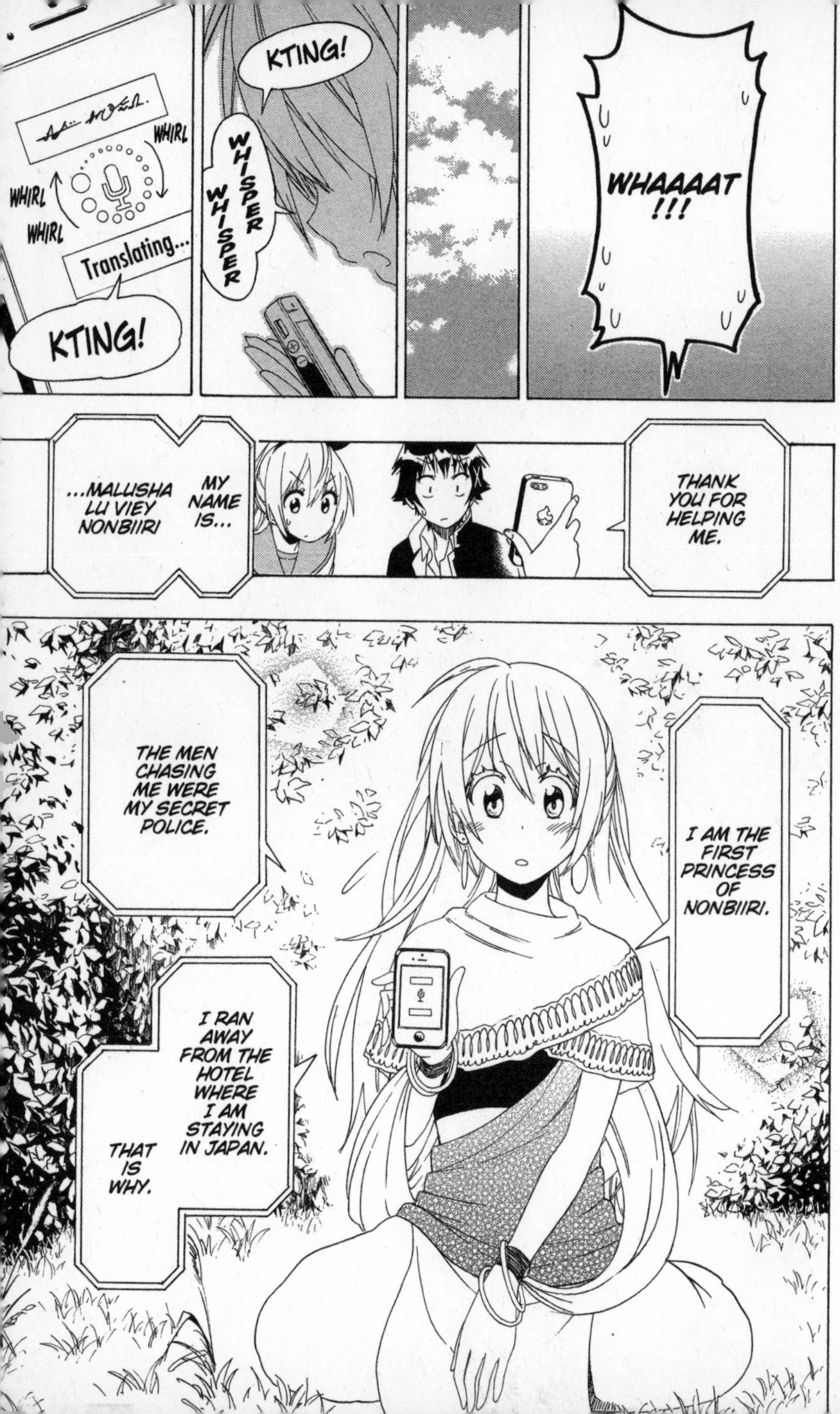
WHAAAAT!!!
KTING!
WHISPER WHISPER
WHIRL
WHIRL
WHIRL
Translating...
KTING!
THANK YOU FOR HELPING ME.
MY NAME IS...
...MALUSHA LU VIEY NONBIIRI
I AM THE FIRST PRINCESS OF NONBIIRI.
THE MEN CHASING ME WERE MY SECRET POLICE.
I RAN AWAY FROM THE HOTEL WHERE I AM STAYING IN JAPAN.
THAT IS WHY.

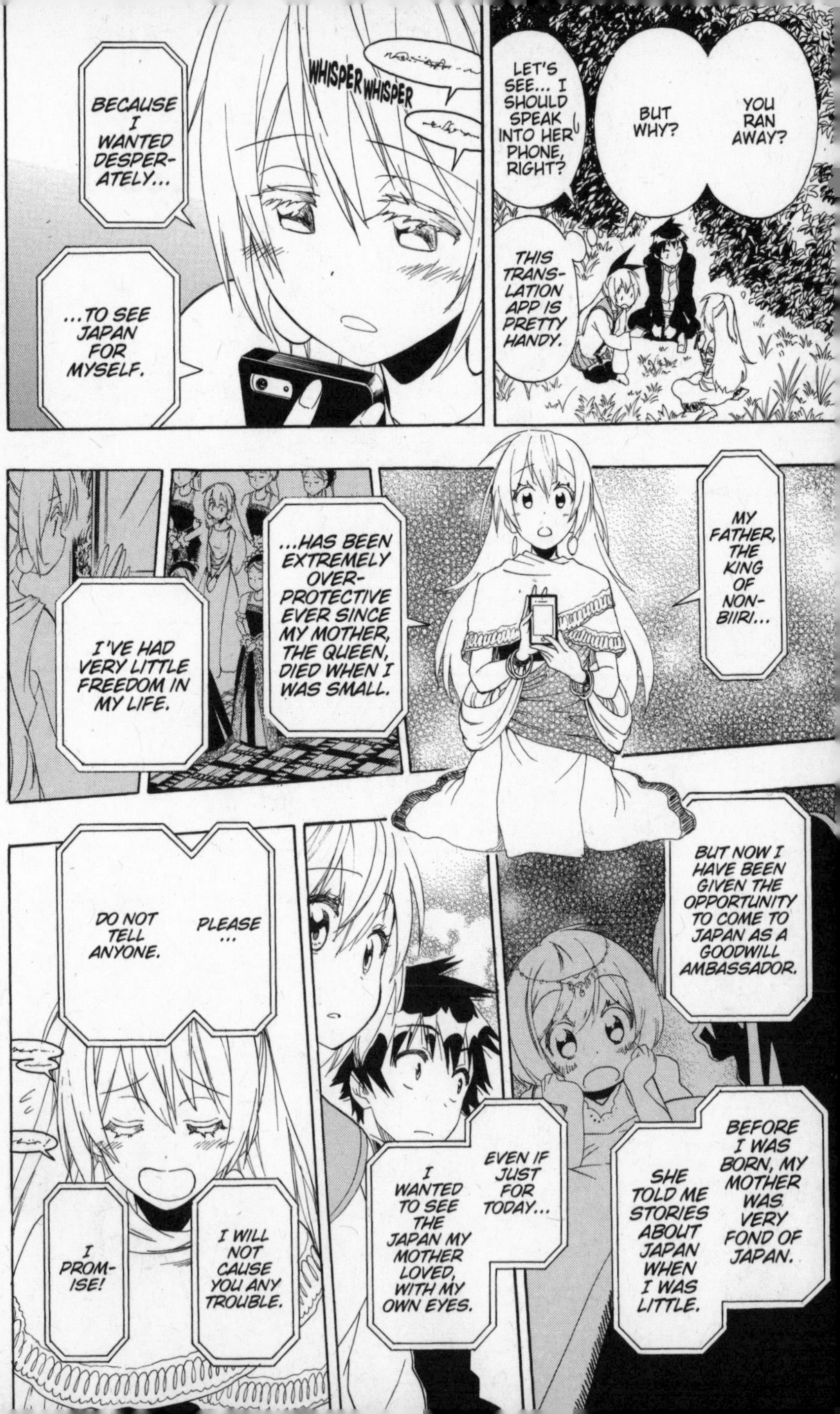
YOU RAN AWAY?
BUT WHY?
LET'S SEE... I SHOULD SPEAK INTO HER PHONE, RIGHT?
THIS TRANSLATION APP IS PRETTY HANDY.
WHISPER WHISPER
BECAUSE I WANTED DESPERATELY...
...TO SEE JAPAN FOR MYSELF.
MY FATHER, THE KING OF NON-BIIRI...
...HAS BEEN EXTREMELY OVERPROTECTIVE EVER SINCE MY MOTHER, THE QUEEN, DIED WHEN I WAS SMALL.
I'VE HAD VERY LITTLE FREEDOM IN MY LIFE.
BUT NOW I HAVE BEEN GIVEN THE OPPORTUNITY TO COME TO JAPAN AS A GOODWILL AMBASSADOR.
BEFORE I WAS BORN, MY MOTHER WAS VERY FOND OF JAPAN.
SHE TOLD ME STORIES ABOUT JAPAN WHEN I WAS LITTLE.
EVEN IF JUST FOR TODAY...
I WANTED TO SEE THE JAPAN MY MOTHER LOVED, WITH MY OWN EYES.
PLEASE...
DO NOT TELL ANYONE.
I WILL NOT CAUSE YOU ANY TROUBLE.
I PROMISE!

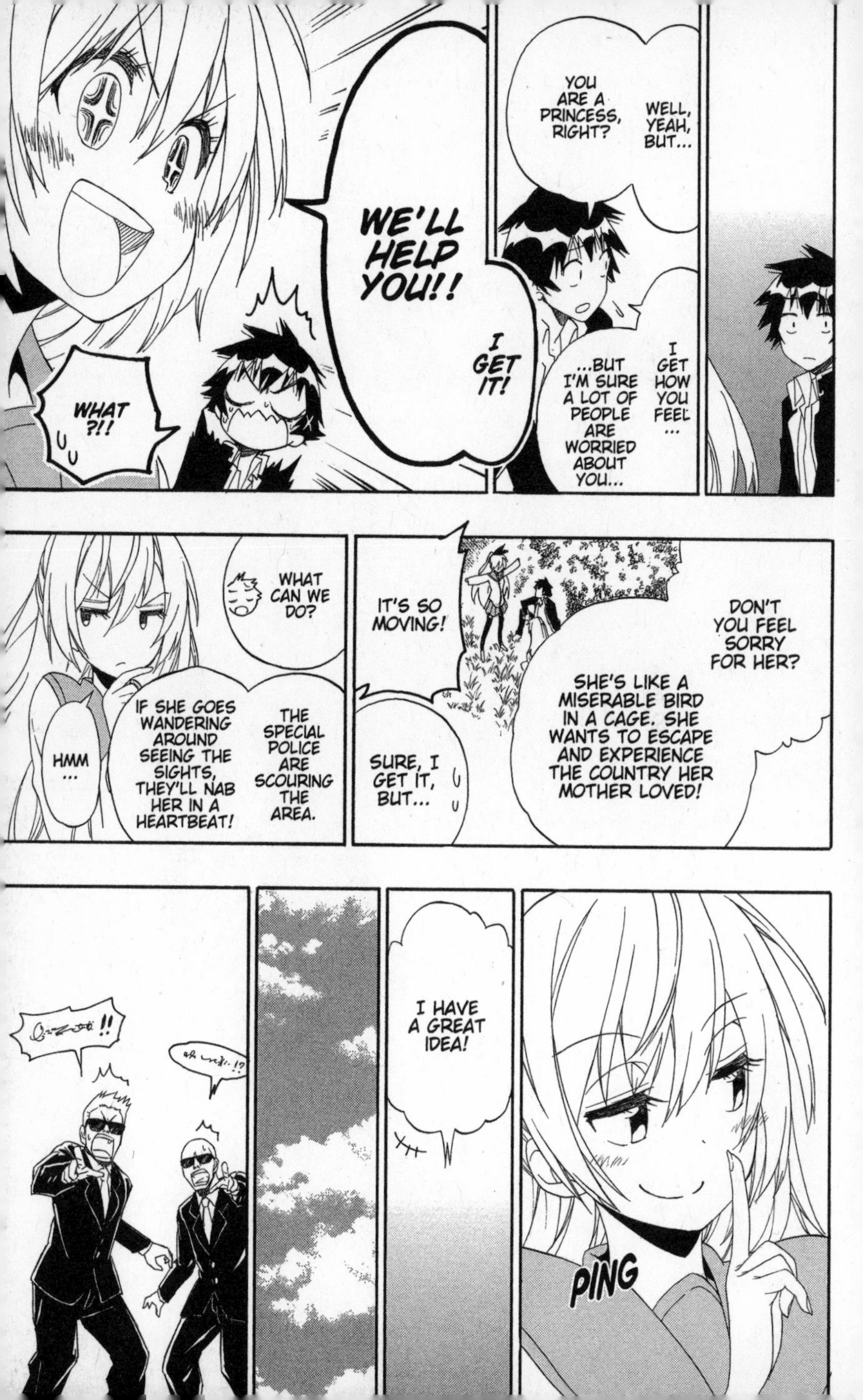
YOU ARE A PRINCESS, RIGHT?
WELL, YEAH, BUT...
I GET HOW YOU FEEL...
...BUT I'M SURE A LOT OF PEOPLE ARE WORRIED ABOUT YOU...
I GET IT!
WE'LL HELP YOU!!
WHAT?!!
DON'T YOU FEEL SORRY FOR HER?
SHE'S LIKE A MISERABLE BIRD IN A CAGE. SHE WANTS TO ESCAPE AND EXPERIENCE THE COUNTRY HER MOTHER LOVED!
IT'S SO MOVING!
SURE, I GET IT, BUT...
WHAT CAN WE DO?
THE SPECIAL POLICE ARE SCOURING THE AREA.
IF SHE GOES WANDERING AROUND SEEING THE SIGHTS, THEY'LL NAB HER IN A HEARTBEAT!
HMM...
PING
I HAVE A GREAT IDEA!

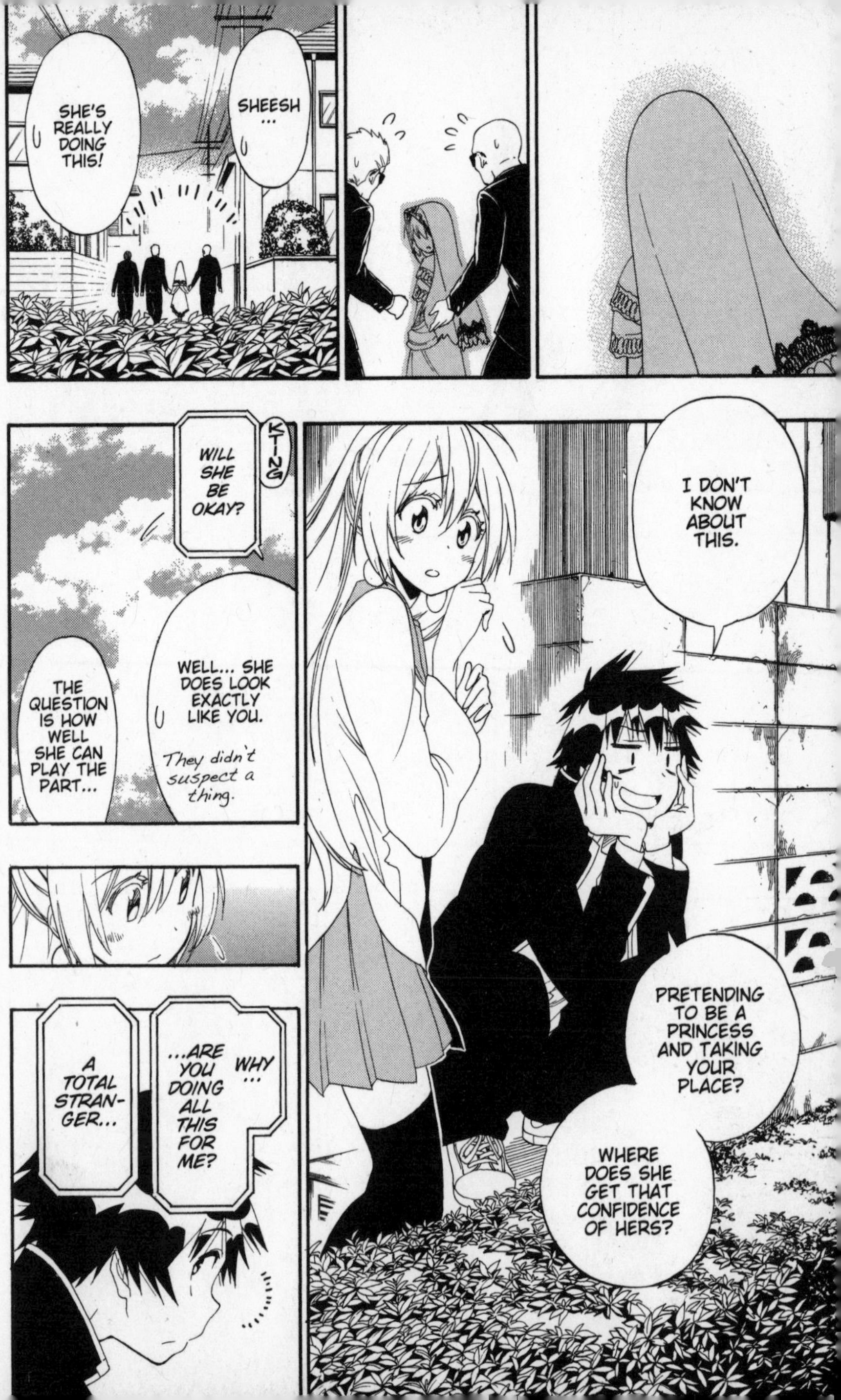
SHEESH...
SHE'S REALLY DOING THIS!
I DON'T KNOW ABOUT THIS.
PRETENDING TO BE A PRINCESS AND TAKING YOUR PLACE?
WHERE DOES SHE GET THAT CONFIDENCE OF HERS?
KTING
WILL SHE BE OKAY?
WELL... SHE DOES LOOK EXACTLY LIKE YOU.
They didn't suspect a thing.
THE QUESTION IS HOW WELL SHE CAN PLAY THE PART...
WHY...
...ARE YOU DOING ALL THIS FOR ME?
A TOTAL STRANGER...

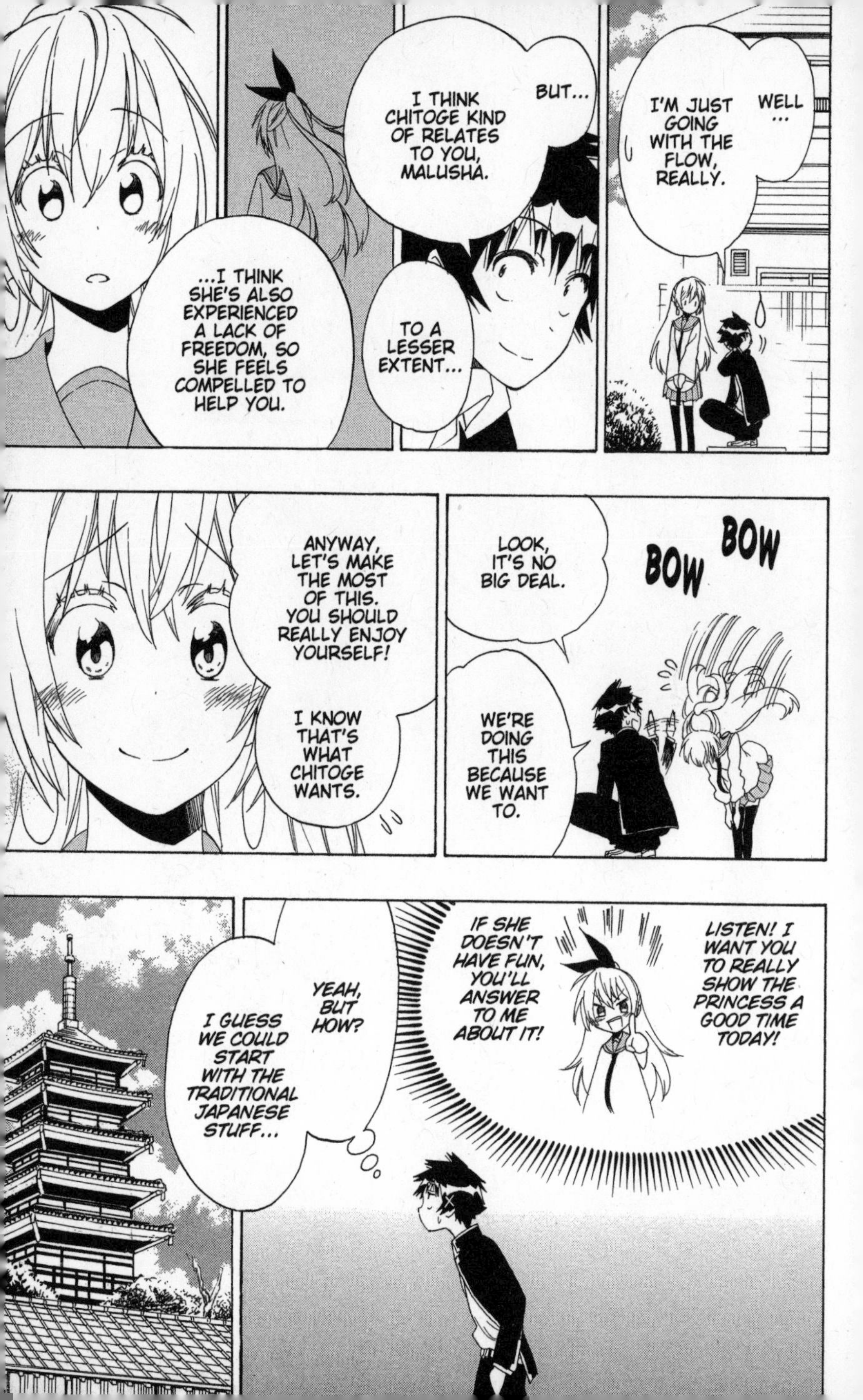
WELL ...
I'M JUST GOING WITH THE FLOW, REALLY.
BUT...
I THINK CHITOGE KIND OF RELATES TO YOU, MALUSHA.
TO A LESSER EXTENT...
...I THINK SHE'S ALSO EXPERIENCED A LACK OF FREEDOM, SO SHE FEELS COMPELLED TO HELP YOU.
BOW
BOW
LOOK, IT'S NO BIG DEAL.
WE'RE DOING THIS BECAUSE WE WANT TO.
ANYWAY, LET'S MAKE THE MOST OF THIS. YOU SHOULD REALLY ENJOY YOURSELF!
I KNOW THAT'S WHAT CHITOGE WANTS.
LISTEN! I WANT YOU TO REALLY SHOW THE PRINCESS A GOOD TIME TODAY!
IF SHE DOESN'T HAVE FUN, YOU'LL ANSWER TO ME ABOUT IT!
YEAH, BUT HOW?
I GUESS WE COULD START WITH THE TRADITIONAL JAPANESE STUFF...

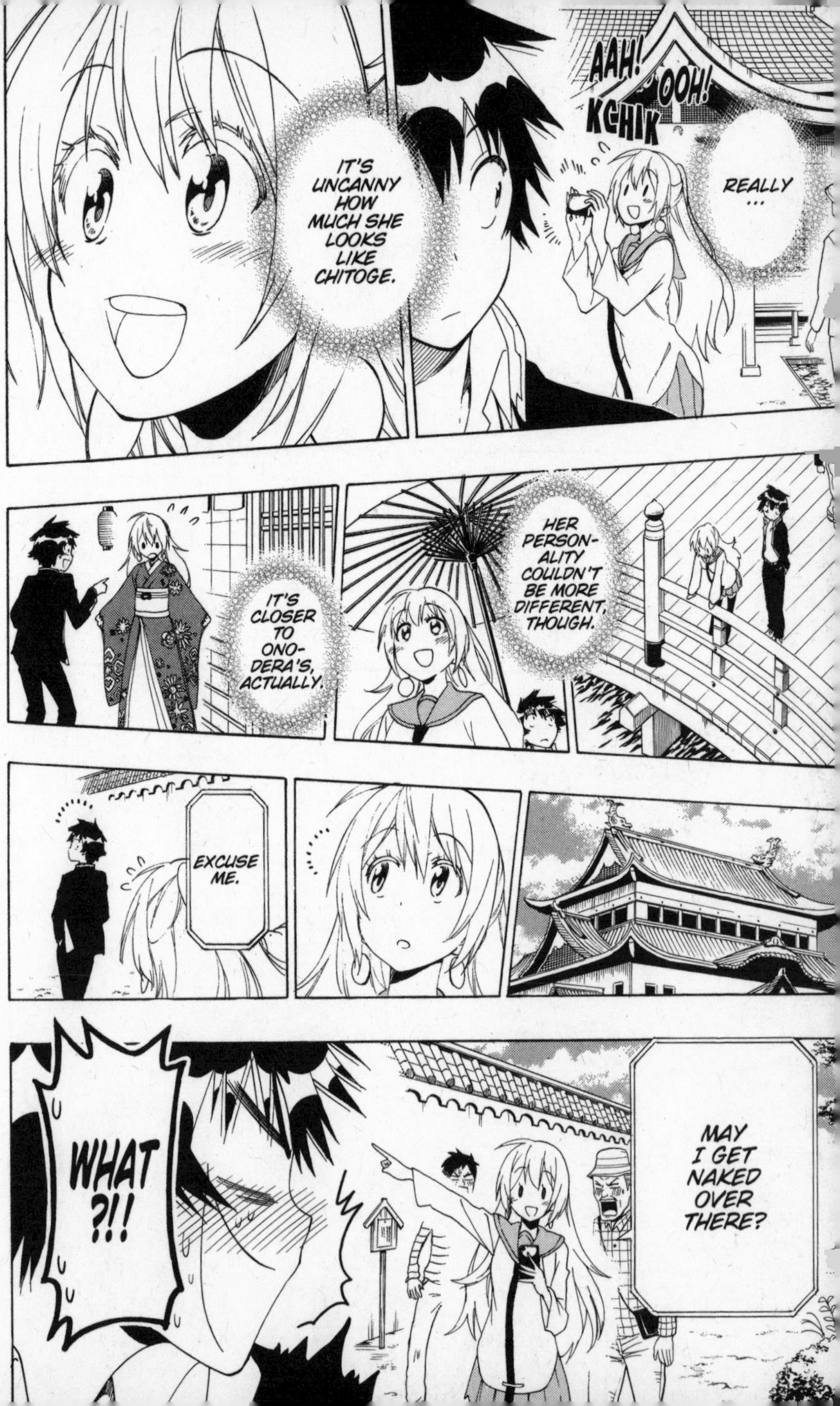
AAH!
OOH!
KCHIK
REALLY ...
IT'S UNCANNY HOW MUCH SHE LOOKS LIKE CHITOGE.
HER PERSONALITY COULDN'T BE MORE DIFFERENT, THOUGH.
IT'S CLOSER TO ONODERA'S, ACTUALLY.
EXCUSE ME.
MAY I GET NAKED OVER THERE?
WHAT ?!!

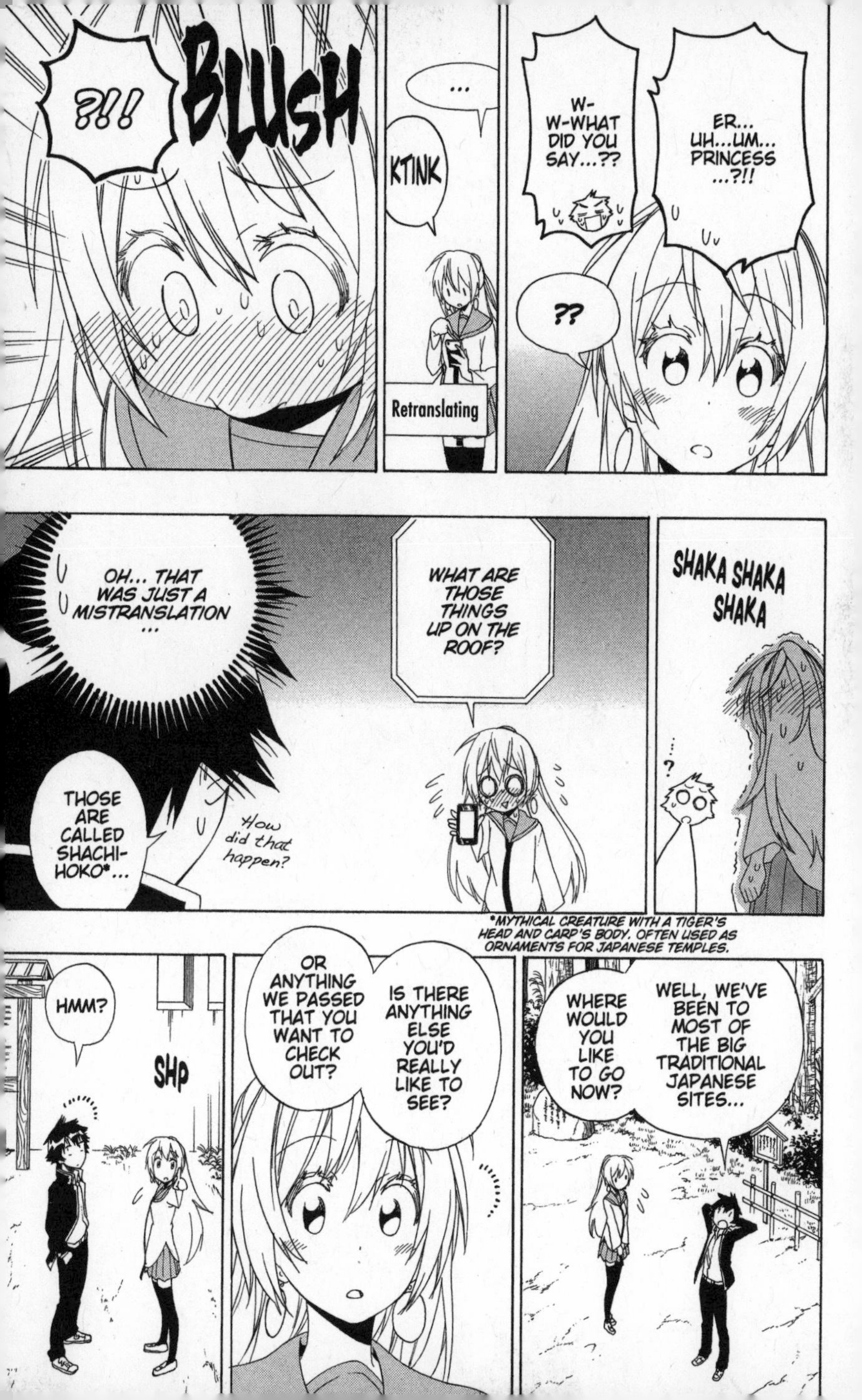
ER... UH...UM... PRINCESS ...?!!
W- W-WHAT DID YOU SAY...??
??
...
KTINK
Retranslating
BLUSH
?!!
SHAKA SHAKA SHAKA
?
WHAT ARE THOSE THINGS UP ON THE ROOF?
OH... THAT WAS JUST A MISTRANSLATION...
How did that happen?
THOSE ARE CALLED SHACHI-HOKO*...
WELL, WE'VE BEEN TO MOST OF THE BIG TRADITIONAL JAPANESE SITES...
WHERE WOULD YOU LIKE TO GO NOW?
IS THERE ANYTHING ELSE YOU'D REALLY LIKE TO SEE?
OR ANYTHING WE PASSED THAT YOU WANT TO CHECK OUT?
SHP
HMM?

*MYTHICAL CREATURE WITH A TIGER'S HEAD AND CARP'S BODY. OFTEN USED AS ORNAMENTS FOR JAPANESE TEMPLES.

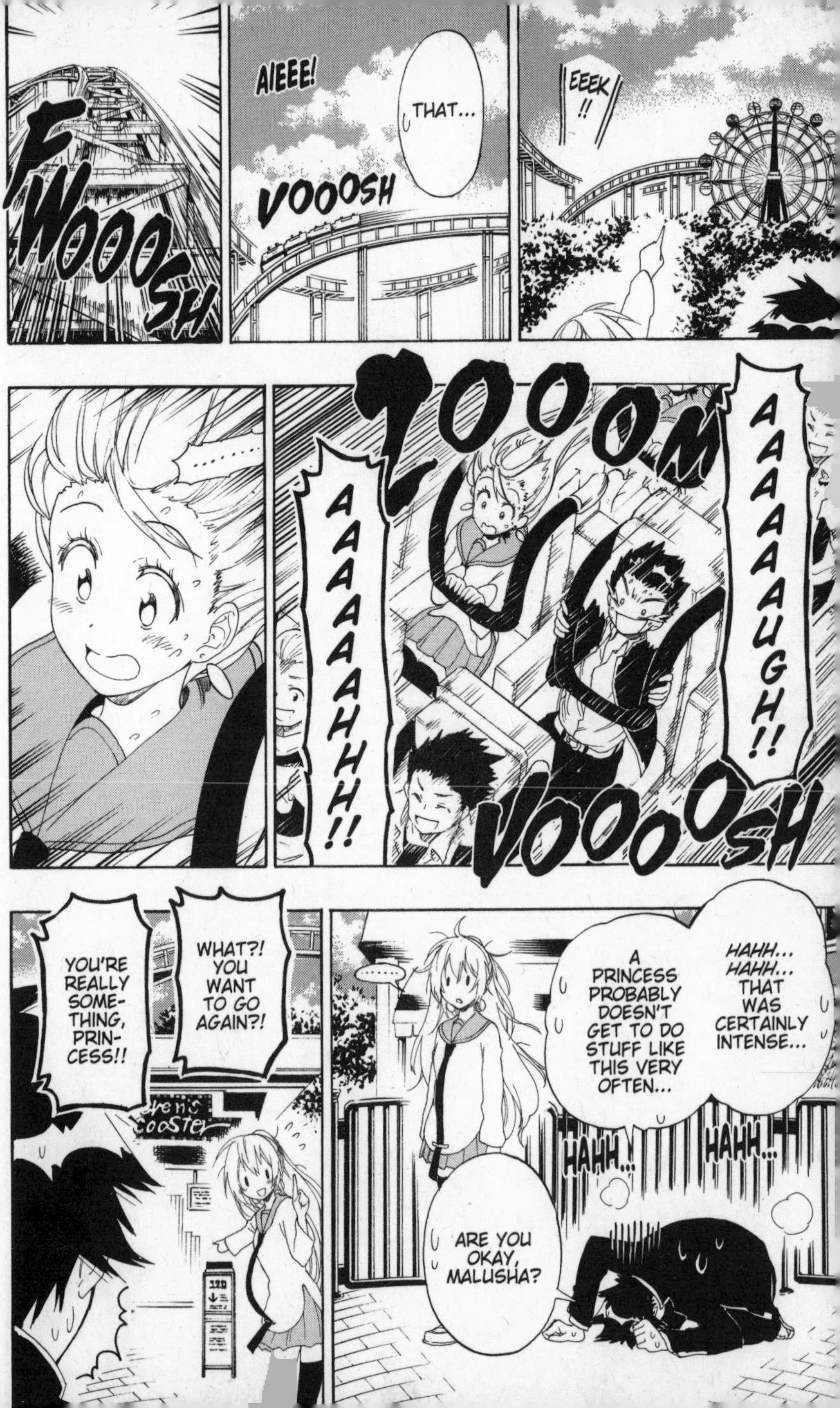
EEEK!!
THAT...
AIEEE!
VOOOSH
FWOOOSH
AAAAAAAUGH!!
ZOOOM
AAAAAAAHHHH!!
VOOOOSH
......
HAHH... HAHH... THAT WAS CERTAINLY INTENSE...
A PRINCESS PROBABLY DOESN'T GET TO DO STUFF LIKE THIS VERY OFTEN...
......
HAHH...
HAHH...
ARE YOU OKAY, MALUSHA?
WHAT?! YOU WANT TO GO AGAIN?!
YOU'RE REALLY SOME-THING, PRIN-CESS!!

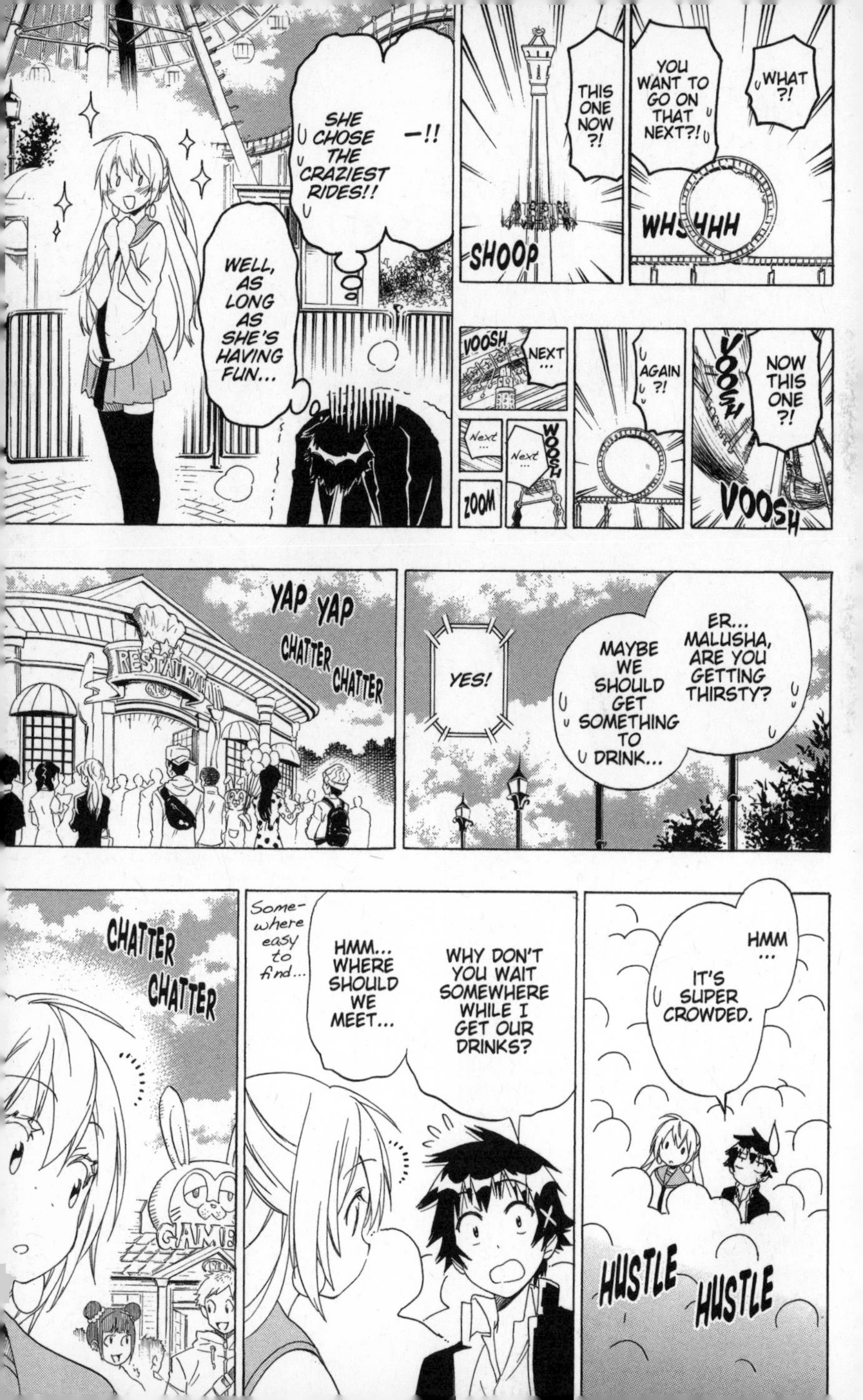
WHAT?!
YOU WANT TO GO ON THAT NEXT?!
WHSHHH
THIS ONE NOW?!
SHOOP
NOW THIS ONE?!
VOOSH
VOOSH
AGAIN?!
VOOSH
NEXT...
Next...
Next...
WOOSH
ZOOM
SHE CHOSE THE CRAZIEST RIDES!!
—!!
WELL, AS LONG AS SHE'S HAVING FUN...
ER... MALUSHA, ARE YOU GETTING THIRSTY?
MAYBE WE SHOULD GET SOMETHING TO DRINK...
YES!
YAP YAP
CHATTER CHATTER
RESTAURANT
HMM...
IT'S SUPER CROWDED.
HUSTLE HUSTLE
WHY DON'T YOU WAIT SOMEWHERE WHILE I GET OUR DRINKS?
HMM... WHERE SHOULD WE MEET...
Somewhere easy to find...
CHATTER CHATTER

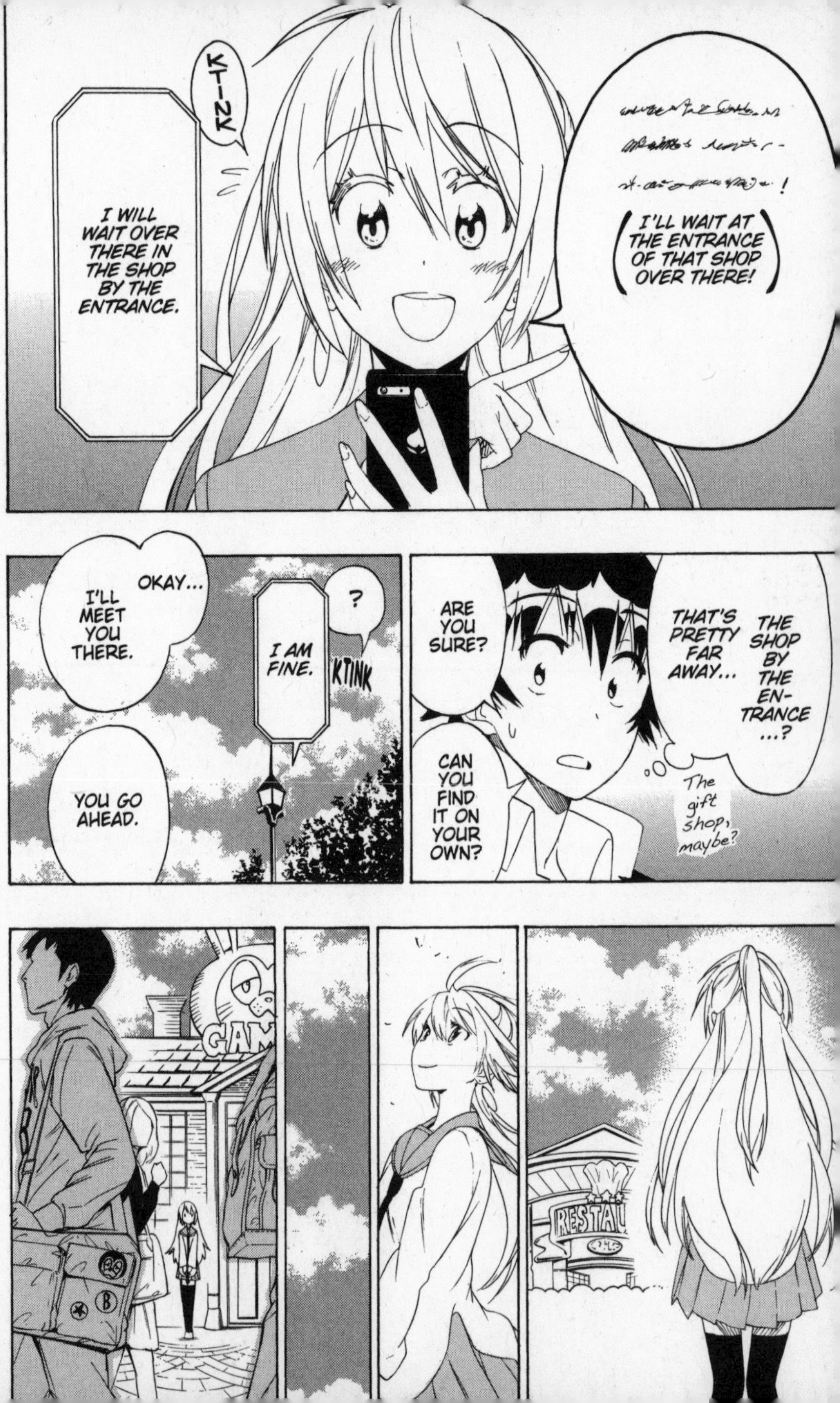
I'LL WAIT AT THE ENTRANCE OF THAT SHOP OVER THERE!
KTINK
I WILL WAIT OVER THERE IN THE SHOP BY THE ENTRANCE.
THE SHOP BY THE EN-TRANCE ...?
THAT'S PRETTY FAR AWAY...
The gift shop, maybe?
ARE YOU SURE?
CAN YOU FIND IT ON YOUR OWN?
?
KTINK
I AM FINE.
OKAY... I'LL MEET YOU THERE.
YOU GO AHEAD.

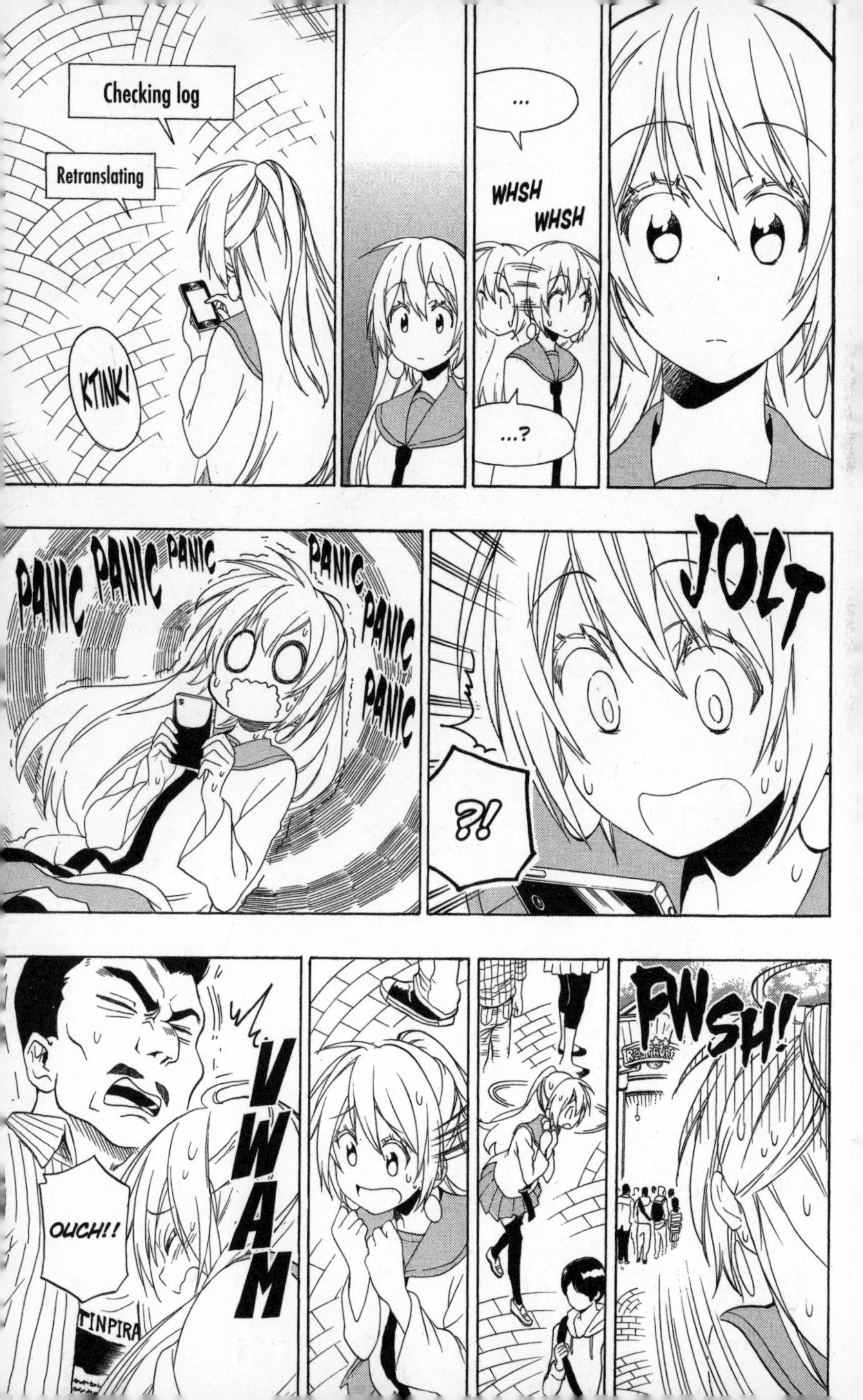
...
WHSH
WHSH
...?
Checking log
Retranslating
KTINK!
JOLT
?!
PANIC PANIC PANIC
PANIC PANIC PANIC
FWSH!
VWAM
OUCH!!
TINPIRA

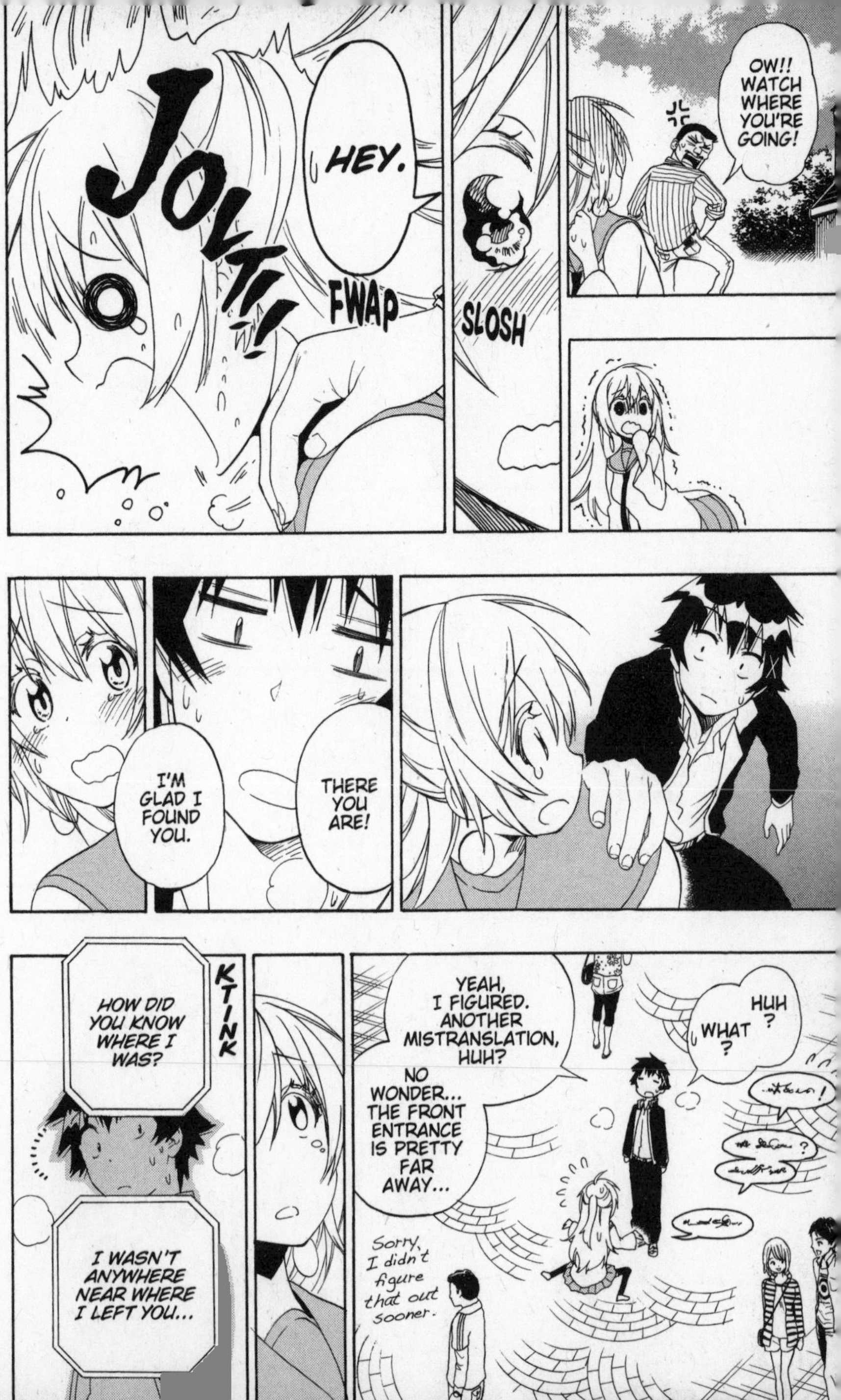
OW!! WATCH WHERE YOU'RE GOING!
SLOSH
HEY.
FWAP
JOLT!!!
THERE YOU ARE!
I'M GLAD I FOUND YOU.
HUH?
WHAT?
YEAH, I FIGURED. ANOTHER MISTRANSLATION, HUH?
NO WONDER... THE FRONT ENTRANCE IS PRETTY FAR AWAY...
Sorry, I didn't figure that out sooner.
KTINK
HOW DID YOU KNOW WHERE I WAS?
I WASN'T ANYWHERE NEAR WHERE I LEFT YOU...

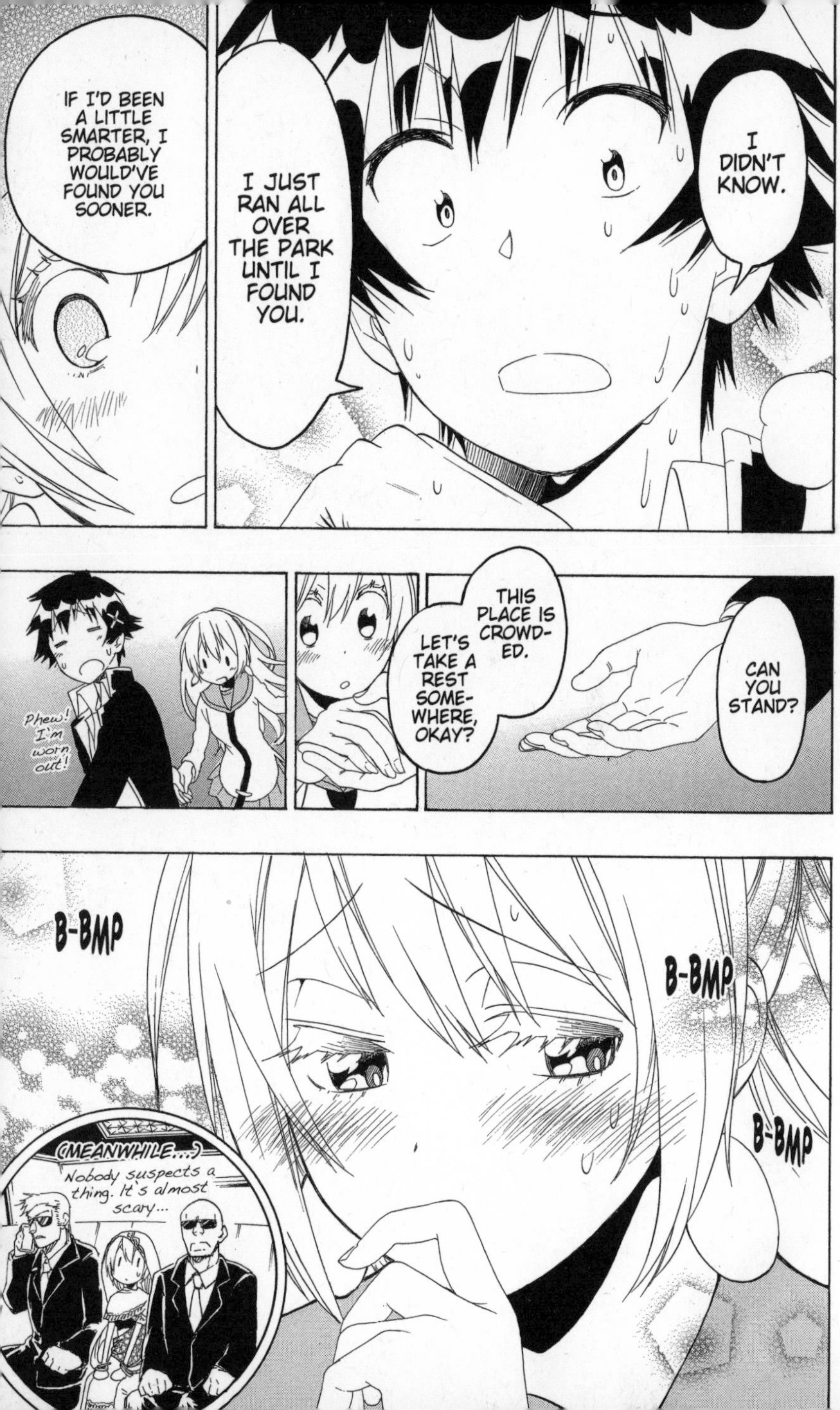
I DIDN'T KNOW.
I JUST RAN ALL OVER THE PARK UNTIL I FOUND YOU.
IF I'D BEEN A LITTLE SMARTER, I PROBABLY WOULD'VE FOUND YOU SOONER.
CAN YOU STAND?
THIS PLACE IS CROWD-ED.
LET'S TAKE A REST SOME-WHERE, OKAY?
Phew! I'm worn out!
B-BMP
B-BMP
B-BMP
(MEANWHILE...)
Nobody suspects a thing. It's almost scary...

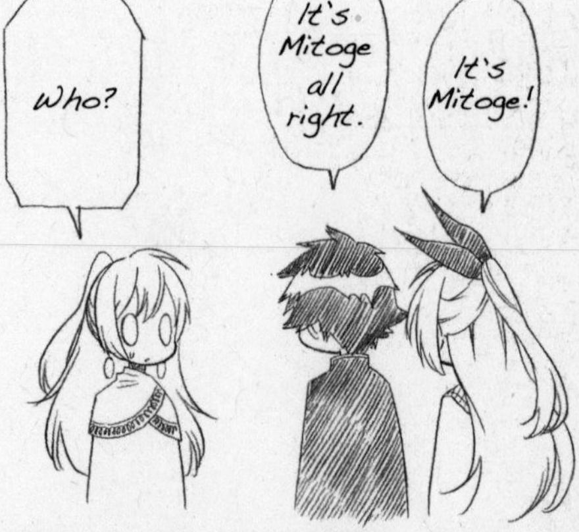
It's Mitoge!
It's Mitoge all right.
Who?

☆ NISEKOI video game now available! ☆

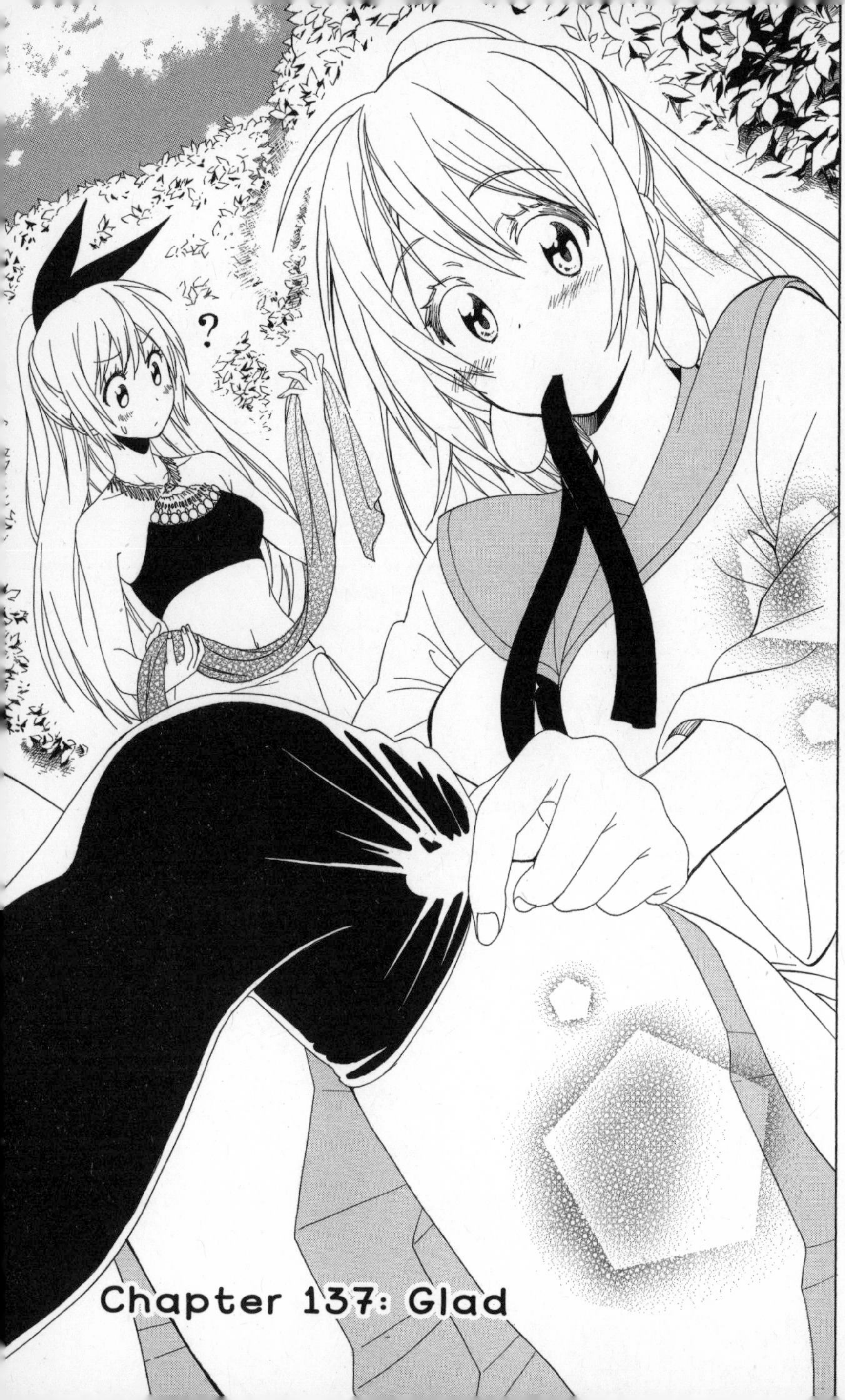
?

Chapter 137: Glad

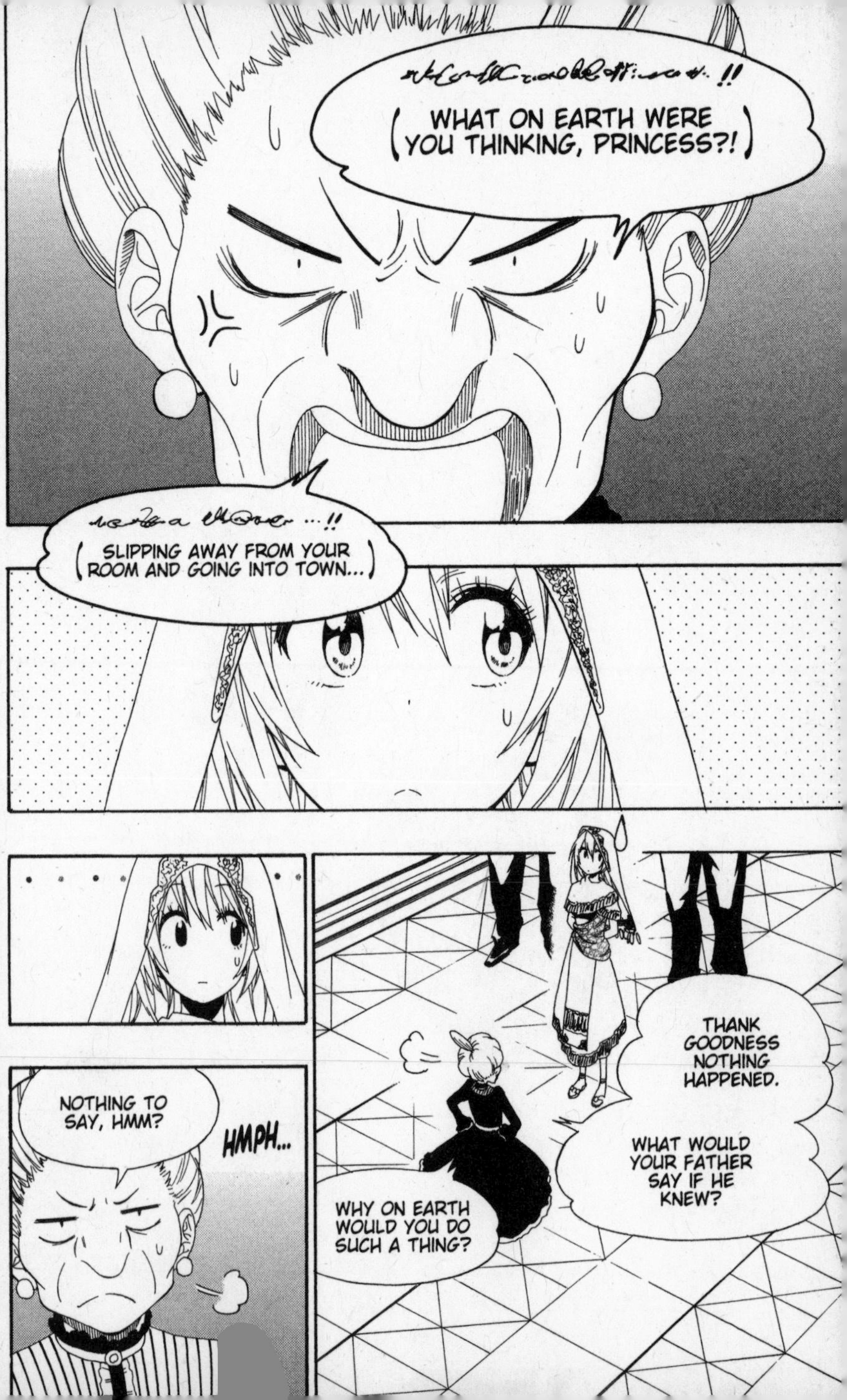
(WHAT ON EARTH WERE YOU THINKING, PRINCESS?!)
(SLIPPING AWAY FROM YOUR ROOM AND GOING INTO TOWN...)
THANK GOODNESS NOTHING HAPPENED.
WHAT WOULD YOUR FATHER SAY IF HE KNEW?
WHY ON EARTH WOULD YOU DO SUCH A THING?
• • • • •
NOTHING TO SAY, HMM?
HMPH...

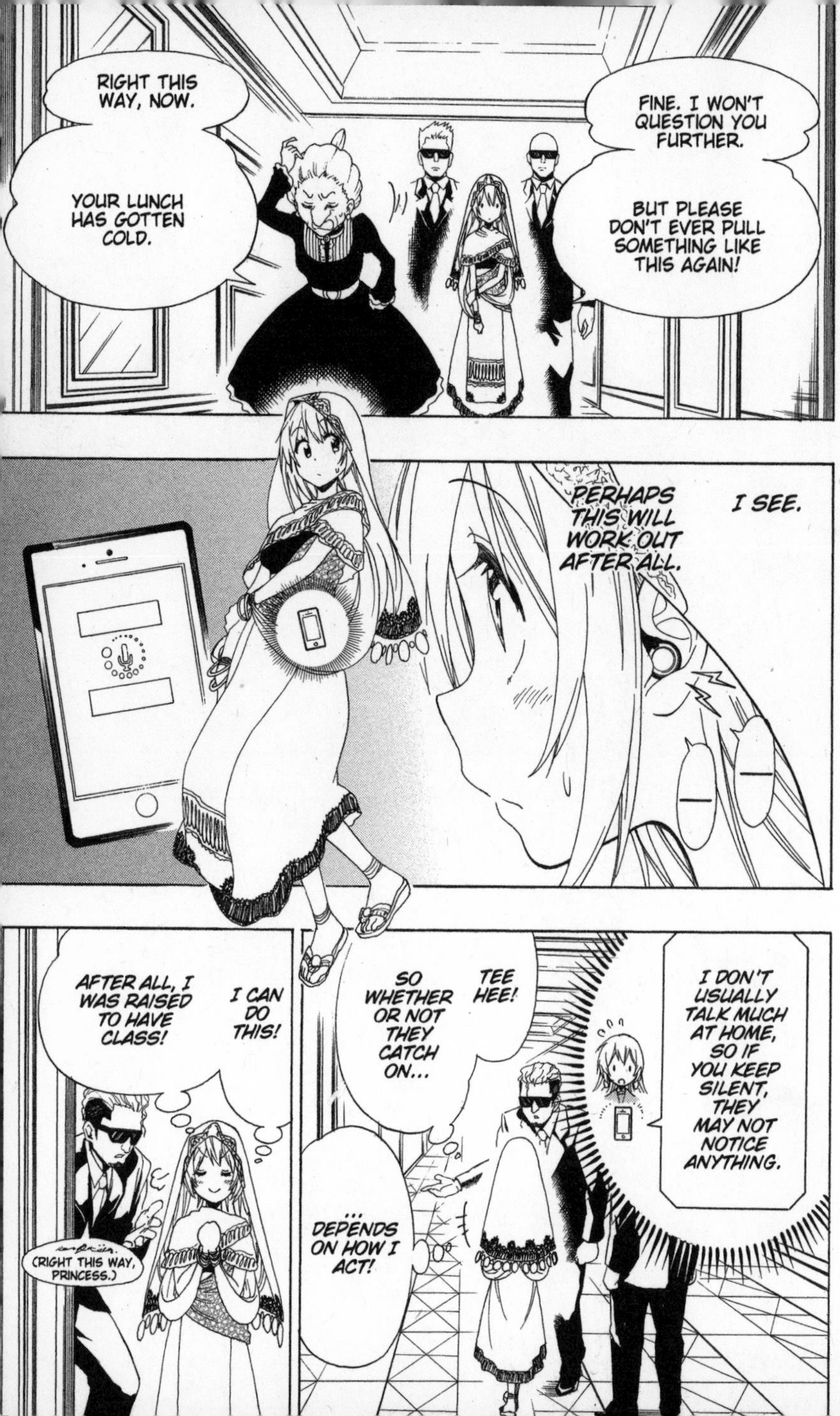
FINE. I WON'T QUESTION YOU FURTHER.
BUT PLEASE DON'T EVER PULL SOMETHING LIKE THIS AGAIN!
RIGHT THIS WAY, NOW.
YOUR LUNCH HAS GOTTEN COLD.
I SEE.
PERHAPS THIS WILL WORK OUT AFTER ALL.
I DON'T USUALLY TALK MUCH AT HOME, SO IF YOU KEEP SILENT, THEY MAY NOT NOTICE ANYTHING.
TEE HEE!
SO WHETHER OR NOT THEY CATCH ON...
...DEPENDS ON HOW I ACT!
I CAN DO THIS!
AFTER ALL, I WAS RAISED TO HAVE CLASS!
(RIGHT THIS WAY, PRINCESS.)

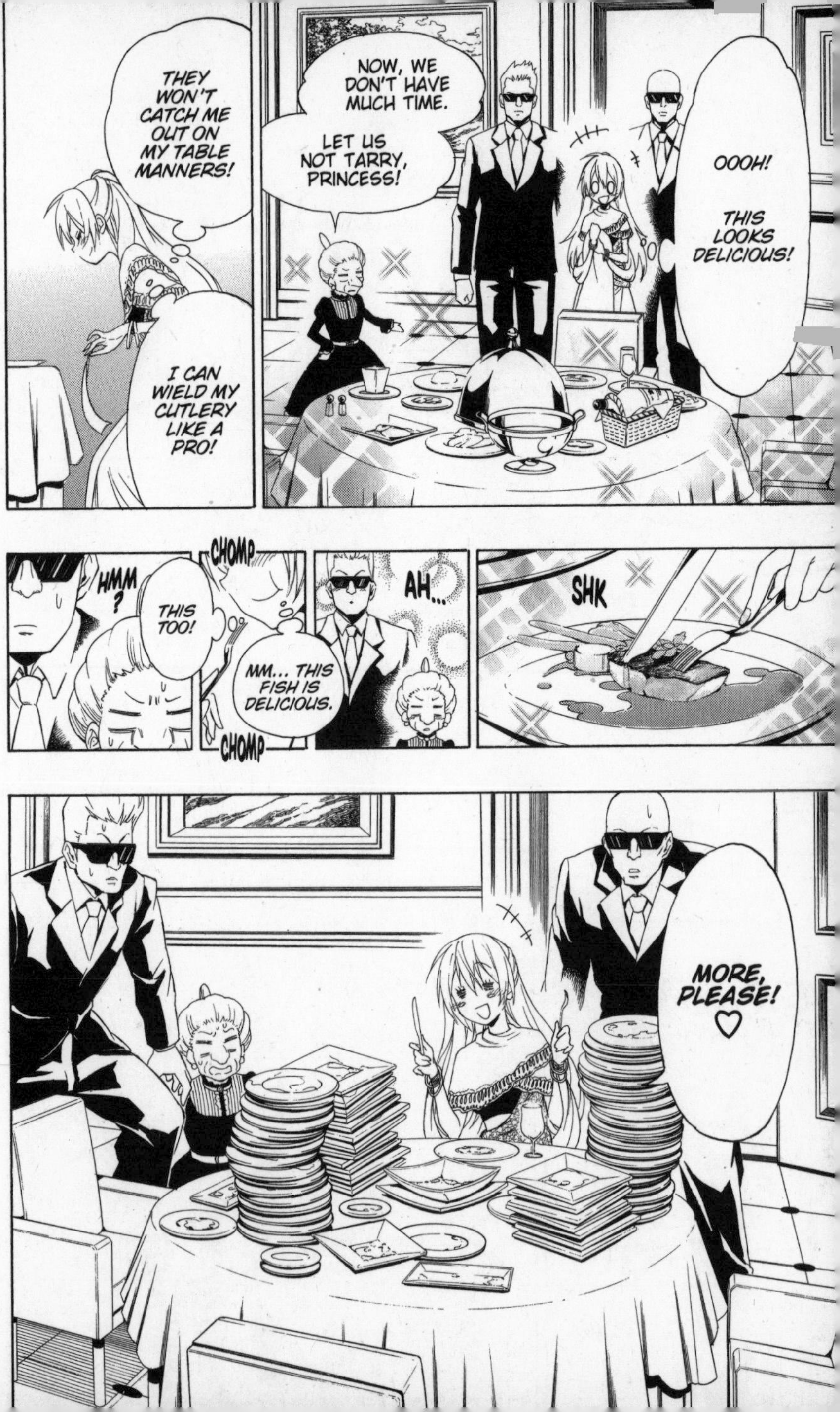
OOOH!
THIS LOOKS DELICIOUS!
NOW, WE DON'T HAVE MUCH TIME.
LET US NOT TARRY, PRINCESS!
THEY WON'T CATCH ME OUT ON MY TABLE MANNERS!
I CAN WIELD MY CUTLERY LIKE A PRO!
SHK
AH...
CHOMP
MM... THIS FISH IS DELICIOUS.
CHOMP
THIS TOO!
HMM?
MORE, PLEASE! ♡

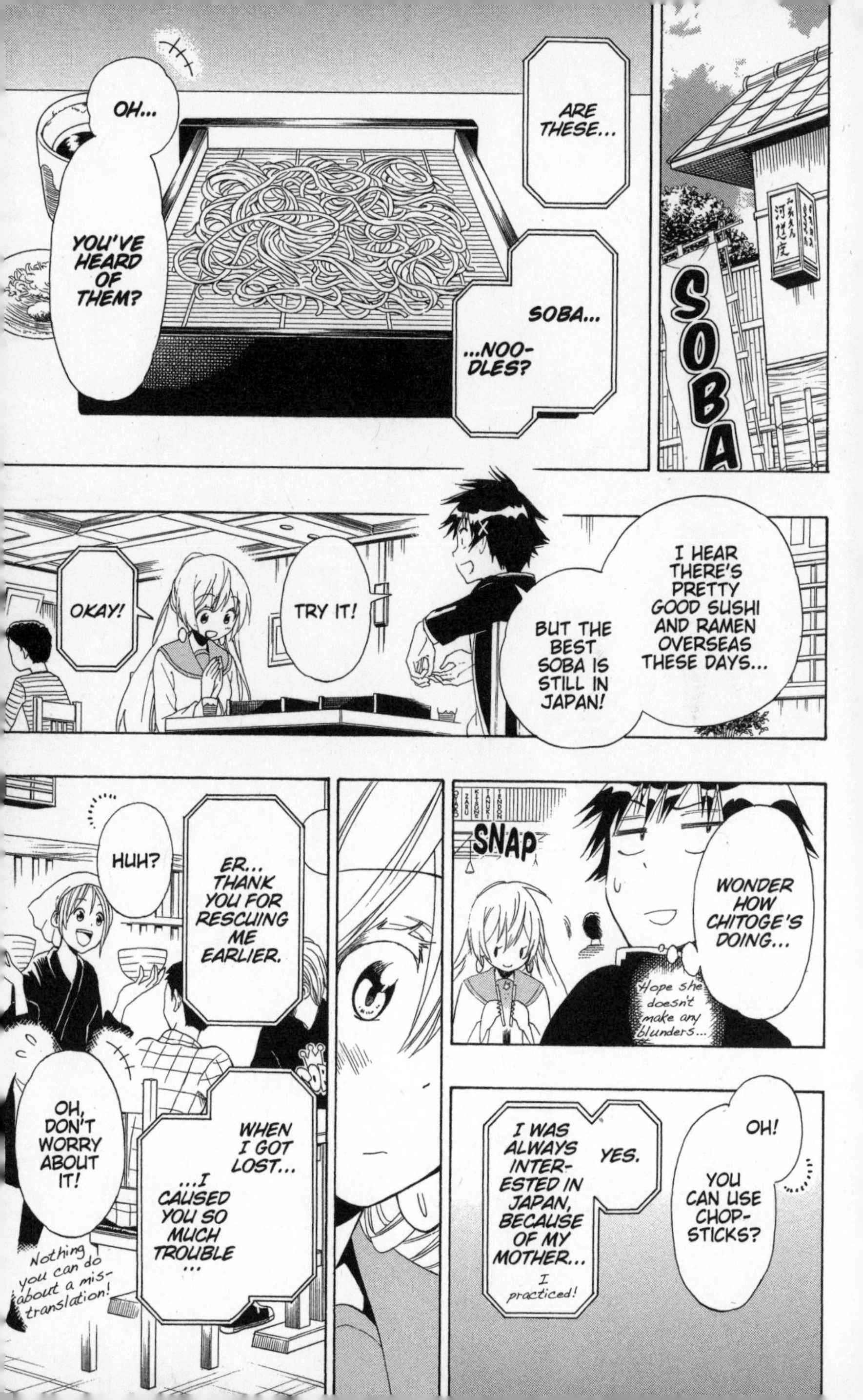
SOBA
ARE THESE...
SOBA...
...NOO-DLES?
OH...
YOU'VE HEARD OF THEM?
I HEAR THERE'S PRETTY GOOD SUSHI AND RAMEN OVERSEAS THESE DAYS...
BUT THE BEST SOBA IS STILL IN JAPAN!
TRY IT!
OKAY!
SNAP
WONDER HOW CHITOGE'S DOING...
Hope she doesn't make any blunders...
OH!
YOU CAN USE CHOP-STICKS?
YES.
I WAS ALWAYS INTER-ESTED IN JAPAN, BECAUSE OF MY MOTHER...
I practiced!
ER... THANK YOU FOR RESCUING ME EARLIER.
HUH?
WHEN I GOT LOST...
...I CAUSED YOU SO MUCH TROUBLE...
OH, DON'T WORRY ABOUT IT!
Nothing you can do about a mis-translation!

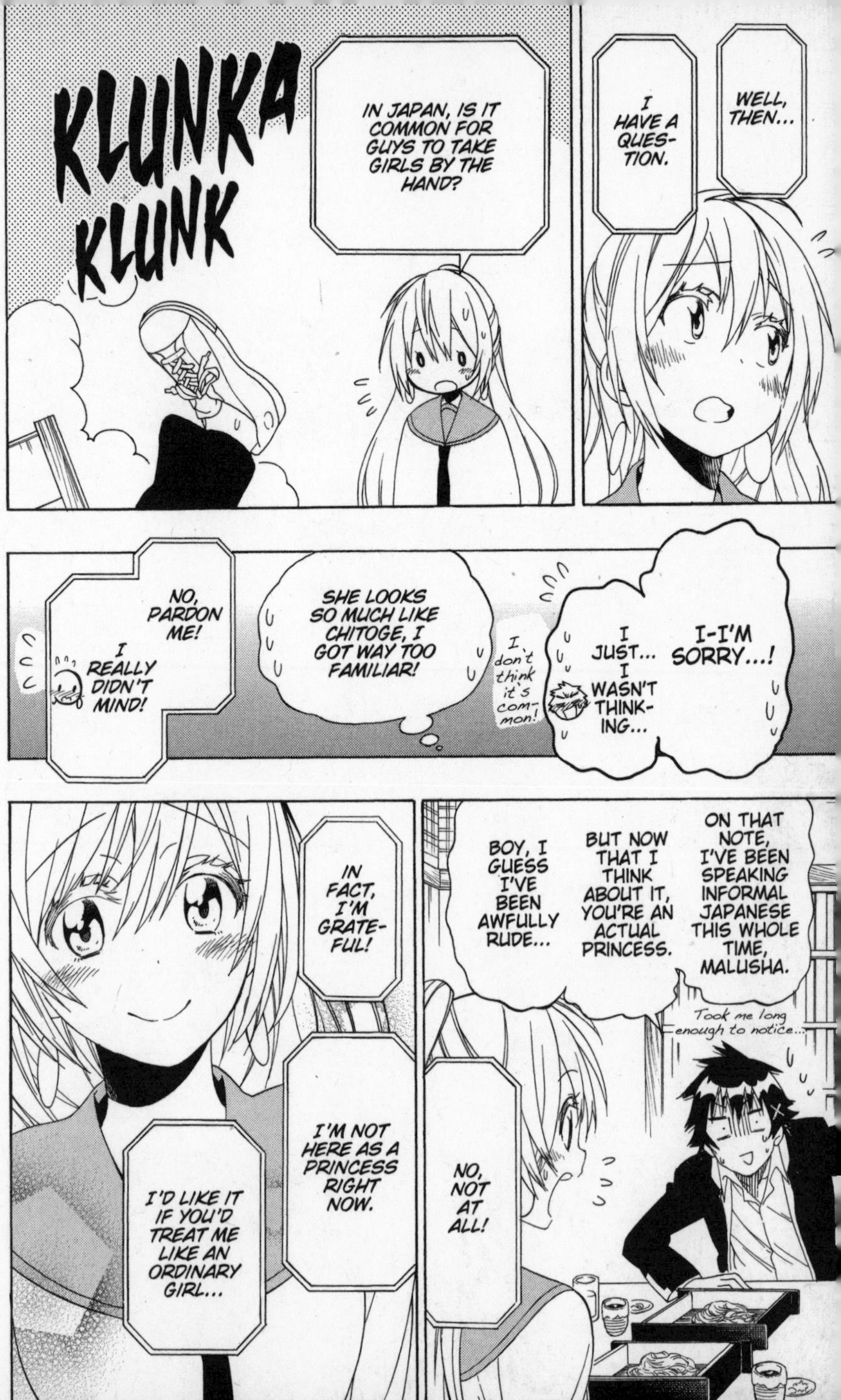
WELL, THEN...
I HAVE A QUESTION.
IN JAPAN, IS IT COMMON FOR GUYS TO TAKE GIRLS BY THE HAND?
KLUNKA KLUNK
I-I'M SORRY...!
I JUST... I WASN'T THINKING...
I don't think it's common!
SHE LOOKS SO MUCH LIKE CHITOGE, I GOT WAY TOO FAMILIAR!
NO, PARDON ME!
I REALLY DIDN'T MIND!
ON THAT NOTE, I'VE BEEN SPEAKING INFORMAL JAPANESE THIS WHOLE TIME, MALUSHA.
BUT NOW THAT I THINK ABOUT IT, YOU'RE AN ACTUAL PRINCESS.
BOY, I GUESS I'VE BEEN AWFULLY RUDE...
Took me long enough to notice...
NO, NOT AT ALL!
IN FACT, I'M GRATEFUL!
I'M NOT HERE AS A PRINCESS RIGHT NOW.
I'D LIKE IT IF YOU'D TREAT ME LIKE AN ORDINARY GIRL...

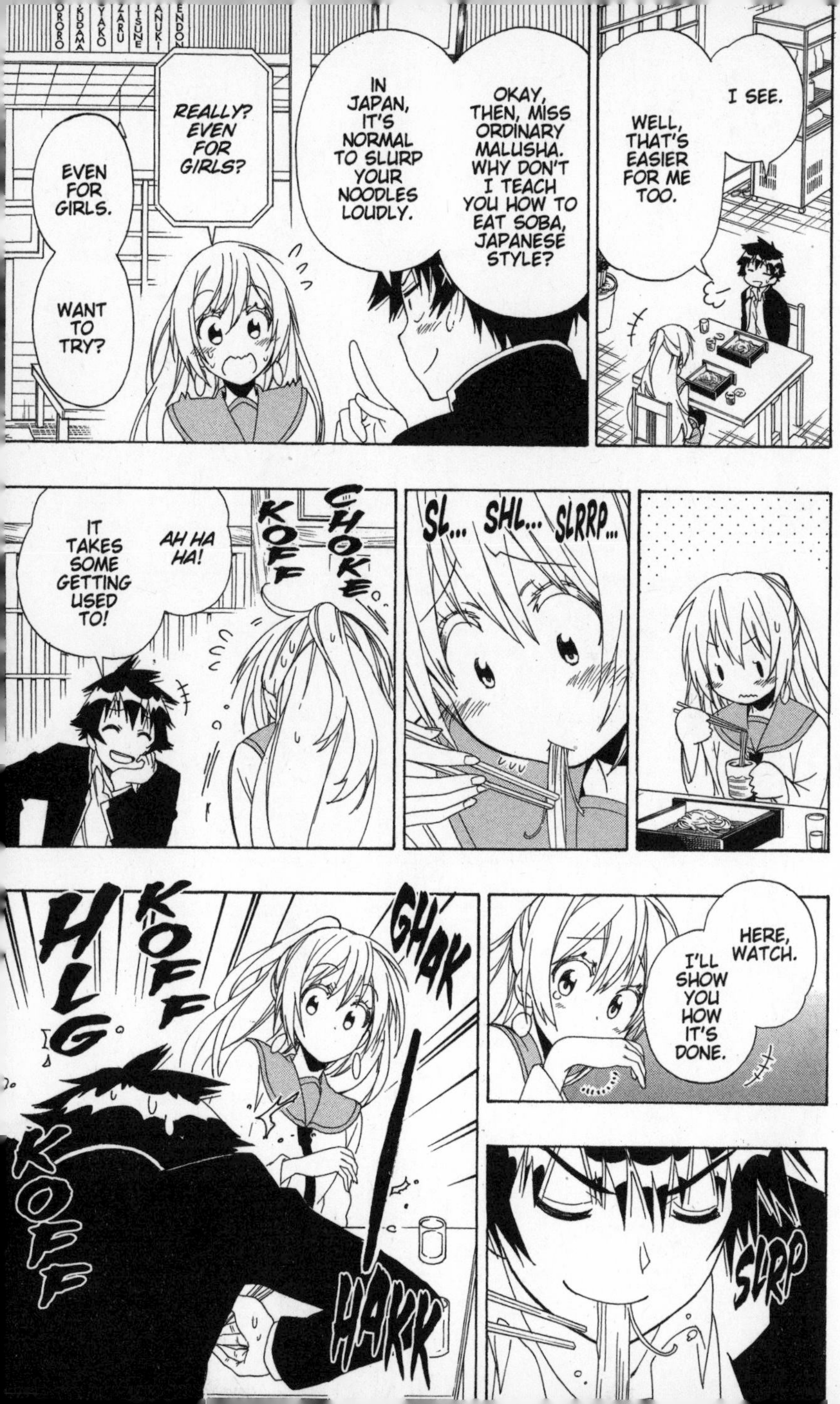

ORORO
KUDAMA
YAKO
ZARU
ITSUNE
ANUKI
ENDON
I SEE.
WELL, THAT'S EASIER FOR ME TOO.
OKAY, THEN, MISS ORDINARY MALUSHA. WHY DON'T I TEACH YOU HOW TO EAT SOBA, JAPANESE STYLE?
IN JAPAN, IT'S NORMAL TO SLURP YOUR NOODLES LOUDLY.
REALLY? EVEN FOR GIRLS?
EVEN FOR GIRLS.
WANT TO TRY?
SL... SHL... SLRRP...
CHOKE
KOFF
AH HA HA!
IT TAKES SOME GETTING USED TO!
HERE, WATCH.
I'LL SHOW YOU HOW IT'S DONE.
SLRP
GHAK
KOFF KOFF
HLG
KOFF KOFF
HAKK

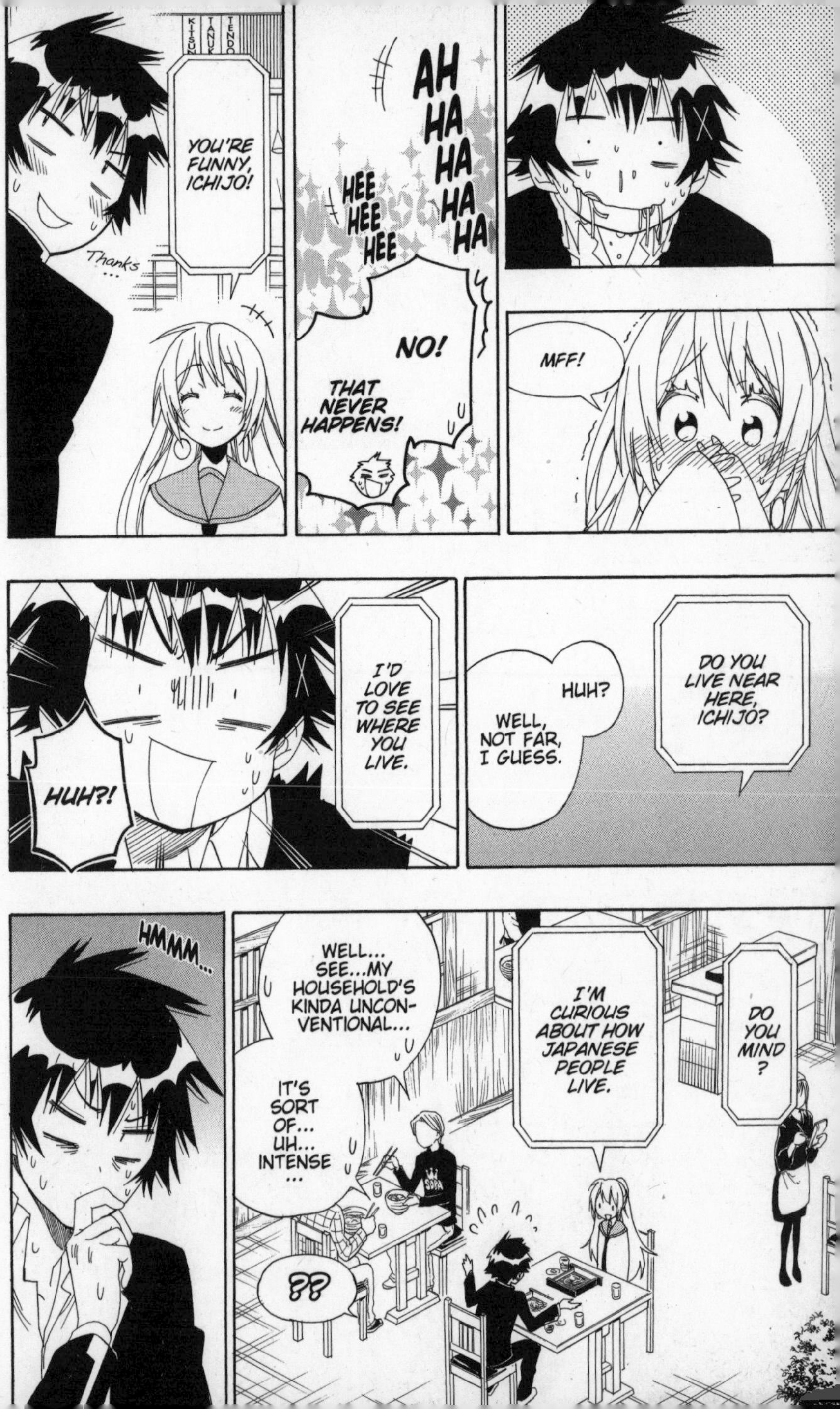
MFF!
AH HA HA HA HA
HEE HEE HEE
NO!
THAT NEVER HAPPENS!
YOU'RE FUNNY, ICHIJO!
Thanks...
DO YOU LIVE NEAR HERE, ICHIJO?
HUH?
WELL, NOT FAR, I GUESS.
I'D LOVE TO SEE WHERE YOU LIVE.
HUH?!
DO YOU MIND?
I'M CURIOUS ABOUT HOW JAPANESE PEOPLE LIVE.
WELL... SEE...MY HOUSEHOLD'S KINDA UNCON-VENTIONAL...
IT'S SORT OF... UH... INTENSE...
??
HMMM...

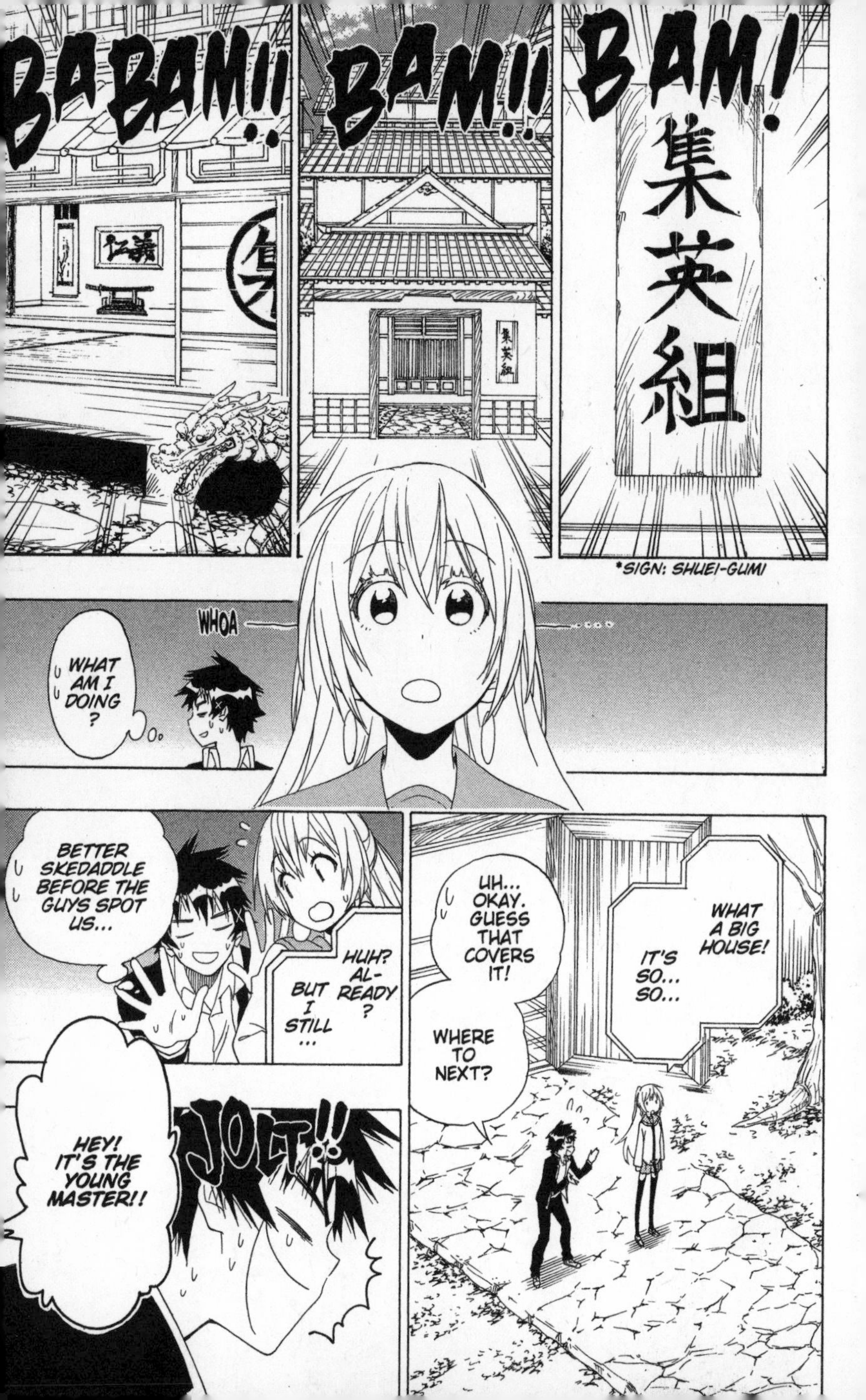
BAM!
集英組
*SIGN: SHUEI-GUMI
BAM!!
BABAM!!
WHOA ———
...
WHAT AM I DOING?
WHAT A BIG HOUSE!
IT'S SO... SO...
UH... OKAY. GUESS THAT COVERS IT!
WHERE TO NEXT?
HUH? AL-READY?
BUT I STILL...
BETTER SKEDADDLE BEFORE THE GUYS SPOT US...
HEY! IT'S THE YOUNG MASTER!!
JOLT!!

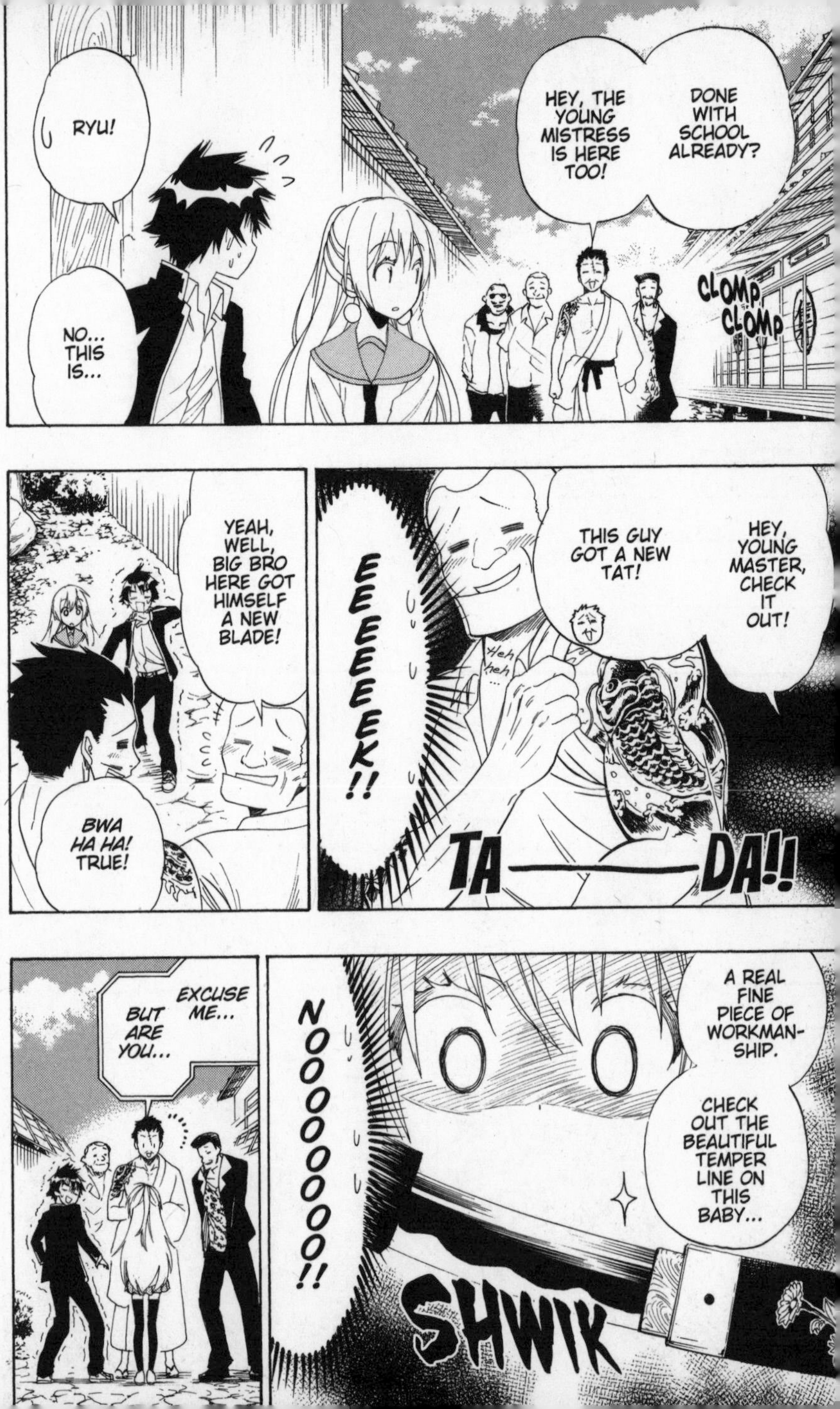
DONE WITH SCHOOL ALREADY?
HEY, THE YOUNG MISTRESS IS HERE TOO!
CLOMP, CLOMP
RYU!
NO... THIS IS...
HEY, YOUNG MASTER, CHECK IT OUT!
THIS GUY GOT A NEW TAT!
Heh heh...
EEEEEEEK!!
TA——DA!!
YEAH, WELL, BIG BRO HERE GOT HIMSELF A NEW BLADE!
BWA HA HA! TRUE!
A REAL FINE PIECE OF WORKMANSHIP.
CHECK OUT THE BEAUTIFUL TEMPER LINE ON THIS BABY...
NOOOOOOOOOO!!
SHWIK
EXCUSE ME...
BUT ARE YOU...

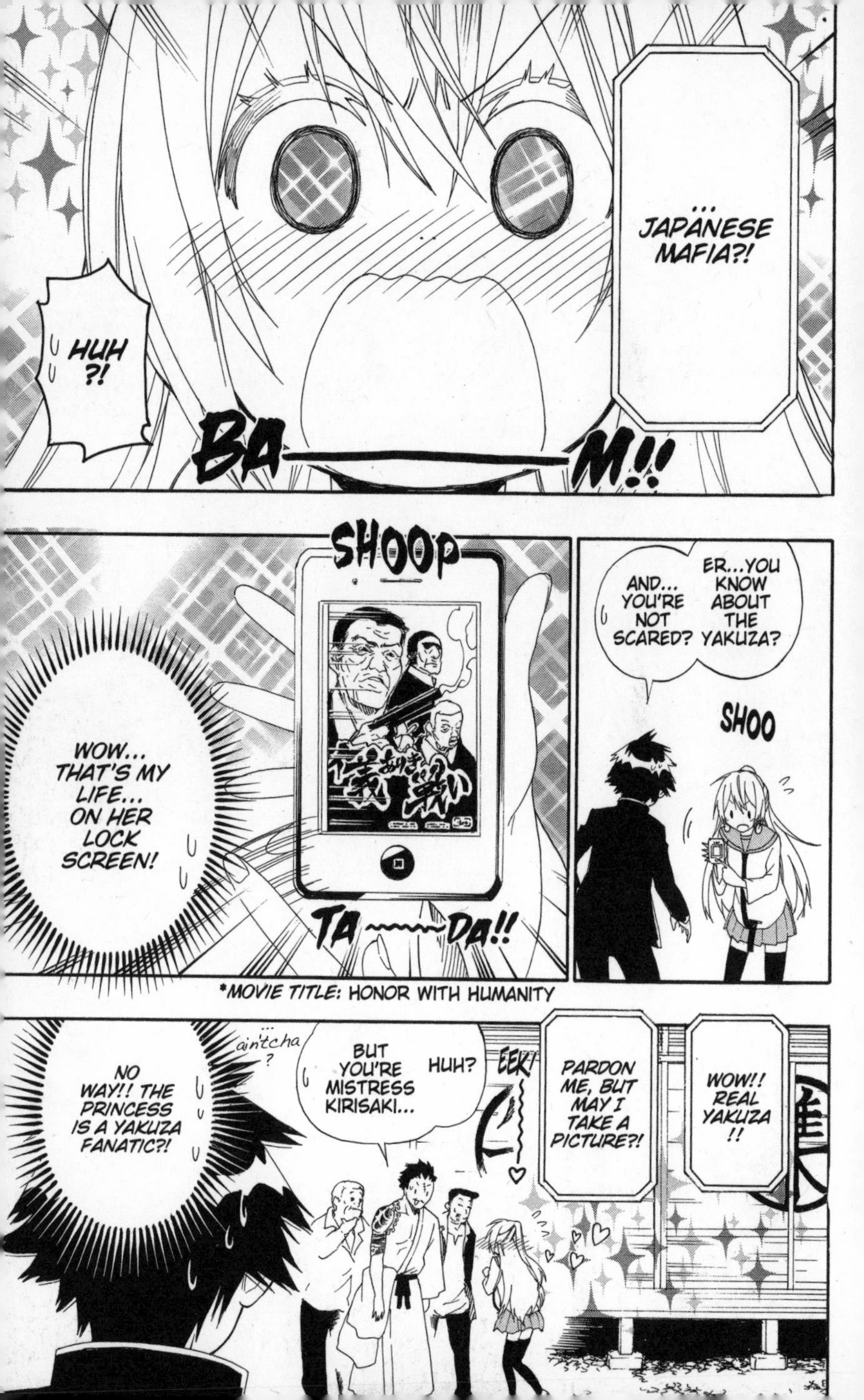
...JAPANESE MAFIA?!
HUH ?!
BA—M!!
ER...YOU KNOW ABOUT THE YAKUZA?
AND... YOU'RE NOT SCARED?
SHOO
SHOOP
WOW... THAT'S MY LIFE... ON HER LOCK SCREEN!
TA——DA!!
WOW!! REAL YAKUZA !!
PARDON ME, BUT MAY I TAKE A PICTURE?!
EEK!
HUH?
BUT YOU'RE MISTRESS KIRISAKI...
...ain'tcha?
NO WAY!! THE PRINCESS IS A YAKUZA FANATIC?!

*MOVIE TITLE: HONOR WITH HUMANITY

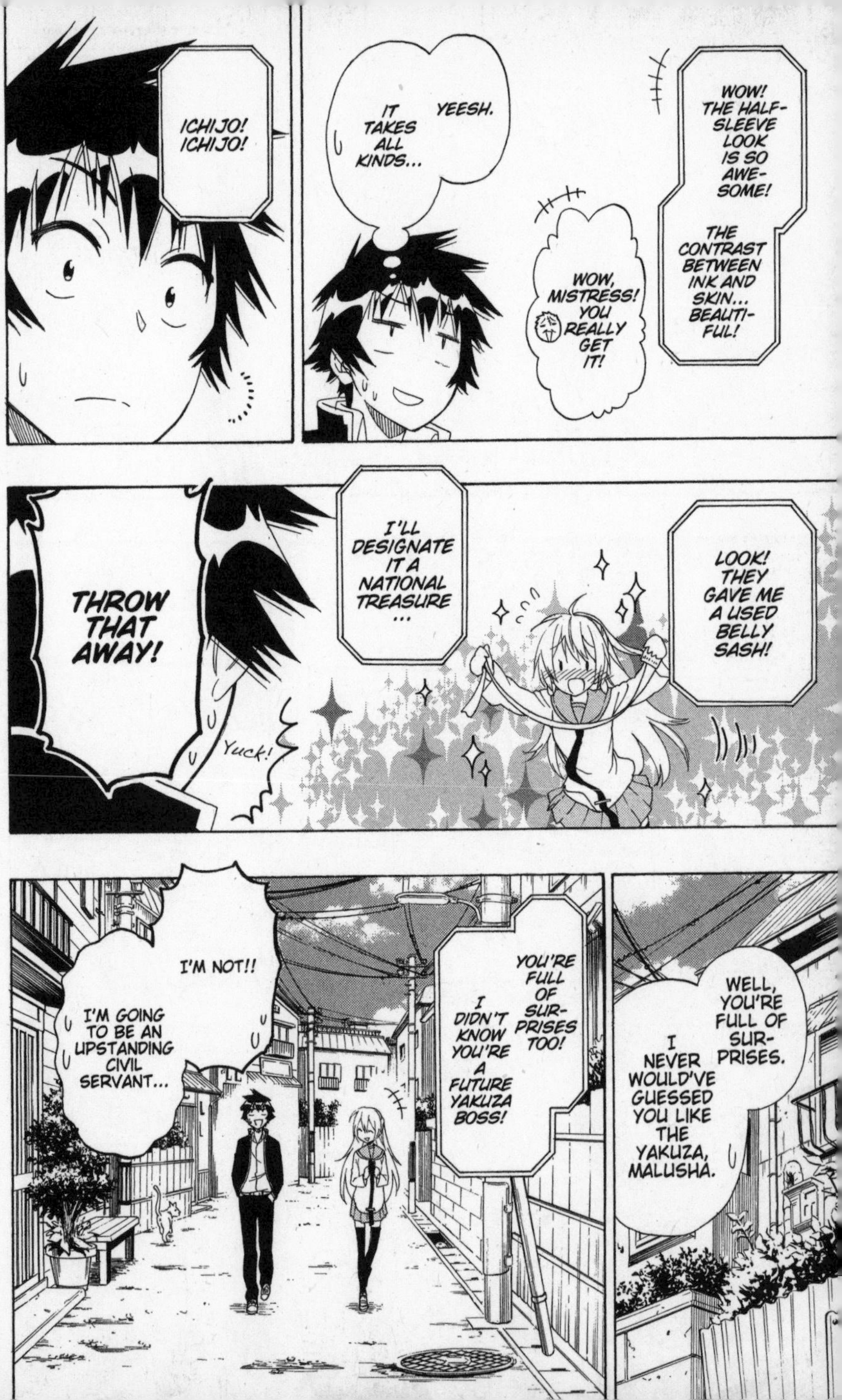
WOW! THE HALF-SLEEVE LOOK IS SO AWESOME!
THE CONTRAST BETWEEN INK AND SKIN... BEAUTIFUL!
WOW, MISTRESS! YOU REALLY GET IT!
YEESH.
IT TAKES ALL KINDS...
ICHIJO! ICHIJO!
LOOK! THEY GAVE ME A USED BELLY SASH!
I'LL DESIGNATE IT A NATIONAL TREASURE...
THROW THAT AWAY!
Yuck!
WELL, YOU'RE FULL OF SURPRISES.
I NEVER WOULD'VE GUESSED YOU LIKE THE YAKUZA, MALUSHA.
YOU'RE FULL OF SURPRISES TOO!
I DIDN'T KNOW YOU'RE A FUTURE YAKUZA BOSS!
I'M NOT!!
I'M GOING TO BE AN UPSTANDING CIVIL SERVANT...

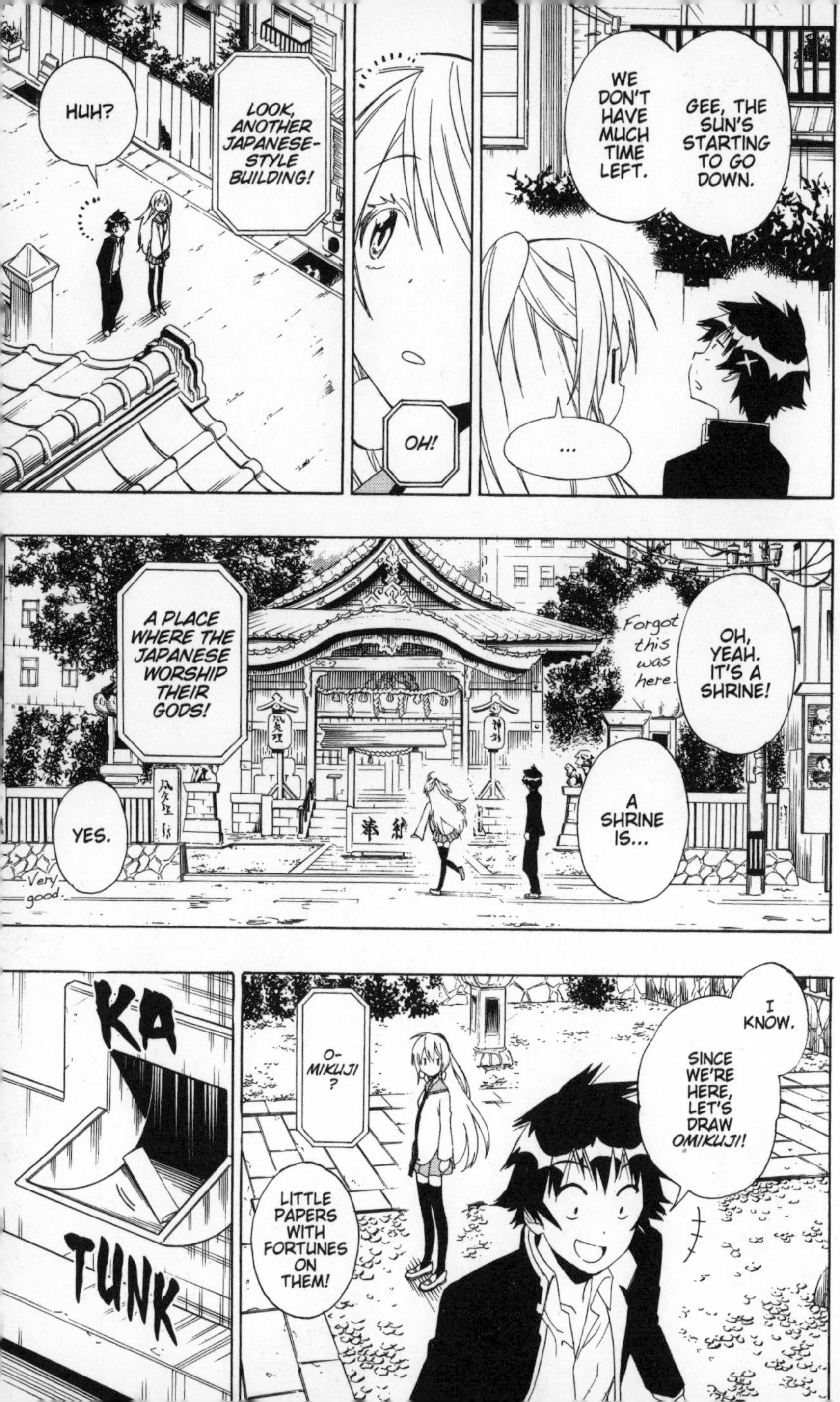
GEE, THE SUN'S STARTING TO GO DOWN.
WE DON'T HAVE MUCH TIME LEFT.
...
OH!
LOOK, ANOTHER JAPANESE-STYLE BUILDING!
HUH?
OH, YEAH. IT'S A SHRINE!
Forgot this was here.
A SHRINE IS...
A PLACE WHERE THE JAPANESE WORSHIP THEIR GODS!
YES.
Very good.
I KNOW.
SINCE WE'RE HERE, LET'S DRAW *OMIKUJI*!
O-MIKUJI?
LITTLE PAPERS WITH FORTUNES ON THEM!
KA
TUNK

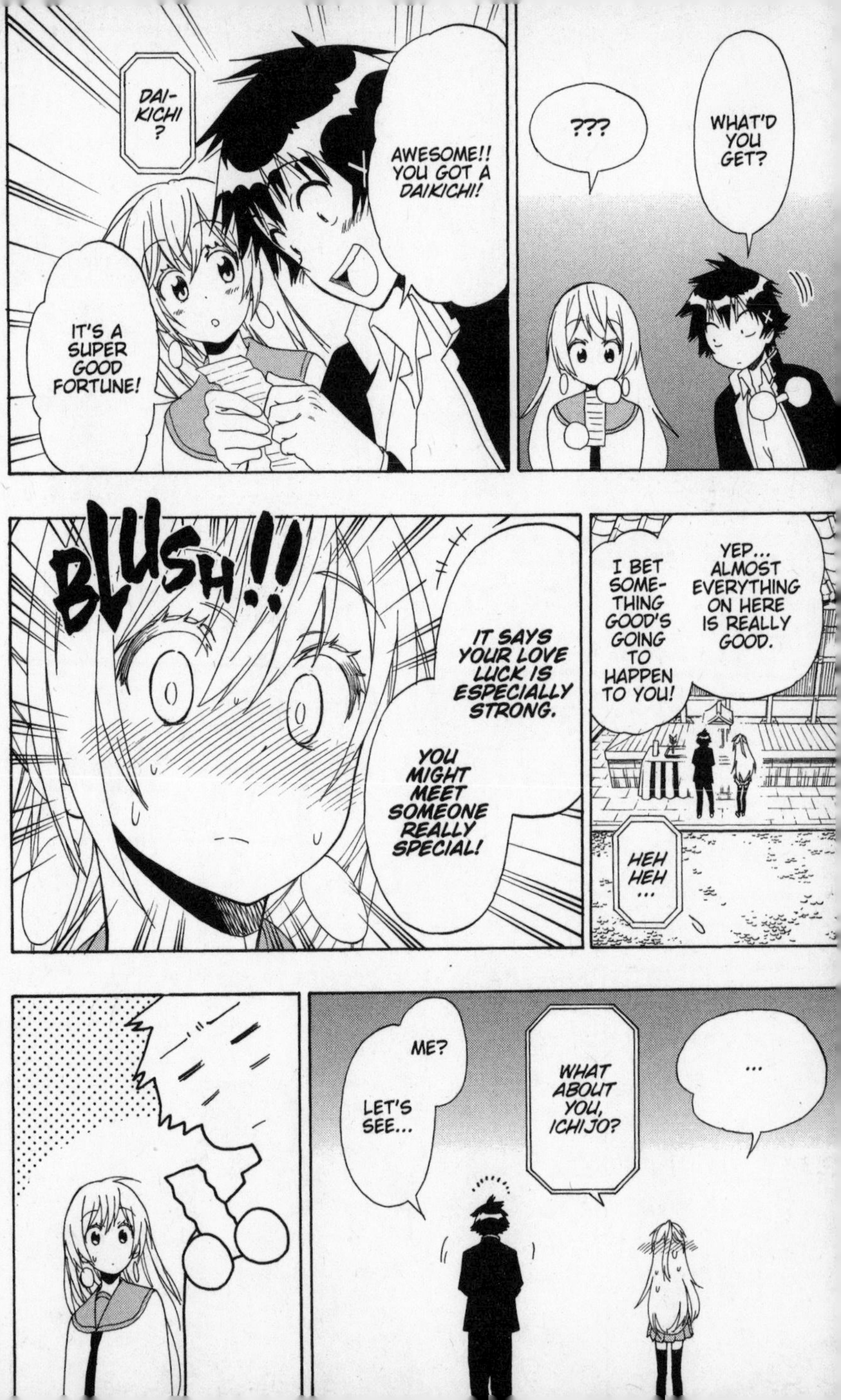
WHAT'D YOU GET?
???
AWESOME!! YOU GOT A DAIKICHI!
DAI-KICHI?
IT'S A SUPER GOOD FORTUNE!
YEP... ALMOST EVERYTHING ON HERE IS REALLY GOOD.
I BET SOME-THING GOOD'S GOING TO HAPPEN TO YOU!
HEH HEH...
IT SAYS YOUR LOVE LUCK IS ESPECIALLY STRONG.
YOU MIGHT MEET SOMEONE REALLY SPECIAL!
BLUSH!!
...
WHAT ABOUT YOU, ICHIJO?
ME?
LET'S SEE...

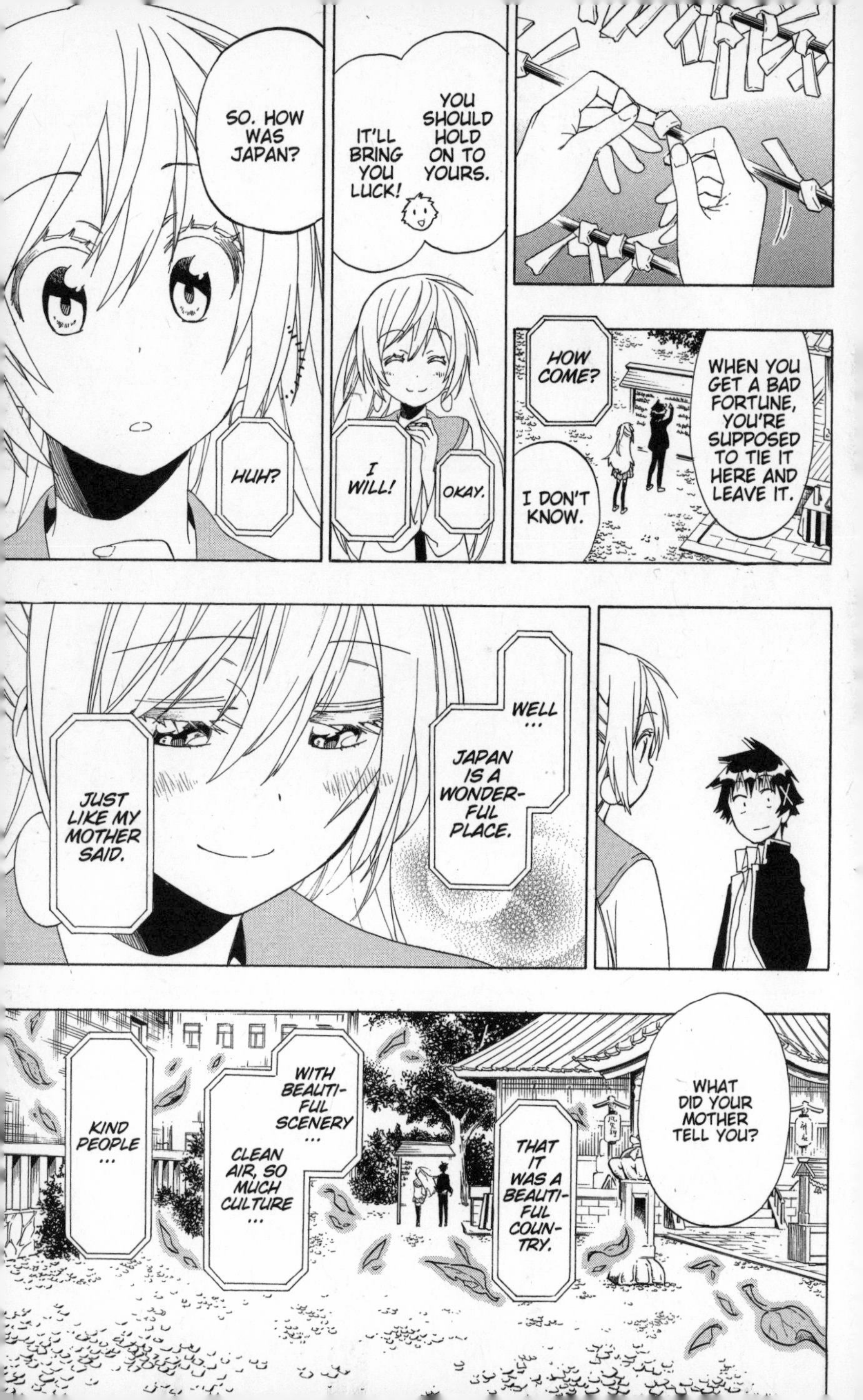
WHEN YOU GET A BAD FORTUNE, YOU'RE SUPPOSED TO TIE IT HERE AND LEAVE IT.
HOW COME?
I DON'T KNOW.
YOU SHOULD HOLD ON TO YOURS.
IT'LL BRING YOU LUCK!
OKAY.
I WILL!
SO. HOW WAS JAPAN?
HUH?
WELL...
JAPAN IS A WONDERFUL PLACE.
JUST LIKE MY MOTHER SAID.
WHAT DID YOUR MOTHER TELL YOU?
THAT IT WAS A BEAUTIFUL COUNTRY.
WITH BEAUTIFUL SCENERY...
CLEAN AIR, SO MUCH CULTURE...
KIND PEOPLE...

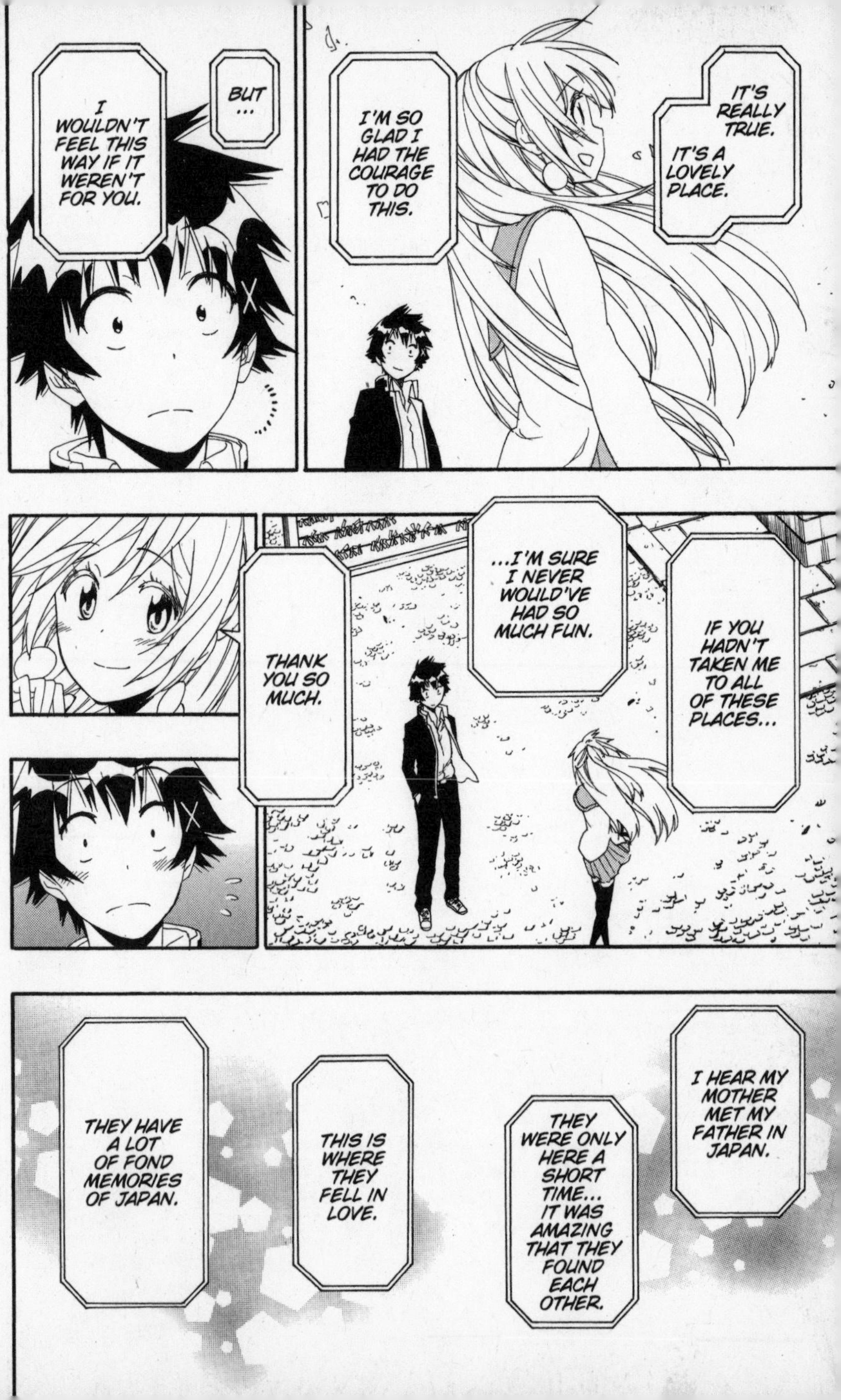
IT'S REALLY TRUE. IT'S A LOVELY PLACE.
I'M SO GLAD I HAD THE COURAGE TO DO THIS.
BUT...
I WOULDN'T FEEL THIS WAY IF IT WEREN'T FOR YOU.
IF YOU HADN'T TAKEN ME TO ALL OF THESE PLACES...
...I'M SURE I NEVER WOULD'VE HAD SO MUCH FUN.
THANK YOU SO MUCH.
I HEAR MY MOTHER MET MY FATHER IN JAPAN.
THEY WERE ONLY HERE A SHORT TIME... IT WAS AMAZING THAT THEY FOUND EACH OTHER.
THIS IS WHERE THEY FELL IN LOVE.
THEY HAVE A LOT OF FOND MEMORIES OF JAPAN.

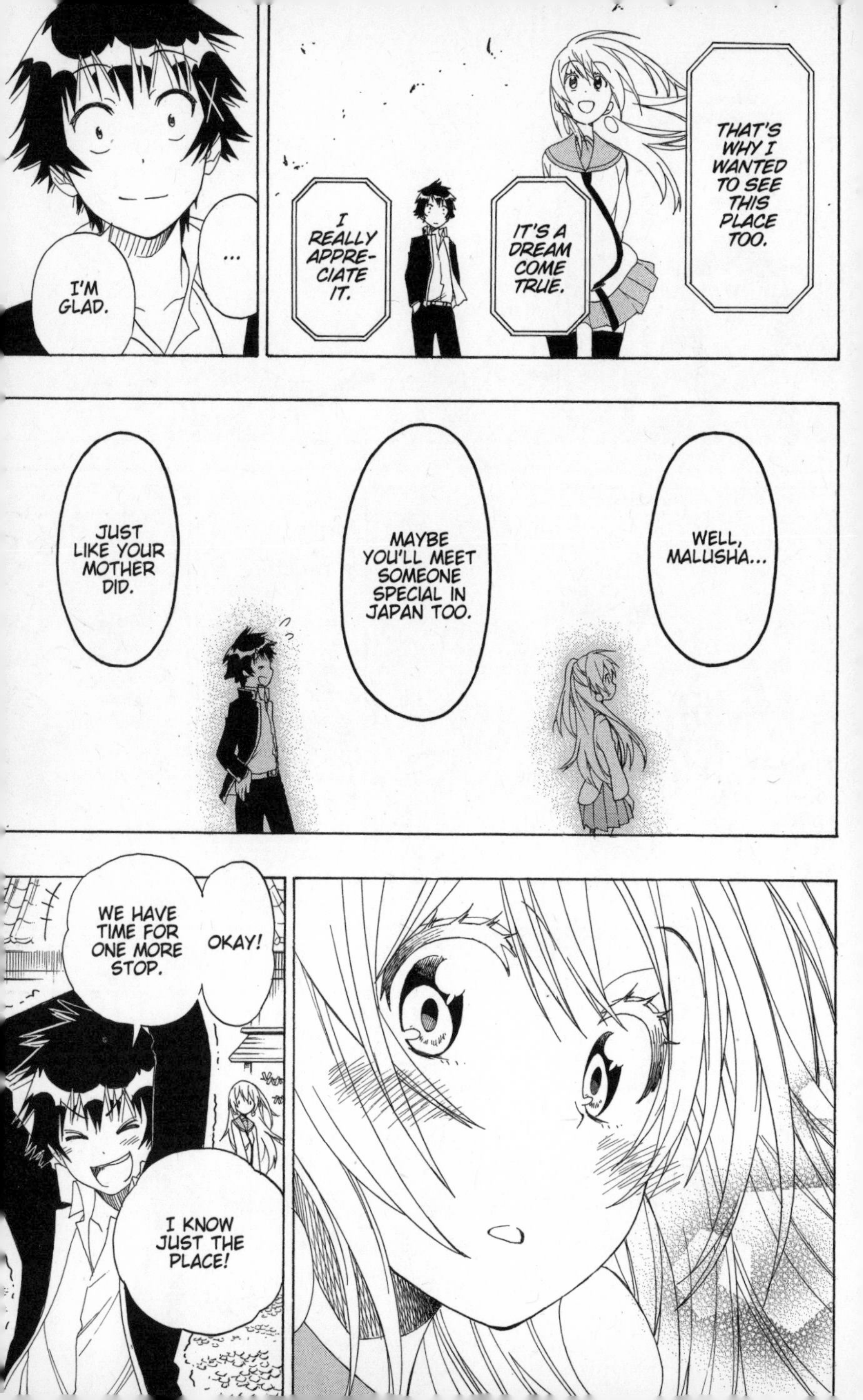
THAT'S WHY I WANTED TO SEE THIS PLACE TOO.
IT'S A DREAM COME TRUE.
I REALLY APPRECIATE IT.
...
I'M GLAD.
WELL, MALUSHA...
MAYBE YOU'LL MEET SOMEONE SPECIAL IN JAPAN TOO.
JUST LIKE YOUR MOTHER DID.
OKAY!
WE HAVE TIME FOR ONE MORE STOP.
I KNOW JUST THE PLACE!

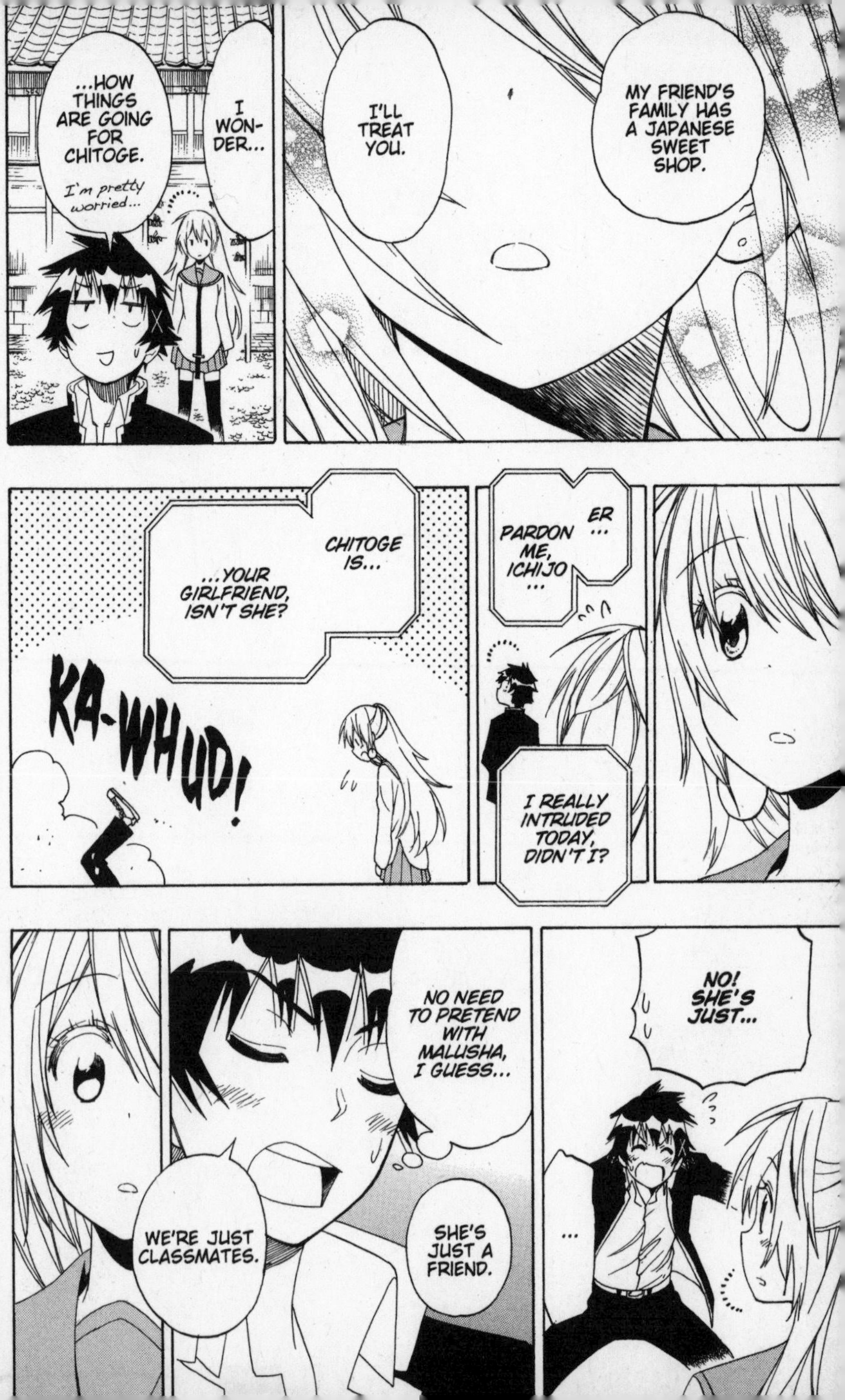
MY FRIEND'S FAMILY HAS A JAPANESE SWEET SHOP.
I'LL TREAT YOU.
I WONDER...
...HOW THINGS ARE GOING FOR CHITOGE.
I'm pretty worried...
ER... PARDON ME, ICHIJO...
I REALLY INTRUDED TODAY, DIDN'T I?
CHITOGE IS...
...YOUR GIRLFRIEND, ISN'T SHE?
KA-WHUD!
NO! SHE'S JUST...
...
NO NEED TO PRETEND WITH MALUSHA, I GUESS...
SHE'S JUST A FRIEND.
WE'RE JUST CLASSMATES.

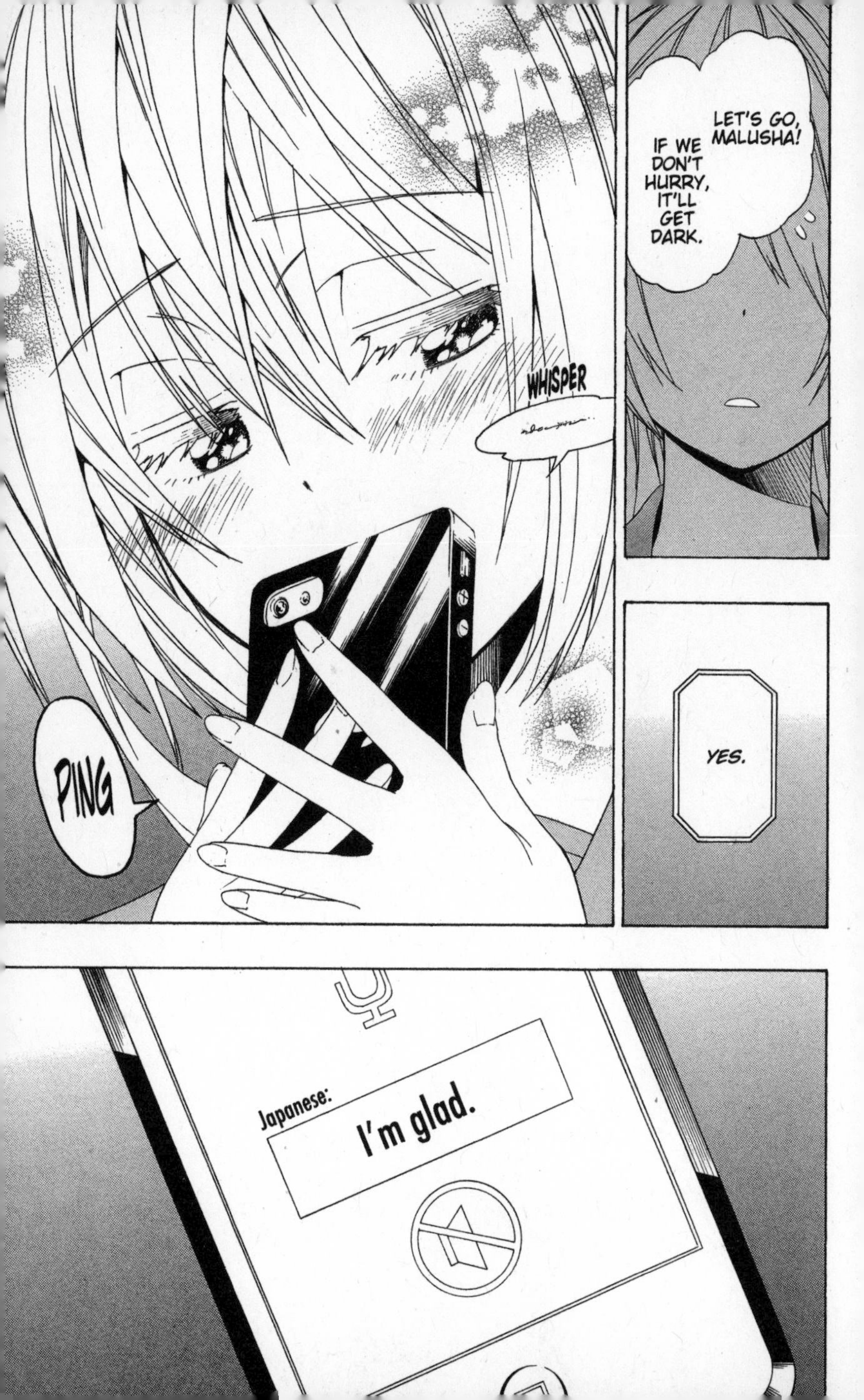
LET'S GO, MALUSHA! IF WE DON'T HURRY, IT'LL GET DARK.
YES.
WHISPER
PING
Japanese:
I'm glad.

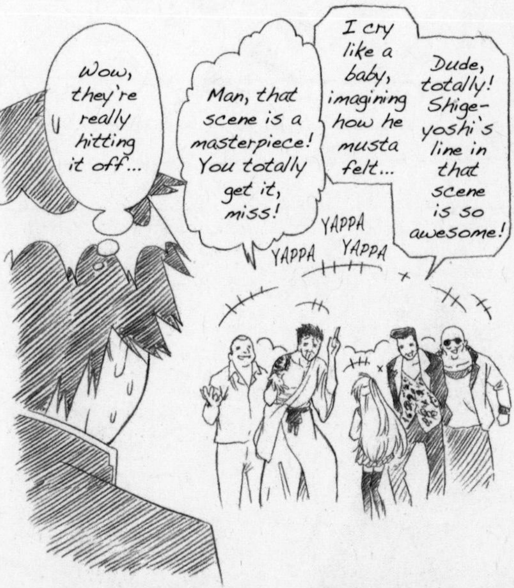
Dude, totally! Shige-yoshi's line in that scene is so awesome!
I cry like a baby, imagining how he musta felt...
Man, that scene is a masterpiece! You totally get it, miss!
YAPPA
YAPPA
YAPPA
Wow, they're really hitting it off...

Chapter 138: Daikichi

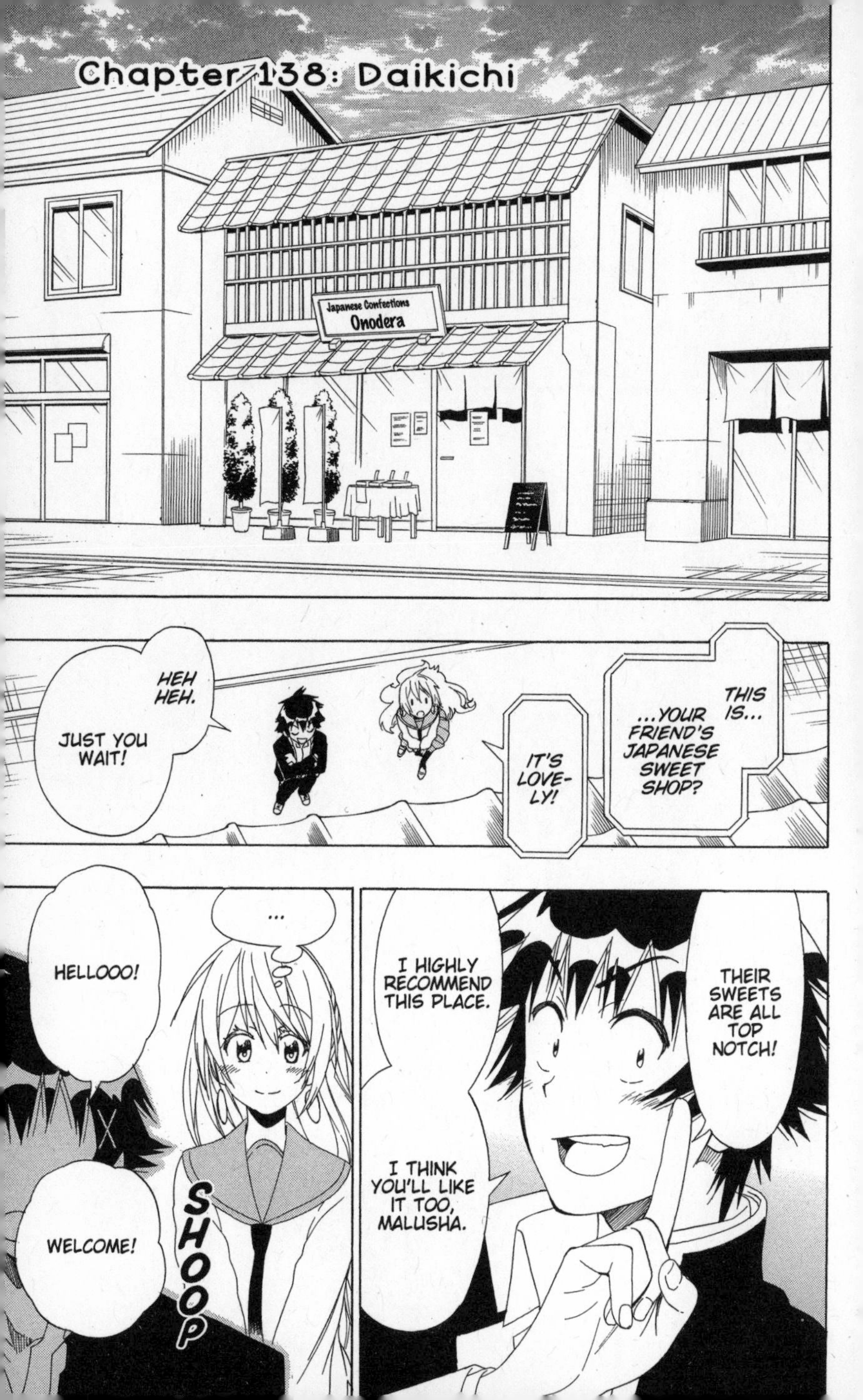
Japanese Confections
Onodera
THIS IS... ...YOUR FRIEND'S JAPANESE SWEET SHOP?
IT'S LOVE-LY!
HEH HEH.
JUST YOU WAIT!
THEIR SWEETS ARE ALL TOP NOTCH!
I HIGHLY RECOMMEND THIS PLACE.
I THINK YOU'LL LIKE IT TOO, MALUSHA.
...
HELLOOO!
SHOOP
WELCOME!

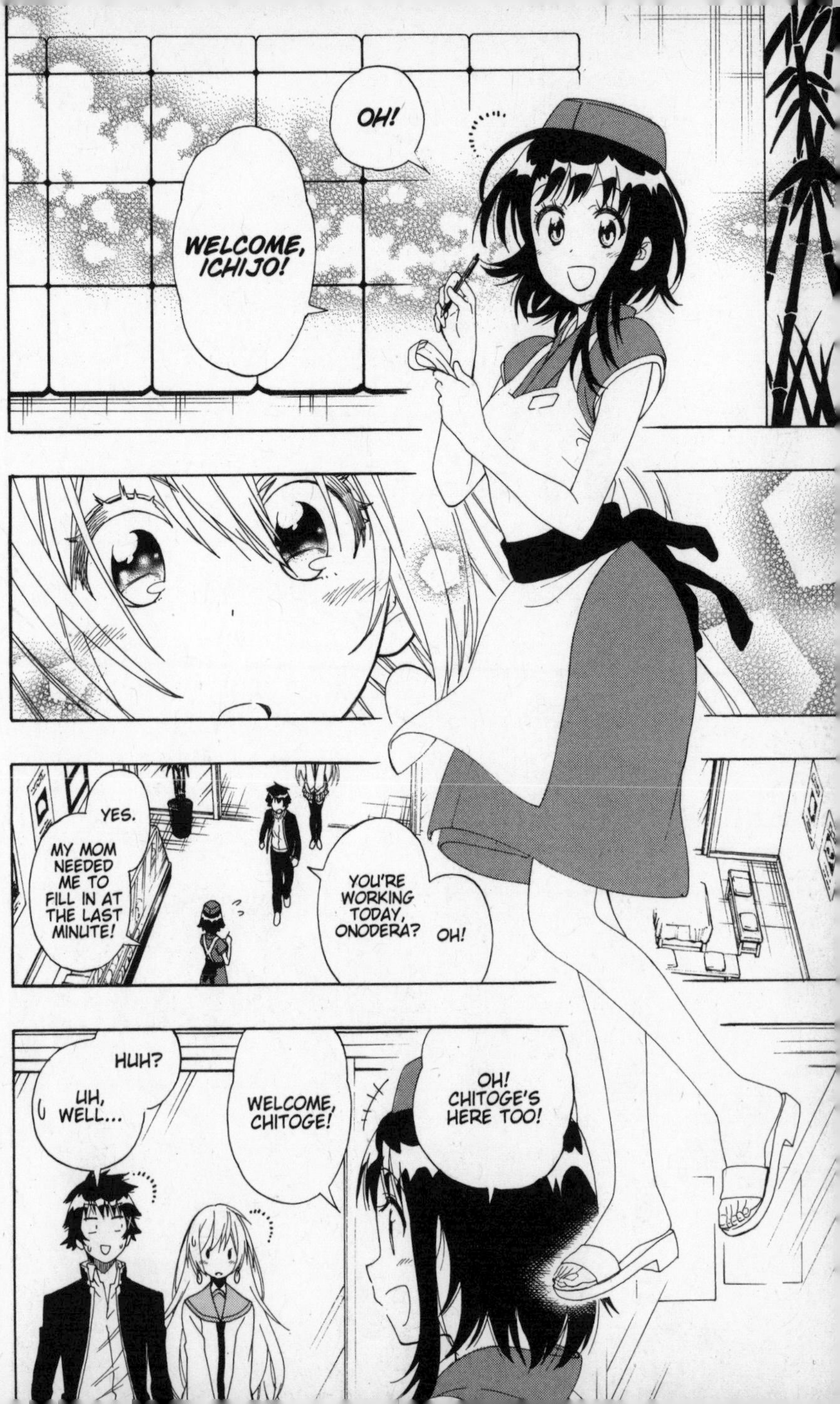
OH!
WELCOME, ICHIJO!
OH!
YOU'RE WORKING TODAY, ONODERA?
YES.
MY MOM NEEDED ME TO FILL IN AT THE LAST MINUTE!
OH! CHITOGE'S HERE TOO!
WELCOME, CHITOGE!
HUH?
UH, WELL...

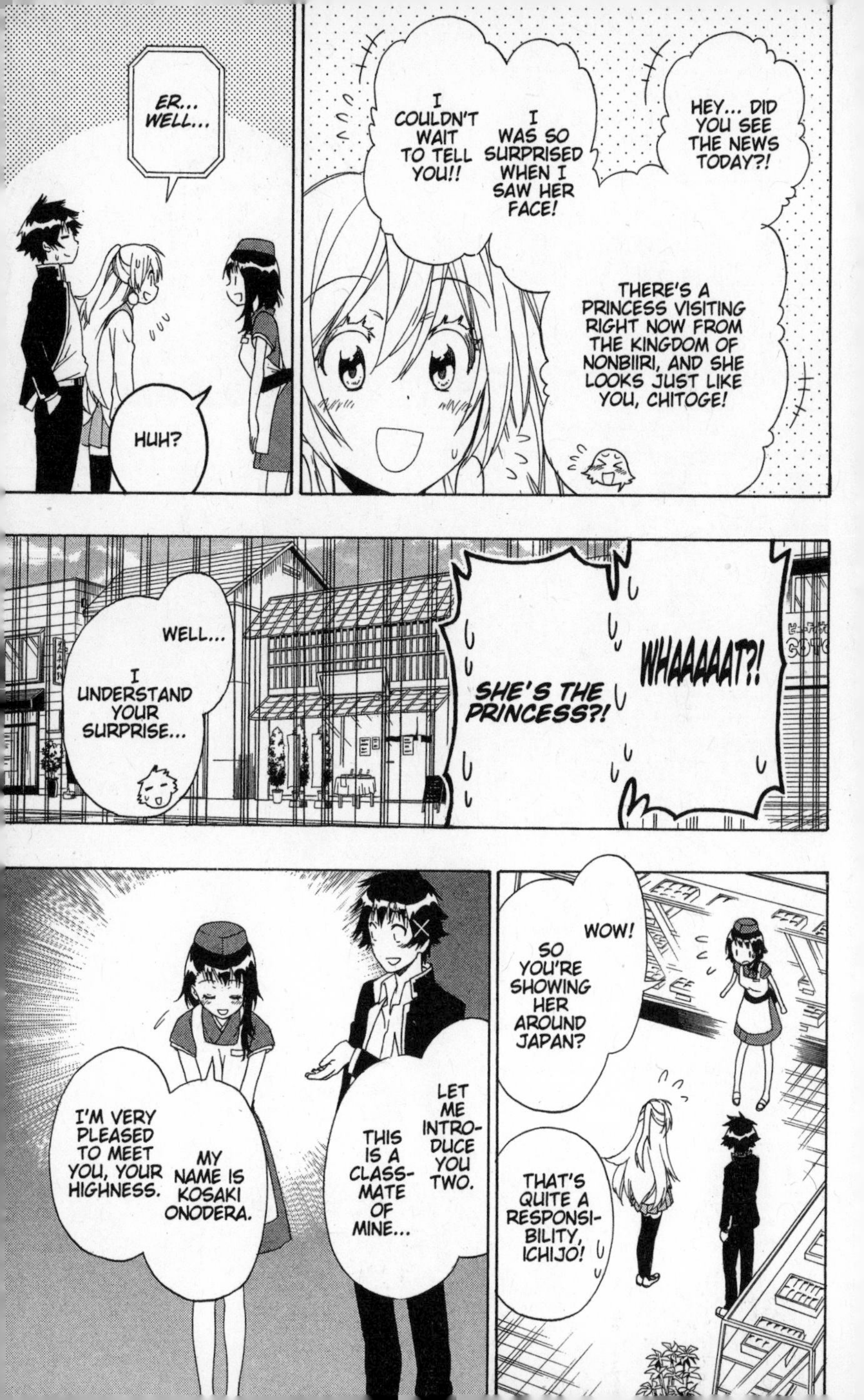
HEY... DID YOU SEE THE NEWS TODAY?!
THERE'S A PRINCESS VISITING RIGHT NOW FROM THE KINGDOM OF NONBIIRI, AND SHE LOOKS JUST LIKE YOU, CHITOGE!
I WAS SO SURPRISED WHEN I SAW HER FACE!
I COULDN'T WAIT TO TELL YOU!!
ER... WELL...
HUH?
WHAAAAAT?!
SHE'S THE PRINCESS?!
WELL...
I UNDERSTAND YOUR SURPRISE...
WOW!
SO YOU'RE SHOWING HER AROUND JAPAN?
THAT'S QUITE A RESPONSIBILITY, ICHIJO!
LET ME INTRODUCE YOU TWO.
THIS IS A CLASSMATE OF MINE...
MY NAME IS KOSAKI ONODERA.
I'M VERY PLEASED TO MEET YOU, YOUR HIGHNESS.

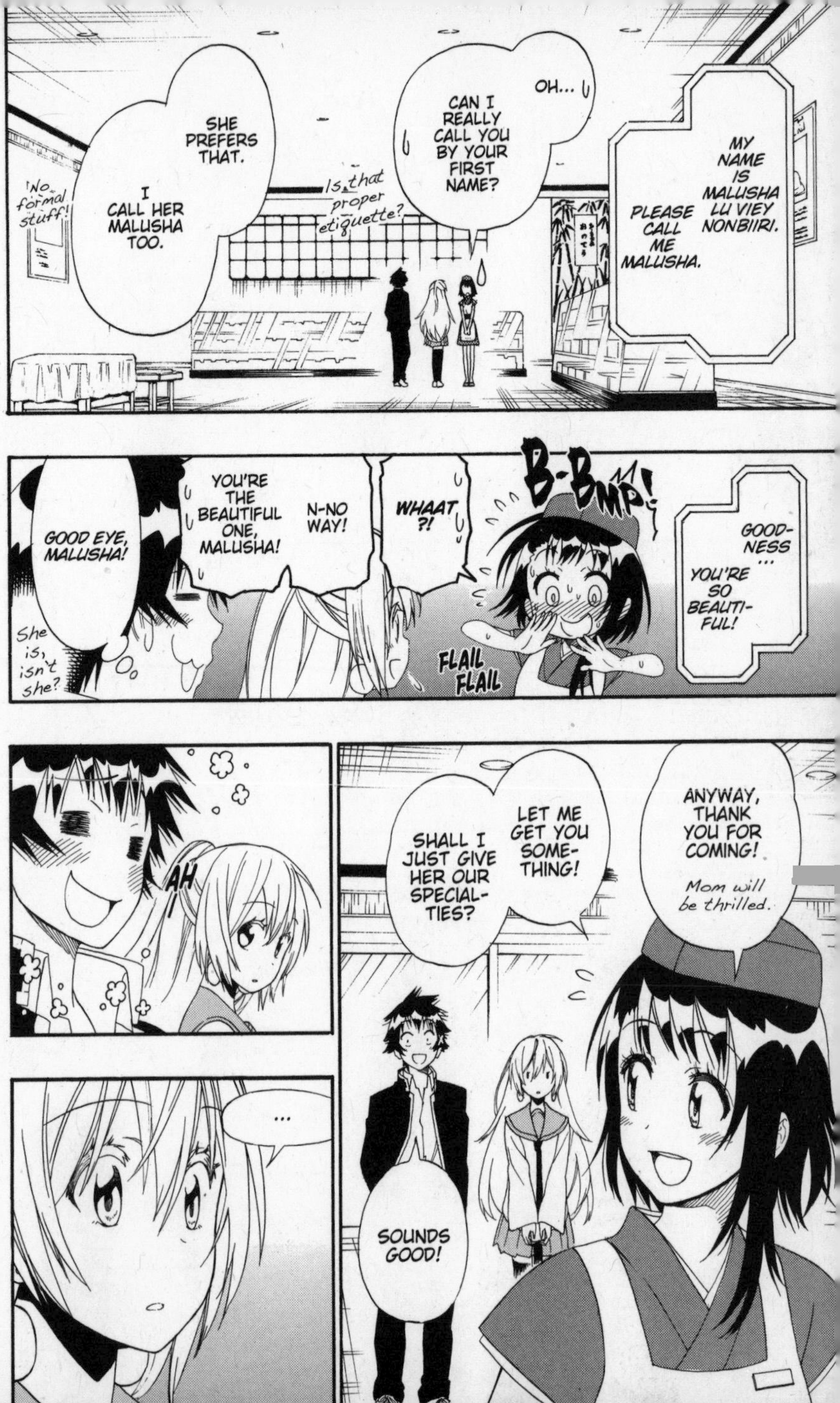
MY NAME IS MALUSHA LU VIEY NONBIIRI.
PLEASE CALL ME MALUSHA.
OH...
CAN I REALLY CALL YOU BY YOUR FIRST NAME?
Is that proper etiquette?
SHE PREFERS THAT.
I CALL HER MALUSHA TOO.
'No formal stuff!'
GOOD-NESS... YOU'RE SO BEAUTI-FUL!
B-BMP!
FLAIL FLAIL
WHAAT?!
N-NO WAY!
YOU'RE THE BEAUTIFUL ONE, MALUSHA!
GOOD EYE, MALUSHA!
She is, isn't she?
ANYWAY, THANK YOU FOR COMING!
Mom will be thrilled.
LET ME GET YOU SOME-THING!
SHALL I JUST GIVE HER OUR SPECIAL-TIES?
SOUNDS GOOD!
AH
...

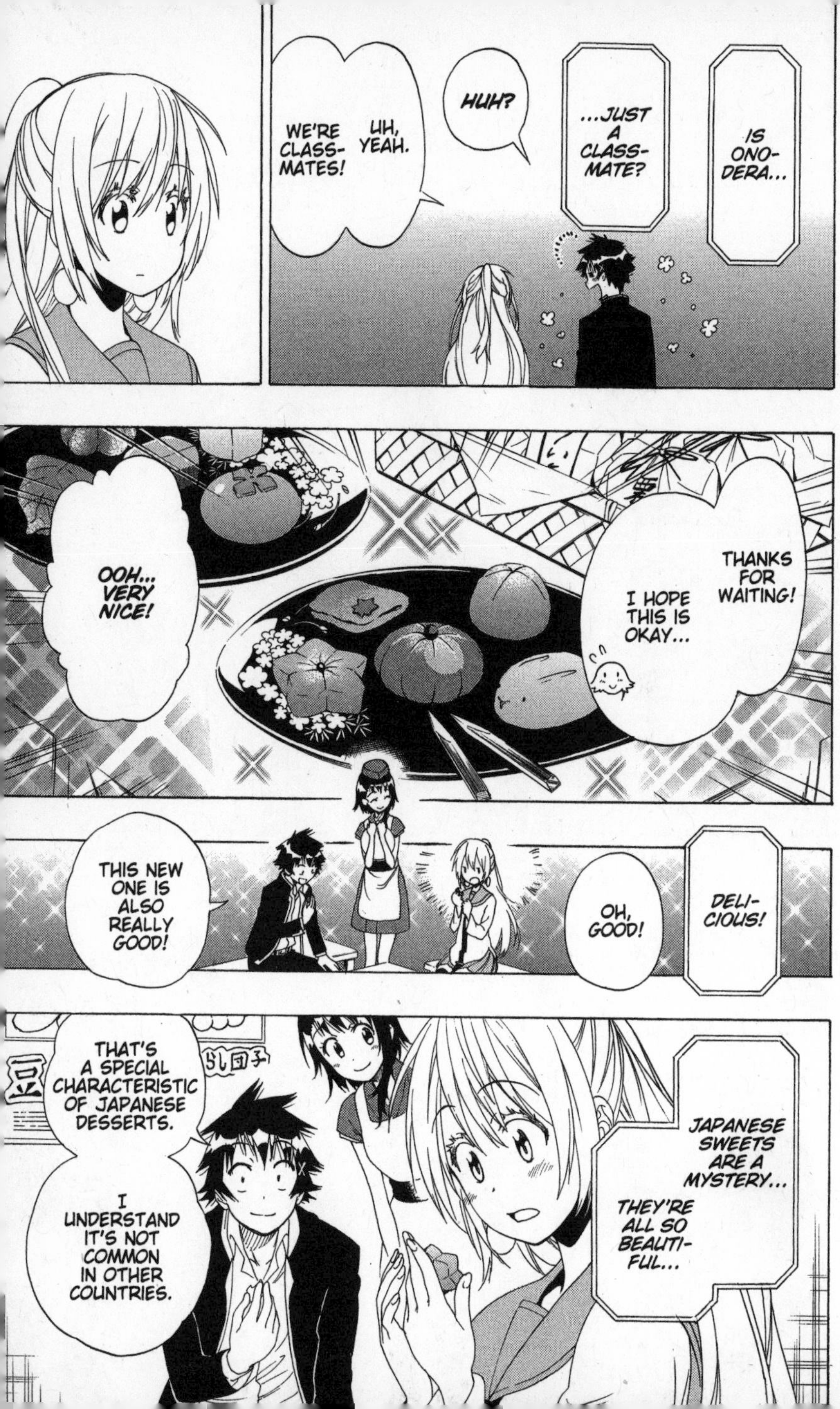
IS ONO-DERA...
...JUST A CLASS-MATE?
HUH?
UH, YEAH.
WE'RE CLASS-MATES!
THANKS FOR WAITING!
I HOPE THIS IS OKAY...
OOH... VERY NICE!
DELI-CIOUS!
OH, GOOD!
THIS NEW ONE IS ALSO REALLY GOOD!
JAPANESE SWEETS ARE A MYSTERY...
THEY'RE ALL SO BEAUTI-FUL...
らし団子
豆
THAT'S A SPECIAL CHARACTERISTIC OF JAPANESE DESSERTS.
I UNDERSTAND IT'S NOT COMMON IN OTHER COUNTRIES.

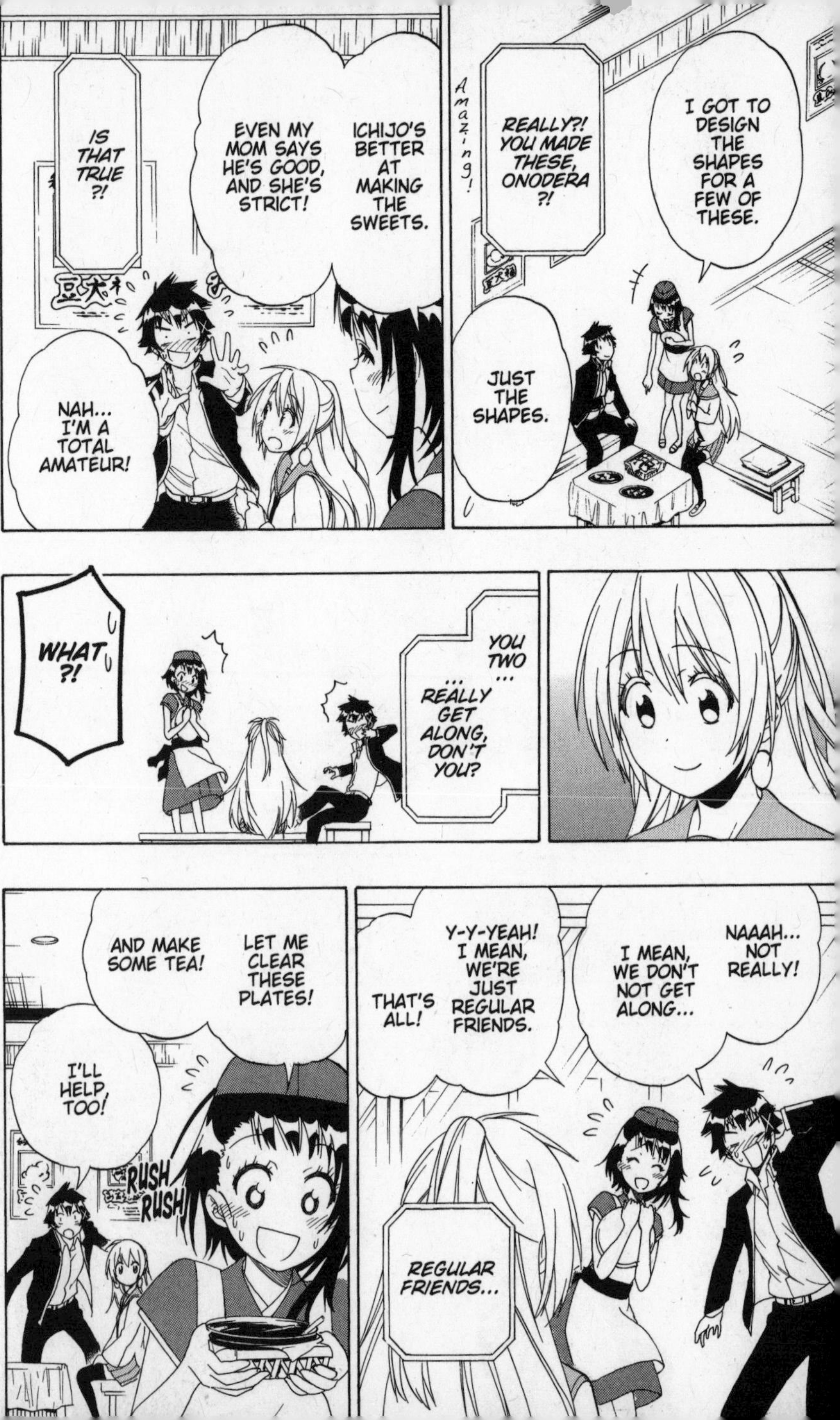
I GOT TO DESIGN THE SHAPES FOR A FEW OF THESE.
REALLY?! YOU MADE THESE, ONODERA?!
Amazing!
JUST THE SHAPES.
ICHIJO'S BETTER AT MAKING THE SWEETS.
EVEN MY MOM SAYS HE'S GOOD, AND SHE'S STRICT!
IS THAT TRUE?!
NAH... I'M A TOTAL AMATEUR!
YOU TWO... REALLY GET ALONG, DON'T YOU?
WHAT?!
NAAAH... NOT REALLY!
I MEAN, WE DON'T NOT GET ALONG...
Y-Y-YEAH! I MEAN, WE'RE JUST REGULAR FRIENDS.
THAT'S ALL!
REGULAR FRIENDS...
LET ME CLEAR THESE PLATES!
AND MAKE SOME TEA!
I'LL HELP, TOO!
RUSH RUSH

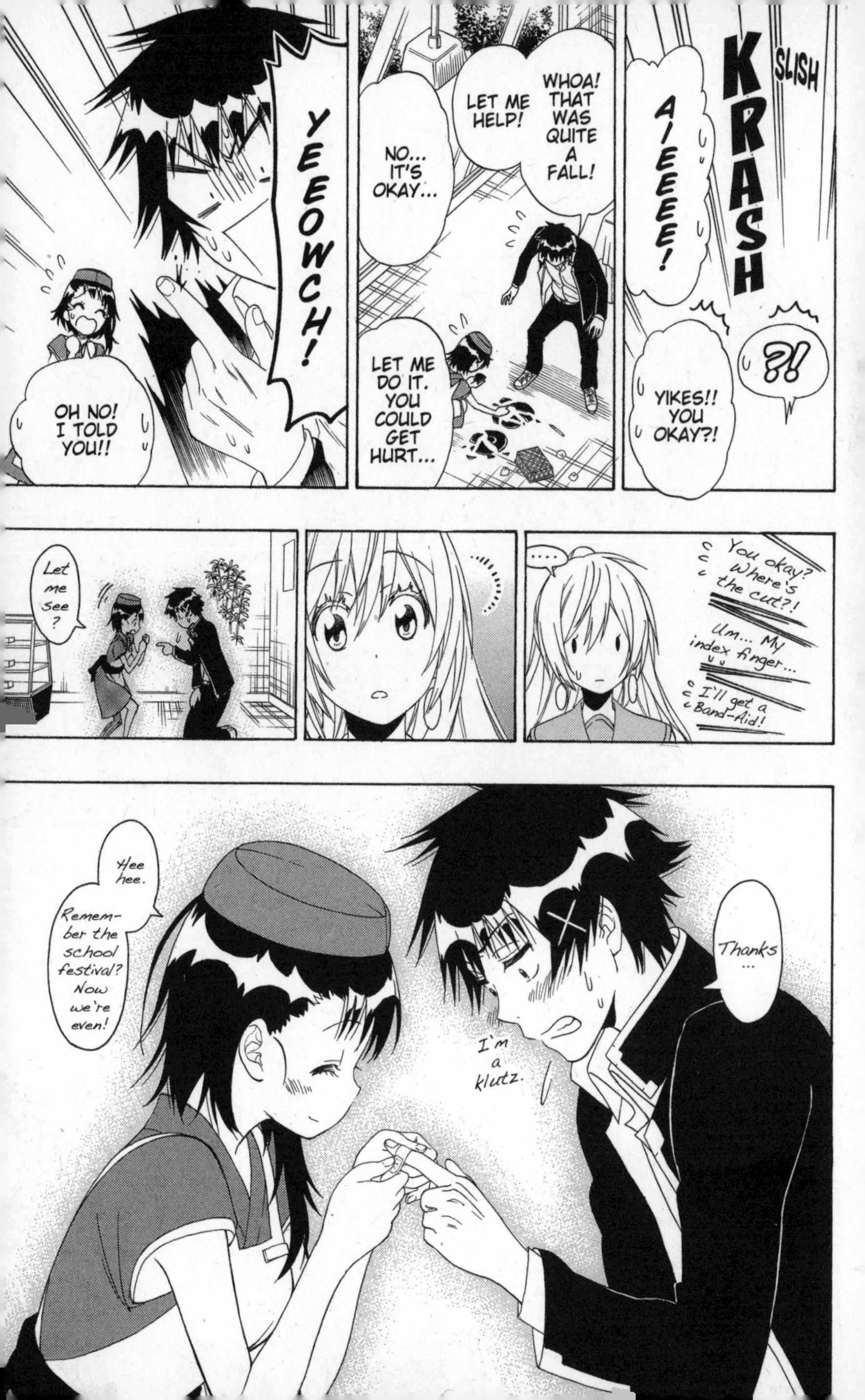
SLISH
KRASH
AIEEEE!
?!
YIKES!! YOU OKAY?!
WHOA! THAT WAS QUITE A FALL!
LET ME HELP!
NO... IT'S OKAY...
LET ME DO IT. YOU COULD GET HURT...
YEEOWCH!
OH NO! I TOLD YOU!!
You okay? Where's the cut?!
Um... My index finger...
I'll get a Band-Aid!
....
Let me see?
Thanks...
I'm a klutz.
Hee hee.
Remember the school festival? Now we're even!

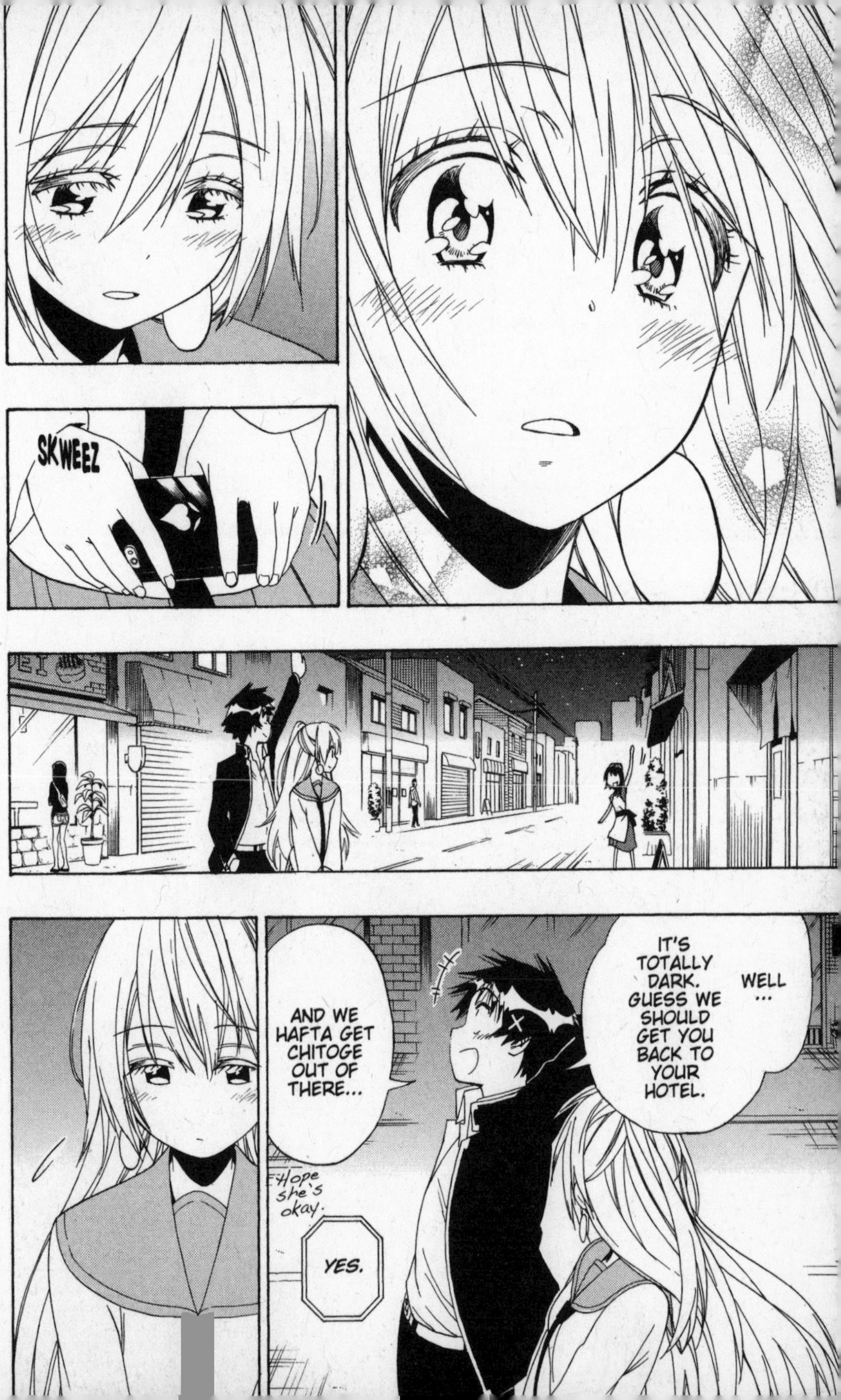
SKWEEZ
WELL ...
IT'S TOTALLY DARK. GUESS WE SHOULD GET YOU BACK TO YOUR HOTEL.
AND WE HAFTA GET CHITOGE OUT OF THERE...
Hope she's okay.
YES.

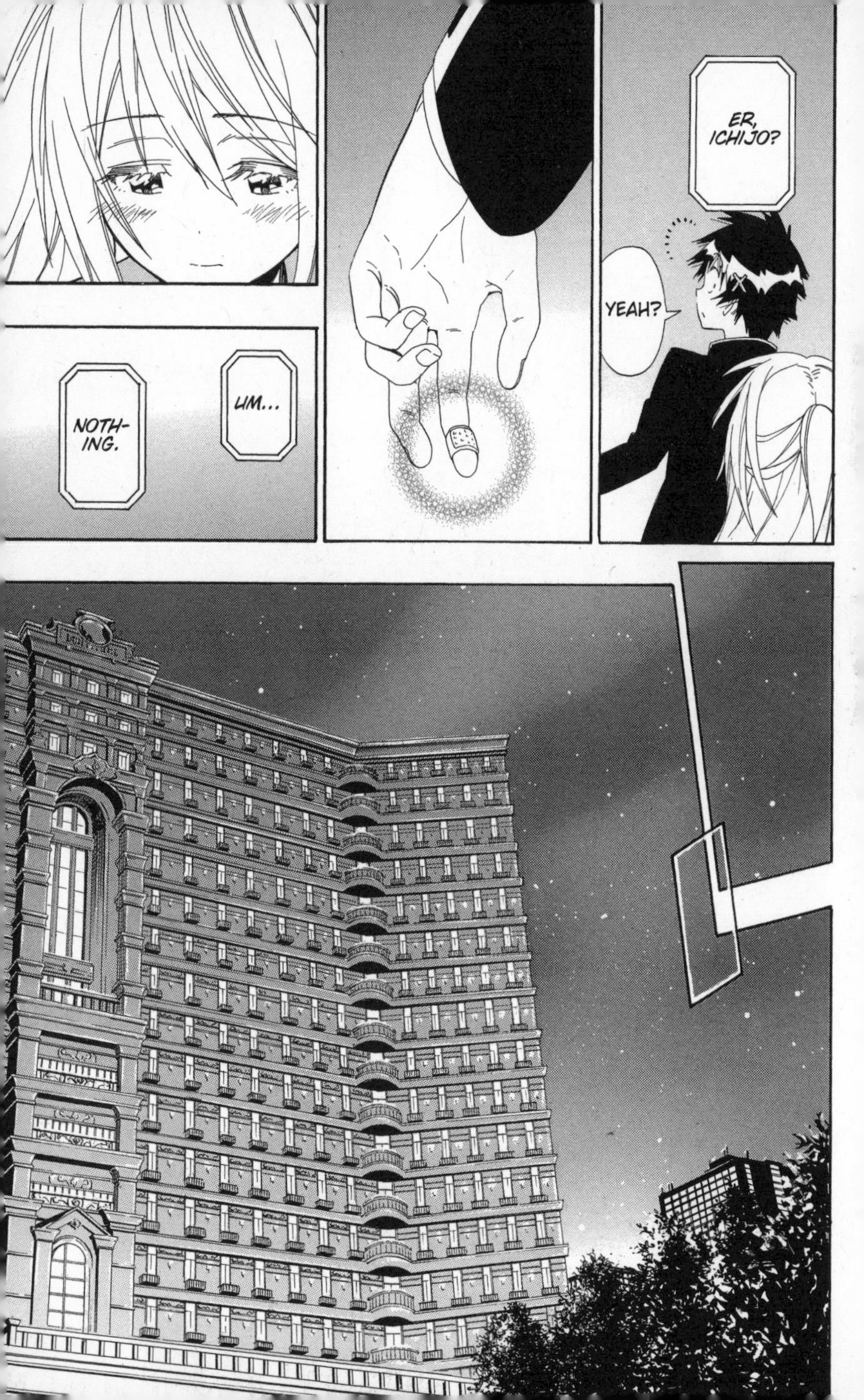
ER, ICHIJO?
YEAH?
UM...
NOTH-ING.

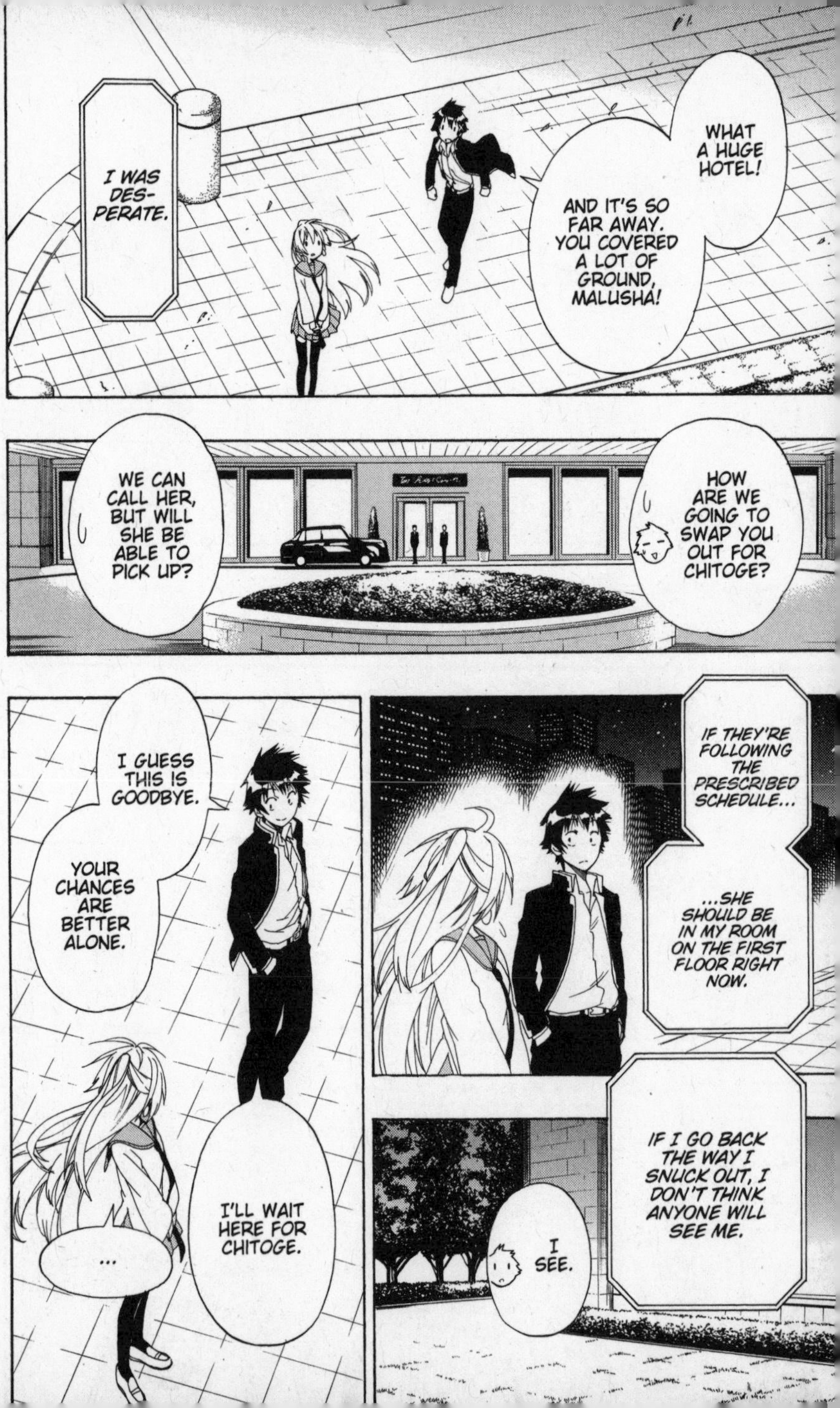
WHAT A HUGE HOTEL!
AND IT'S SO FAR AWAY. YOU COVERED A LOT OF GROUND, MALUSHA!
I WAS DES-PERATE.
HOW ARE WE GOING TO SWAP YOU OUT FOR CHITOGE?
WE CAN CALL HER, BUT WILL SHE BE ABLE TO PICK UP?
IF THEY'RE FOLLOWING THE PRESCRIBED SCHEDULE...
...SHE SHOULD BE IN MY ROOM ON THE FIRST FLOOR RIGHT NOW.
IF I GO BACK THE WAY I SNUCK OUT, I DON'T THINK ANYONE WILL SEE ME.
I SEE.
I GUESS THIS IS GOODBYE.
YOUR CHANCES ARE BETTER ALONE.
I'LL WAIT HERE FOR CHITOGE.
...

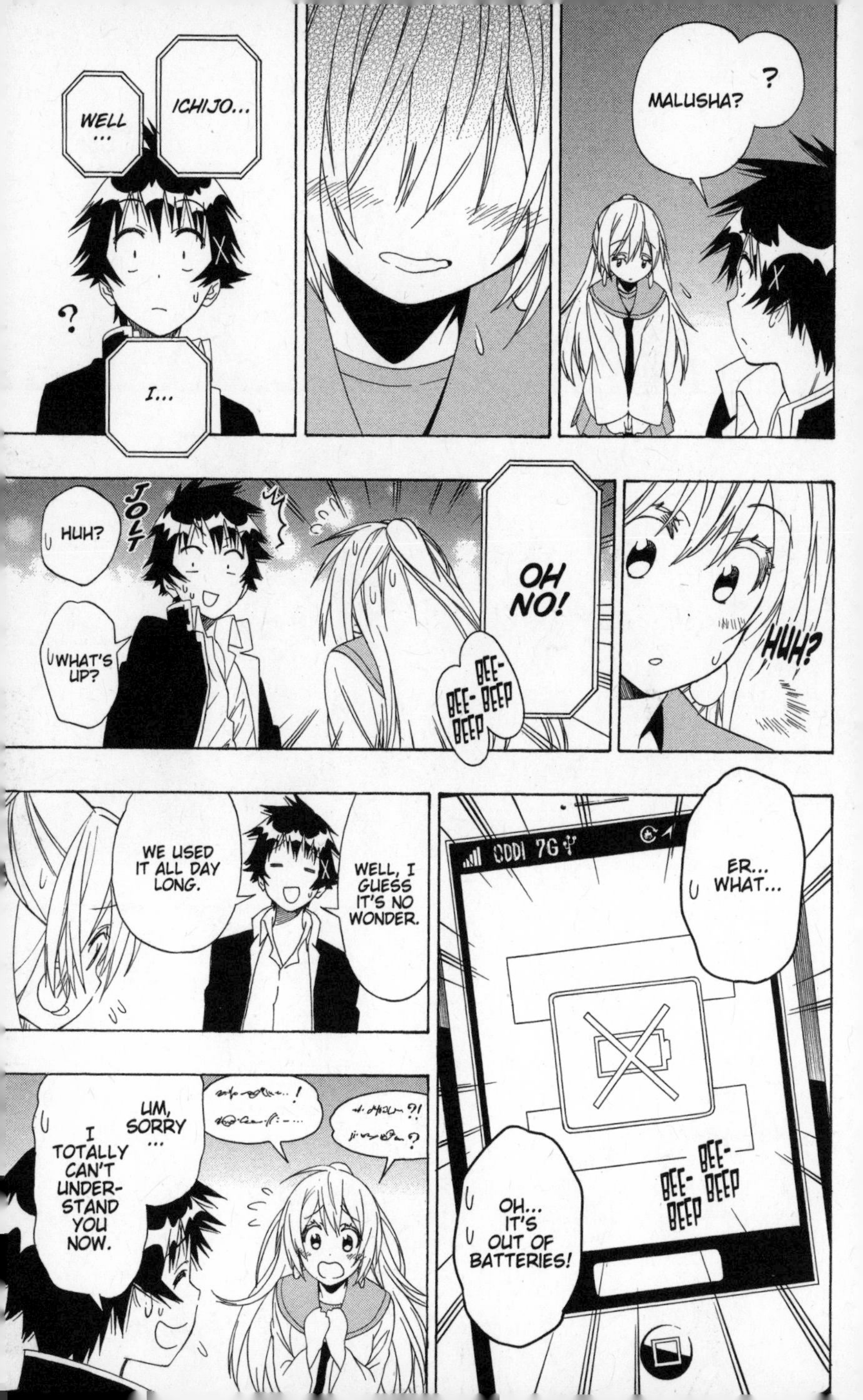
?
MALUSHA?
ICHIJO...
WELL...
?
I...
HUH?
OH NO!
BEE-BEEP BEE-BEEP
JOLT
HUH?
WHAT'S UP?
ER... WHAT...
BEE-BEEP BEE-BEEP
OH... IT'S OUT OF BATTERIES!
WELL, I GUESS IT'S NO WONDER.
WE USED IT ALL DAY LONG.
UM, SORRY...
I TOTALLY CAN'T UNDERSTAND YOU NOW.

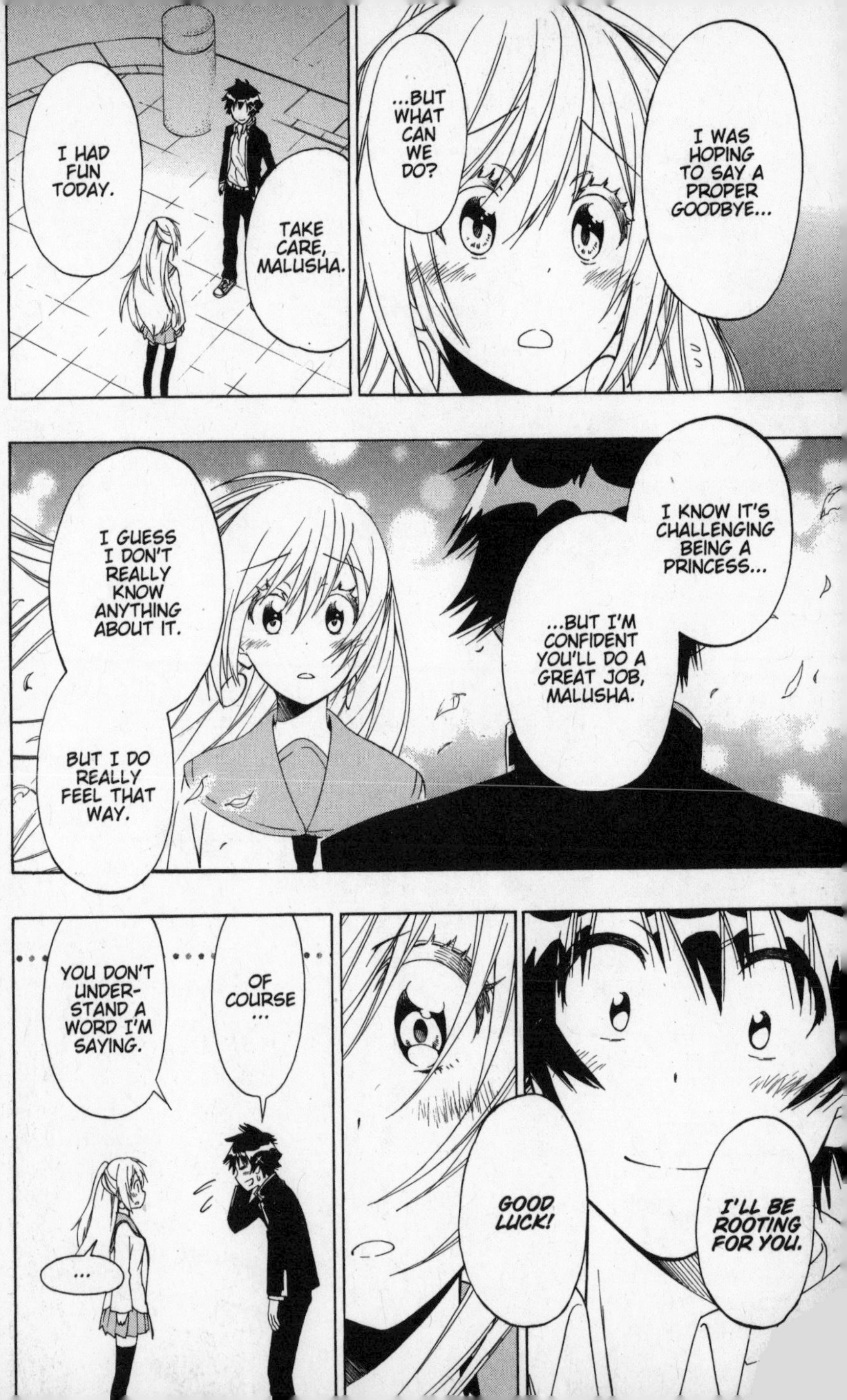
I WAS HOPING TO SAY A PROPER GOODBYE...
...BUT WHAT CAN WE DO?
I HAD FUN TODAY.
TAKE CARE, MALUSHA.
I KNOW IT'S CHALLENGING BEING A PRINCESS...
...BUT I'M CONFIDENT YOU'LL DO A GREAT JOB, MALUSHA.
I GUESS I DON'T REALLY KNOW ANYTHING ABOUT IT.
BUT I DO REALLY FEEL THAT WAY.
I'LL BE ROOTING FOR YOU.
GOOD LUCK!
OF COURSE ...
YOU DON'T UNDER-STAND A WORD I'M SAYING.
...

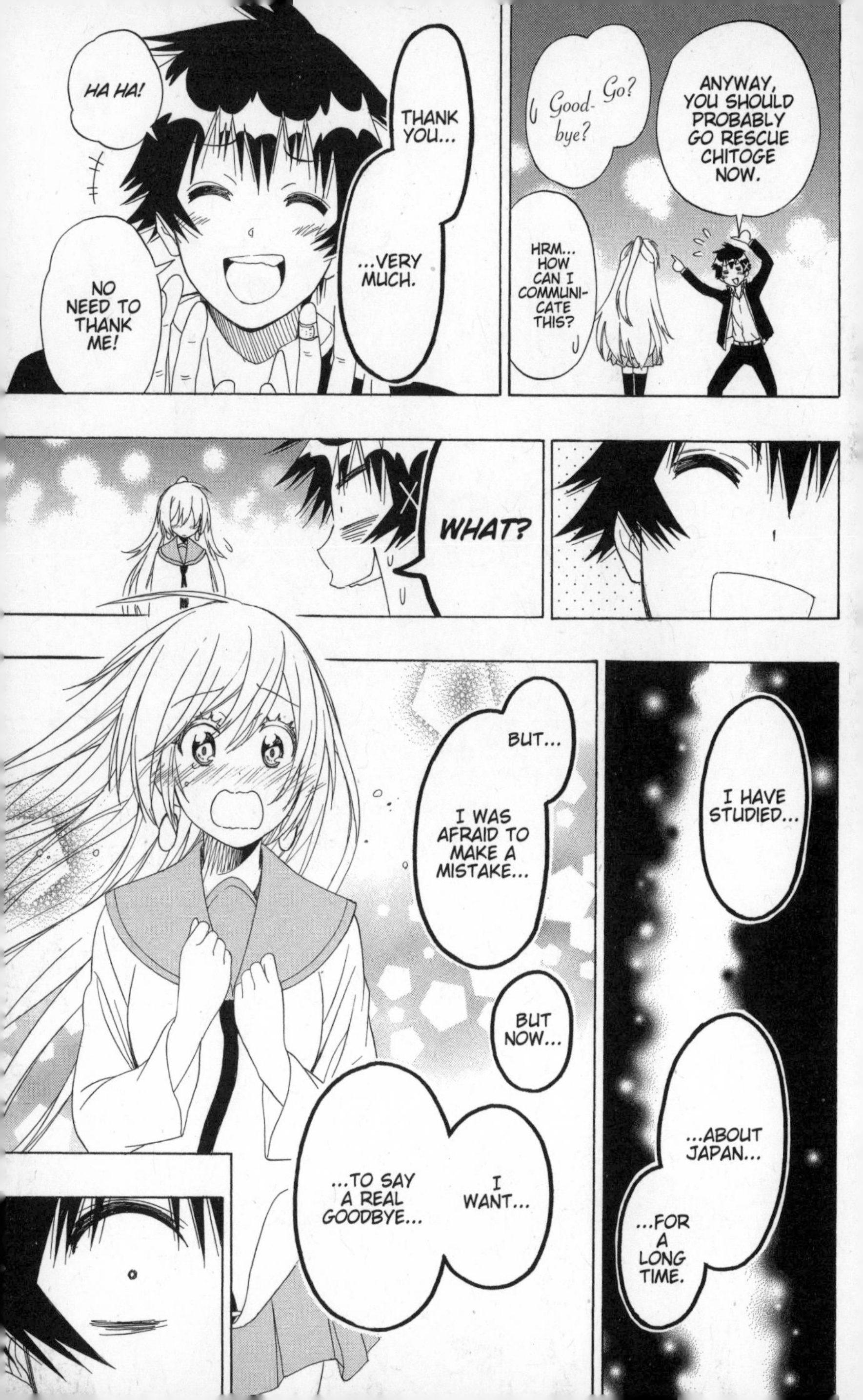
ANYWAY, YOU SHOULD PROBABLY GO RESCUE CHITOGE NOW.
Go? Good-bye?
HRM... HOW CAN I COMMUNICATE THIS?
THANK YOU...
...VERY MUCH.
HA HA!
NO NEED TO THANK ME!
WHAT?
I HAVE STUDIED...
...ABOUT JAPAN...
...FOR A LONG TIME.
BUT...
I WAS AFRAID TO MAKE A MISTAKE...
BUT NOW...
I WANT...
...TO SAY A REAL GOODBYE...

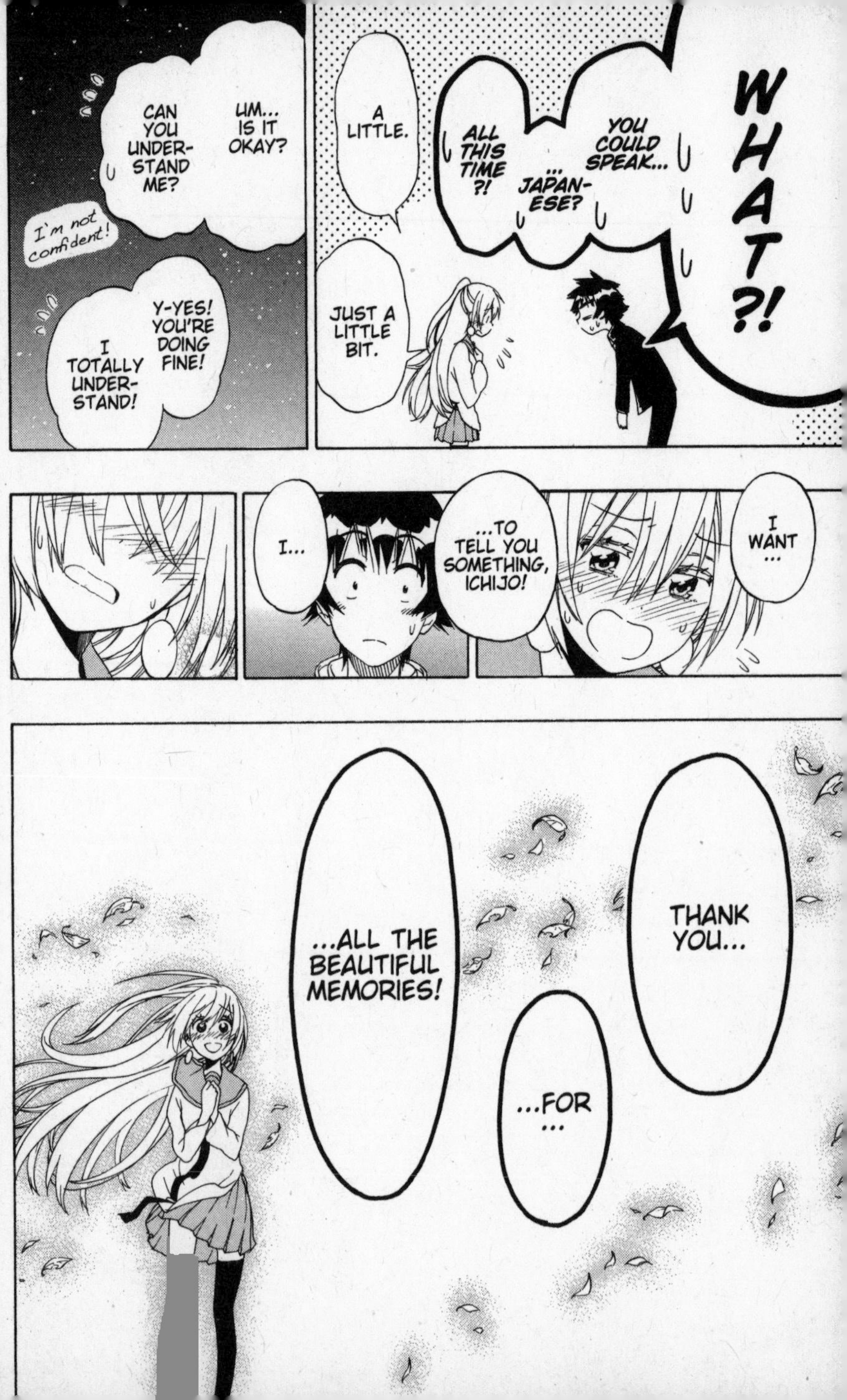
WHAT?!
YOU COULD SPEAK... ...JAPANESE?
ALL THIS TIME?!
A LITTLE.
JUST A LITTLE BIT.
UM... IS IT OKAY?
CAN YOU UNDERSTAND ME?
I'm not confident!
Y-YES! YOU'RE DOING FINE!
I TOTALLY UNDERSTAND!
I WANT...
...TO TELL YOU SOMETHING, ICHIJO!
I...
THANK YOU...
...FOR...
...ALL THE BEAUTIFUL MEMORIES!

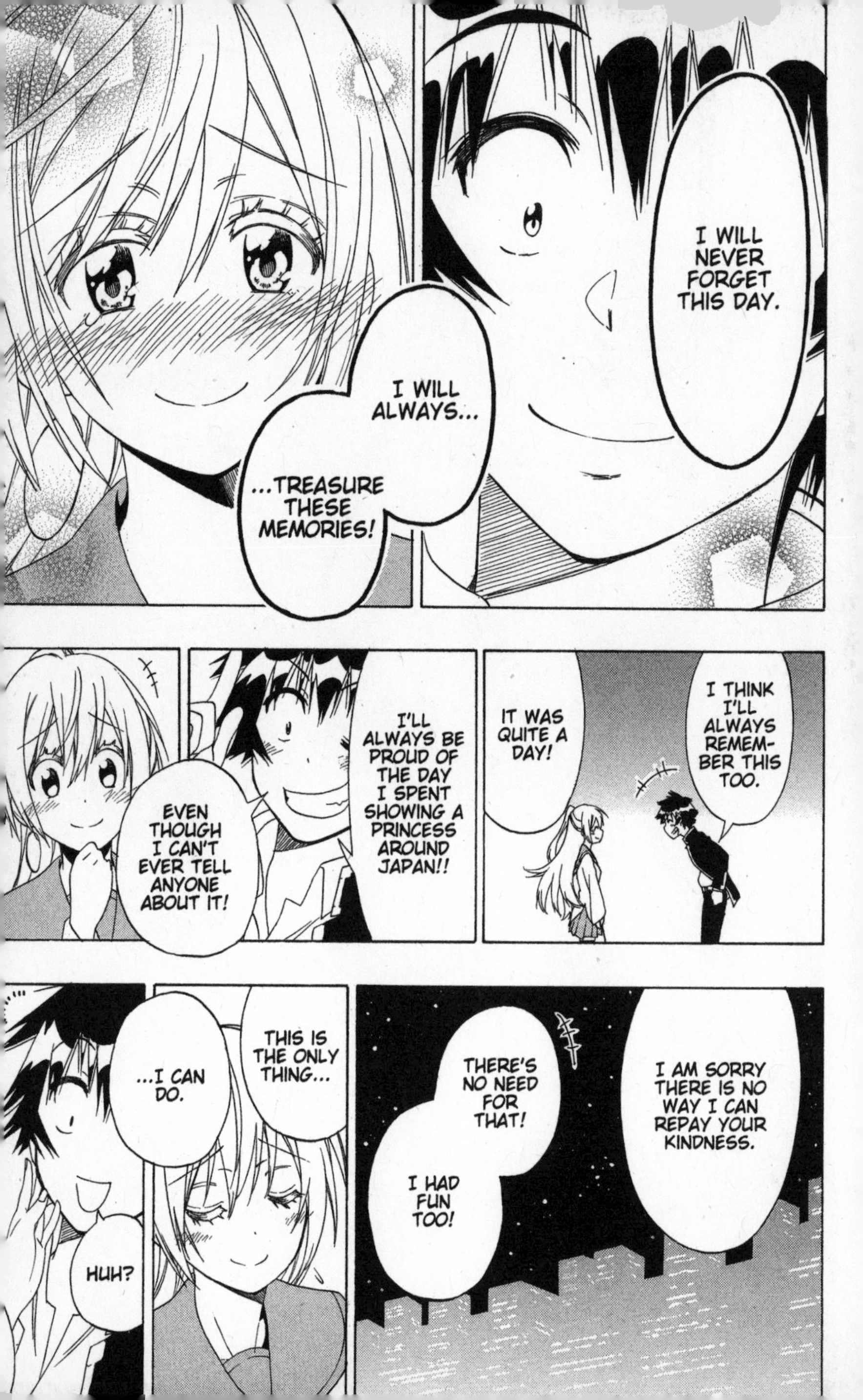
I WILL NEVER FORGET THIS DAY.
I WILL ALWAYS...
...TREASURE THESE MEMORIES!
I THINK I'LL ALWAYS REMEMBER THIS TOO.
IT WAS QUITE A DAY!
I'LL ALWAYS BE PROUD OF THE DAY I SPENT SHOWING A PRINCESS AROUND JAPAN!!
EVEN THOUGH I CAN'T EVER TELL ANYONE ABOUT IT!
I AM SORRY THERE IS NO WAY I CAN REPAY YOUR KINDNESS.
THERE'S NO NEED FOR THAT!
I HAD FUN TOO!
THIS IS THE ONLY THING...
...I CAN DO.
...
HUH?

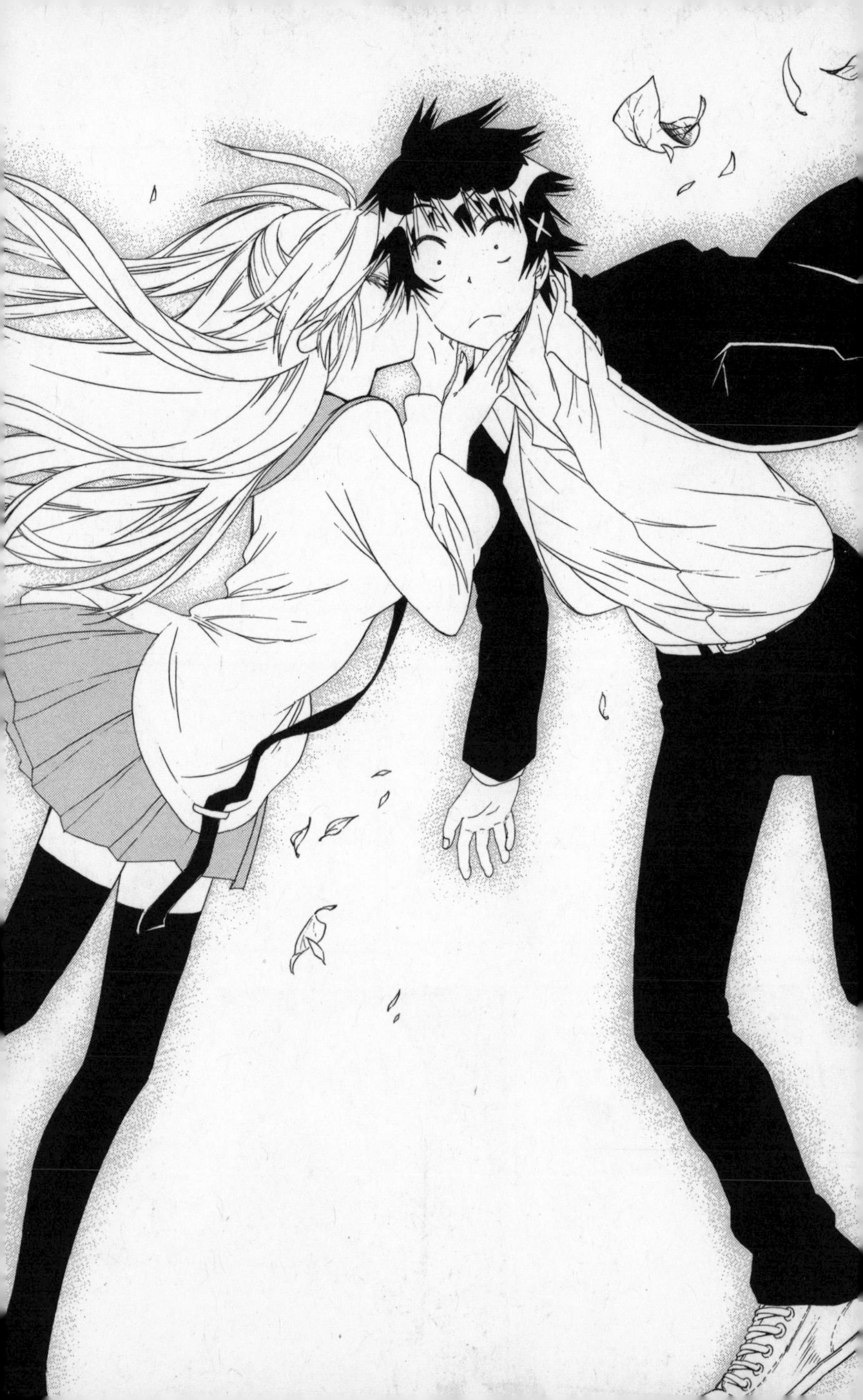

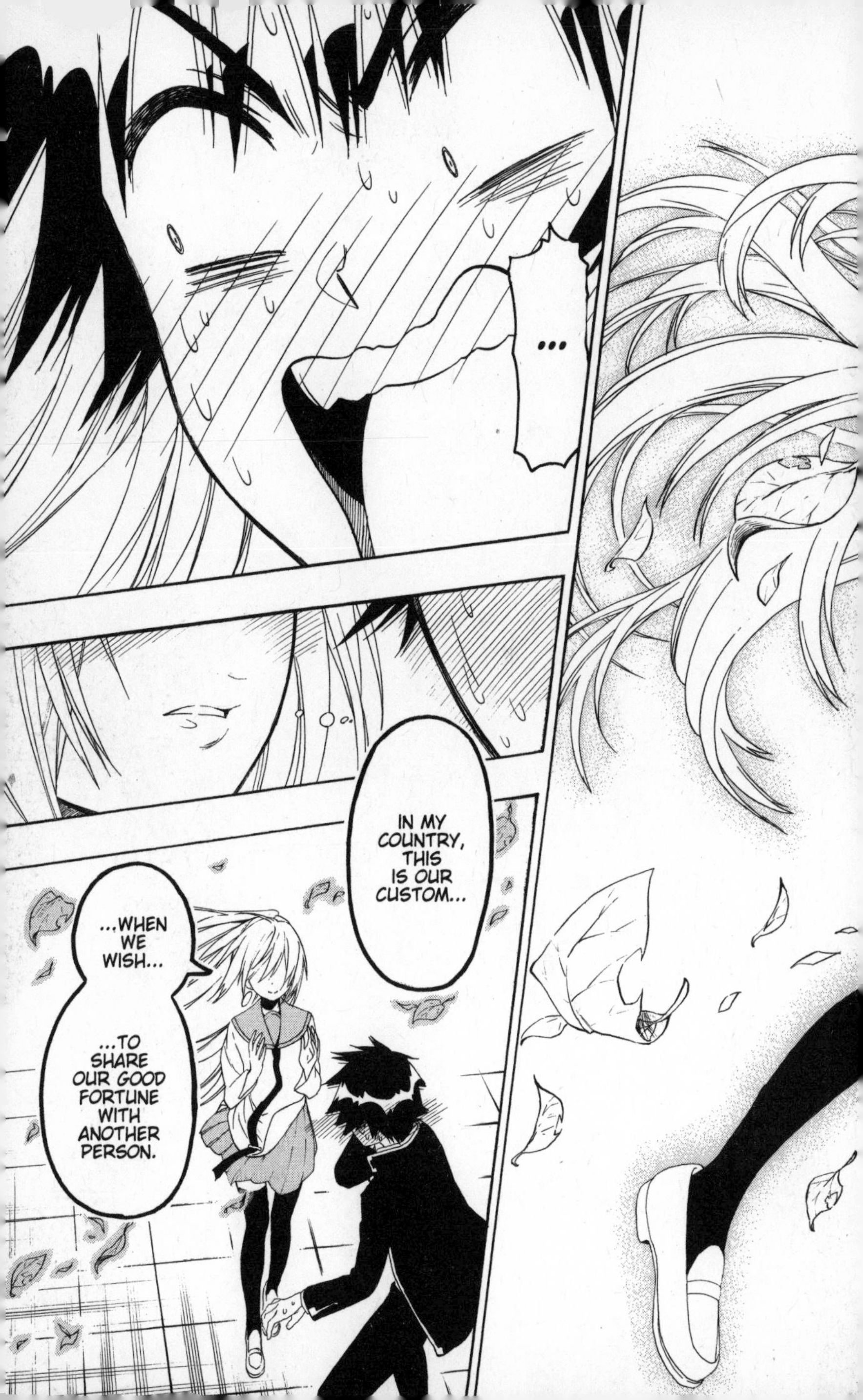
...
IN MY COUNTRY, THIS IS OUR CUSTOM...
...WHEN WE WISH...
...TO SHARE OUR GOOD FORTUNE WITH ANOTHER PERSON.

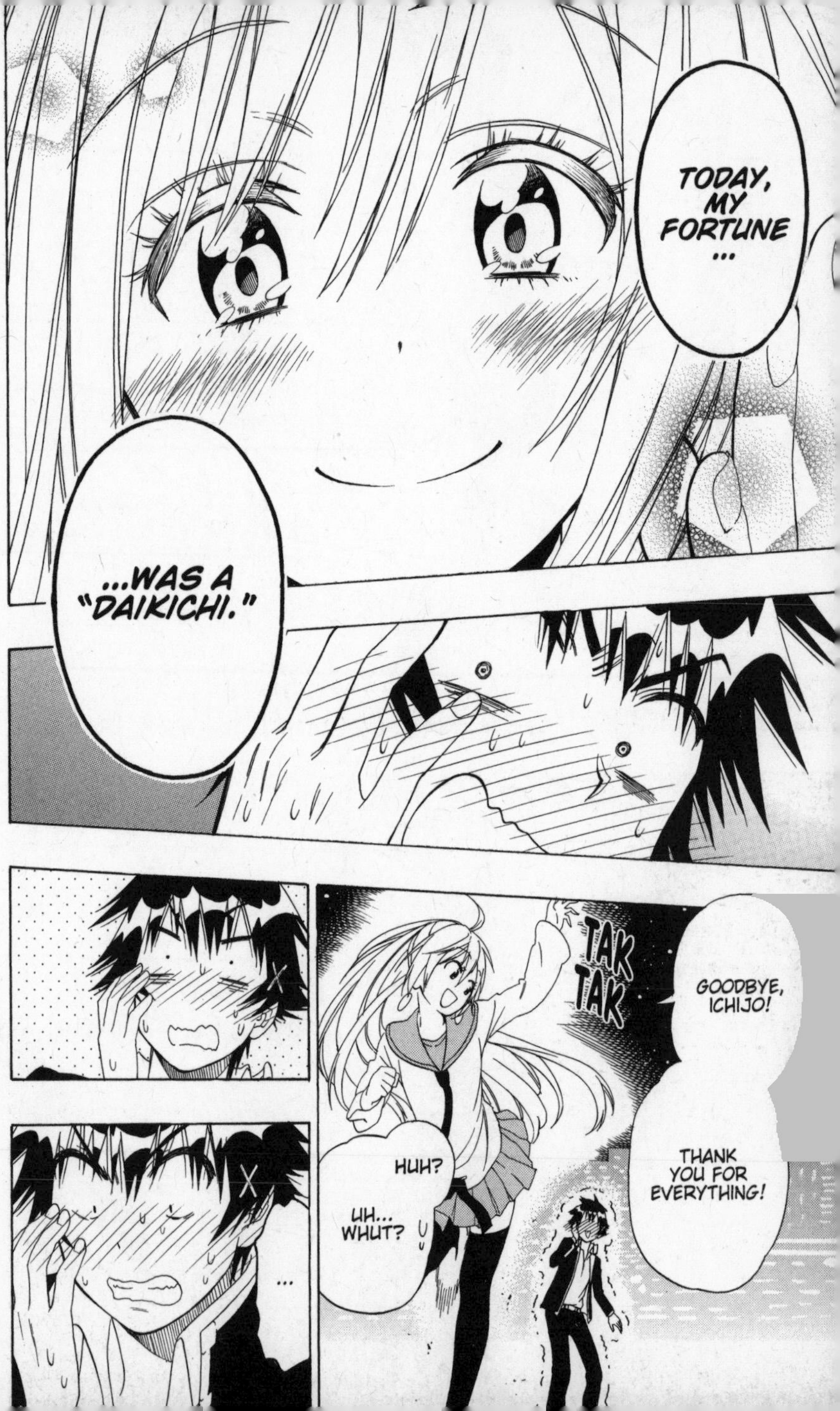
TODAY, MY FORTUNE ...
...WAS A "DAIKICHI."
GOODBYE, ICHIJO!
TAK TAK
THANK YOU FOR EVERYTHING!
HUH?
UH... WHUT?
...

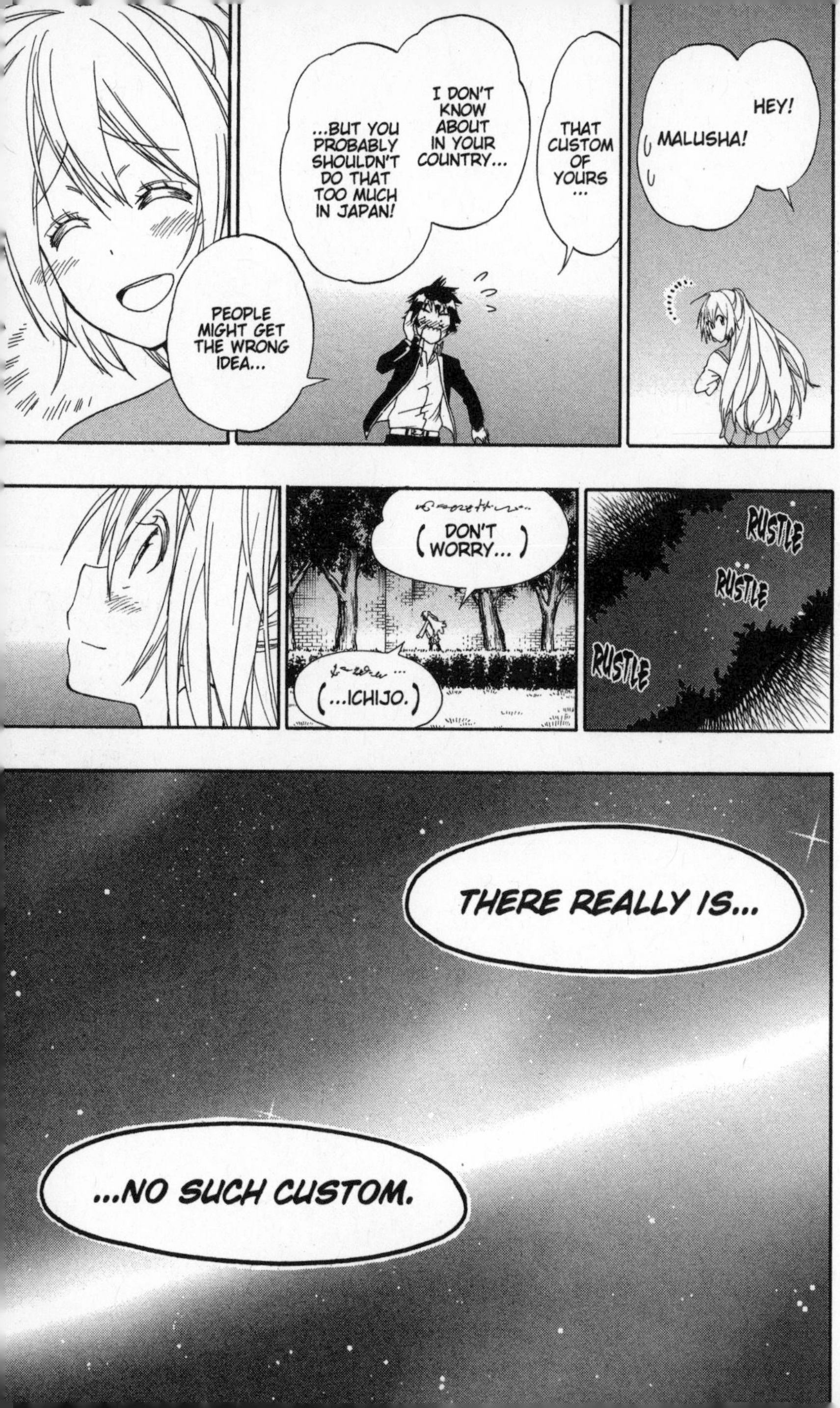
HEY! MALUSHA!
THAT CUSTOM OF YOURS...
I DON'T KNOW ABOUT IN YOUR COUNTRY...
...BUT YOU PROBABLY SHOULDN'T DO THAT TOO MUCH IN JAPAN!
PEOPLE MIGHT GET THE WRONG IDEA...
RUSTLE
RUSTLE
RUSTLE
(DON'T WORRY...)
(...ICHIJO.)
THERE REALLY IS...
...NO SUCH CUSTOM.

Chapter 139: Speech

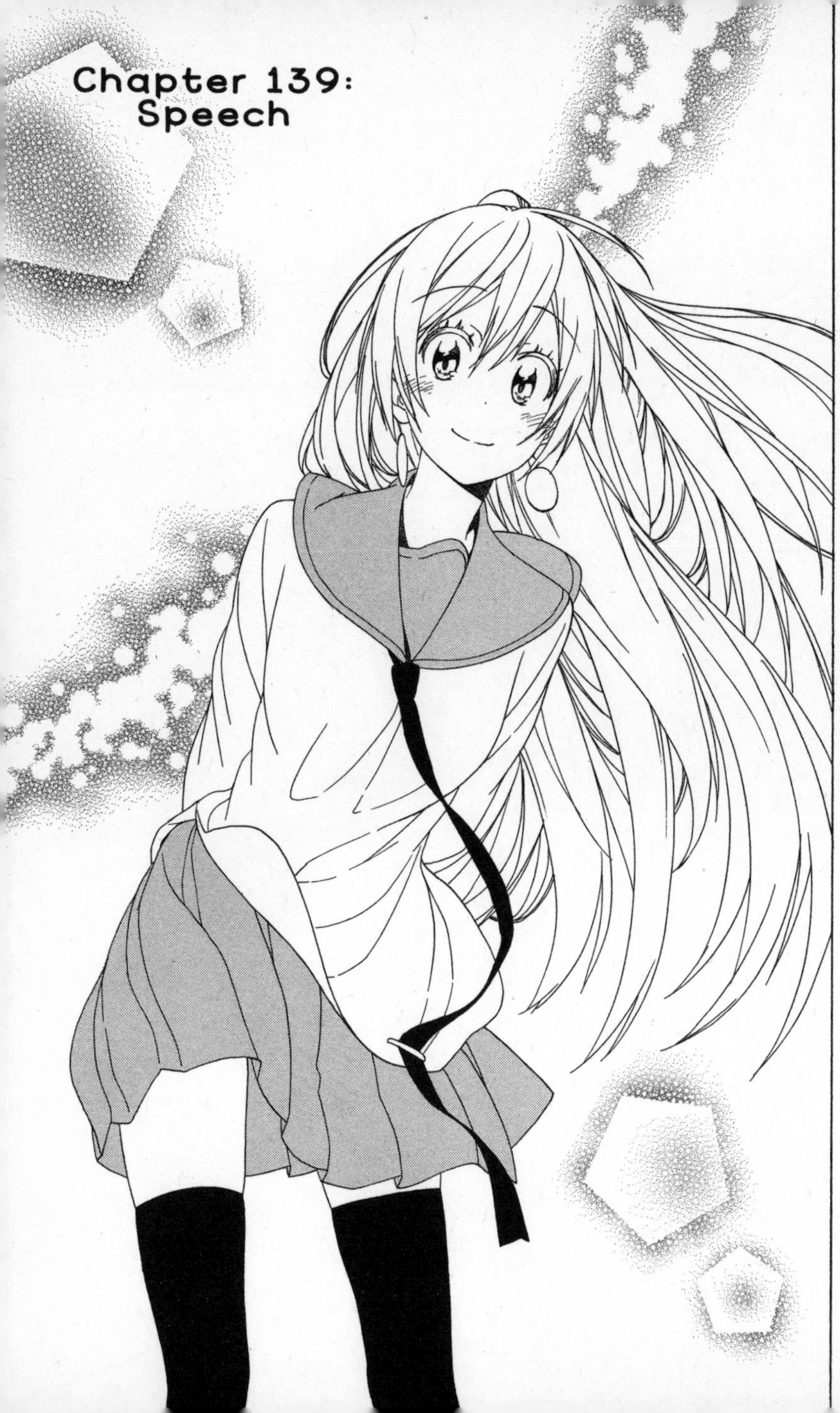

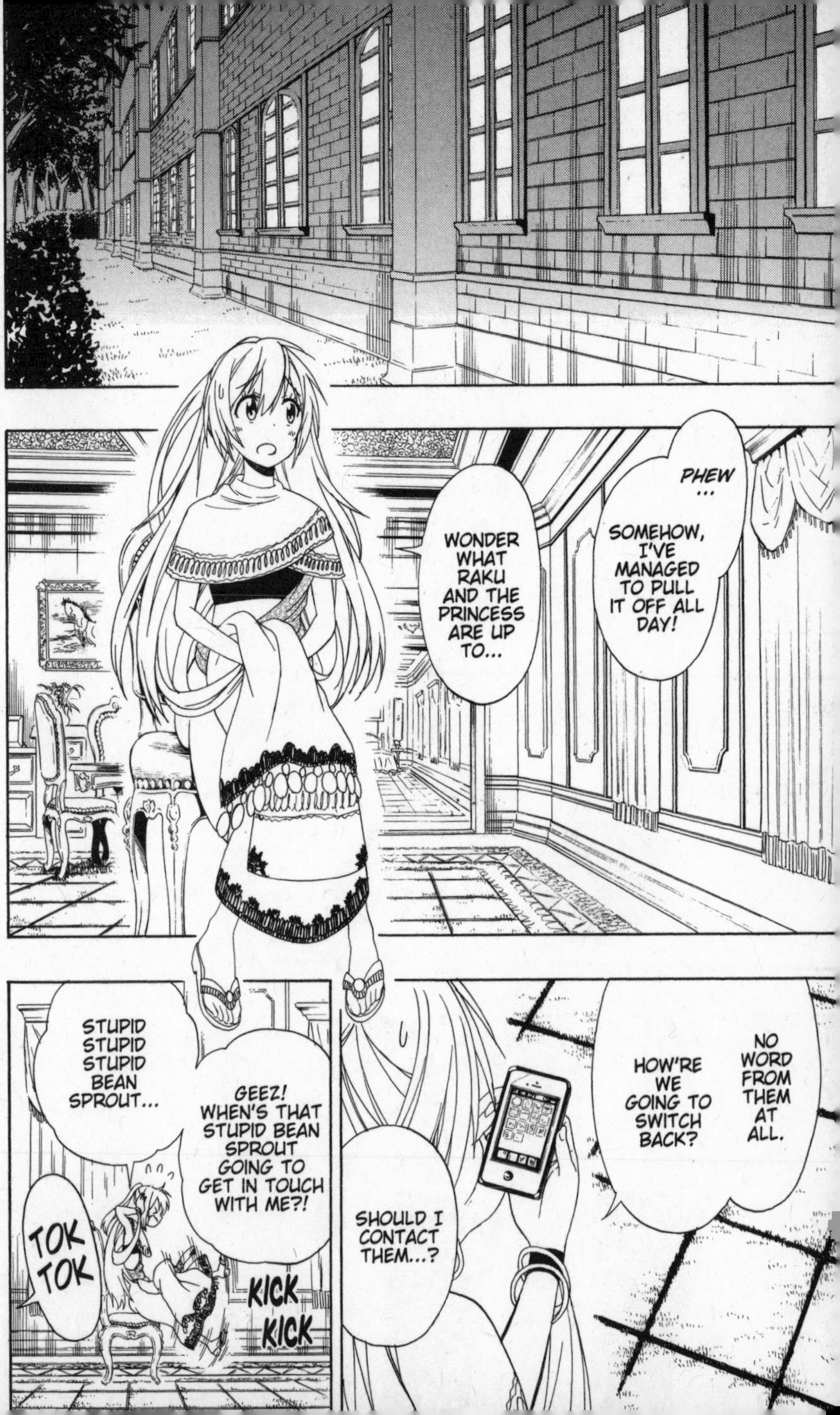
PHEW ... SOMEHOW, I'VE MANAGED TO PULL IT OFF ALL DAY!
WONDER WHAT RAKU AND THE PRINCESS ARE UP TO...
NO WORD FROM THEM AT ALL.
HOW'RE WE GOING TO SWITCH BACK?
SHOULD I CONTACT THEM...?
GEEZ! WHEN'S THAT STUPID BEAN SPROUT GOING TO GET IN TOUCH WITH ME?!
STUPID STUPID STUPID BEAN SPROUT...
KICK KICK
TOK TOK

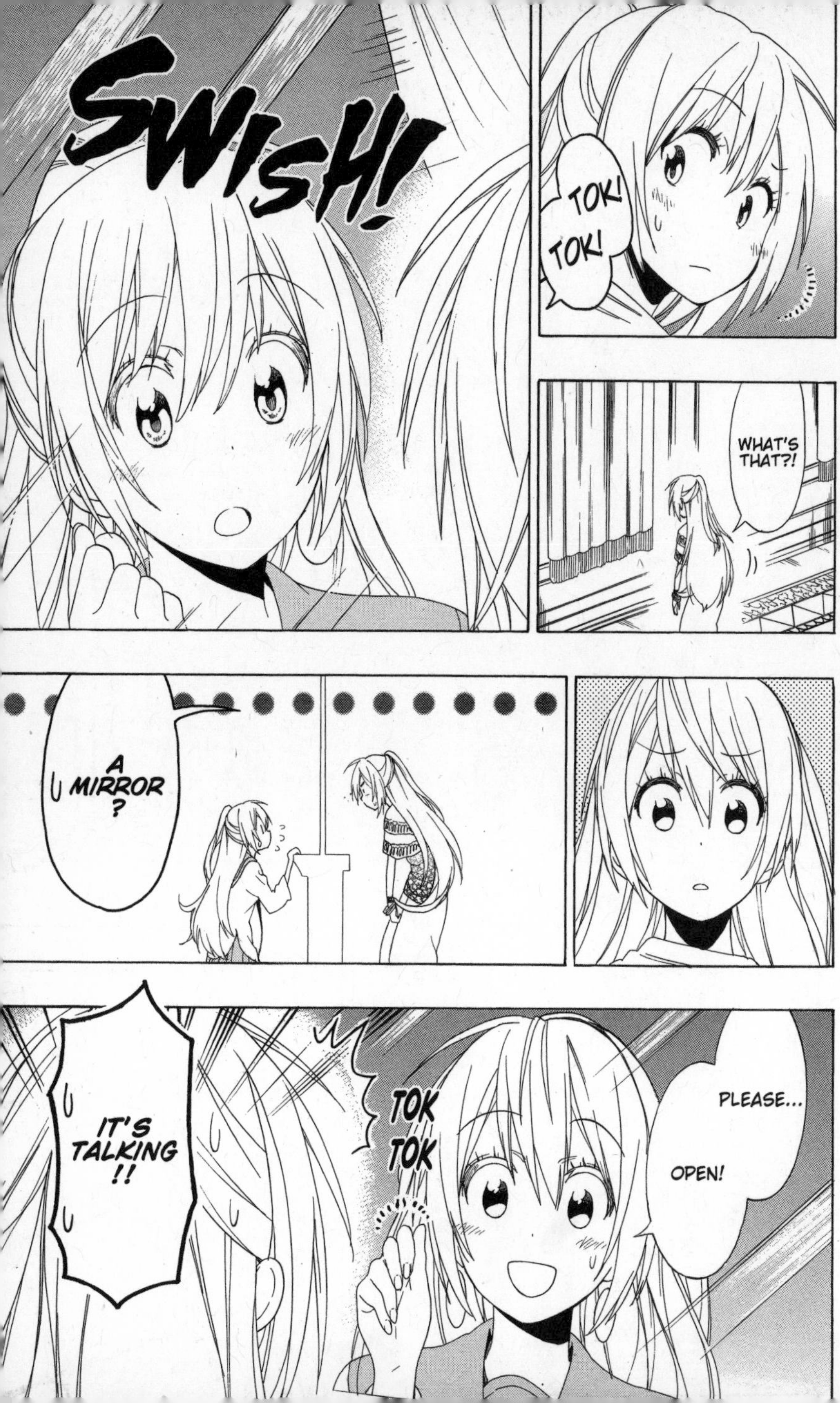
TOK! TOK!
WHAT'S THAT?!
SWISH!
A MIRROR?
PLEASE... OPEN!
TOK TOK
IT'S TALKING!!

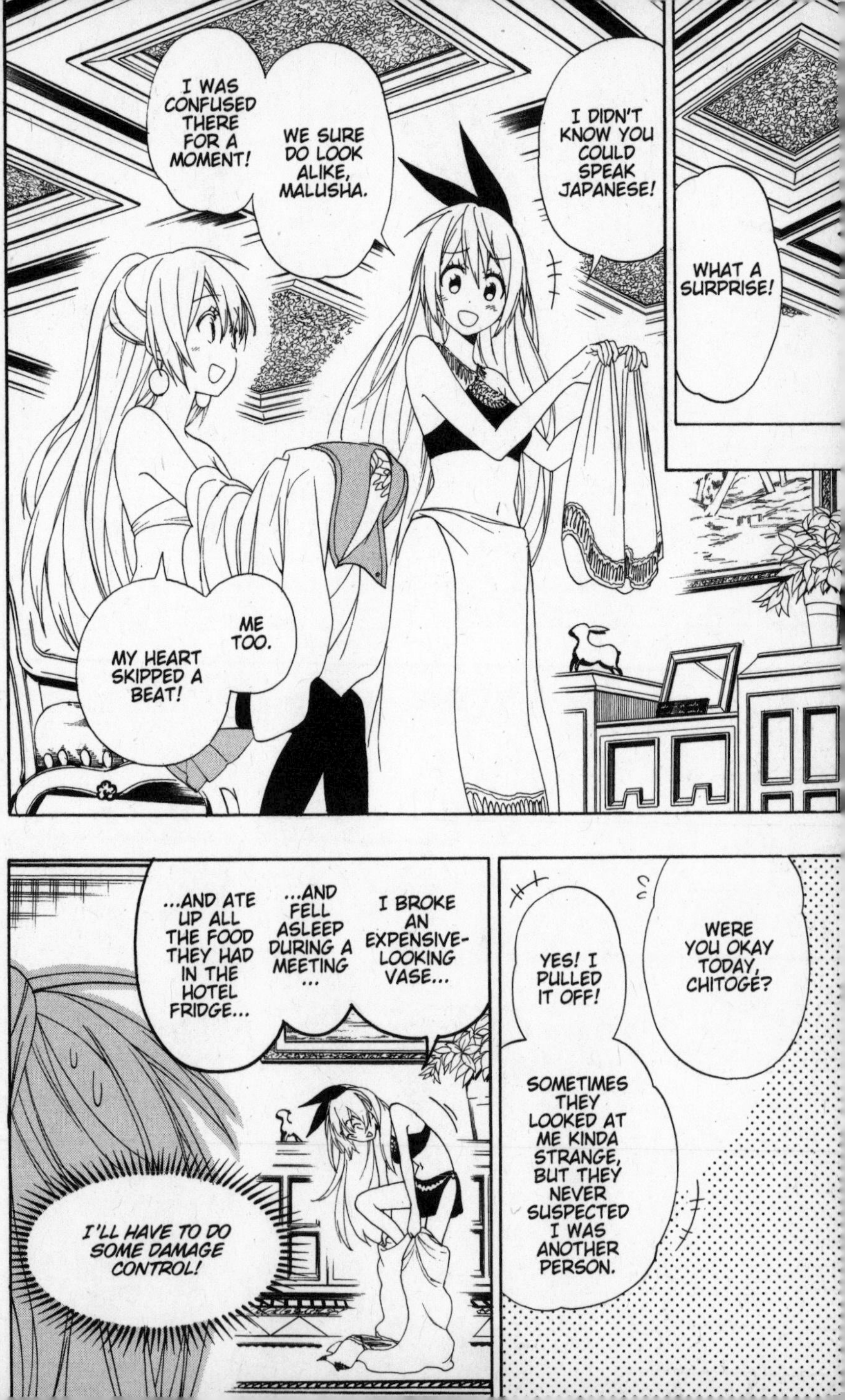
I DIDN'T KNOW YOU COULD SPEAK JAPANESE!
WHAT A SURPRISE!
WE SURE DO LOOK ALIKE, MALUSHA.
I WAS CONFUSED THERE FOR A MOMENT!
ME TOO.
MY HEART SKIPPED A BEAT!
WERE YOU OKAY TODAY, CHITOGE?
YES! I PULLED IT OFF!
SOMETIMES THEY LOOKED AT ME KINDA STRANGE, BUT THEY NEVER SUSPECTED I WAS ANOTHER PERSON.
I BROKE AN EXPENSIVE-LOOKING VASE...
...AND FELL ASLEEP DURING A MEETING...
...AND ATE UP ALL THE FOOD THEY HAD IN THE HOTEL FRIDGE...
I'LL HAVE TO DO SOME DAMAGE CONTROL!

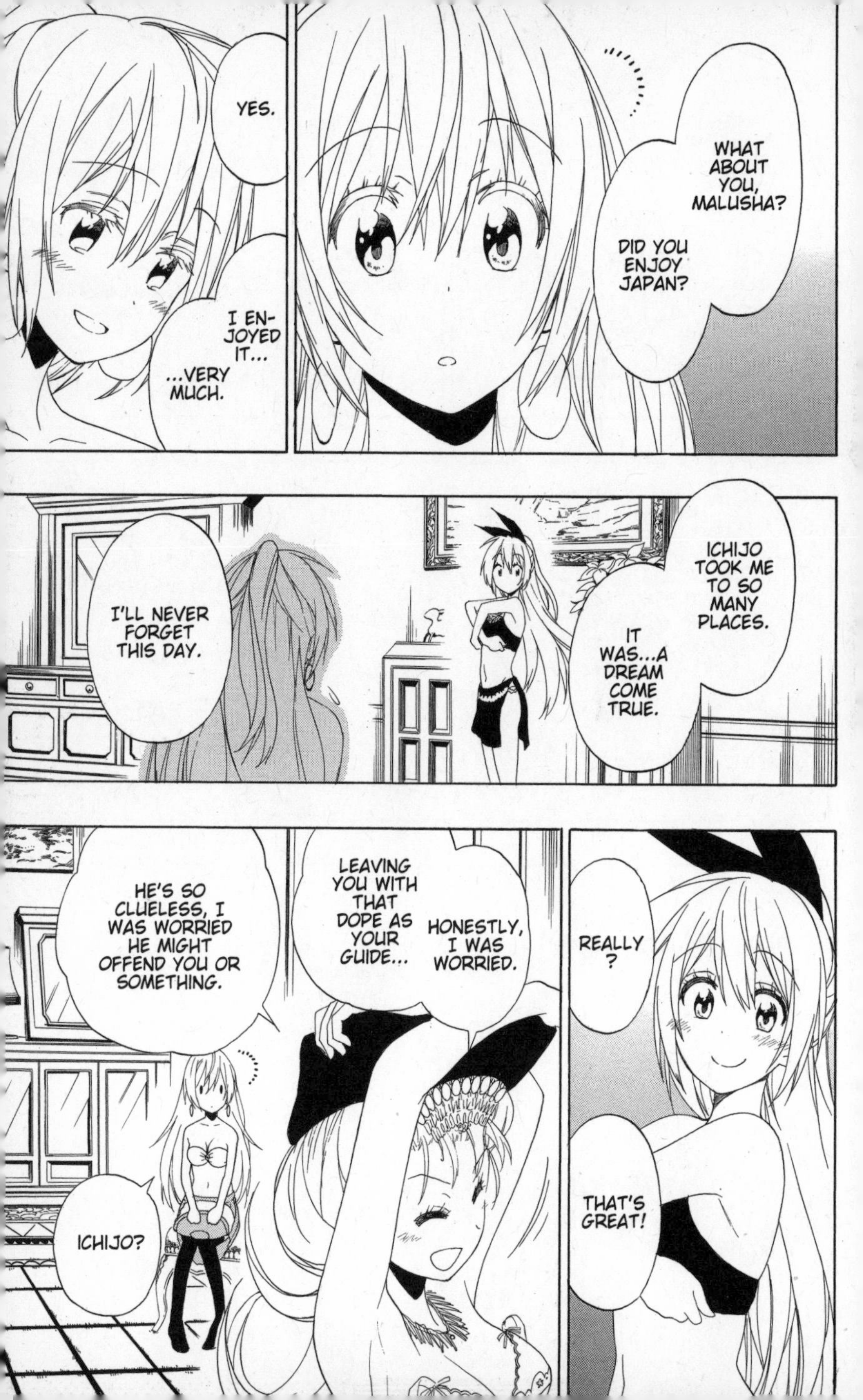
WHAT ABOUT YOU, MALUSHA?
DID YOU ENJOY JAPAN?
YES.
I EN-JOYED IT...
...VERY MUCH.
ICHIJO TOOK ME TO SO MANY PLACES.
IT WAS...A DREAM COME TRUE.
I'LL NEVER FORGET THIS DAY.
REALLY?
THAT'S GREAT!
HONESTLY, I WAS WORRIED.
LEAVING YOU WITH THAT DOPE AS YOUR GUIDE...
HE'S SO CLUELESS, I WAS WORRIED HE MIGHT OFFEND YOU OR SOMETHING.
ICHIJO?

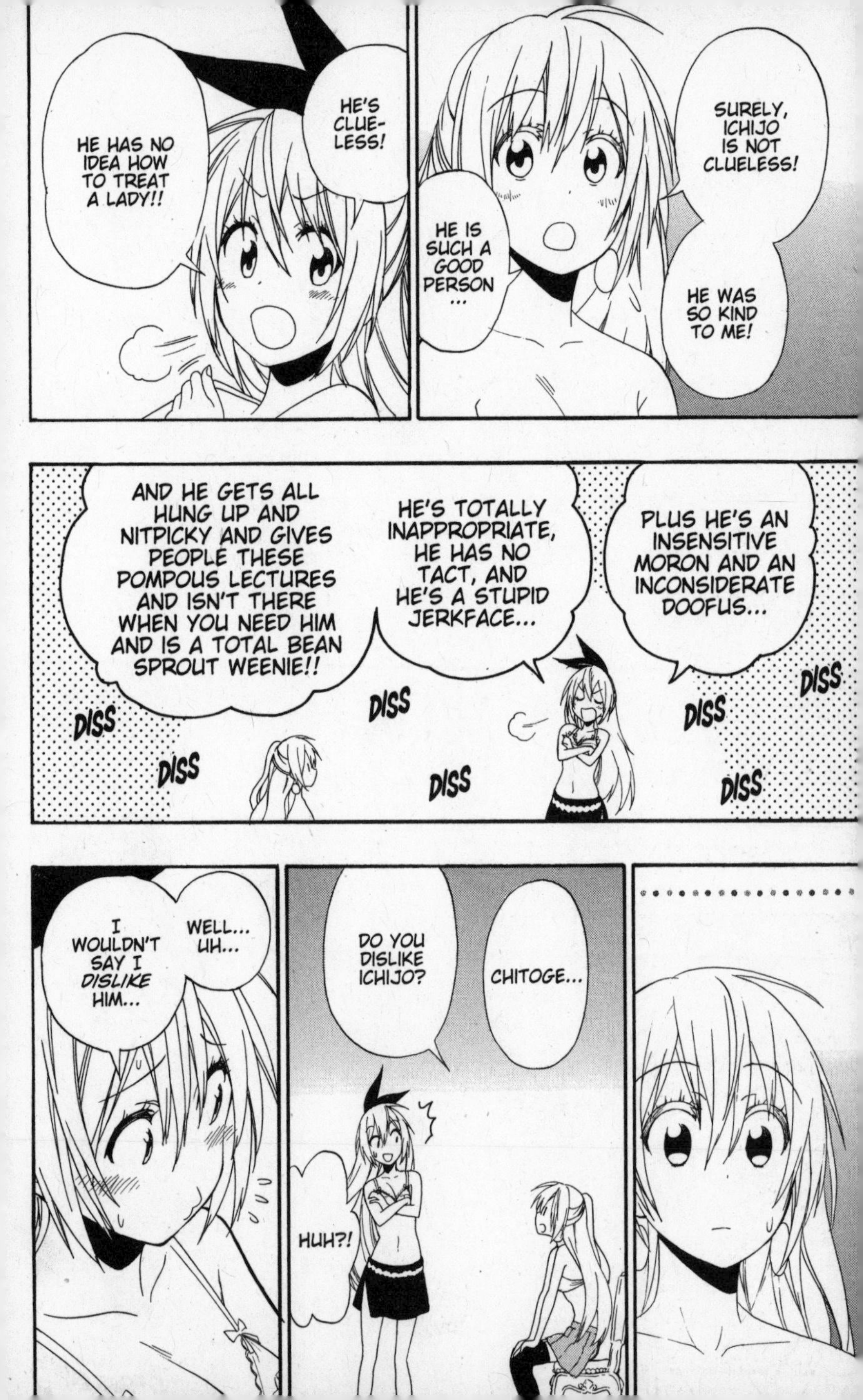
SURELY, ICHIJO IS NOT CLUELESS!
HE WAS SO KIND TO ME!
HE IS SUCH A GOOD PERSON...
HE'S CLUELESS!
HE HAS NO IDEA HOW TO TREAT A LADY!!
PLUS HE'S AN INSENSITIVE MORON AND AN INCONSIDERATE DOOFUS...
HE'S TOTALLY INAPPROPRIATE, HE HAS NO TACT, AND HE'S A STUPID JERKFACE...
AND HE GETS ALL HUNG UP AND NITPICKY AND GIVES PEOPLE THESE POMPOUS LECTURES AND ISN'T THERE WHEN YOU NEED HIM AND IS A TOTAL BEAN SPROUT WEENIE!!
DISS
DISS
DISS
DISS
DISS
DISS
DISS
....
CHITOGE...
DO YOU DISLIKE ICHIJO?
HUH?!
WELL... UH...
I WOULDN'T SAY I *DISLIKE* HIM...

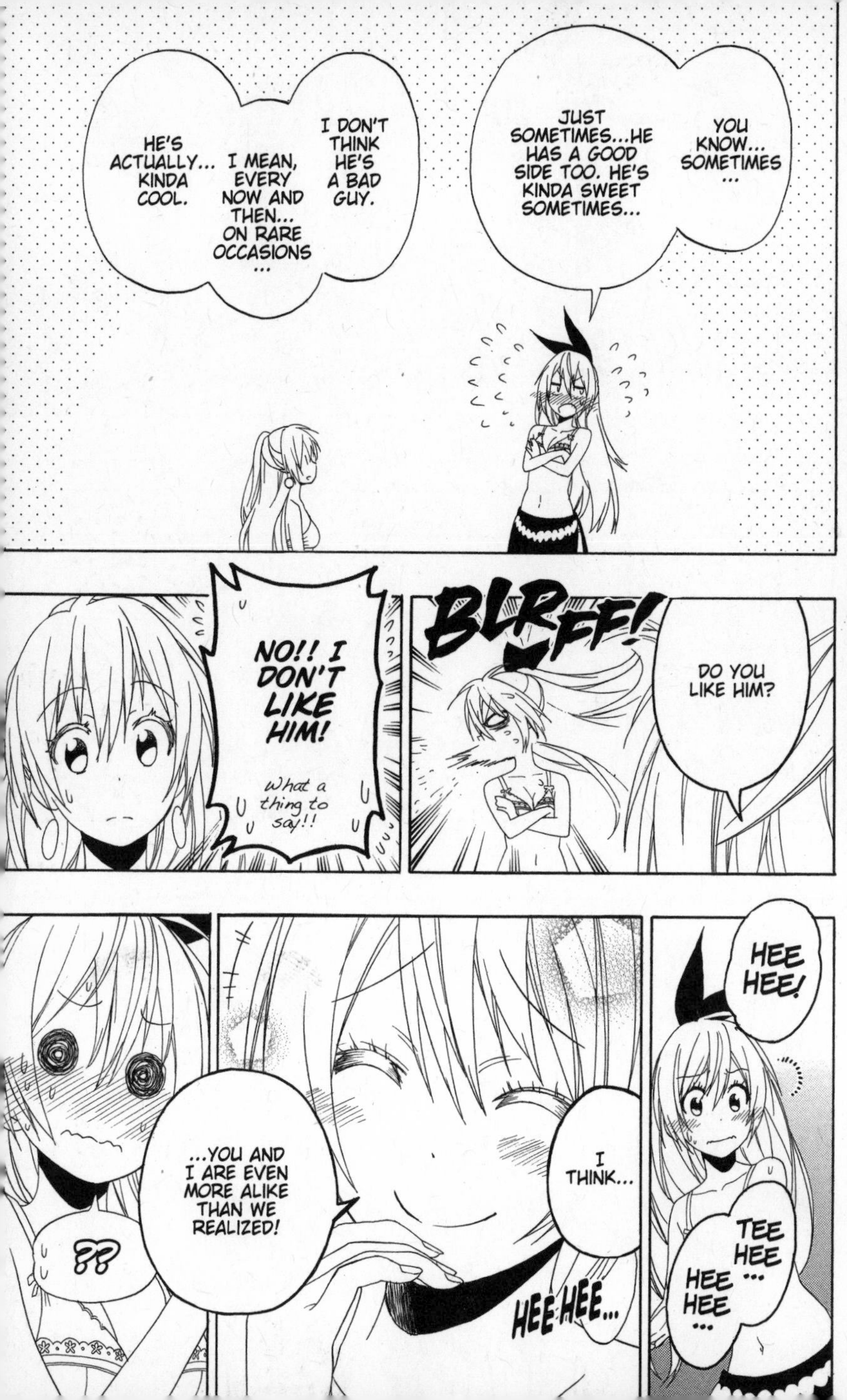
YOU KNOW... SOMETIMES...
JUST SOMETIMES...HE HAS A GOOD SIDE TOO. HE'S KINDA SWEET SOMETIMES...
I DON'T THINK HE'S A BAD GUY.
I MEAN, EVERY NOW AND THEN... ON RARE OCCASIONS...
HE'S ACTUALLY... KINDA COOL.
DO YOU LIKE HIM?
BLRFF!
NO!! I DON'T LIKE HIM!
What a thing to say!!
HEE HEE!
TEE HEE...
HEE HEE...
I THINK...
...YOU AND I ARE EVEN MORE ALIKE THAN WE REALIZED!
HEE HEE...
??

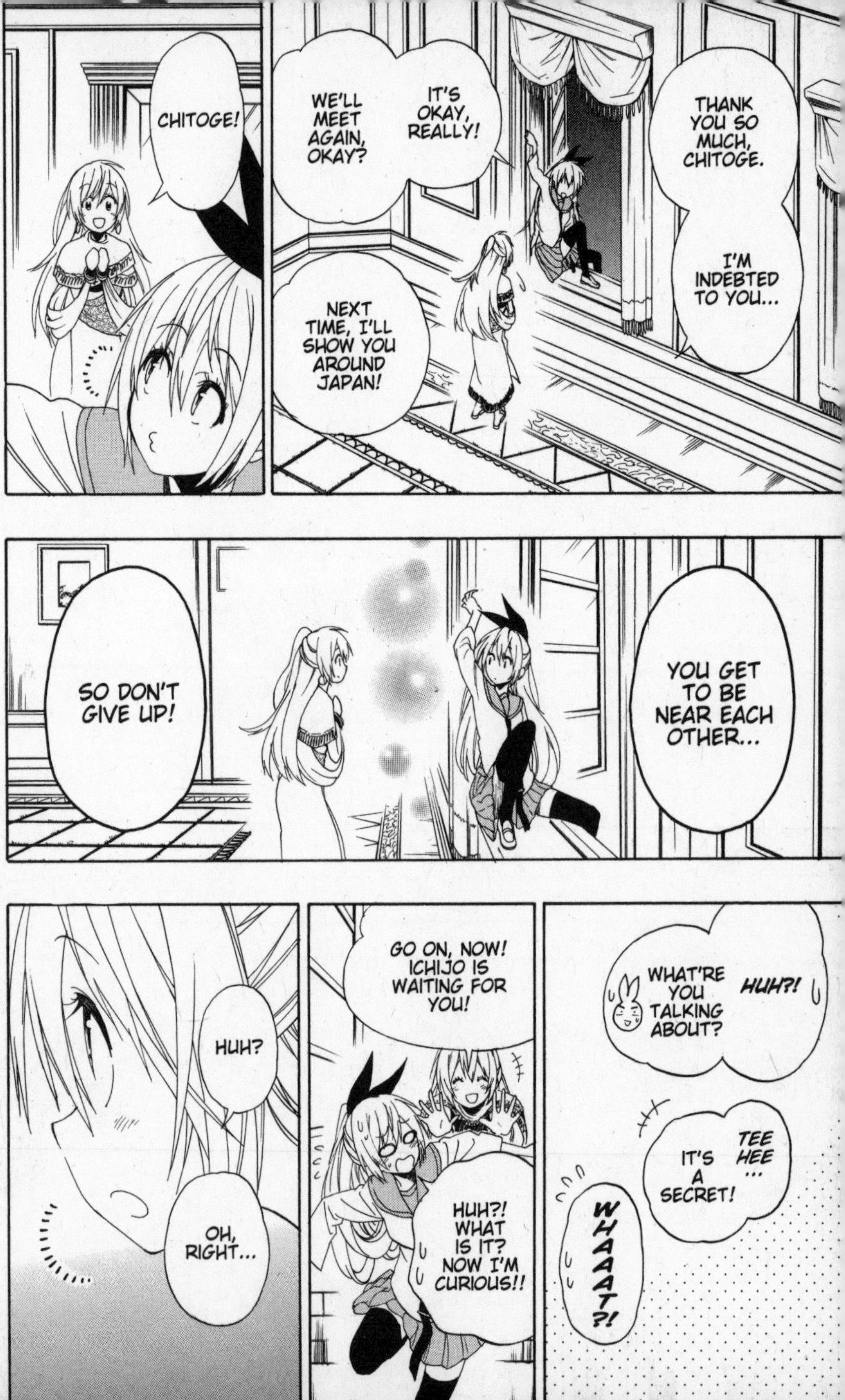
THANK YOU SO MUCH, CHITOGE.
I'M INDEBTED TO YOU...
IT'S OKAY, REALLY!
WE'LL MEET AGAIN, OKAY?
NEXT TIME, I'LL SHOW YOU AROUND JAPAN!
CHITOGE!
YOU GET TO BE NEAR EACH OTHER...
SO DON'T GIVE UP!
HUH?!
WHAT'RE YOU TALKING ABOUT?
TEE HEE...
IT'S A SECRET!
WHAAAAT?!
GO ON, NOW! ICHIJO IS WAITING FOR YOU!
HUH?! WHAT IS IT? NOW I'M CURIOUS!!
HUH?
OH, RIGHT...

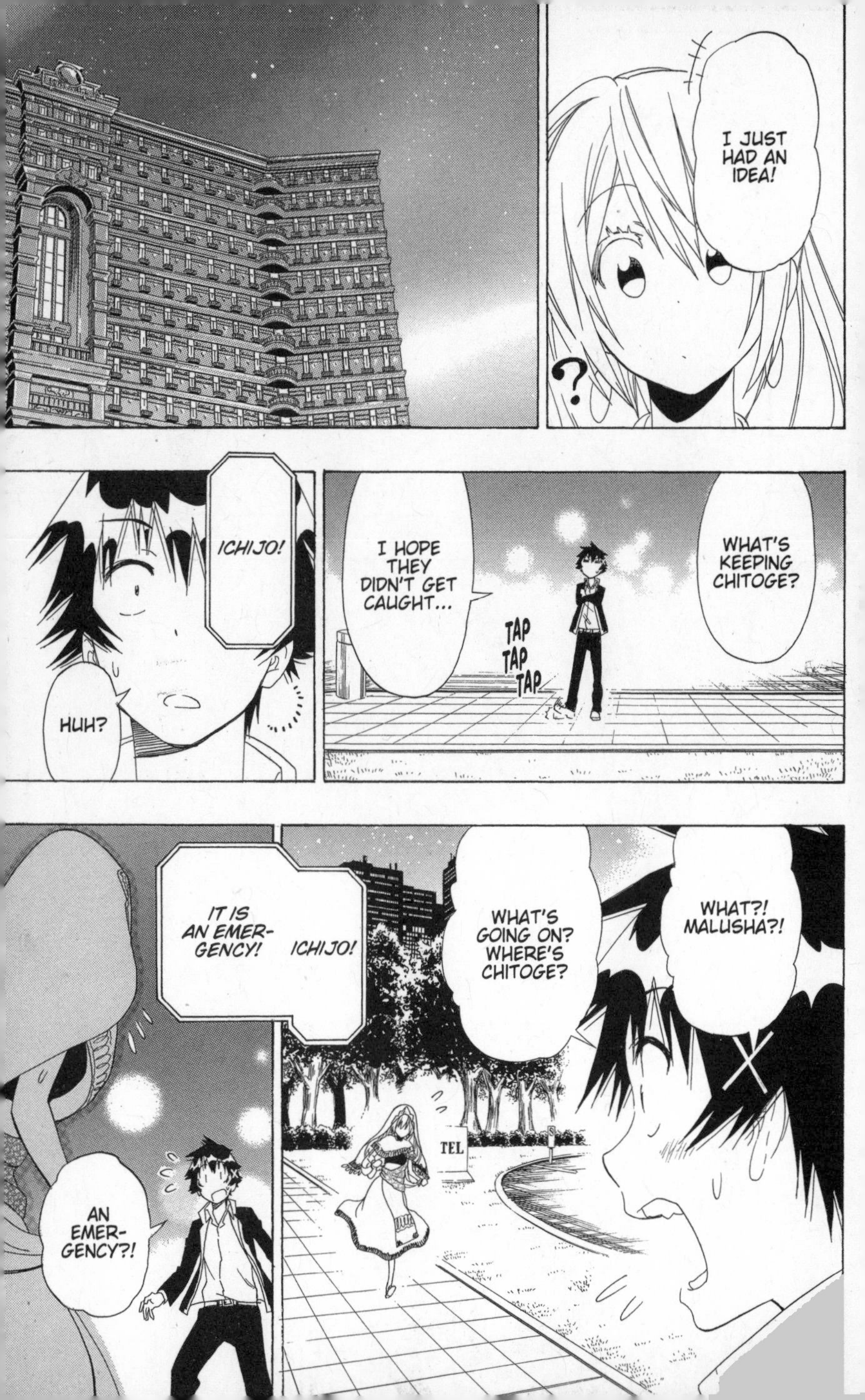
I JUST HAD AN IDEA!
WHAT'S KEEPING CHITOGE?
I HOPE THEY DIDN'T GET CAUGHT...
TAP TAP TAP
ICHIJO!
HUH?
WHAT?! MALUSHA?!
WHAT'S GOING ON? WHERE'S CHITOGE?
ICHIJO!
IT IS AN EMERGENCY!
AN EMERGENCY?!
TEL

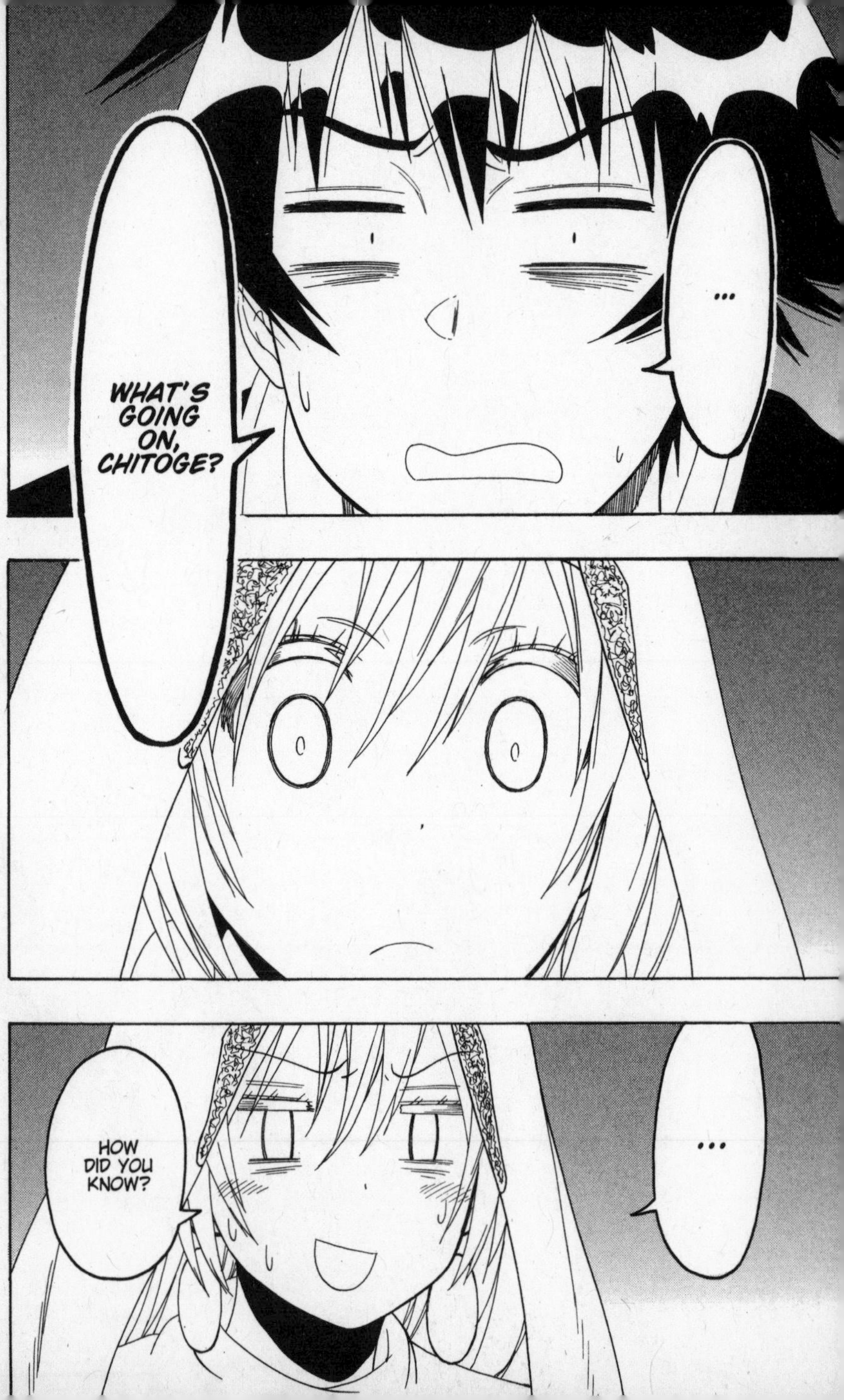
...
WHAT'S GOING ON, CHITOGE?
...
HOW DID YOU KNOW?

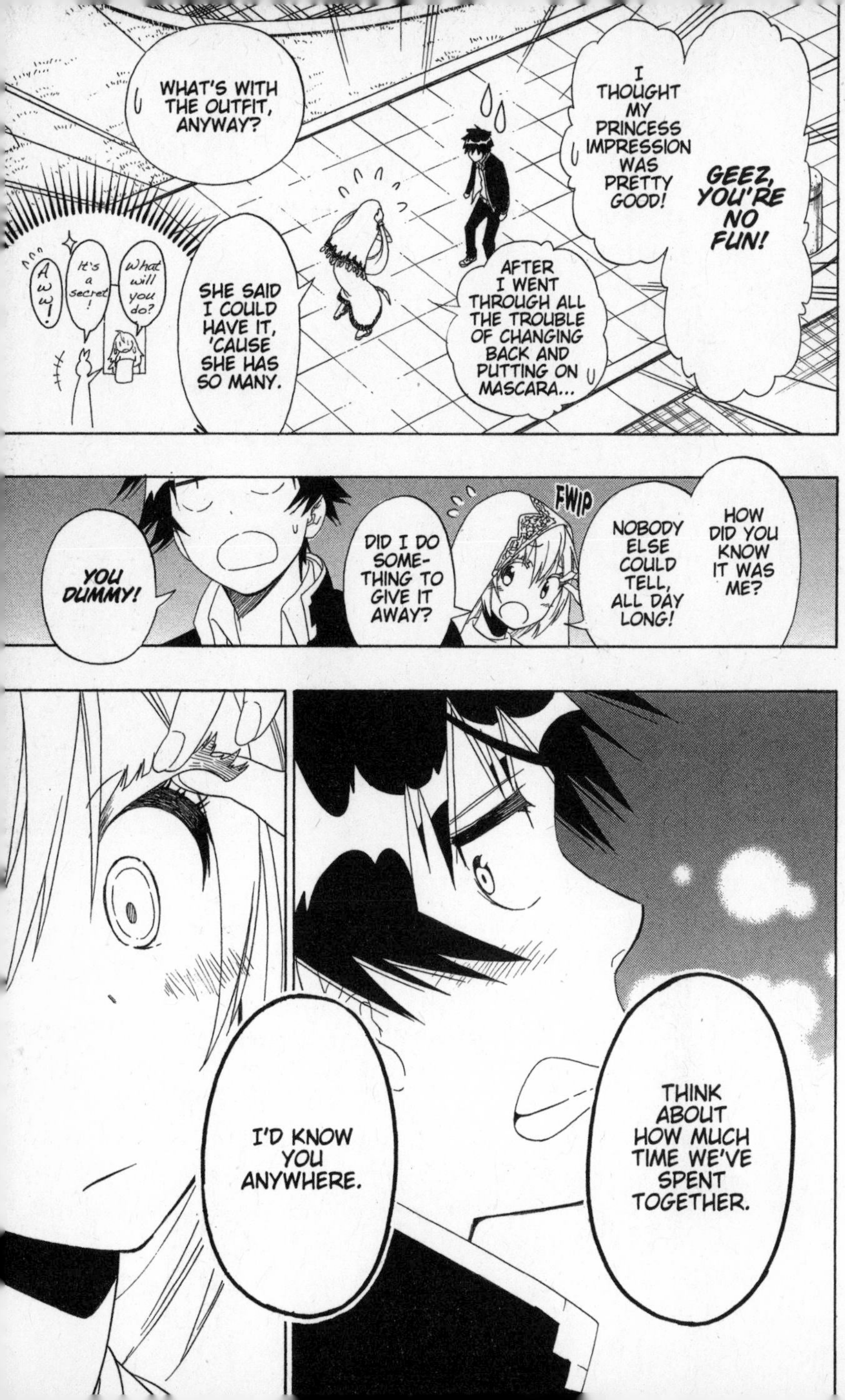
I THOUGHT MY PRINCESS IMPRESSION WAS PRETTY GOOD!
GEEZ, YOU'RE NO FUN!
AFTER I WENT THROUGH ALL THE TROUBLE OF CHANGING BACK AND PUTTING ON MASCARA...
WHAT'S WITH THE OUTFIT, ANYWAY?
SHE SAID I COULD HAVE IT, 'CAUSE SHE HAS SO MANY.
What will you do?
It's a secret!
Aww!
HOW DID YOU KNOW IT WAS ME?
NOBODY ELSE COULD TELL, ALL DAY LONG!
FWIP
DID I DO SOMETHING TO GIVE IT AWAY?
YOU DUMMY!
THINK ABOUT HOW MUCH TIME WE'VE SPENT TOGETHER.
I'D KNOW YOU ANYWHERE.

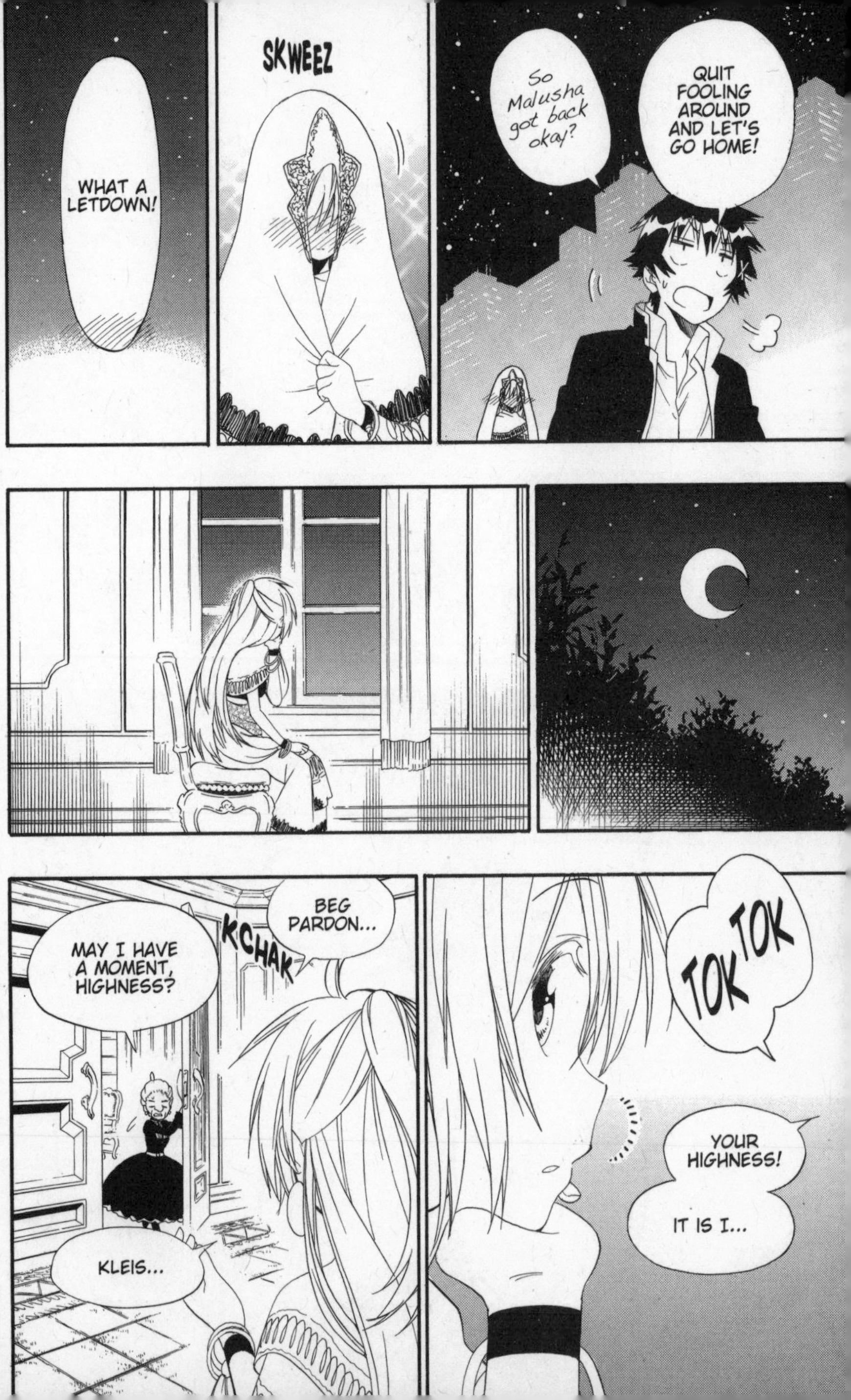
QUIT FOOLING AROUND AND LET'S GO HOME!
So Malusha got back okay?
SKWEEZ
WHAT A LETDOWN!
TOK TOK
YOUR HIGHNESS!
IT IS I...
BEG PARDON...
KCHAK
MAY I HAVE A MOMENT, HIGHNESS?
KLEIS...

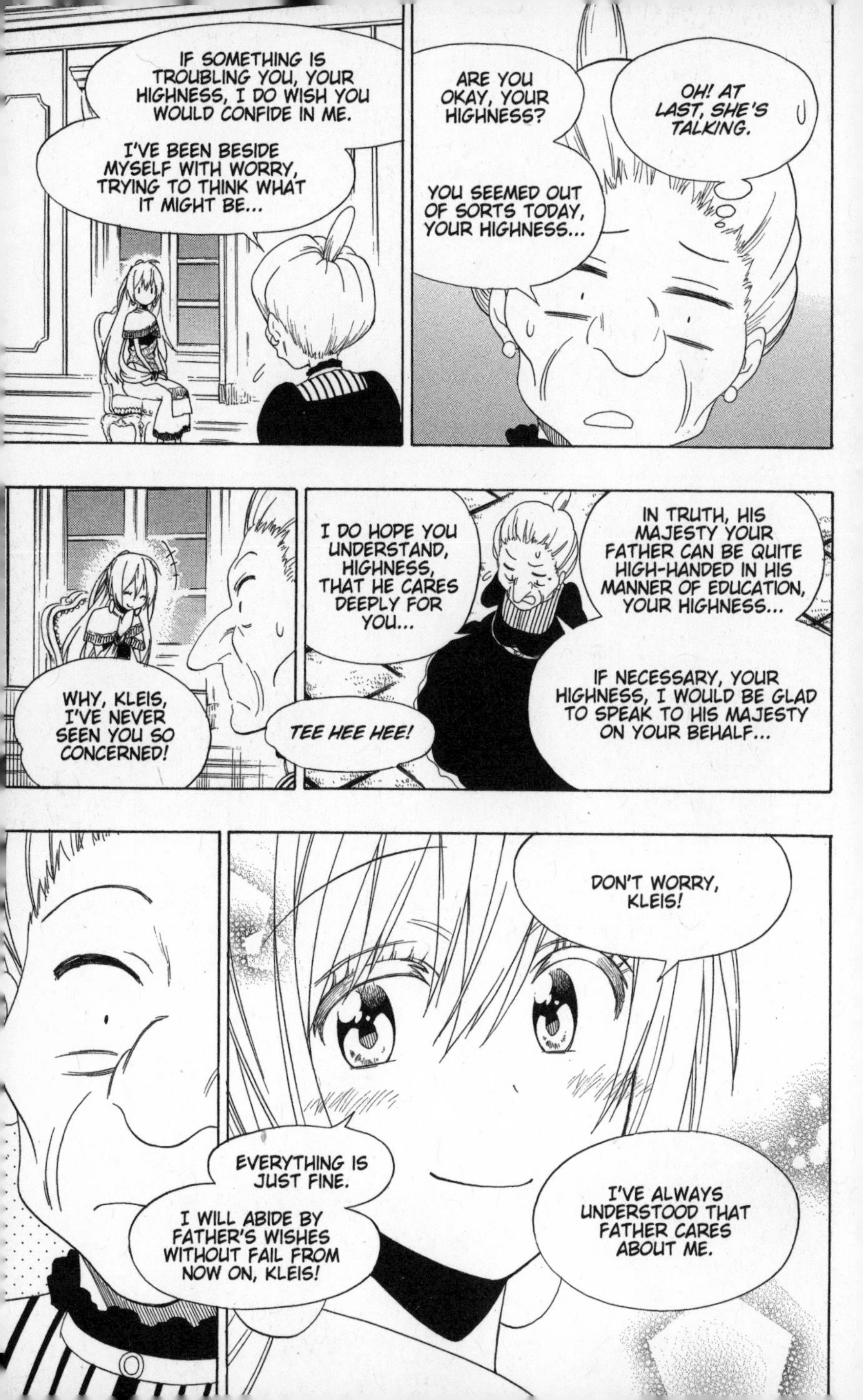
OH! AT LAST, SHE'S TALKING.
ARE YOU OKAY, YOUR HIGHNESS?
YOU SEEMED OUT OF SORTS TODAY, YOUR HIGHNESS...
IF SOMETHING IS TROUBLING YOU, YOUR HIGHNESS, I DO WISH YOU WOULD CONFIDE IN ME.
I'VE BEEN BESIDE MYSELF WITH WORRY, TRYING TO THINK WHAT IT MIGHT BE...
IN TRUTH, HIS MAJESTY YOUR FATHER CAN BE QUITE HIGH-HANDED IN HIS MANNER OF EDUCATION, YOUR HIGHNESS...
I DO HOPE YOU UNDERSTAND, HIGHNESS, THAT HE CARES DEEPLY FOR YOU...
IF NECESSARY, YOUR HIGHNESS, I WOULD BE GLAD TO SPEAK TO HIS MAJESTY ON YOUR BEHALF...
TEE HEE HEE!
WHY, KLEIS, I'VE NEVER SEEN YOU SO CONCERNED!
DON'T WORRY, KLEIS!
I'VE ALWAYS UNDERSTOOD THAT FATHER CARES ABOUT ME.
EVERYTHING IS JUST FINE.
I WILL ABIDE BY FATHER'S WISHES WITHOUT FAIL FROM NOW ON, KLEIS!

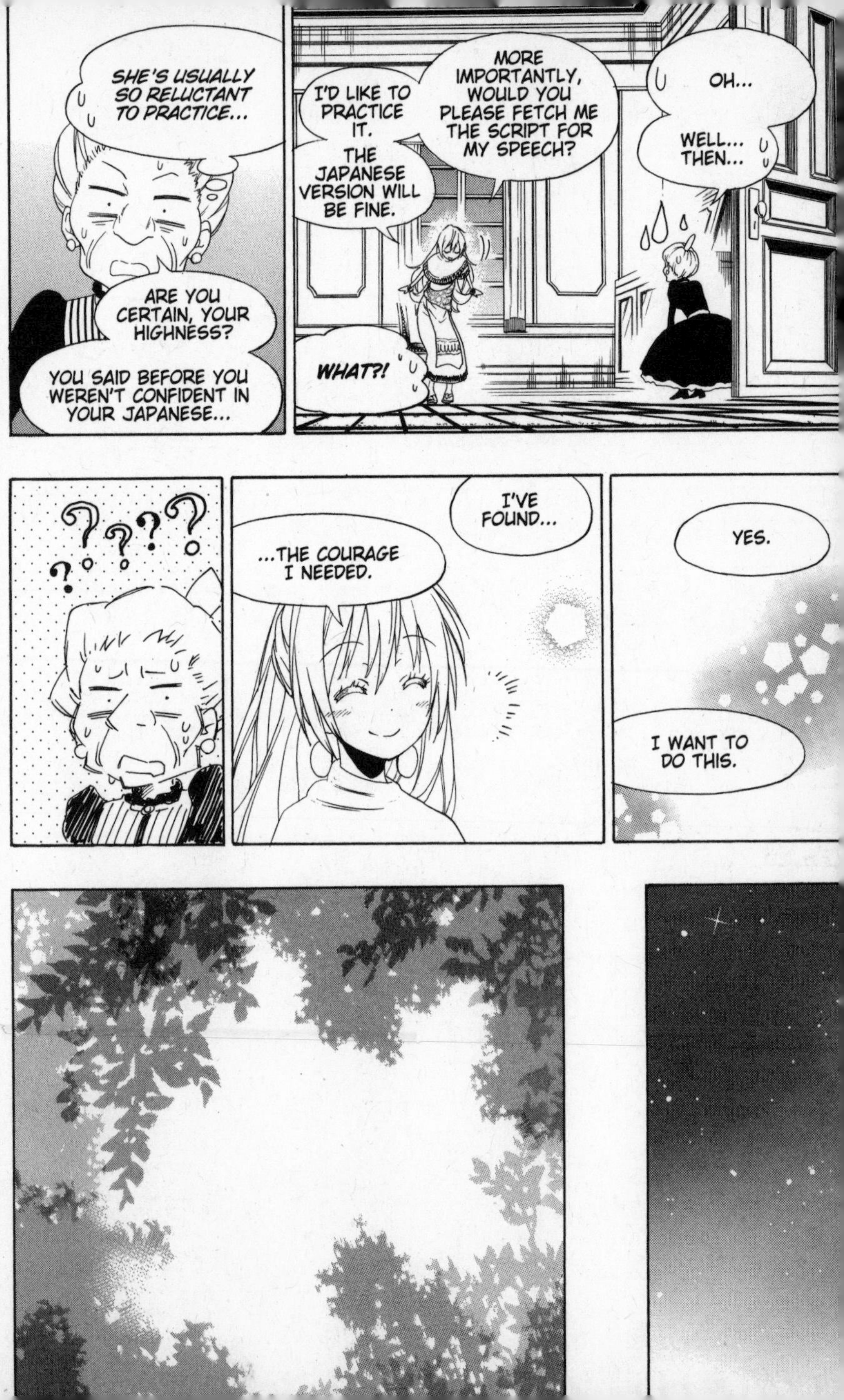
OH...
WELL... THEN...
MORE IMPORTANTLY, WOULD YOU PLEASE FETCH ME THE SCRIPT FOR MY SPEECH?
I'D LIKE TO PRACTICE IT.
THE JAPANESE VERSION WILL BE FINE.
WHAT?!
SHE'S USUALLY SO RELUCTANT TO PRACTICE...
ARE YOU CERTAIN, YOUR HIGHNESS?
YOU SAID BEFORE YOU WEREN'T CONFIDENT IN YOUR JAPANESE...
YES.
I WANT TO DO THIS.
I'VE FOUND...
...THE COURAGE I NEEDED.

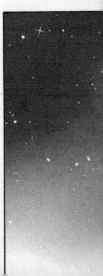

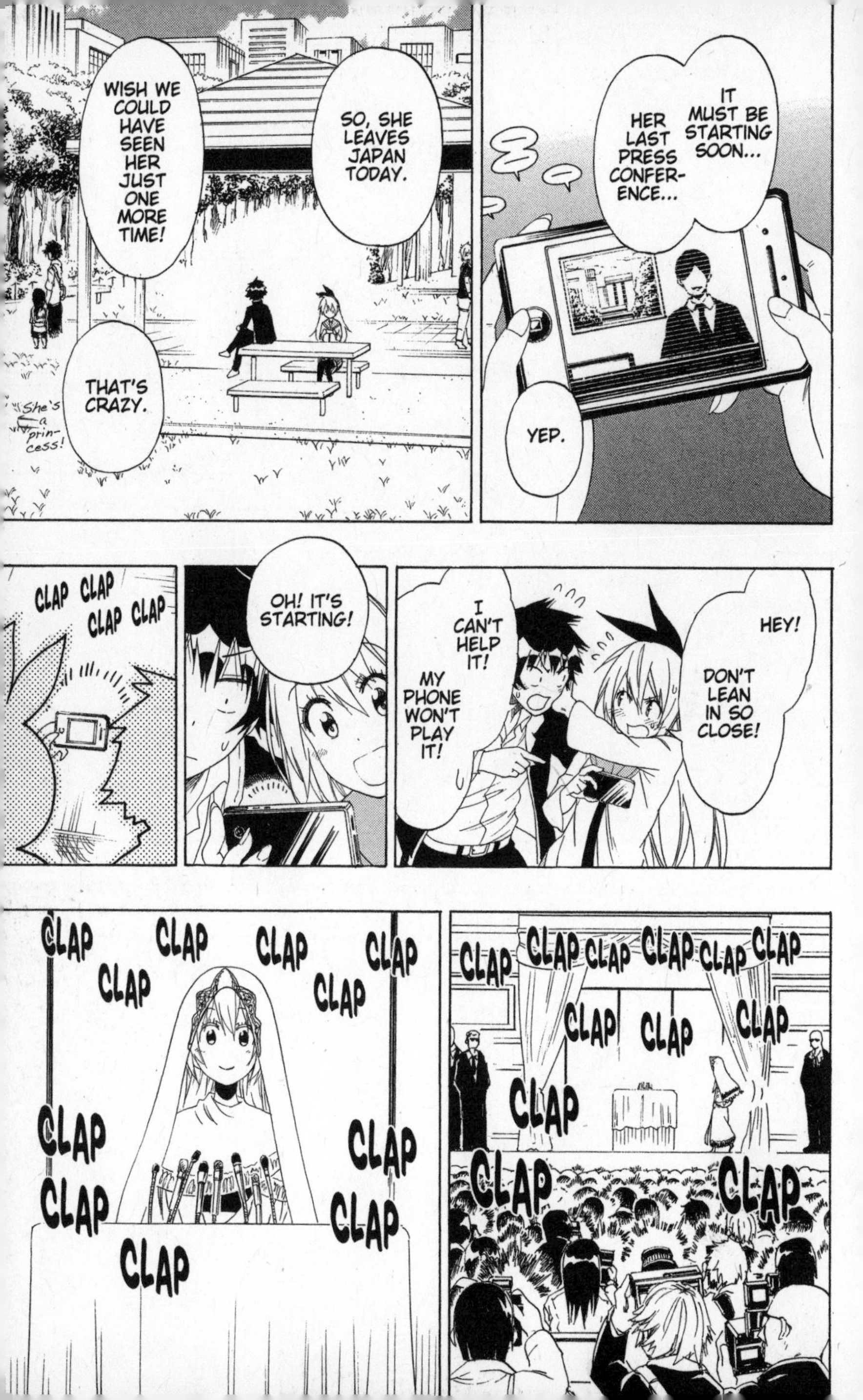
IT MUST BE STARTING SOON...
HER LAST PRESS CONFERENCE...
YEP.
SO, SHE LEAVES JAPAN TODAY.
WISH WE COULD HAVE SEEN HER JUST ONE MORE TIME!
THAT'S CRAZY.
She's a princess!
HEY!
DON'T LEAN IN SO CLOSE!
I CAN'T HELP IT!
MY PHONE WON'T PLAY IT!
OH! IT'S STARTING!
CLAP CLAP
CLAP CLAP
CLAP CLAP CLAP CLAP CLAP CLAP
CLAP CLAP CLAP
CLAP
CLAP CLAP
CLAP CLAP CLAP CLAP
CLAP CLAP
CLAP CLAP
CLAP CLAP
CLAP

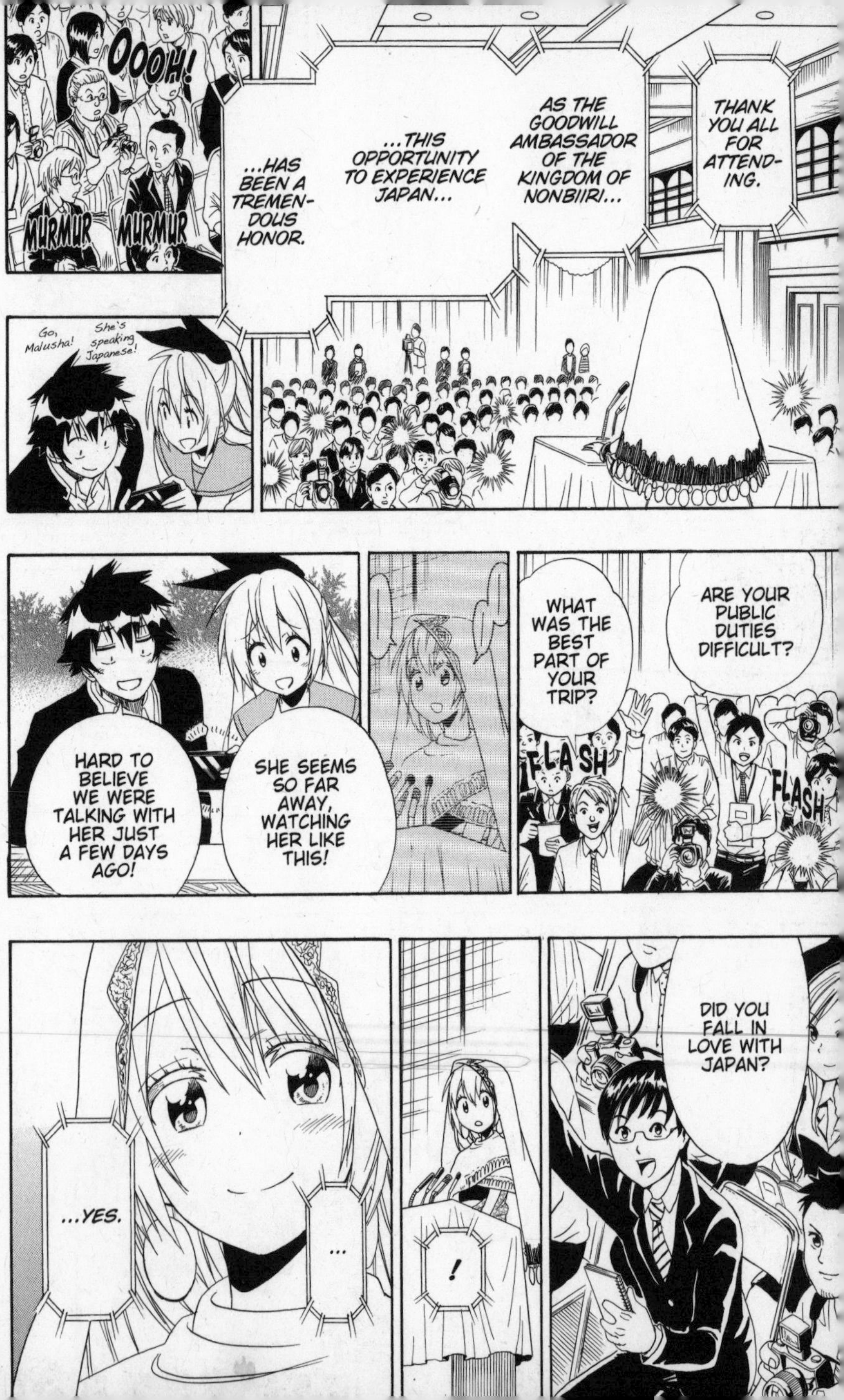
THANK YOU ALL FOR ATTENDING.
AS THE GOODWILL AMBASSADOR OF THE KINGDOM OF NONBIIRI...
...THIS OPPORTUNITY TO EXPERIENCE JAPAN...
...HAS BEEN A TREMENDOUS HONOR.
OOOH!
MURMUR
MURMUR
She's speaking Japanese!
Go, Malusha!
ARE YOUR PUBLIC DUTIES DIFFICULT?
WHAT WAS THE BEST PART OF YOUR TRIP?
FLASH
FLASH
SHE SEEMS SO FAR AWAY, WATCHING HER LIKE THIS!
HARD TO BELIEVE WE WERE TALKING WITH HER JUST A FEW DAYS AGO!
DID YOU FALL IN LOVE WITH JAPAN?
!
...
...YES.

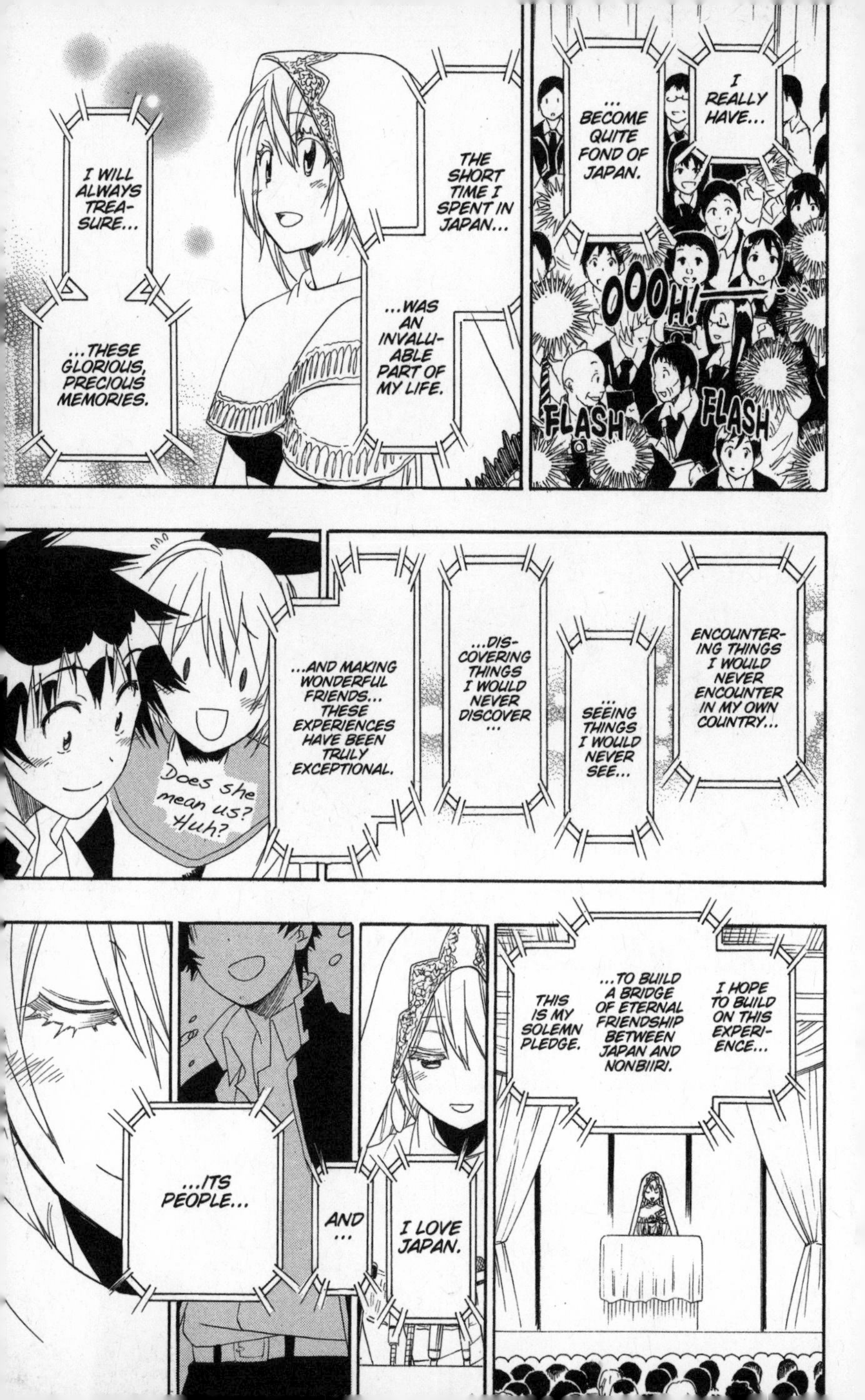

I REALLY HAVE...
...BECOME QUITE FOND OF JAPAN.
OOOH!
FLASH
FLASH
THE SHORT TIME I SPENT IN JAPAN...
...WAS AN INVALUABLE PART OF MY LIFE.
I WILL ALWAYS TREASURE...
...THESE GLORIOUS, PRECIOUS MEMORIES.
ENCOUNTERING THINGS I WOULD NEVER ENCOUNTER IN MY OWN COUNTRY...
...SEEING THINGS I WOULD NEVER SEE...
...DISCOVERING THINGS I WOULD NEVER DISCOVER...
...AND MAKING WONDERFUL FRIENDS... THESE EXPERIENCES HAVE BEEN TRULY EXCEPTIONAL.
Does she mean us? Huh?
I HOPE TO BUILD ON THIS EXPERIENCE...
...TO BUILD A BRIDGE OF ETERNAL FRIENDSHIP BETWEEN JAPAN AND NONBIIRI.
THIS IS MY SOLEMN PLEDGE.
I LOVE JAPAN.
AND...
...ITS PEOPLE...

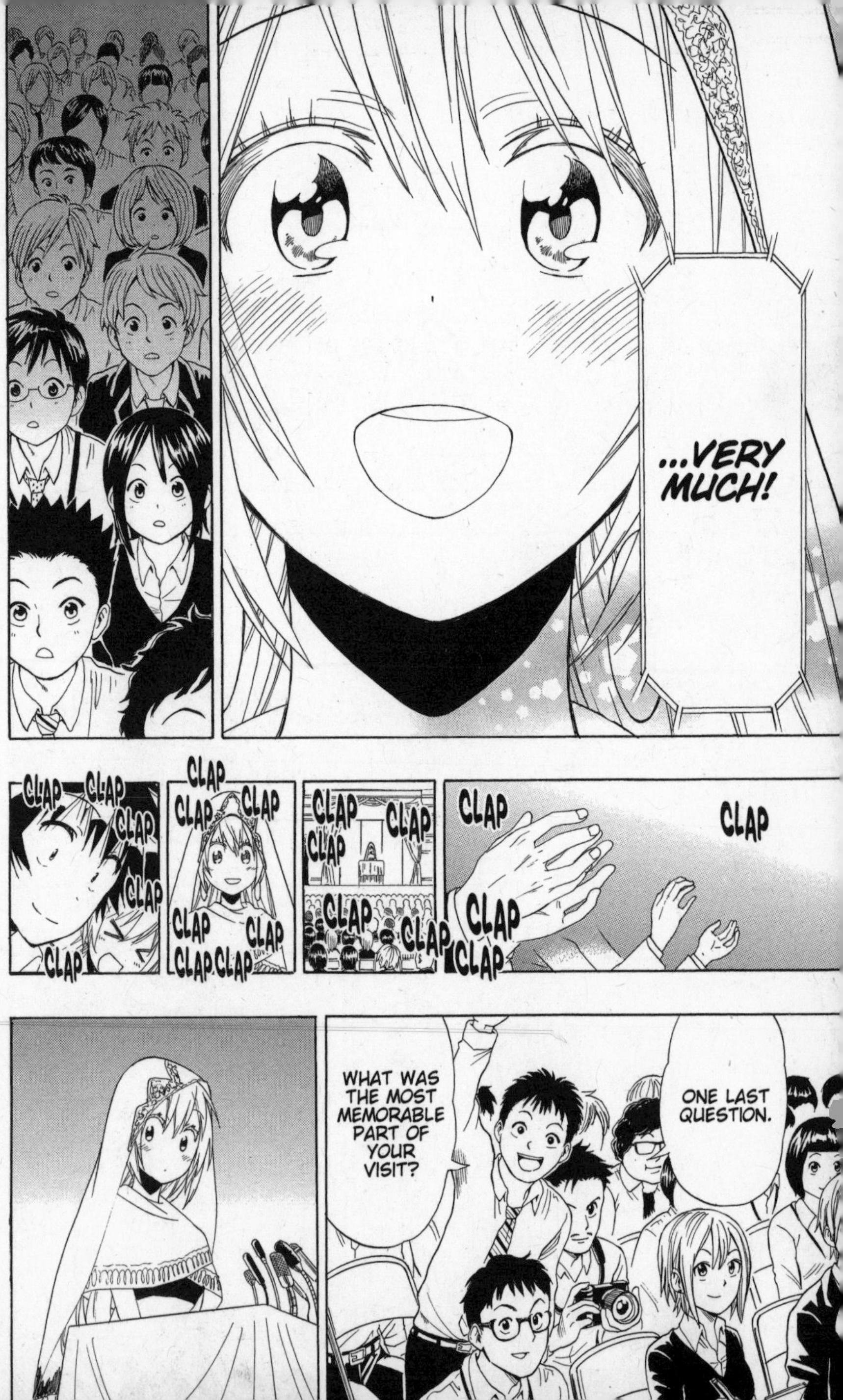
...VERY MUCH!
CLAP
CLAP
CLAP
CLAP
CLAP
CLAP
CLAP
CLAP
CLAP
CLAP
CLAP
CLAP
CLAP
CLAP
CLAP
CLAP
CLAP
CLAP
CLAP
CLAP
CLAP
CLAP
ONE LAST QUESTION.
WHAT WAS THE MOST MEMORABLE PART OF YOUR VISIT?

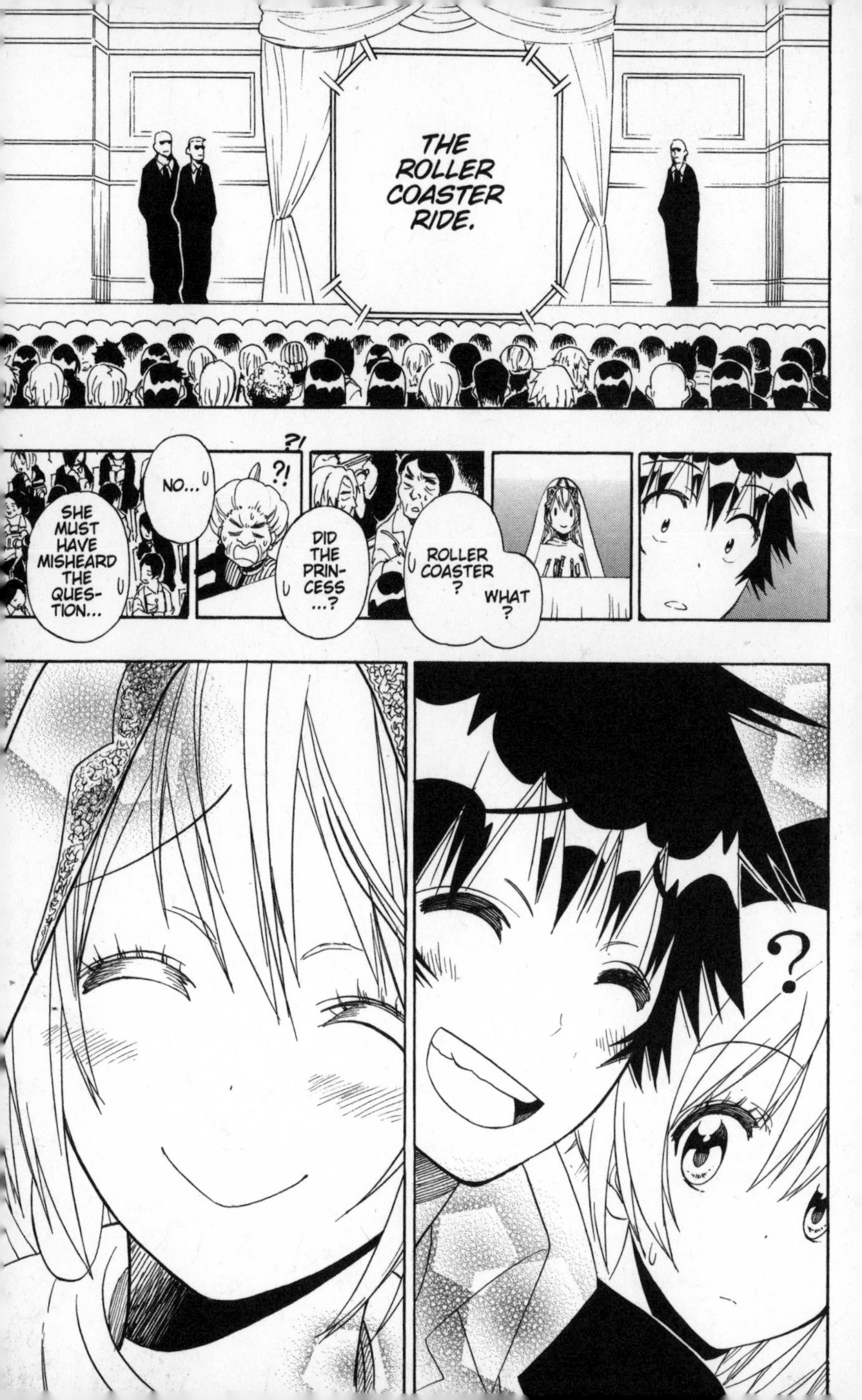
THE ROLLER COASTER RIDE.
ROLLER COASTER?
WHAT?
DID THE PRINCESS...?
?!
?!
NO...
SHE MUST HAVE MISHEARD THE QUESTION...
?

☆ Later that day ☆ 🐰

Raku: "So what did you do with your day after the switch?"

Chitoge: "Oh, I toured all around. As friendship ambassador, I visited a lot of cultural sites. Castles, shrines...and I had soba noodles for lunch at a yummy place near the amusemet park."

Raku: "Oh, man!! We were right in the same area!!"

That coulda been bad!!

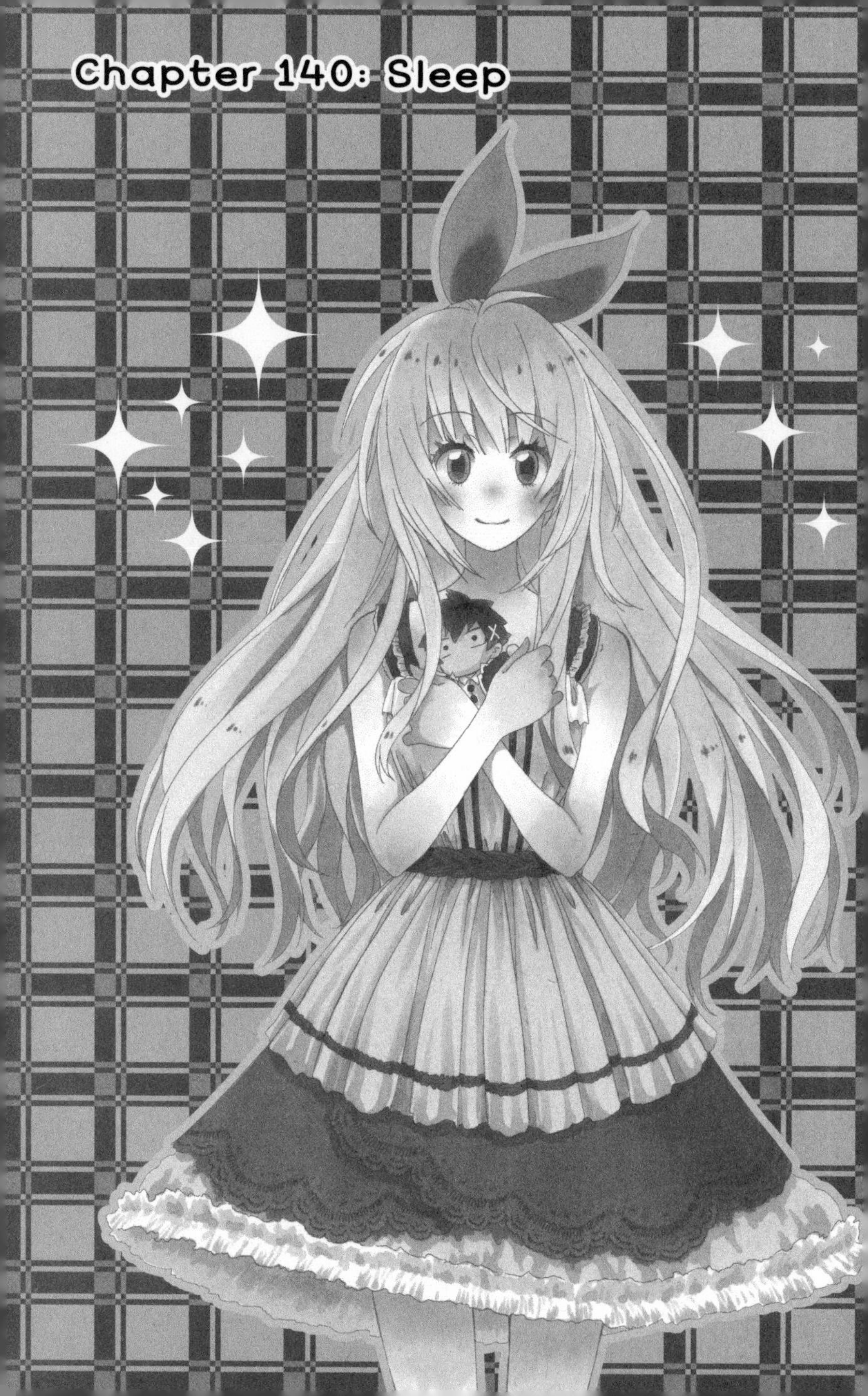
Chapter 140: Sleep

NISEKOI
False Love

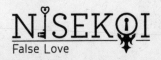

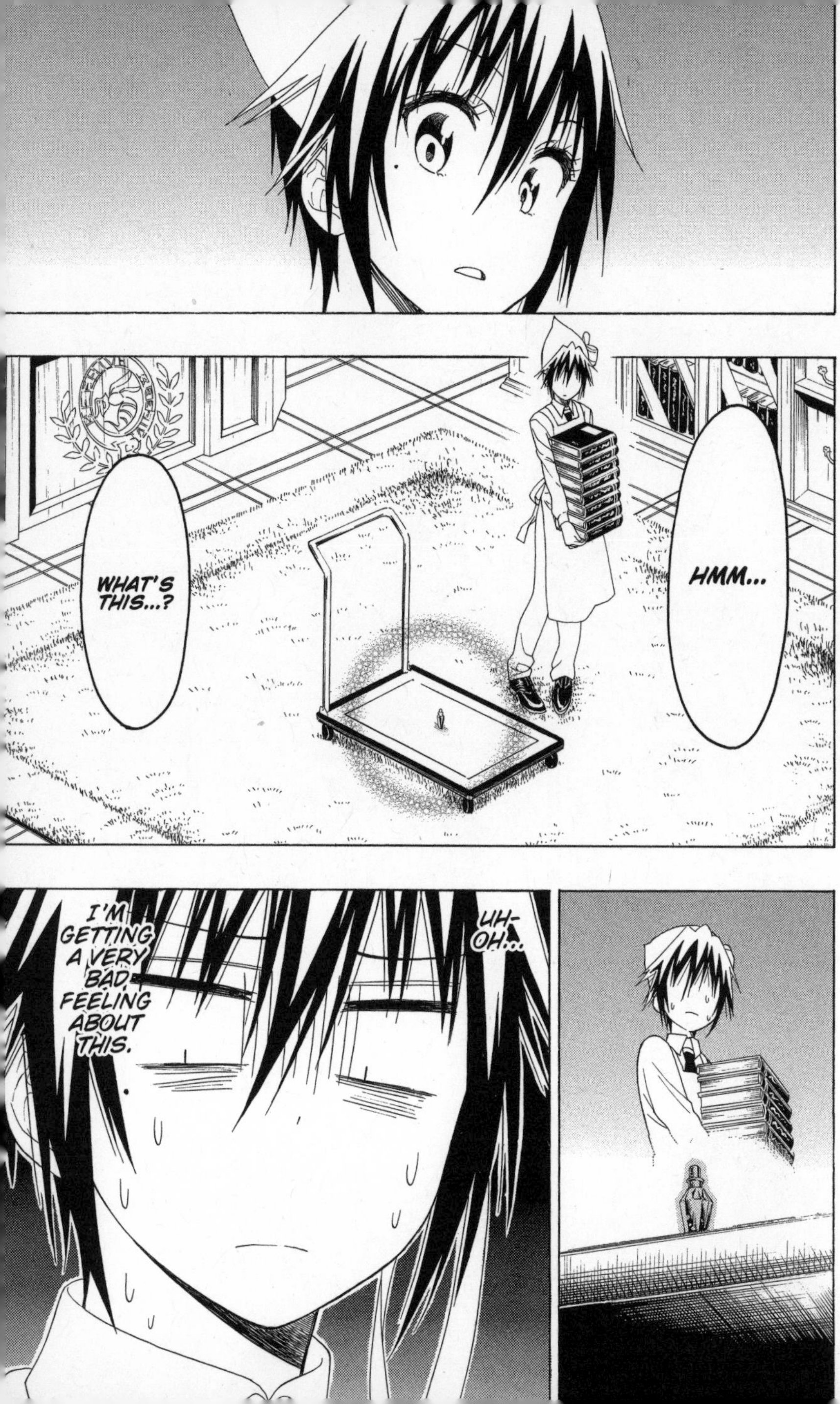
HMM...
WHAT'S THIS...?
UH-OH...
I'M GETTING A VERY BAD FEELING ABOUT THIS.

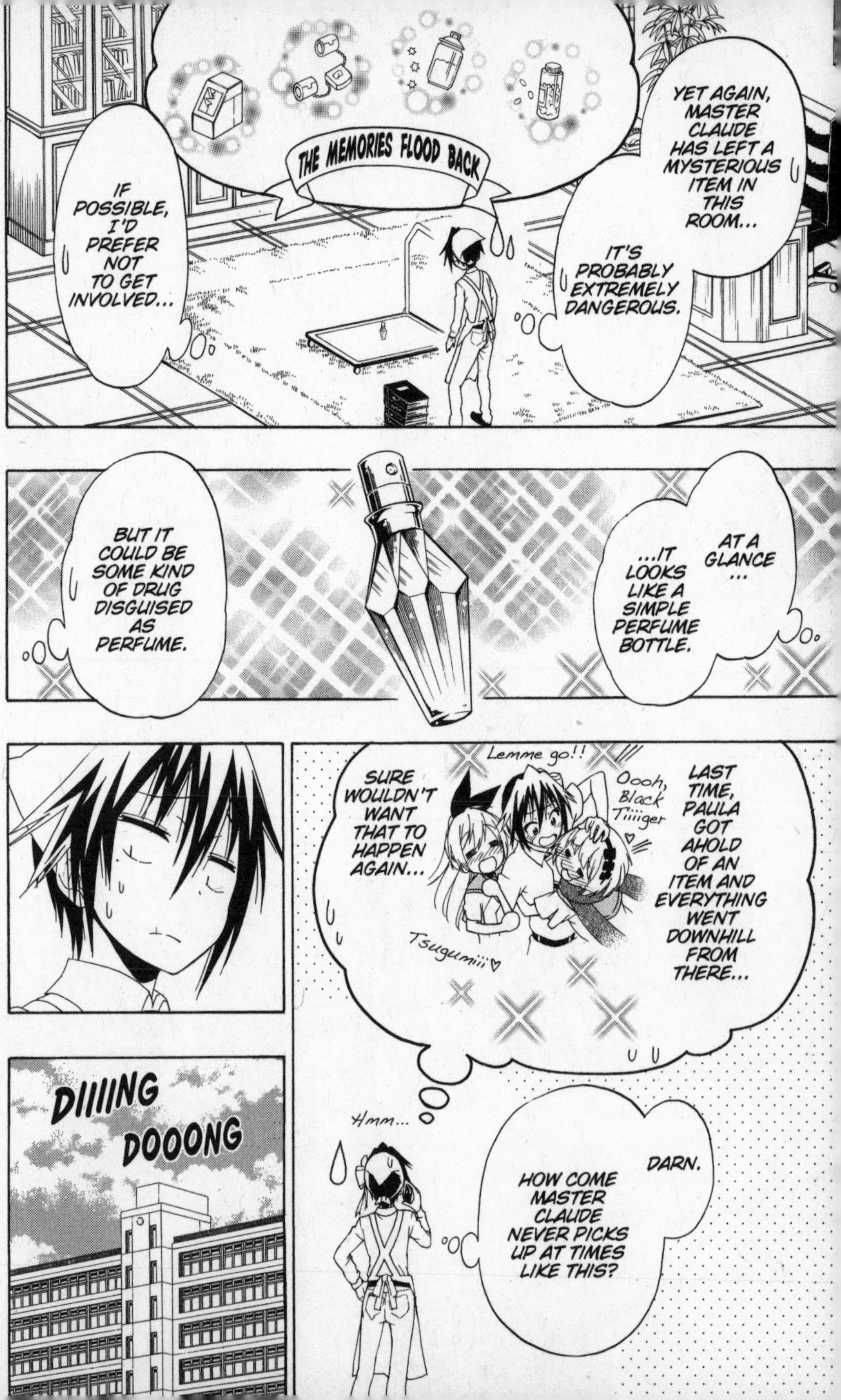
YET AGAIN, MASTER CLAUDE HAS LEFT A MYSTERIOUS ITEM IN THIS ROOM...
THE MEMORIES FLOOD BACK
IT'S PROBABLY EXTREMELY DANGEROUS.
IF POSSIBLE, I'D PREFER NOT TO GET INVOLVED...
AT A GLANCE...
...IT LOOKS LIKE A SIMPLE PERFUME BOTTLE.
BUT IT COULD BE SOME KIND OF DRUG DISGUISED AS PERFUME.
LAST TIME, PAULA GOT AHOLD OF AN ITEM AND EVERYTHING WENT DOWNHILL FROM THERE...
Oooh, Black Tiiiiger
Lemme go!!
SURE WOULDN'T WANT THAT TO HAPPEN AGAIN...
Tsugumiii♥
DARN.
HOW COME MASTER CLAUDE NEVER PICKS UP AT TIMES LIKE THIS?
Hmm...
DIIIING
DOOONG

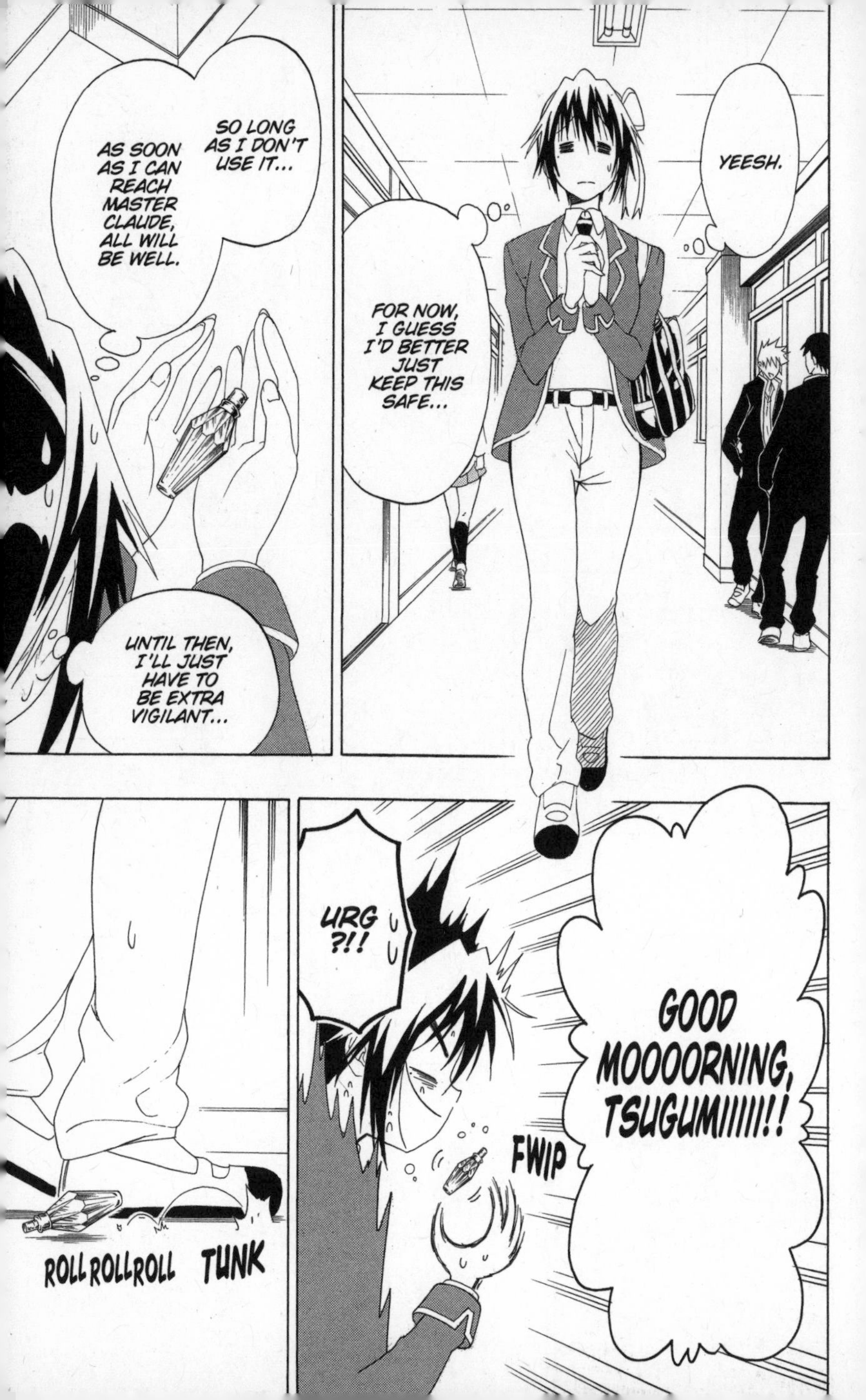
YEESH.
FOR NOW, I GUESS I'D BETTER JUST KEEP THIS SAFE...
SO LONG AS I DON'T USE IT...
AS SOON AS I CAN REACH MASTER CLAUDE, ALL WILL BE WELL.
UNTIL THEN, I'LL JUST HAVE TO BE EXTRA VIGILANT...
GOOD MOOOORNING, TSUGUMIIIIII!!
URG ?!!
FWIP
ROLLROLLROLL
TUNK

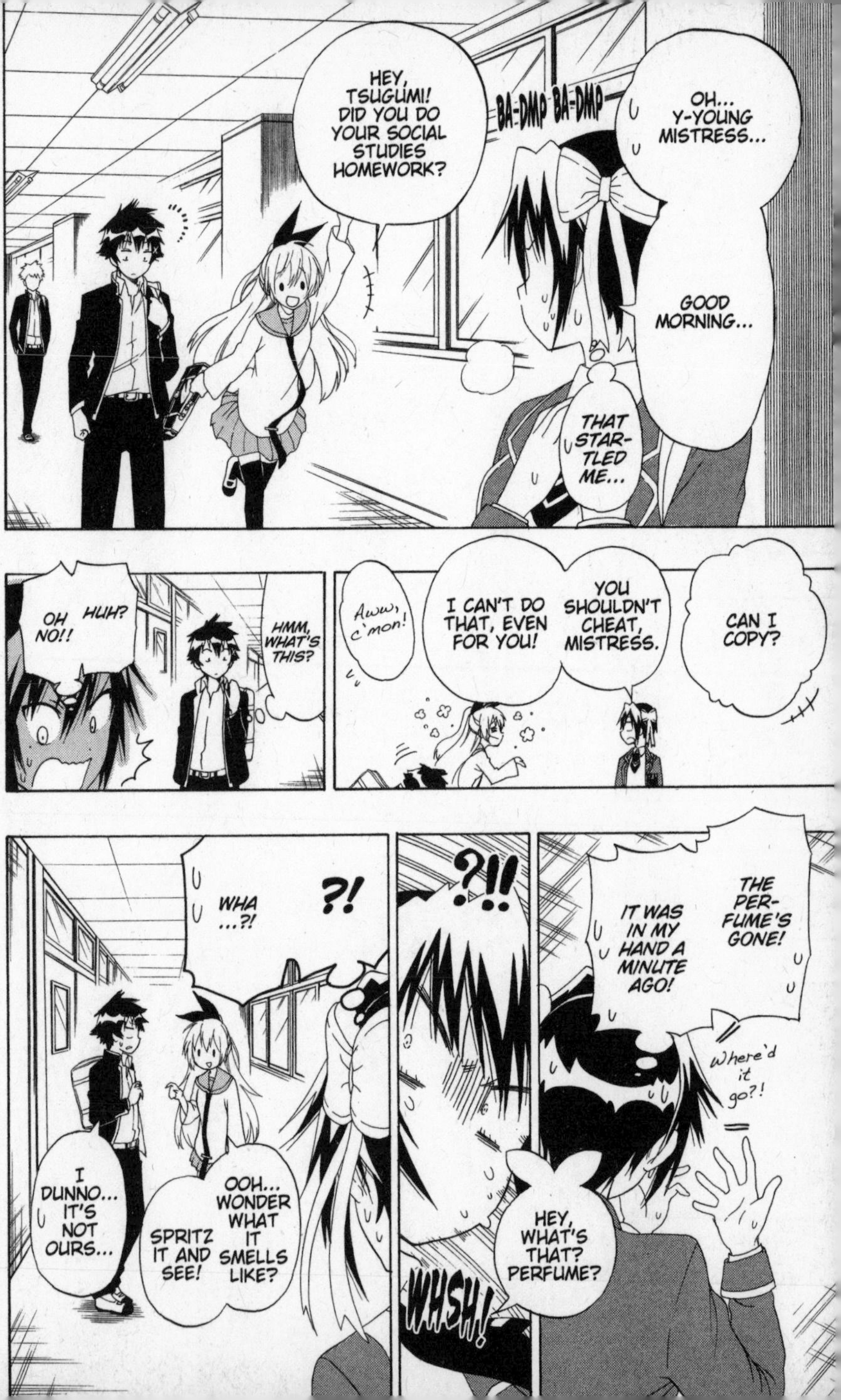
OH... Y-YOUNG MISTRESS...
GOOD MORNING...
THAT STARTLED ME...
BA-DMP BA-DMP
HEY, TSUGUMI! DID YOU DO YOUR SOCIAL STUDIES HOMEWORK?
CAN I COPY?
YOU SHOULDN'T CHEAT, MISTRESS.
I CAN'T DO THAT, EVEN FOR YOU!
Aww, c'mon!
HMM, WHAT'S THIS?
HUH?
OH NO!!
THE PERFUME'S GONE!
IT WAS IN MY HAND A MINUTE AGO!
Where'd it go?!
?!!
HEY, WHAT'S THAT? PERFUME?
WHSH!
?!
WHA ...?!
OOH... WONDER WHAT IT SMELLS LIKE?
SPRITZ IT AND SEE!
I DUNNO... IT'S NOT OURS...

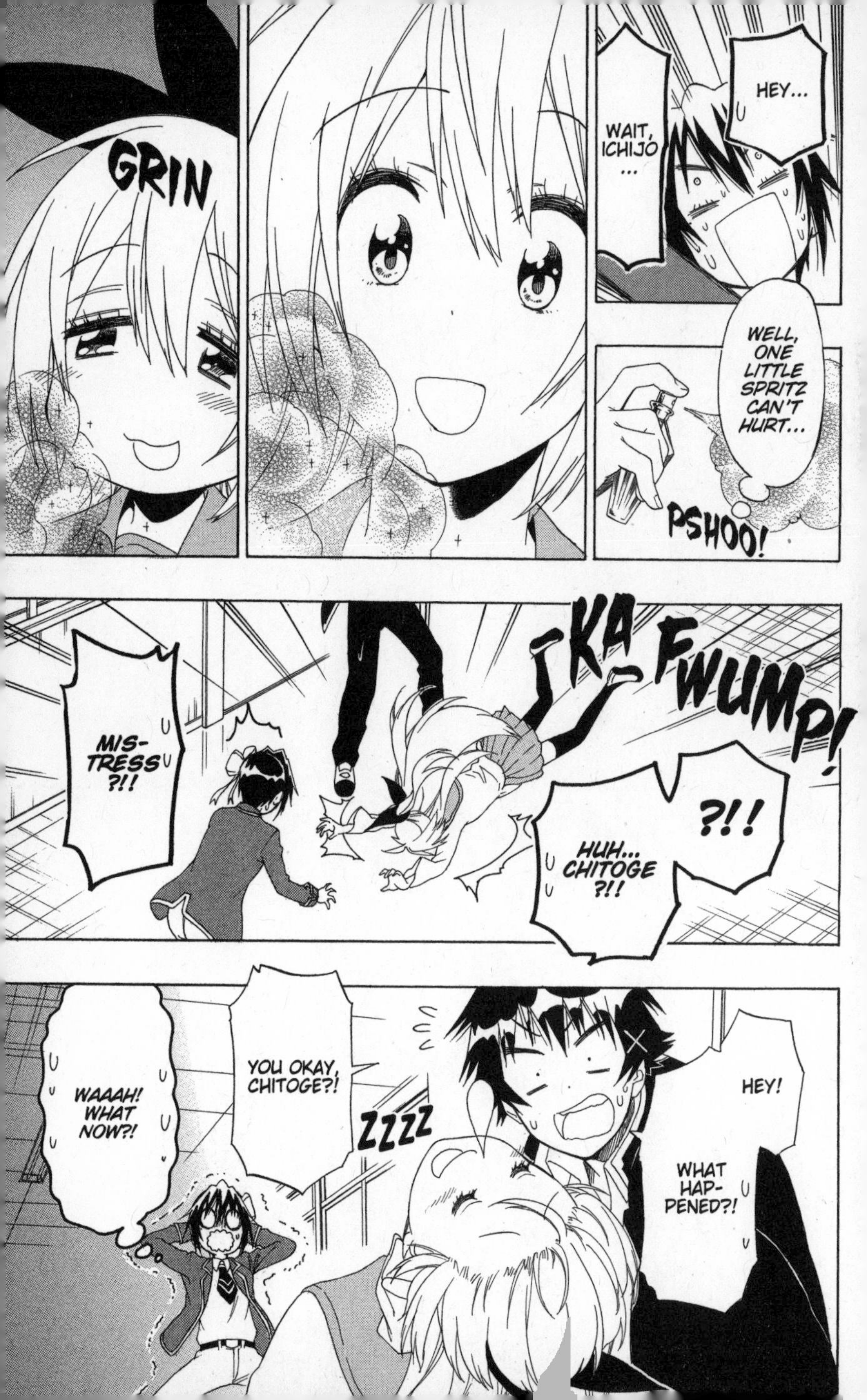
HEY...
WAIT, ICHIJO...
WELL, ONE LITTLE SPRITZ CAN'T HURT...
PSHOO!
GRIN
KA-FWUMP!
?!!
HUH... CHITOGE?!!
MIS-TRESS?!!
HEY!
WHAT HAP-PENED?!
ZZZZ
YOU OKAY, CHITOGE?!
WAAAH! WHAT NOW?!

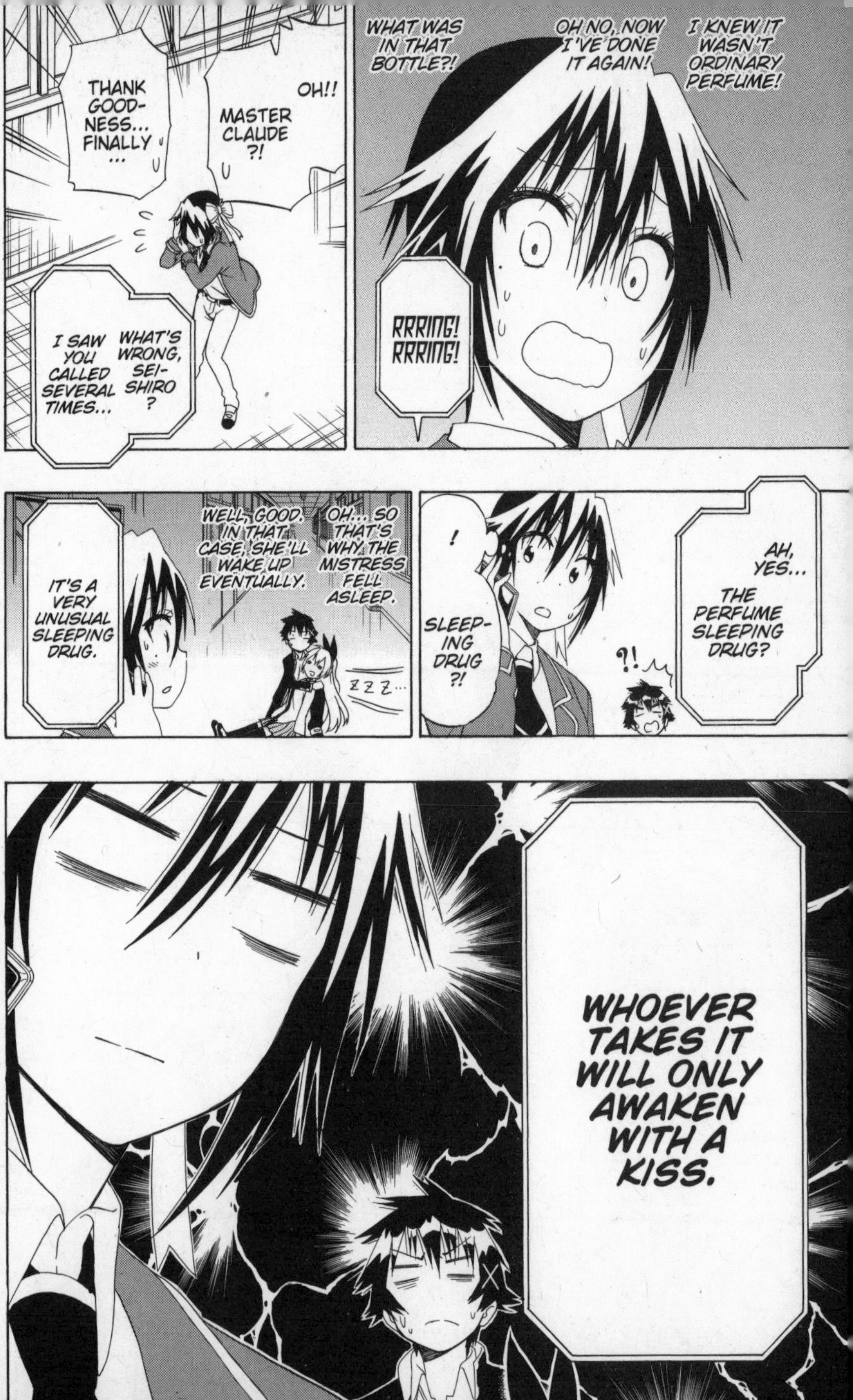
I KNEW IT WASN'T ORDINARY PERFUME!
OH NO, NOW I'VE DONE IT AGAIN!
WHAT WAS IN THAT BOTTLE?!
RRRING! RRRING!
OH!!
MASTER CLAUDE ?!
THANK GOODNESS... FINALLY...
WHAT'S WRONG, SEI-SHIRO?
I SAW YOU CALLED SEVERAL TIMES...
AH, YES... THE PERFUME SLEEPING DRUG?
?!
!
SLEEPING DRUG?!
OH... SO THAT'S WHY THE MISTRESS FELL ASLEEP.
WELL, GOOD. IN THAT CASE, SHE'LL WAKE UP EVENTUALLY.
IT'S A VERY UNUSUAL SLEEPING DRUG.
Z Z Z...
WHOEVER TAKES IT WILL ONLY AWAKEN WITH A KISS.

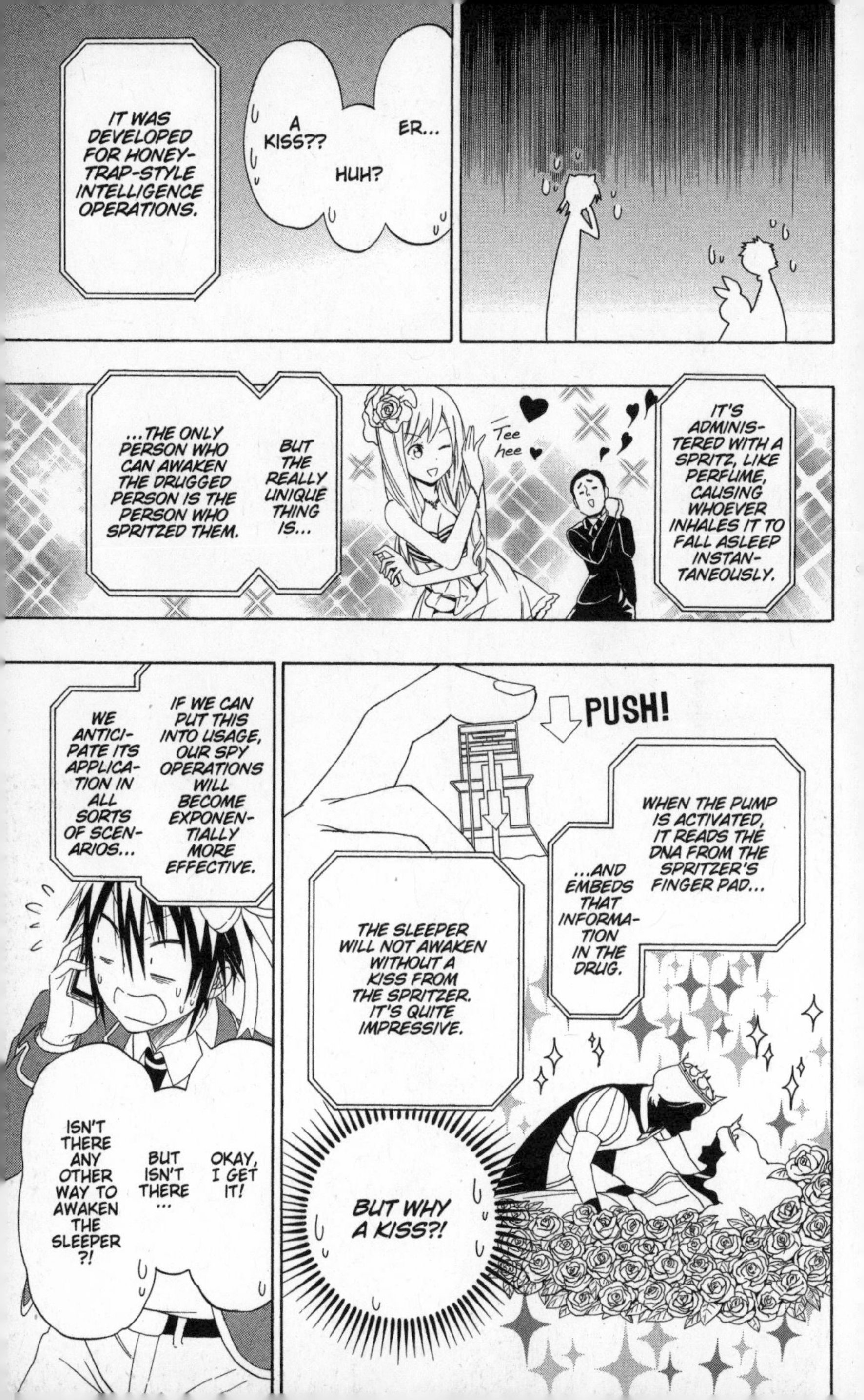
ER...
A KISS??
HUH?
IT WAS DEVELOPED FOR HONEY-TRAP-STYLE INTELLIGENCE OPERATIONS.
IT'S ADMINISTERED WITH A SPRITZ, LIKE PERFUME, CAUSING WHOEVER INHALES IT TO FALL ASLEEP INSTANTANEOUSLY.
Tee hee
BUT THE REALLY UNIQUE THING IS...
...THE ONLY PERSON WHO CAN AWAKEN THE DRUGGED PERSON IS THE PERSON WHO SPRITZED THEM.
PUSH!
WHEN THE PUMP IS ACTIVATED, IT READS THE DNA FROM THE SPRITZER'S FINGER PAD...
...AND EMBEDS THAT INFORMATION IN THE DRUG.
THE SLEEPER WILL NOT AWAKEN WITHOUT A KISS FROM THE SPRITZER. IT'S QUITE IMPRESSIVE.
BUT WHY A KISS?!
IF WE CAN PUT THIS INTO USAGE, OUR SPY OPERATIONS WILL BECOME EXPONENTIALLY MORE EFFECTIVE.
WE ANTICIPATE ITS APPLICATION IN ALL SORTS OF SCENARIOS...
OKAY, I GET IT!
BUT ISN'T THERE...
ISN'T THERE ANY OTHER WAY TO AWAKEN THE SLEEPER?!

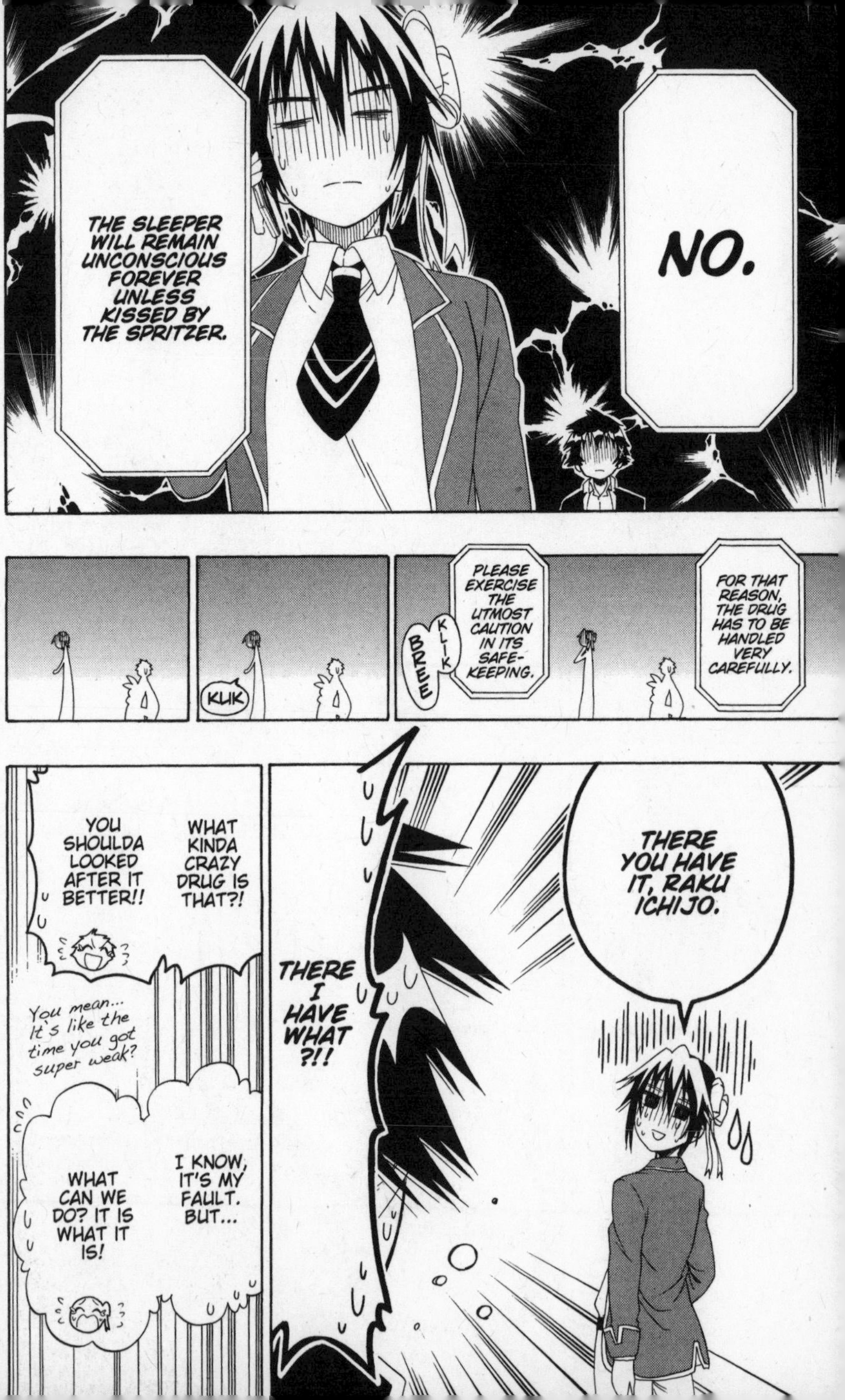
NO.
THE SLEEPER WILL REMAIN UNCONSCIOUS FOREVER UNLESS KISSED BY THE SPRITZER.
FOR THAT REASON, THE DRUG HAS TO BE HANDLED VERY CAREFULLY.
PLEASE EXERCISE THE UTMOST CAUTION IN ITS SAFE-KEEPING.
KLIK
BREE
KLIK
THERE YOU HAVE IT, RAKU ICHIJO.
THERE I HAVE WHAT ?!!
WHAT KINDA CRAZY DRUG IS THAT?!
YOU SHOULDA LOOKED AFTER IT BETTER!!
You mean... It's like the time you got super weak?
I KNOW, IT'S MY FAULT. BUT...
WHAT CAN WE DO? IT IS WHAT IT IS!

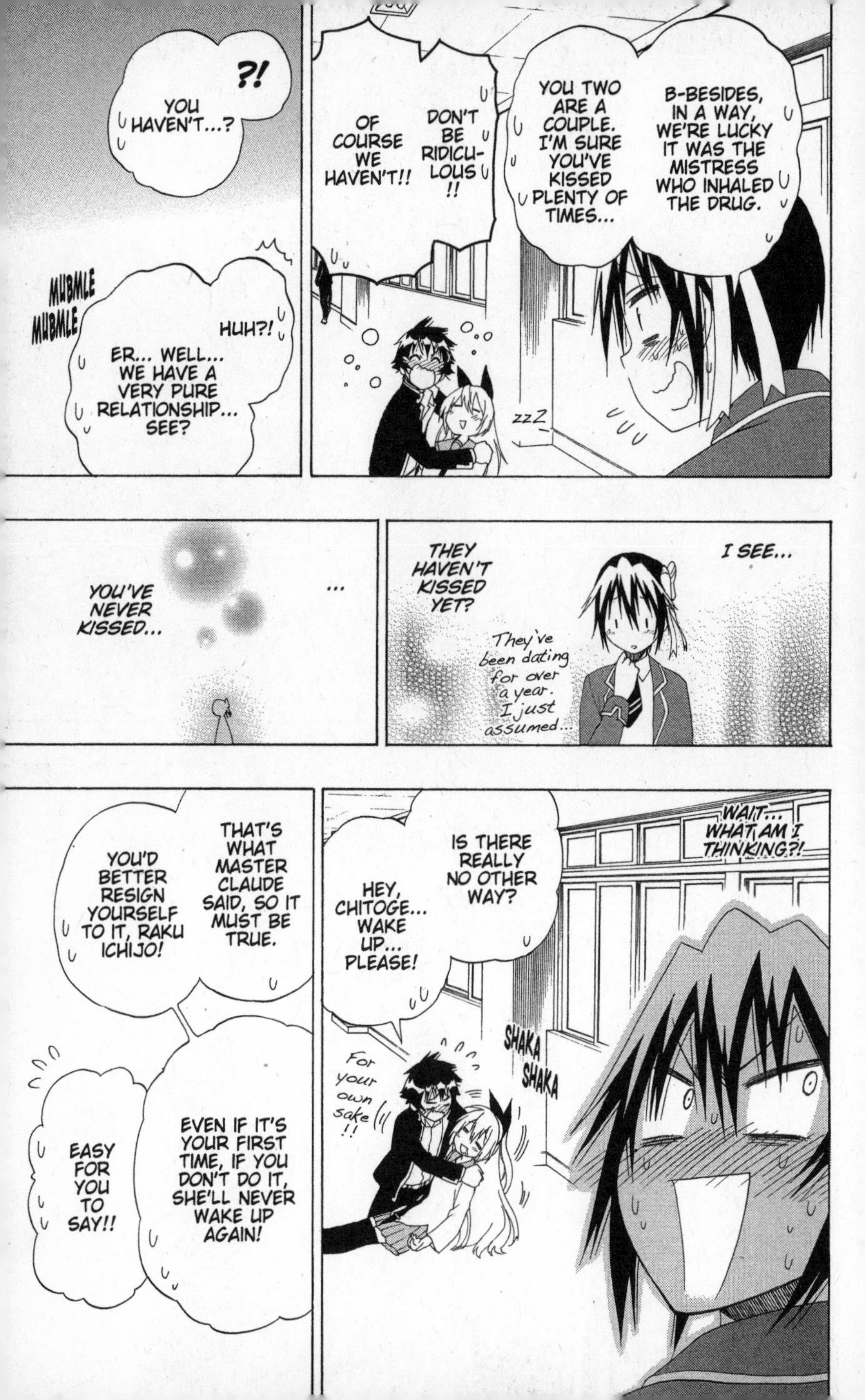
B-BESIDES, IN A WAY, WE'RE LUCKY IT WAS THE MISTRESS WHO INHALED THE DRUG.
YOU TWO ARE A COUPLE. I'M SURE YOU'VE KISSED PLENTY OF TIMES...
DON'T BE RIDICULOUS!!
OF COURSE WE HAVEN'T!!
zzZ
?!
YOU HAVEN'T...?
HUH?!
ER... WELL... WE HAVE A VERY PURE RELATIONSHIP... SEE?
MUBMLE MUBMLE
I SEE...
THEY HAVEN'T KISSED YET?
They've been dating for over a year. I just assumed...
...
YOU'VE NEVER KISSED...
WAIT... WHAT AM I THINKING?!
IS THERE REALLY NO OTHER WAY?
HEY, CHITOGE... WAKE UP... PLEASE!
SHAKA SHAKA
For your own sake!!
THAT'S WHAT MASTER CLAUDE SAID, SO IT MUST BE TRUE.
YOU'D BETTER RESIGN YOURSELF TO IT, RAKU ICHIJO!
EVEN IF IT'S YOUR FIRST TIME, IF YOU DON'T DO IT, SHE'LL NEVER WAKE UP AGAIN!
EASY FOR YOU TO SAY!!

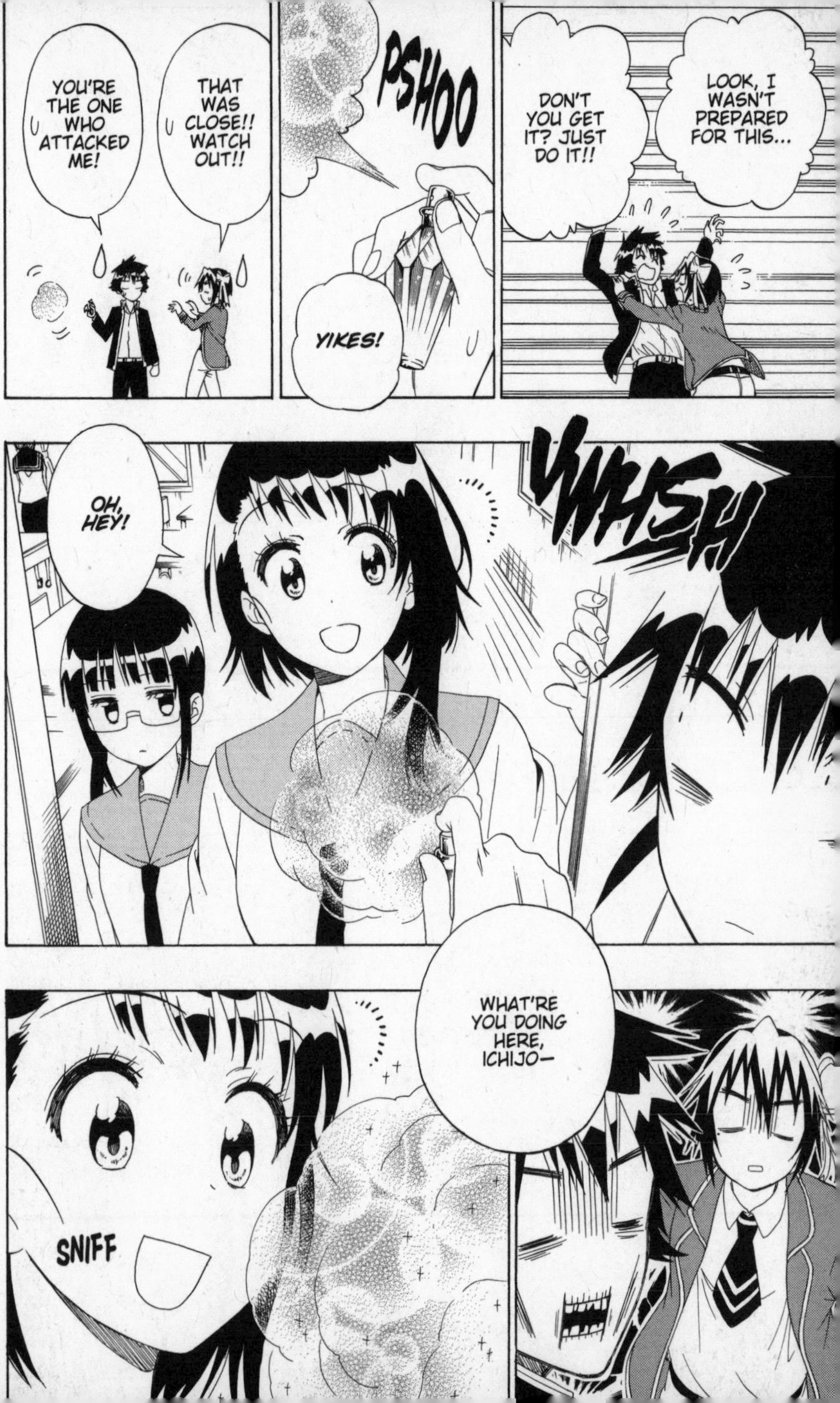
LOOK, I WASN'T PREPARED FOR THIS...
DON'T YOU GET IT? JUST DO IT!!
PSHOO
YIKES!
THAT WAS CLOSE!! WATCH OUT!!
YOU'RE THE ONE WHO ATTACKED ME!
VWISH
OH, HEY!
WHAT'RE YOU DOING HERE, ICHIJO—
SNIFF

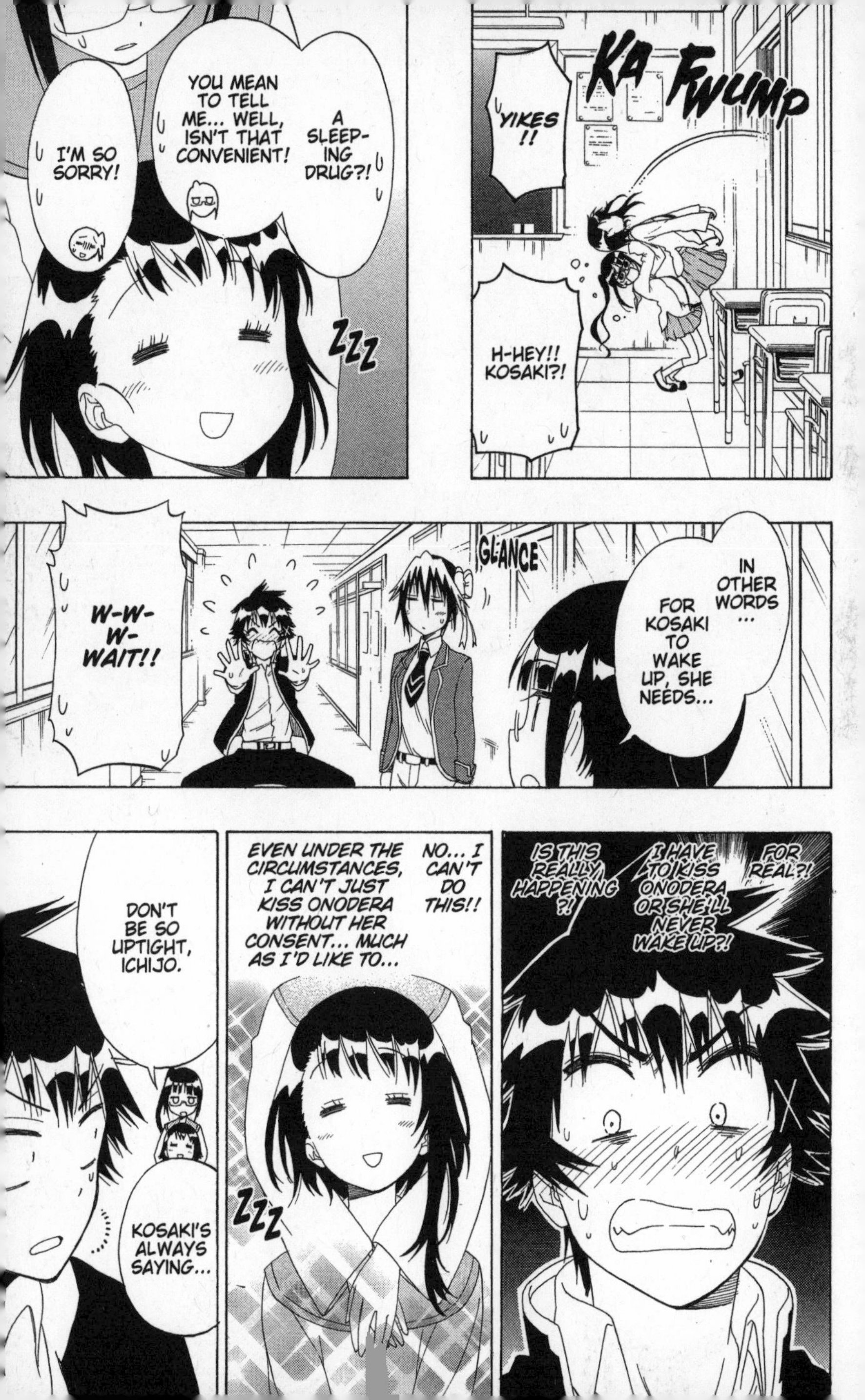
KA FWUMP
YIKES!!
H-HEY!! KOSAKI?!
A SLEEPING DRUG?!
YOU MEAN TO TELL ME... WELL, ISN'T THAT CONVENIENT!
I'M SO SORRY!
ZZZ
IN OTHER WORDS... FOR KOSAKI TO WAKE UP, SHE NEEDS...
GLANCE
W-W-W-WAIT!!
FOR REAL?!
I HAVE TO KISS ONODERA OR SHE'LL NEVER WAKE UP?!
IS THIS REALLY HAPPENING?!
NO... I CAN'T DO THIS!!
EVEN UNDER THE CIRCUMSTANCES, I CAN'T JUST KISS ONODERA WITHOUT HER CONSENT... MUCH AS I'D LIKE TO...
ZZZ
DON'T BE SO UPTIGHT, ICHIJO.
KOSAKI'S ALWAYS SAYING...

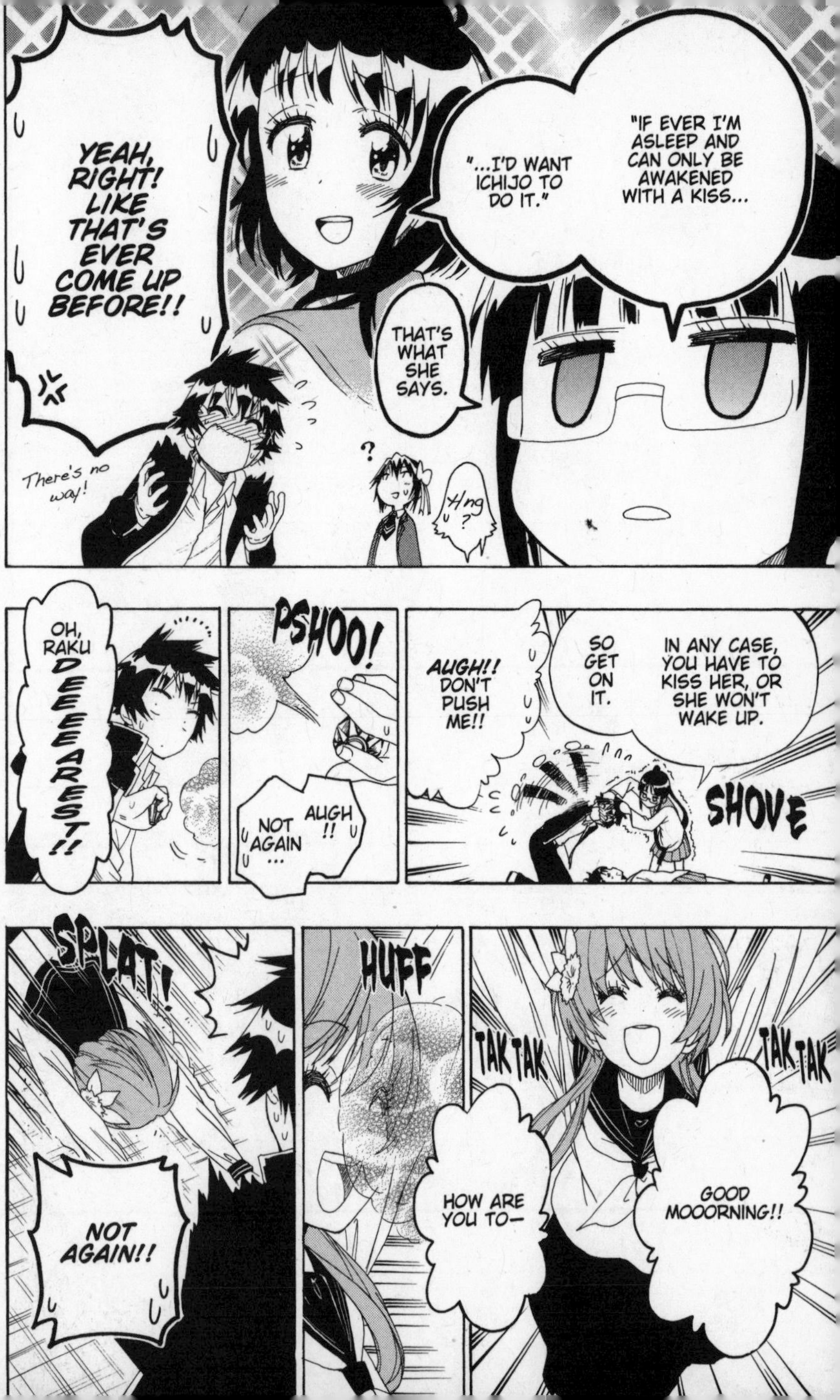
"IF EVER I'M ASLEEP AND CAN ONLY BE AWAKENED WITH A KISS...
"...I'D WANT ICHIJO TO DO IT."
THAT'S WHAT SHE SAYS.
YEAH, RIGHT! LIKE THAT'S EVER COME UP BEFORE!!
Hng?
There's no way!
IN ANY CASE, YOU HAVE TO KISS HER, OR SHE WON'T WAKE UP.
SO GET ON IT.
AUGH!! DON'T PUSH ME!!
SHOVE
PSHOO!
AUGH!!
NOT AGAIN...
OH, RAKU DEEEEAREST!!
TAK TAK
TAK TAK
GOOD MOOORNING!!
HUFF
HOW ARE YOU TO—
SPLAT!
NOT AGAIN!!

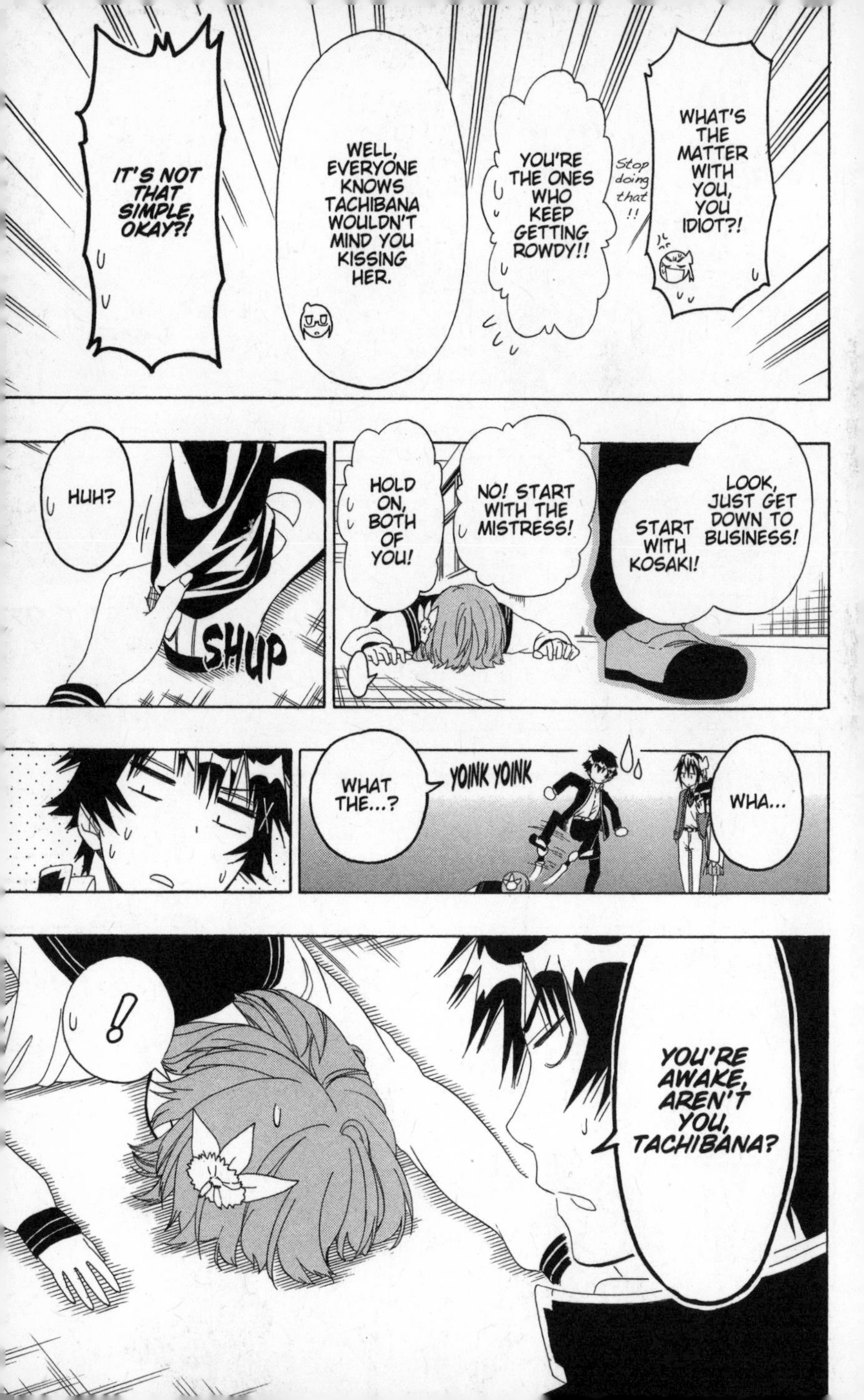
WHAT'S THE MATTER WITH YOU, YOU IDIOT?!
Stop doing that!!
YOU'RE THE ONES WHO KEEP GETTING ROWDY!!
WELL, EVERYONE KNOWS TACHIBANA WOULDN'T MIND YOU KISSING HER.
IT'S NOT THAT SIMPLE, OKAY?!
LOOK, JUST GET DOWN TO BUSINESS!
START WITH KOSAKI!
NO! START WITH THE MISTRESS!
HOLD ON, BOTH OF YOU!
HUH?
SHUP
WHA...
YOINK YOINK
WHAT THE...?
YOU'RE AWAKE, AREN'T YOU, TACHIBANA?
!

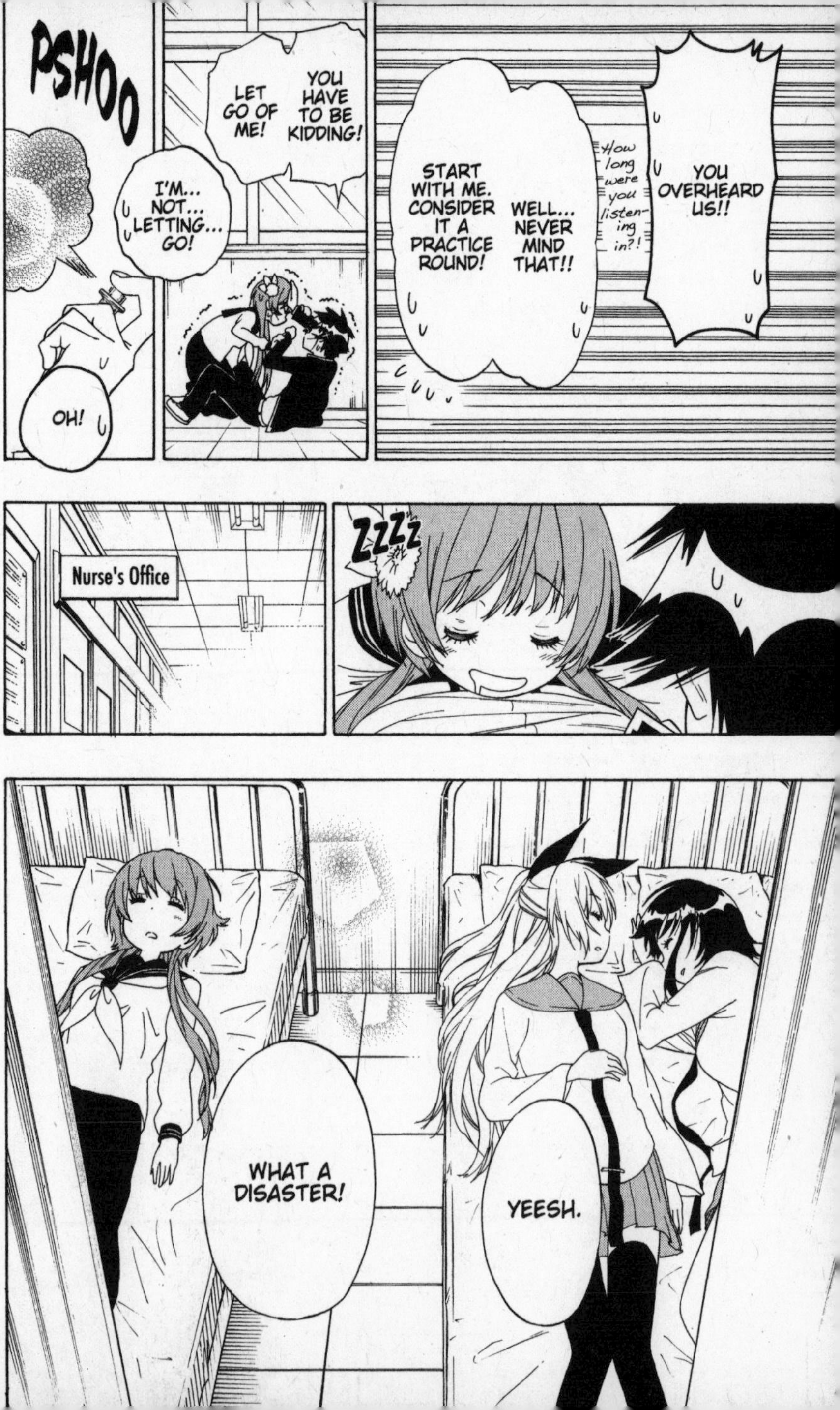
YOU OVERHEARD US!!
How long were you listening in?!
WELL... NEVER MIND THAT!!
START WITH ME. CONSIDER IT A PRACTICE ROUND!
YOU HAVE TO BE KIDDING!
LET GO OF ME!
I'M... NOT... LETTING... GO!
PSHOO
OH!
ZZZZ
Nurse's Office
YEESH.
WHAT A DISASTER!

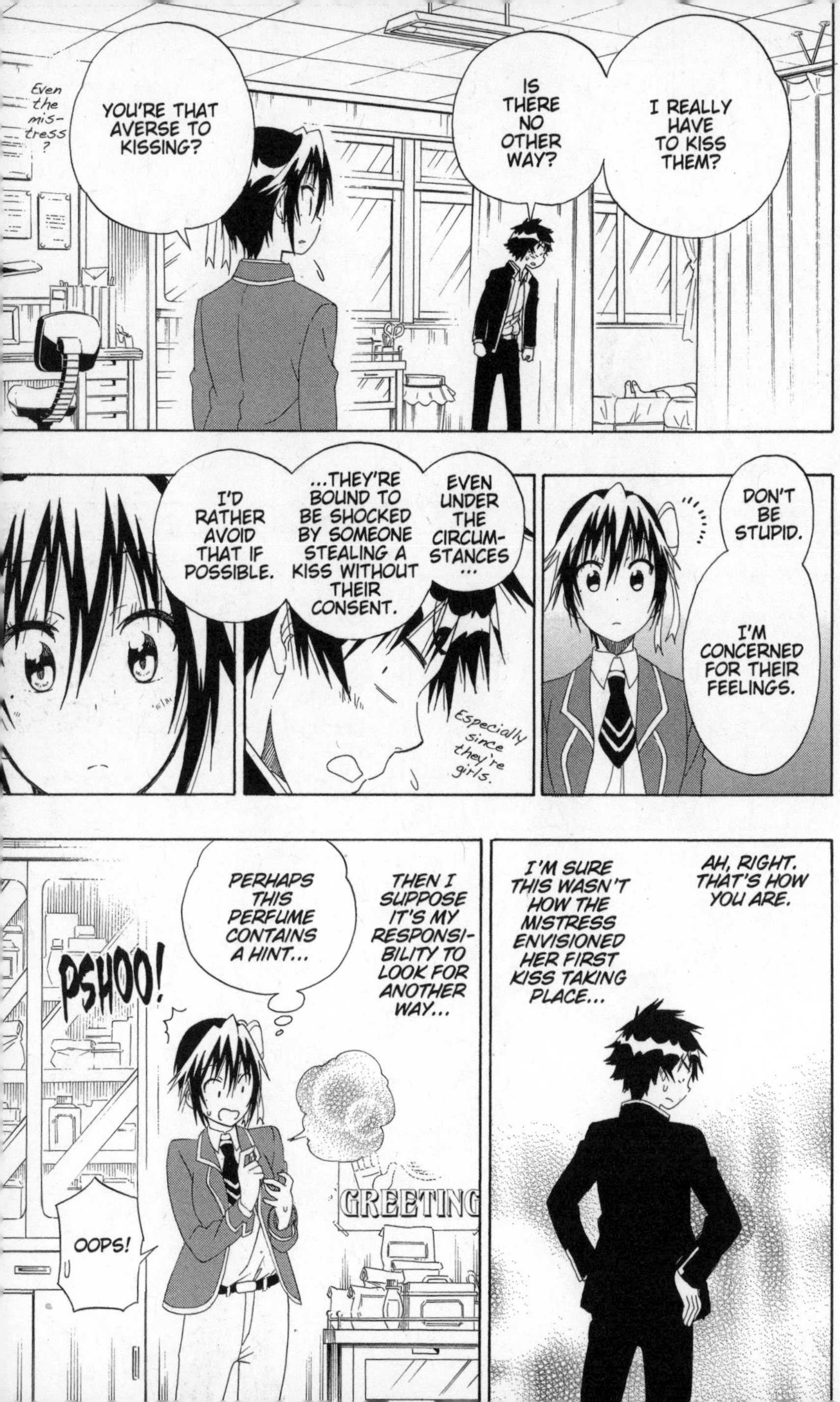
I REALLY HAVE TO KISS THEM?
IS THERE NO OTHER WAY?
YOU'RE THAT AVERSE TO KISSING?
Even the mis-tress?
DON'T BE STUPID.
I'M CONCERNED FOR THEIR FEELINGS.
EVEN UNDER THE CIRCUM-STANCES...
...THEY'RE BOUND TO BE SHOCKED BY SOMEONE STEALING A KISS WITHOUT THEIR CONSENT.
Especially since they're girls.
I'D RATHER AVOID THAT IF POSSIBLE.
AH, RIGHT. THAT'S HOW YOU ARE.
I'M SURE THIS WASN'T HOW THE MISTRESS ENVISIONED HER FIRST KISS TAKING PLACE...
THEN I SUPPOSE IT'S MY RESPONSI-BILITY TO LOOK FOR ANOTHER WAY...
PERHAPS THIS PERFUME CONTAINS A HINT...
PSHOO!
GREETING
OOPS!

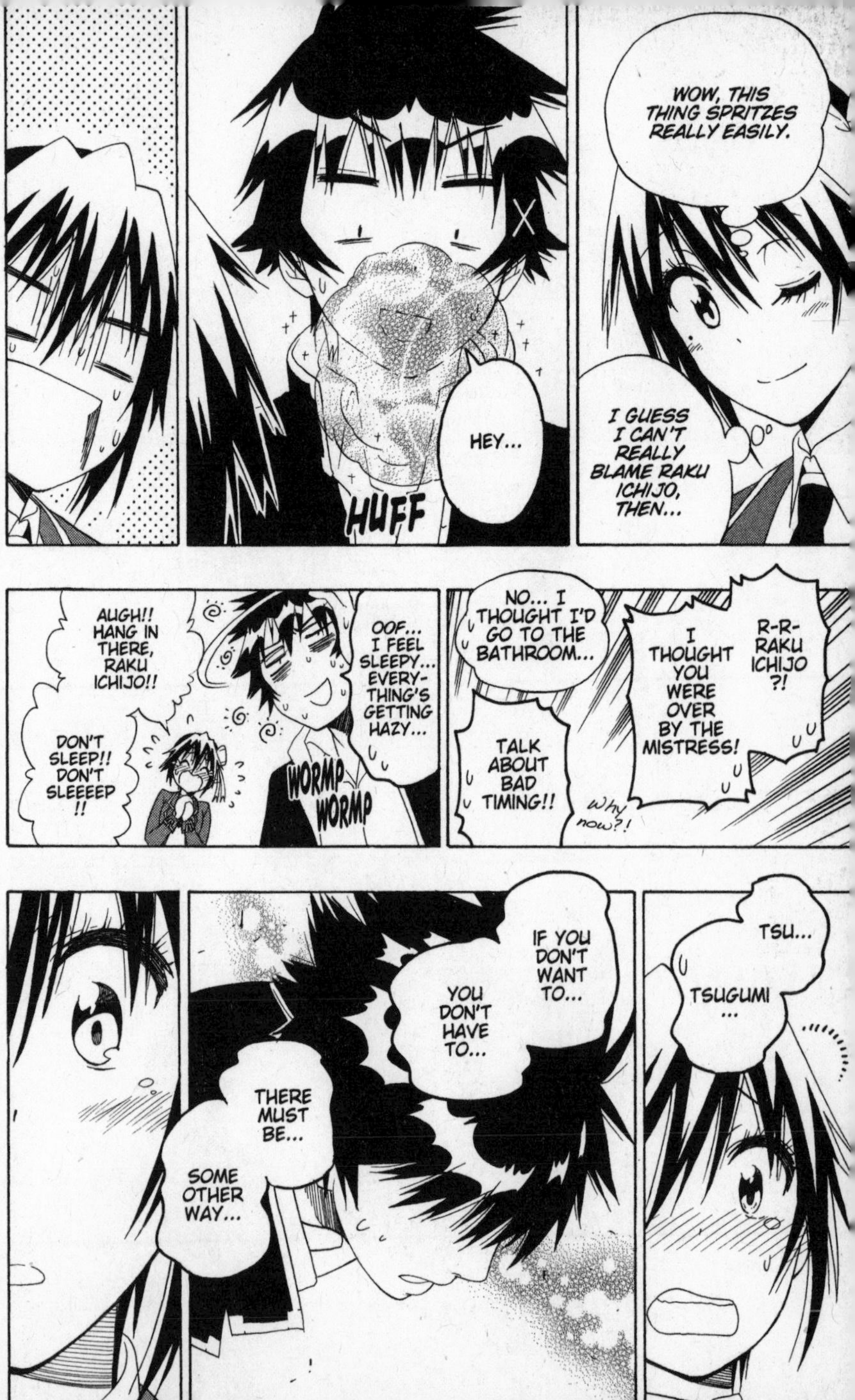
WOW, THIS THING SPRITZES REALLY EASILY.
I GUESS I CAN'T REALLY BLAME RAKU ICHIJO, THEN...
HEY...
HUFF
R-R-RAKU ICHIJO?!
I THOUGHT YOU WERE OVER BY THE MISTRESS!
NO... I THOUGHT I'D GO TO THE BATHROOM...
TALK ABOUT BAD TIMING!!
Why now?!
OOF... I FEEL SLEEPY... EVERY-THING'S GETTING HAZY...
WORMP WORMP
AUGH!! HANG IN THERE, RAKU ICHIJO!!
DON'T SLEEP!! DON'T SLEEEEP!!
TSU...
TSUGUMI...
......
IF YOU DON'T WANT TO...
YOU DON'T HAVE TO...
THERE MUST BE...
SOME OTHER WAY...

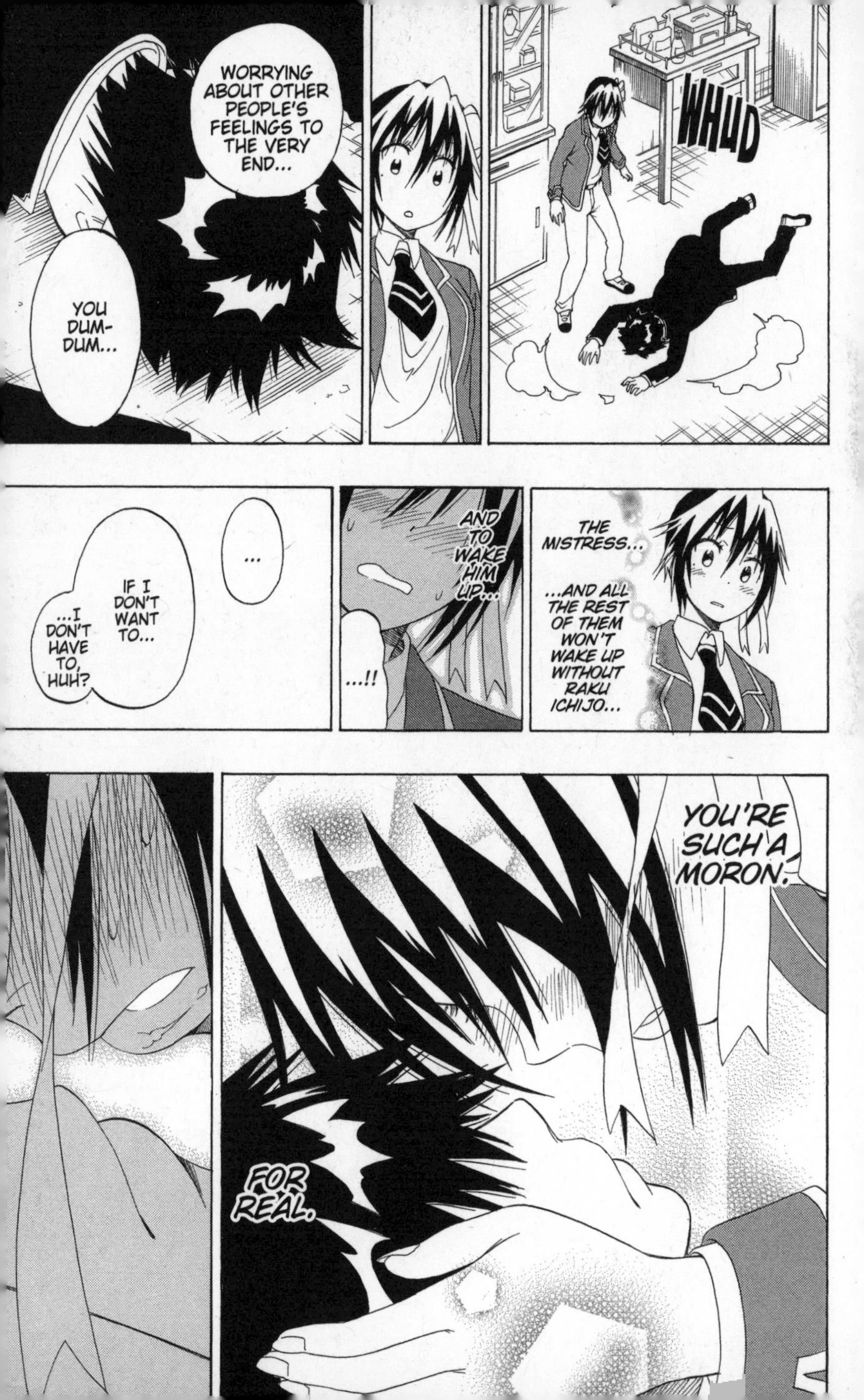
WHUD
WORRYING ABOUT OTHER PEOPLE'S FEELINGS TO THE VERY END...
YOU DUM-DUM...
THE MISTRESS...
...AND ALL THE REST OF THEM WON'T WAKE UP WITHOUT RAKU ICHIJO...
AND TO WAKE HIM UP...
...!!
...
IF I DON'T WANT TO...
...I DON'T HAVE TO, HUH?
YOU'RE SUCH A MORON.
FOR REAL.

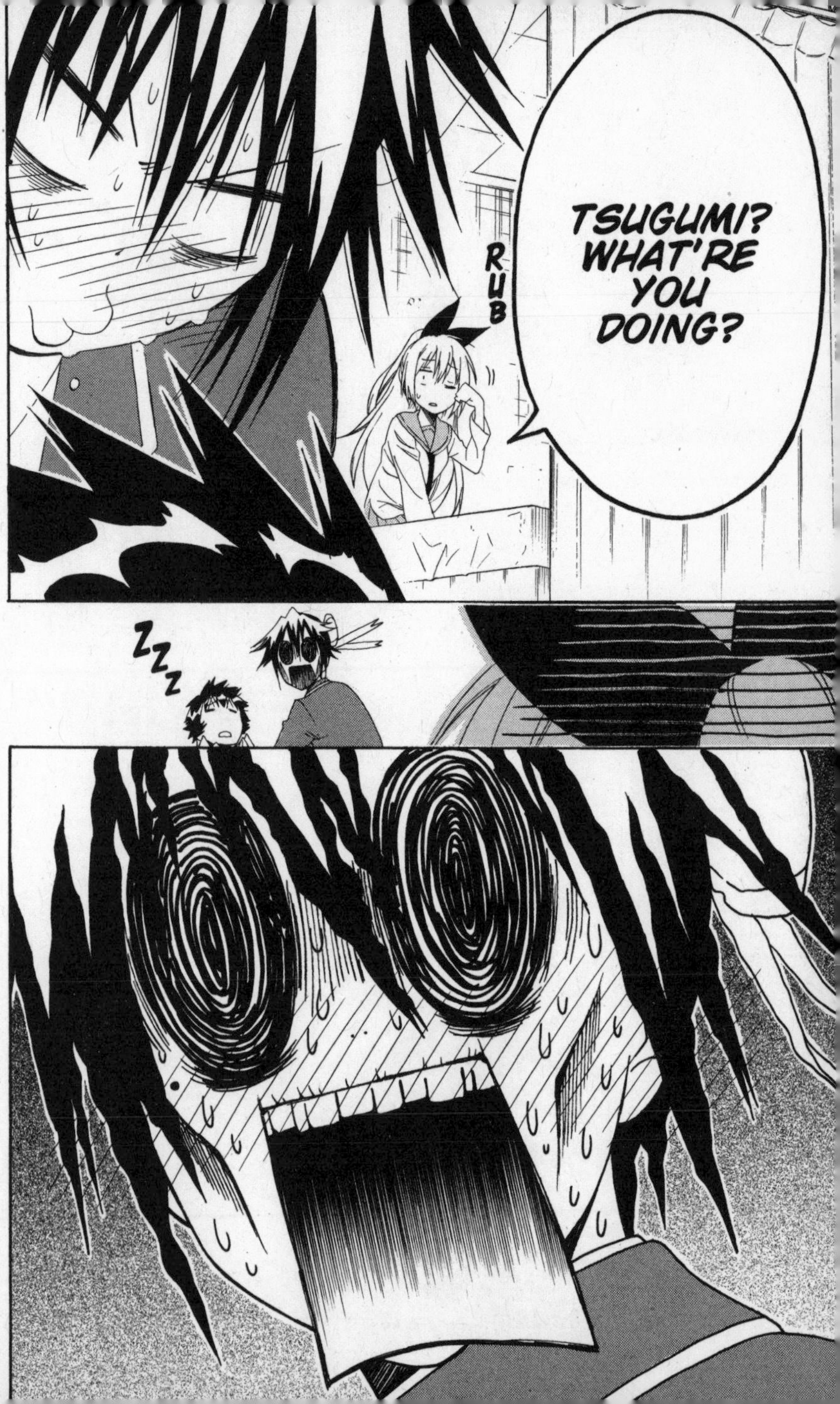
TSUGUMI? WHAT'RE YOU DOING?
RUB
ZZZ

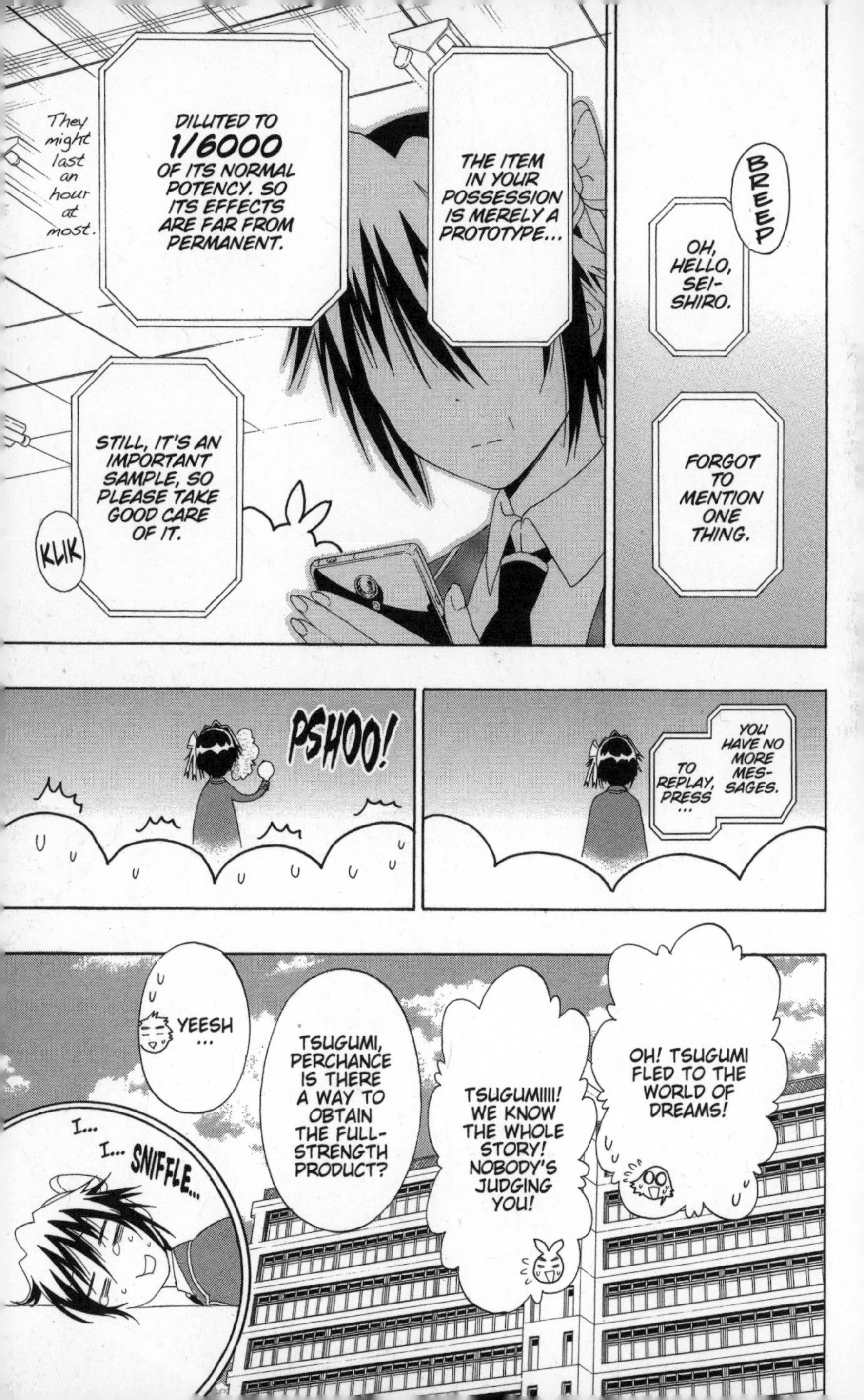
BREEP
OH, HELLO, SEI-SHIRO.
FORGOT TO MENTION ONE THING.
THE ITEM IN YOUR POSSESSION IS MERELY A PROTOTYPE...
DILUTED TO 1/6000 OF ITS NORMAL POTENCY. SO ITS EFFECTS ARE FAR FROM PERMANENT.
They might last an hour at most.
STILL, IT'S AN IMPORTANT SAMPLE, SO PLEASE TAKE GOOD CARE OF IT.
KLIK
YOU HAVE NO MORE MES-SAGES.
TO REPLAY, PRESS ...
PSHOO!
OH! TSUGUMI FLED TO THE WORLD OF DREAMS!
TSUGUMIIII! WE KNOW THE WHOLE STORY! NOBODY'S JUDGING YOU!
TSUGUMI, PERCHANCE IS THERE A WAY TO OBTAIN THE FULL-STRENGTH PRODUCT?
YEESH ...
I... I... SNIFFLE...

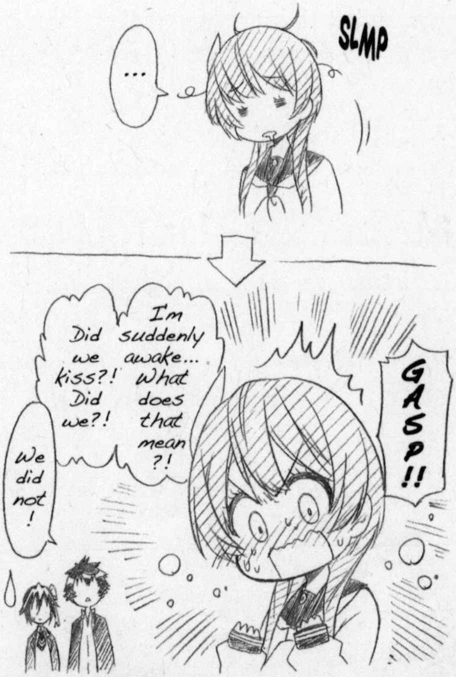
SLMP
...
GASP!!
I'm suddenly awake... What does that mean?!
Did we kiss?! Did we?!
We did not!

Chapter 141: Sincere

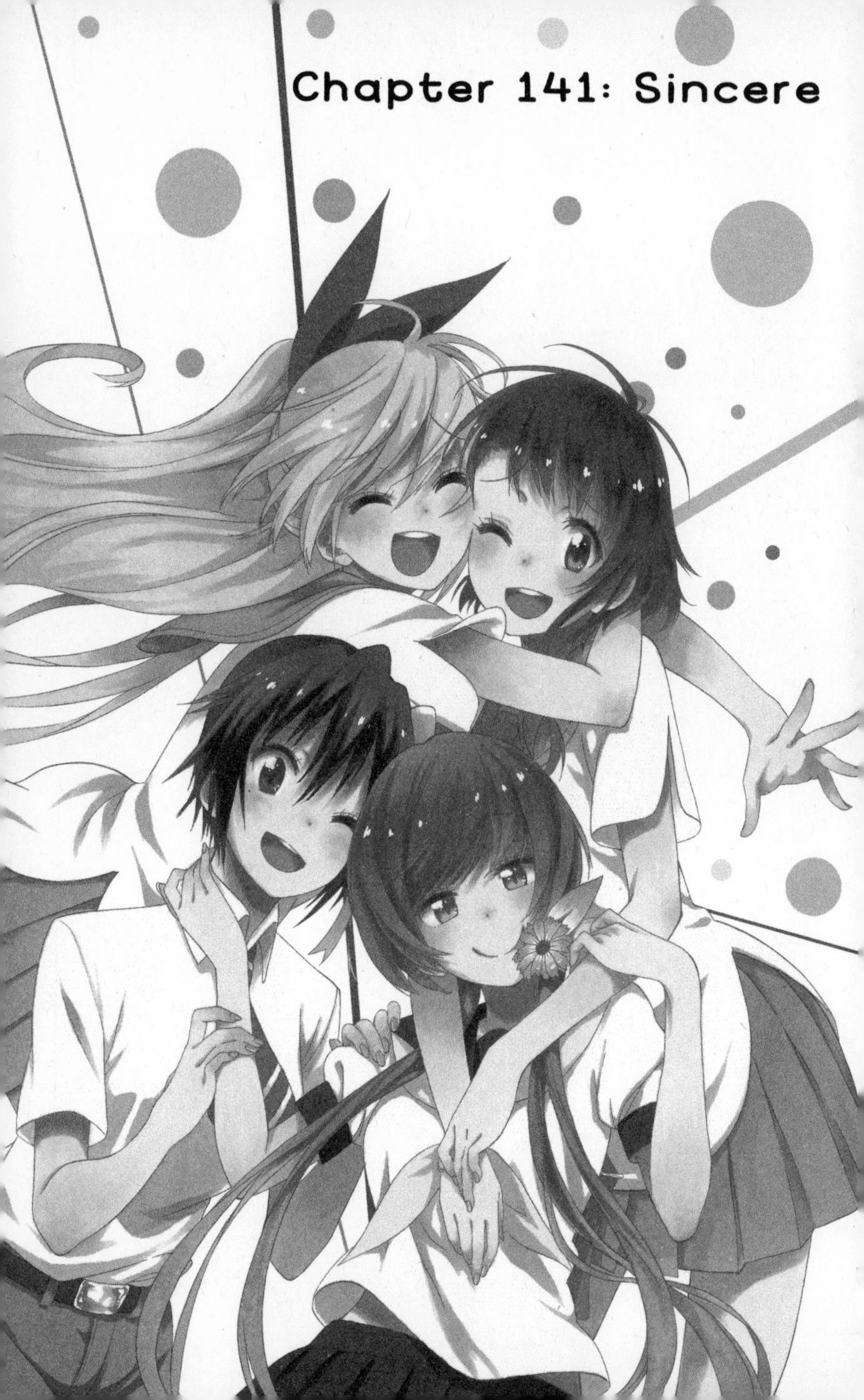

NISEKOI
False Love

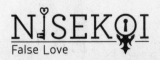

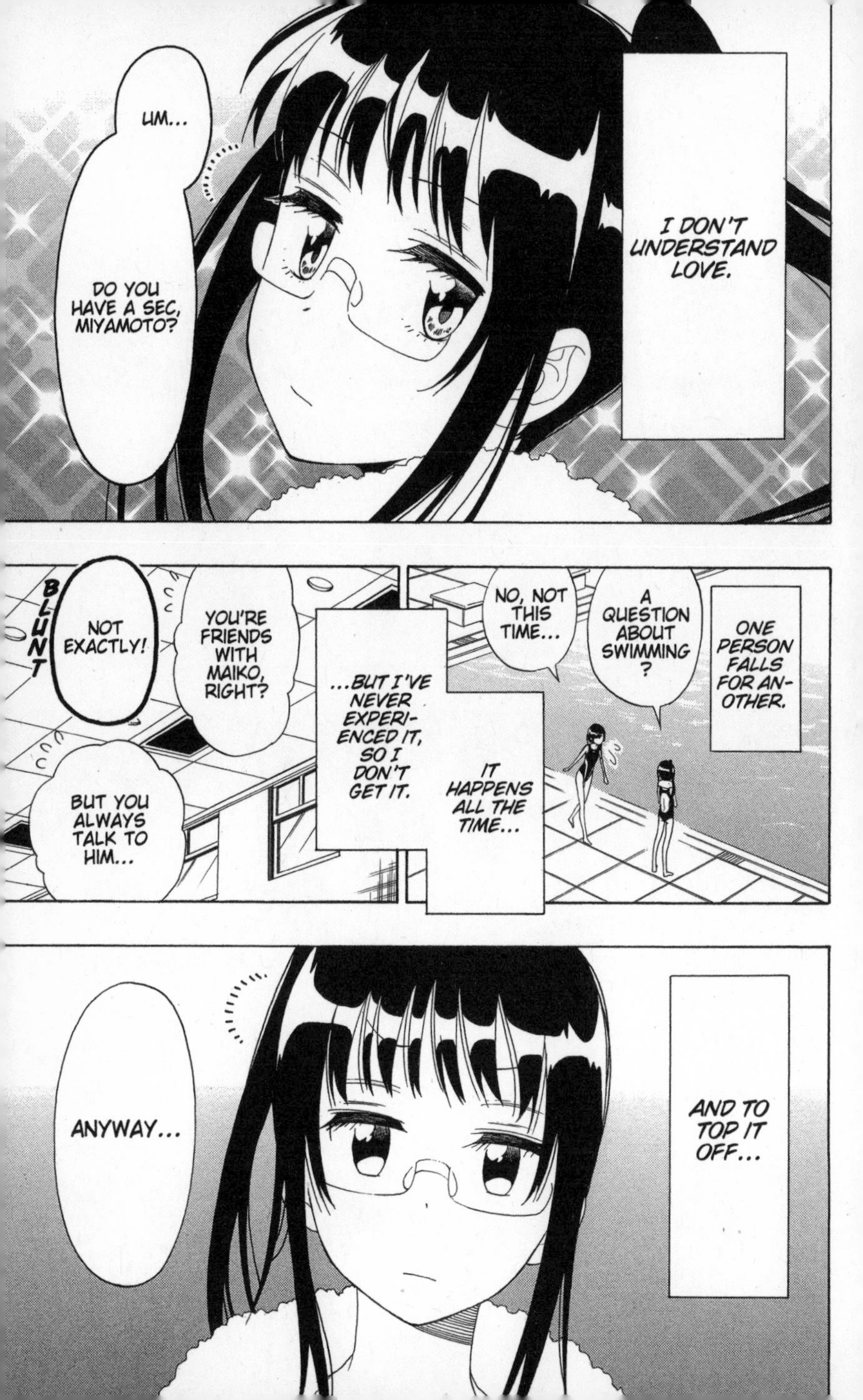
I DON'T UNDERSTAND LOVE.
UM...
DO YOU HAVE A SEC, MIYAMOTO?
ONE PERSON FALLS FOR AN-OTHER.
A QUESTION ABOUT SWIMMING?
NO, NOT THIS TIME...
IT HAPPENS ALL THE TIME...
...BUT I'VE NEVER EXPERI-ENCED IT, SO I DON'T GET IT.
YOU'RE FRIENDS WITH MAIKO, RIGHT?
BLUNT
NOT EXACTLY!
BUT YOU ALWAYS TALK TO HIM...
AND TO TOP IT OFF...
ANYWAY...

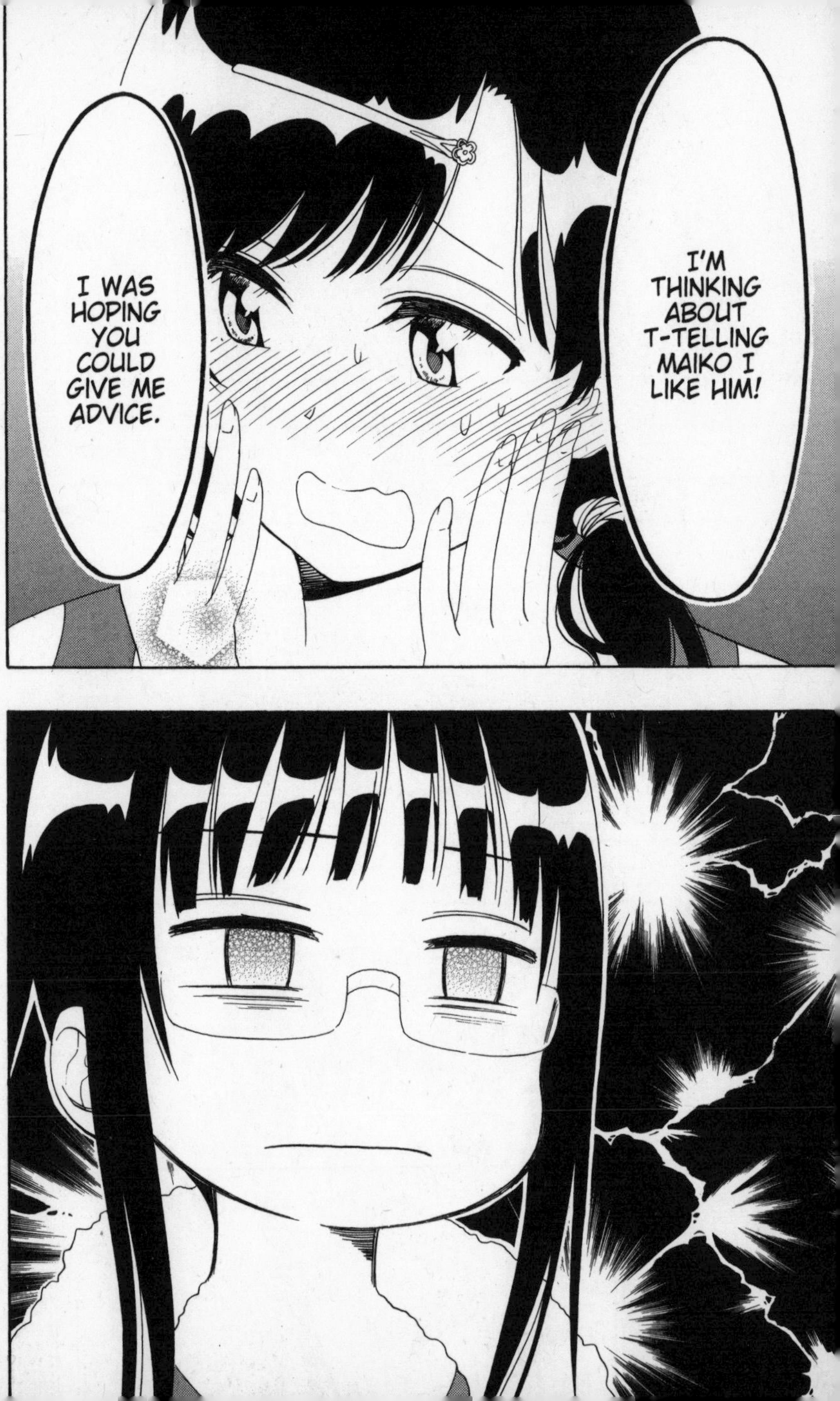
I'M THINKING ABOUT T-TELLING MAIKO I LIKE HIM!
I WAS HOPING YOU COULD GIVE ME ADVICE.

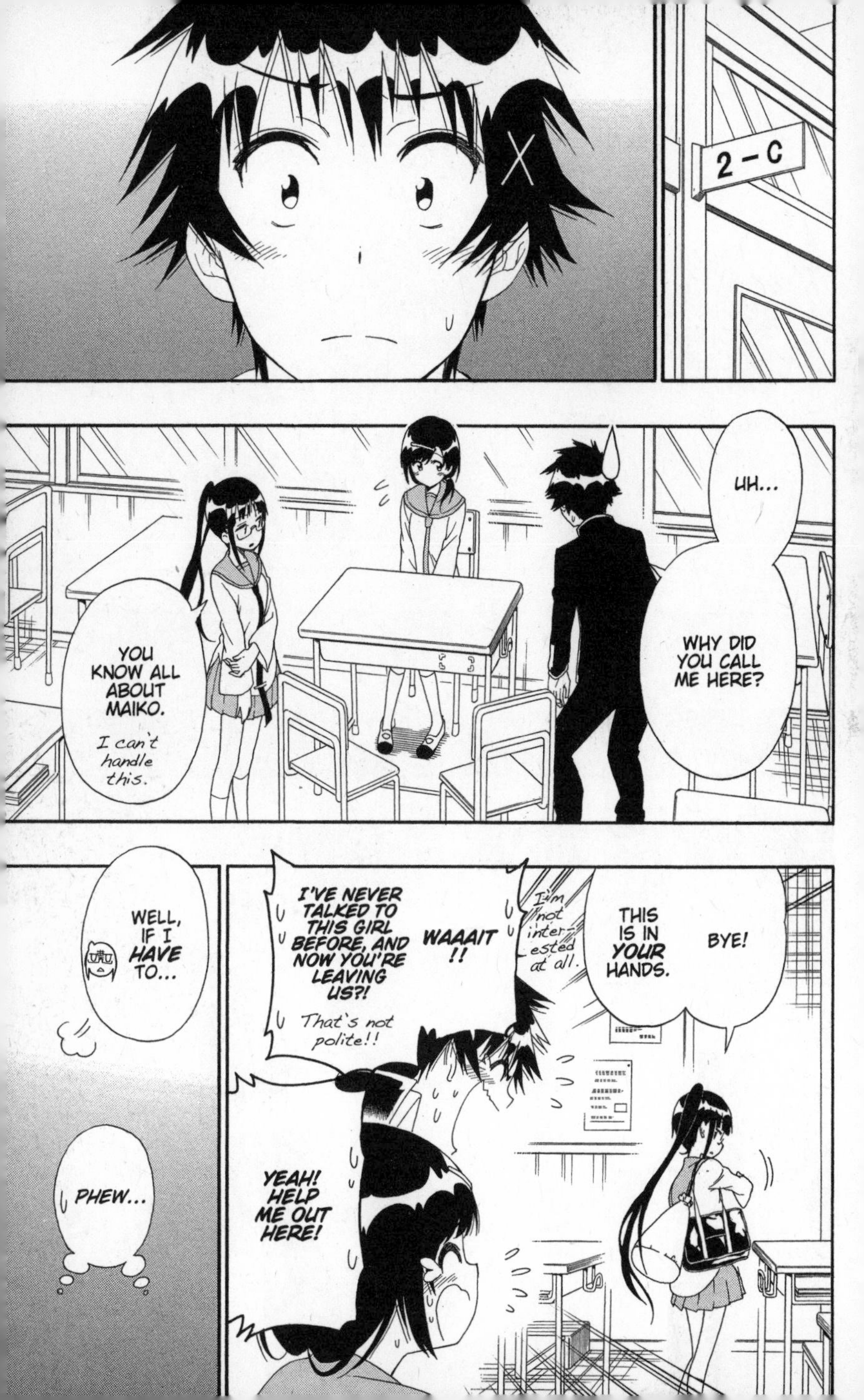

2 – C
UH...
WHY DID YOU CALL ME HERE?
YOU KNOW ALL ABOUT MAIKO.
I can't handle this.
THIS IS IN YOUR HANDS.
BYE!
I'm not interested at all.
WAAAIT!!
I'VE NEVER TALKED TO THIS GIRL BEFORE, AND NOW YOU'RE LEAVING US?!
That's not polite!!
YEAH! HELP ME OUT HERE!
WELL, IF I HAVE TO...
PHEW...

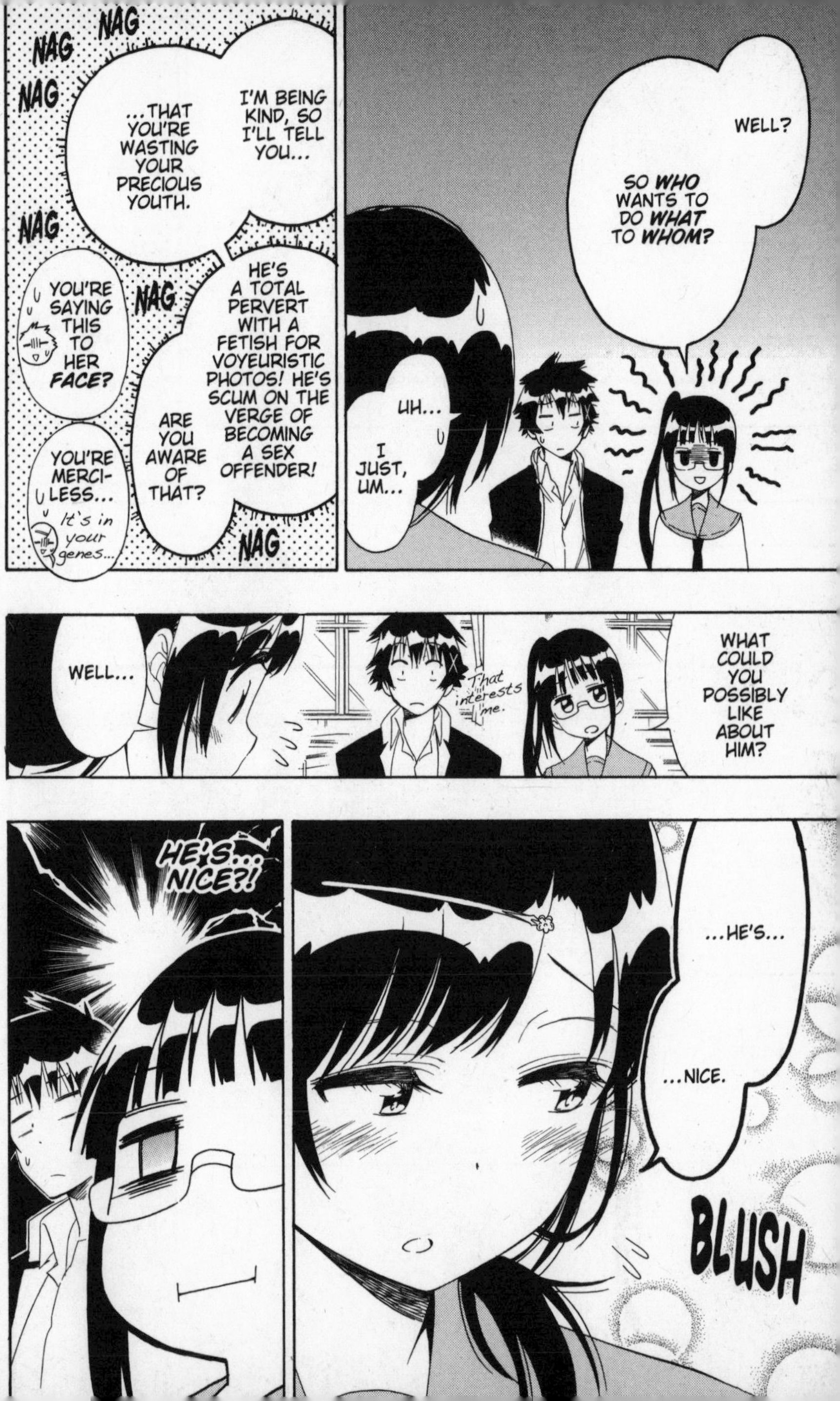
WELL?
SO WHO WANTS TO DO WHAT TO WHOM?
UH...
I JUST, UM...
I'M BEING KIND, SO I'LL TELL YOU...
...THAT YOU'RE WASTING YOUR PRECIOUS YOUTH.
NAG NAG NAG NAG NAG NAG
HE'S A TOTAL PERVERT WITH A FETISH FOR VOYEURISTIC PHOTOS! HE'S SCUM ON THE VERGE OF BECOMING A SEX OFFENDER!
ARE YOU AWARE OF THAT?
YOU'RE SAYING THIS TO HER FACE?
YOU'RE MERCILESS...
It's in your genes...
WHAT COULD YOU POSSIBLY LIKE ABOUT HIM?
That interests me.
WELL...
...HE'S...
...NICE.
BLUSH
HE'S... NICE?!

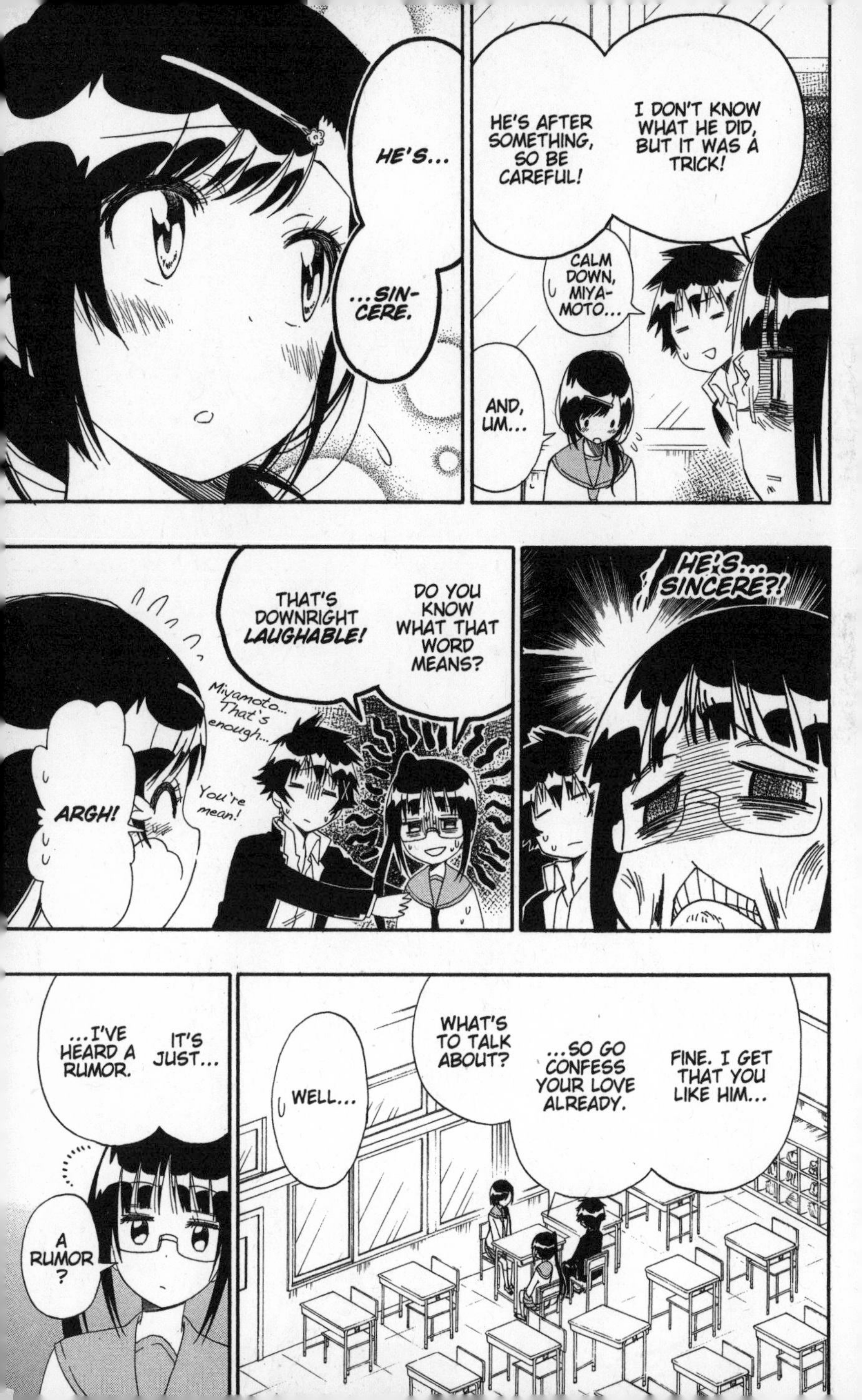
I DON'T KNOW WHAT HE DID, BUT IT WAS A TRICK!
HE'S AFTER SOMETHING, SO BE CAREFUL!
CALM DOWN, MIYA-MOTO...
AND, UM...
HE'S...
...SIN-CERE.
HE'S... SINCERE?!
DO YOU KNOW WHAT THAT WORD MEANS?
THAT'S DOWNRIGHT LAUGHABLE!
Miyamoto... That's enough...
You're mean!
ARGH!
FINE. I GET THAT YOU LIKE HIM...
...SO GO CONFESS YOUR LOVE ALREADY.
WHAT'S TO TALK ABOUT?
WELL...
IT'S JUST...
...I'VE HEARD A RUMOR.
A RUMOR?

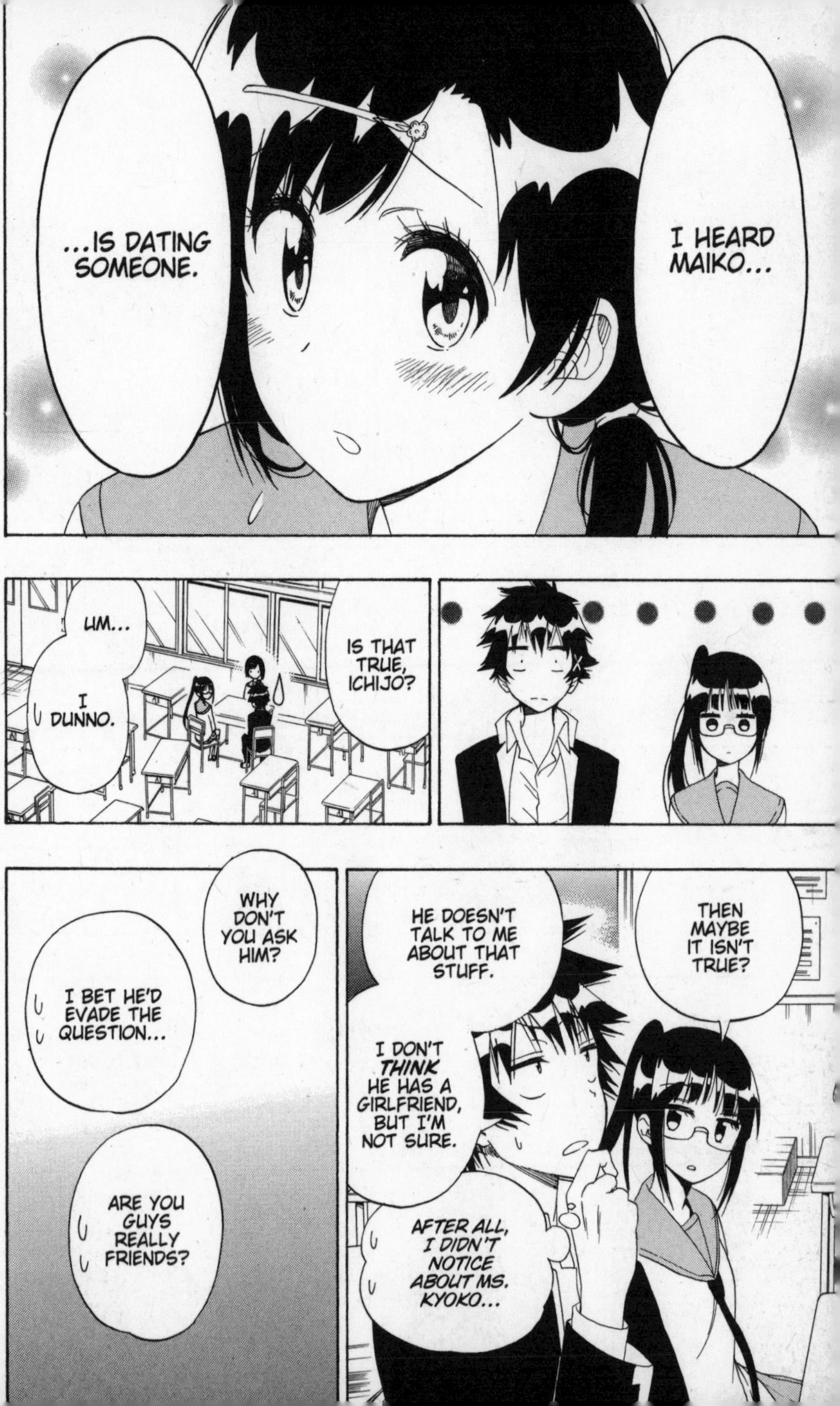
I HEARD MAIKO...
...IS DATING SOMEONE.
IS THAT TRUE, ICHIJO?
UM...
I DUNNO.
THEN MAYBE IT ISN'T TRUE?
HE DOESN'T TALK TO ME ABOUT THAT STUFF.
I DON'T *THINK* HE HAS A GIRLFRIEND, BUT I'M NOT SURE.
AFTER ALL, I DIDN'T NOTICE ABOUT MS. KYOKO...
WHY DON'T YOU ASK HIM?
I BET HE'D EVADE THE QUESTION...
ARE YOU GUYS REALLY FRIENDS?

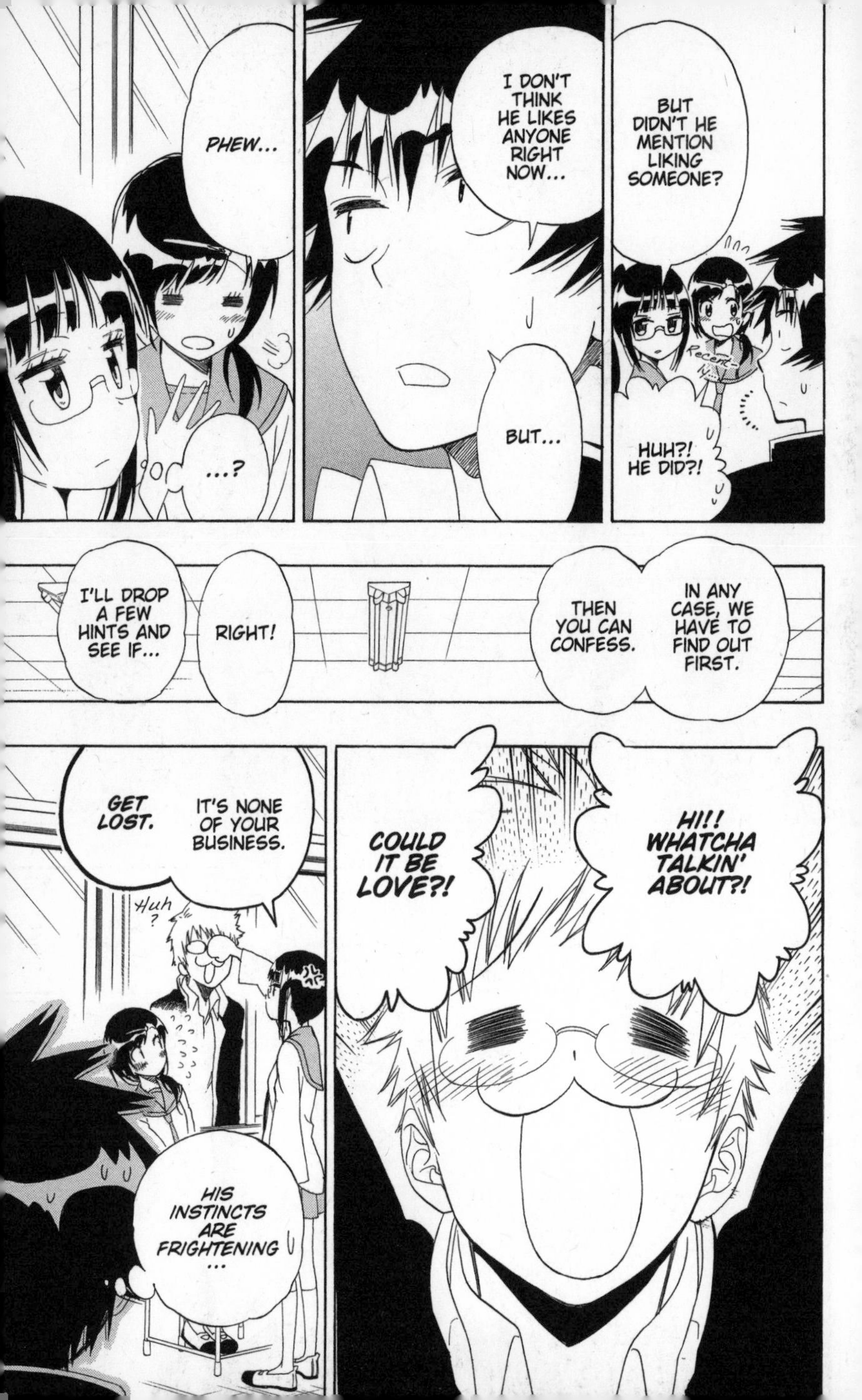
BUT DIDN'T HE MENTION LIKING SOMEONE?
Recent-ly...
HUH?! HE DID?!
I DON'T THINK HE LIKES ANYONE RIGHT NOW...
BUT...
PHEW...
...?
IN ANY CASE, WE HAVE TO FIND OUT FIRST.
THEN YOU CAN CONFESS.
RIGHT!
I'LL DROP A FEW HINTS AND SEE IF...
HI!! WHATCHA TALKIN' ABOUT?!
COULD IT BE LOVE?!
IT'S NONE OF YOUR BUSINESS.
GET LOST.
Huh?
HIS INSTINCTS ARE FRIGHTENING...

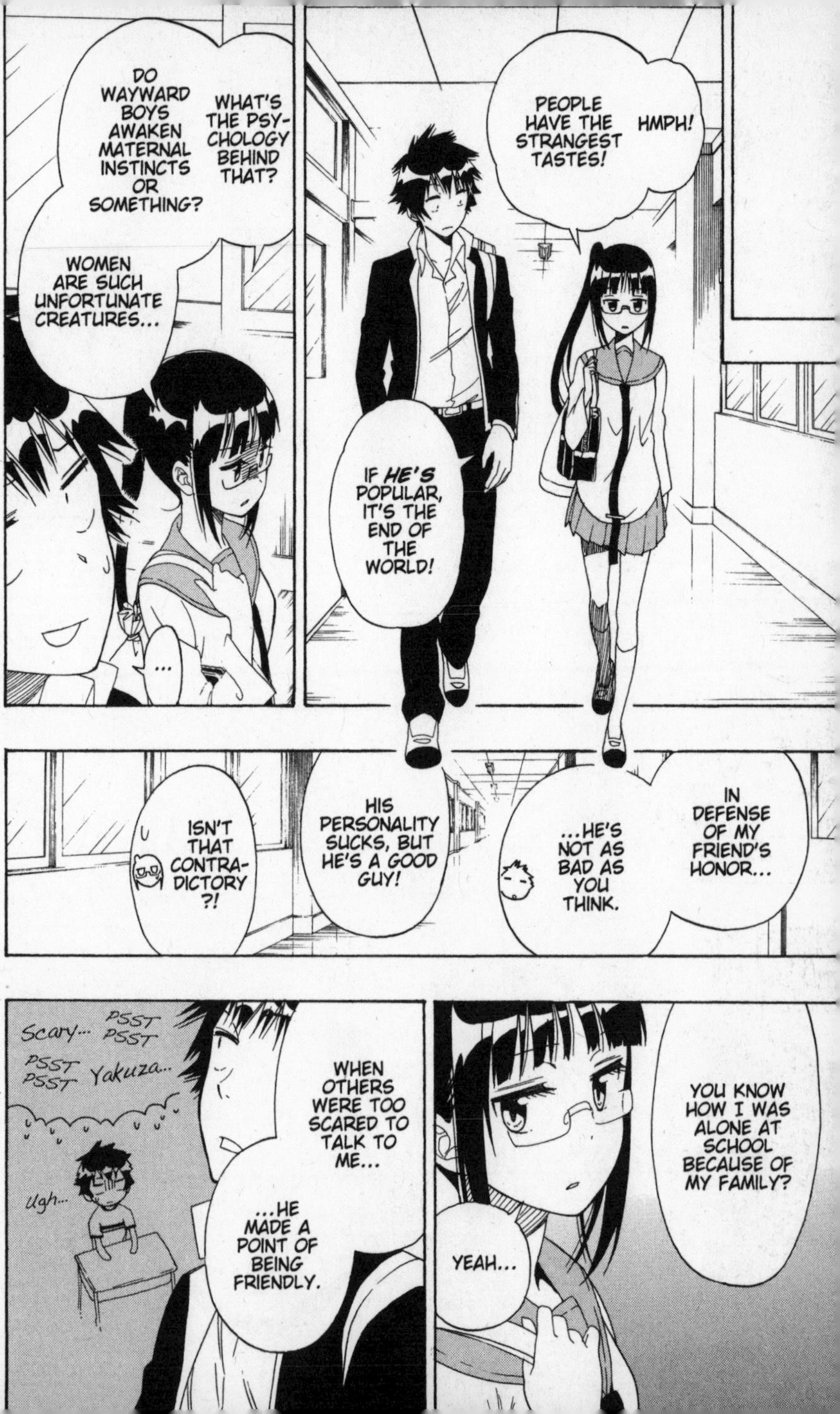
HMPH!
PEOPLE HAVE THE STRANGEST TASTES!
IF *HE'S* POPULAR, IT'S THE END OF THE WORLD!
WHAT'S THE PSY-CHOLOGY BEHIND THAT?
DO WAYWARD BOYS AWAKEN MATERNAL INSTINCTS OR SOMETHING?
WOMEN ARE SUCH UNFORTUNATE CREATURES...
...
IN DEFENSE OF MY FRIEND'S HONOR...
...HE'S NOT AS BAD AS YOU THINK.
HIS PERSONALITY SUCKS, BUT HE'S A GOOD GUY!
ISN'T THAT CONTRA-DICTORY ?!
YOU KNOW HOW I WAS ALONE AT SCHOOL BECAUSE OF MY FAMILY?
YEAH...
WHEN OTHERS WERE TOO SCARED TO TALK TO ME...
...HE MADE A POINT OF BEING FRIENDLY.
PSST PSST
Scary...
PSST PSST
Yakuza...
Ugh...

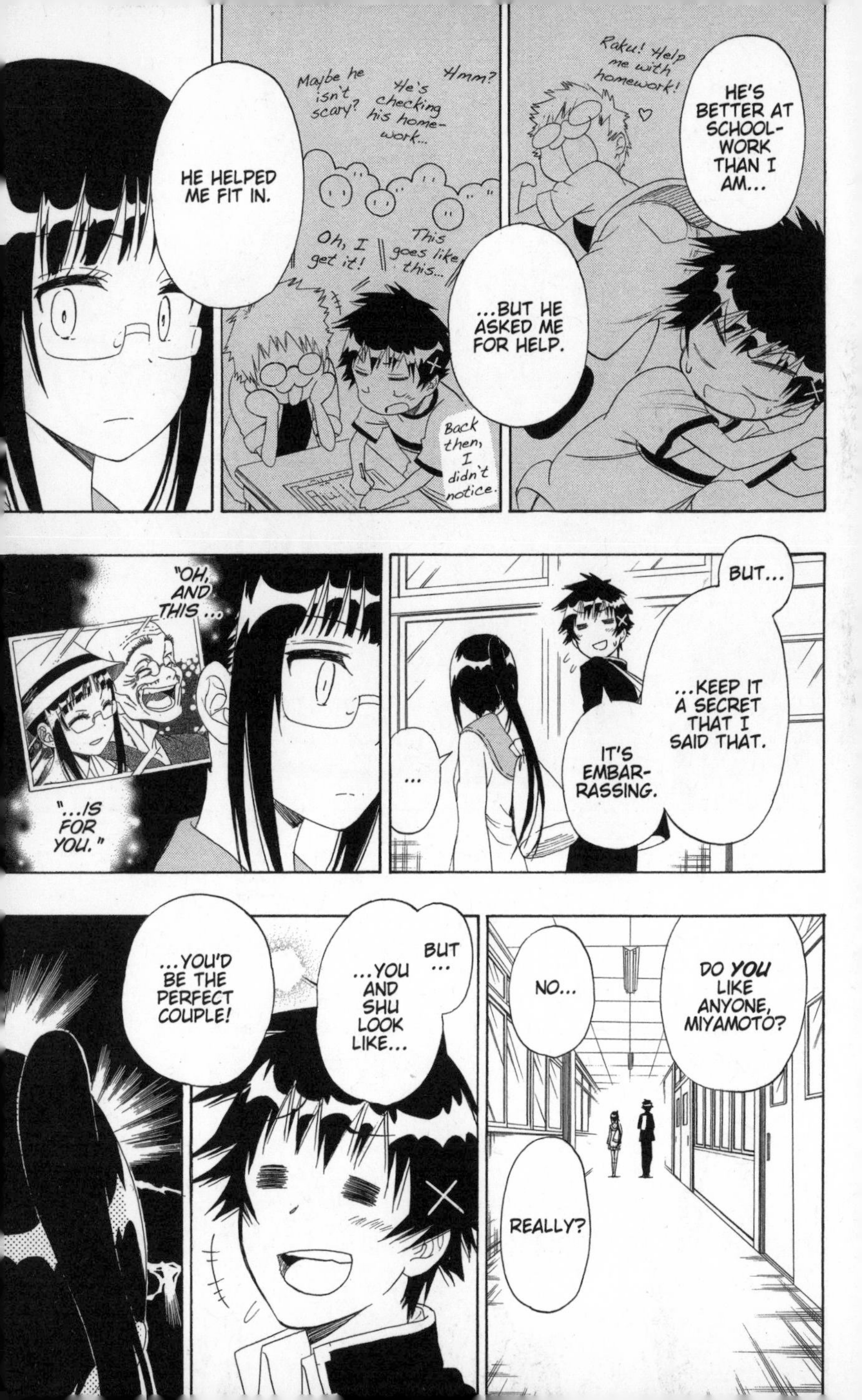
Raku! Help me with homework! ♡
HE'S BETTER AT SCHOOL-WORK THAN I AM...
...BUT HE ASKED ME FOR HELP.
Hmm?
He's checking his home-work...
Maybe he isn't scary?
This goes like this...
Oh, I get it!
Back then, I didn't notice.
HE HELPED ME FIT IN.
BUT...
...KEEP IT A SECRET THAT I SAID THAT.
IT'S EMBAR-RASSING.
...
"OH, AND THIS...
"...IS FOR YOU."
DO YOU LIKE ANYONE, MIYAMOTO?
NO...
REALLY?
BUT...
...YOU AND SHU LOOK LIKE...
...YOU'D BE THE PERFECT COUPLE!

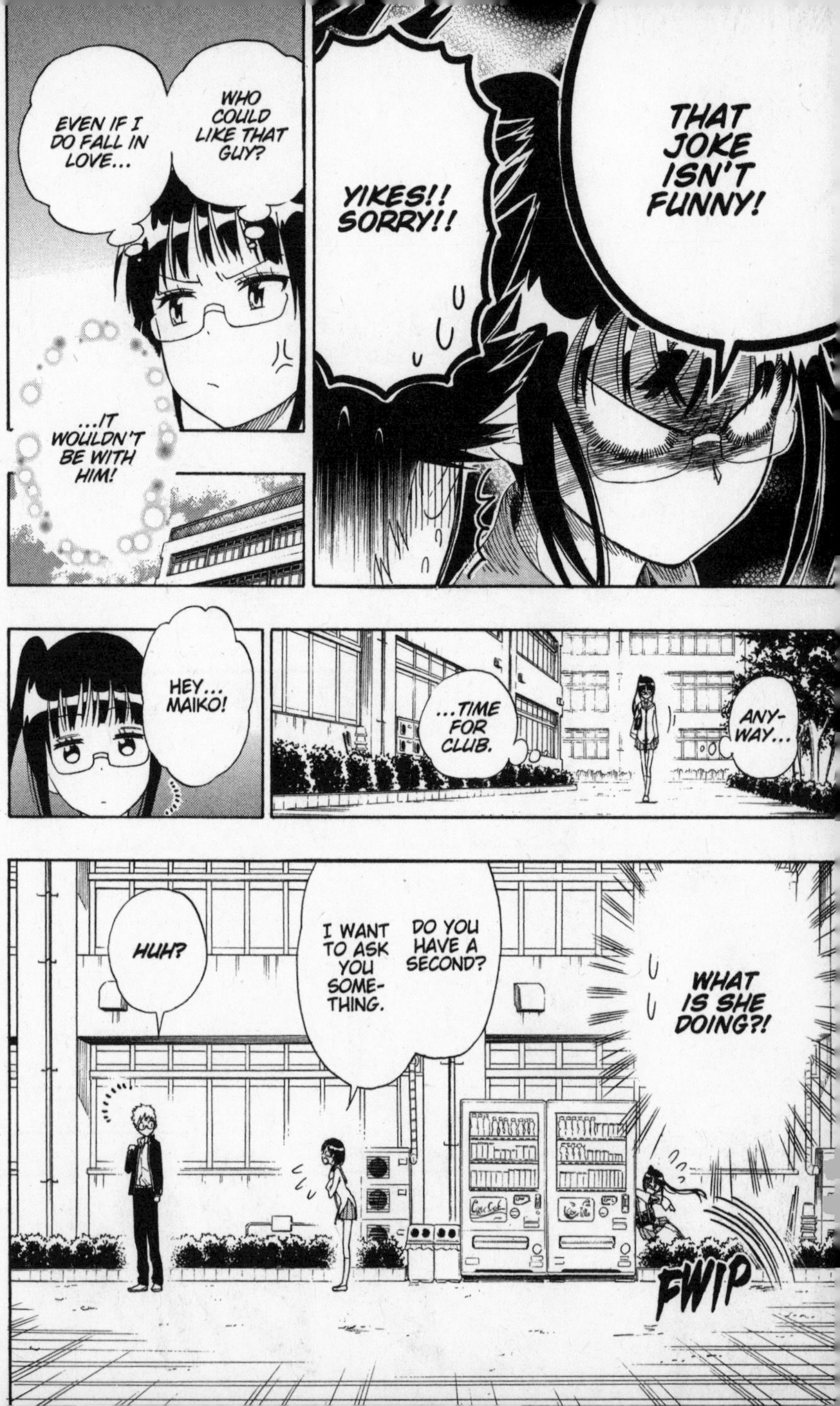
THAT JOKE ISN'T FUNNY!
YIKES!! SORRY!!
WHO COULD LIKE THAT GUY?
EVEN IF I DO FALL IN LOVE...
...IT WOULDN'T BE WITH HIM!
ANY-WAY...
...TIME FOR CLUB.
HEY... MAIKO!
WHAT IS SHE DOING?!
FWIP
DO YOU HAVE A SECOND?
I WANT TO ASK YOU SOME-THING.
HUH?

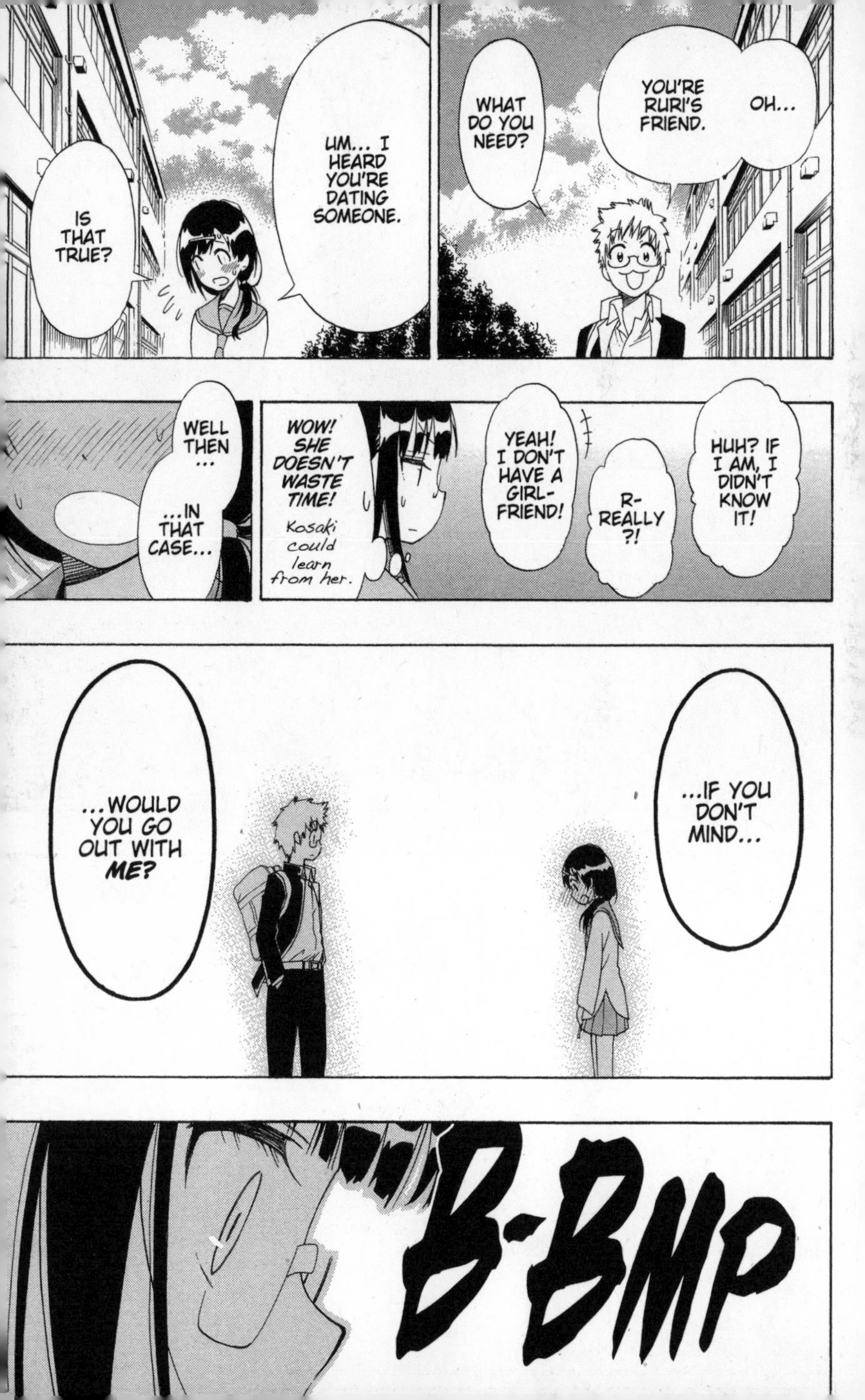
OH...
YOU'RE RURI'S FRIEND.
WHAT DO YOU NEED?
UM... I HEARD YOU'RE DATING SOMEONE.
IS THAT TRUE?
HUH? IF I AM, I DIDN'T KNOW IT!
R-REALLY?!
YEAH! I DON'T HAVE A GIRL-FRIEND!
WOW! SHE DOESN'T WASTE TIME!
Kosaki could learn from her.
WELL THEN...
...IN THAT CASE...
...IF YOU DON'T MIND...
...WOULD YOU GO OUT WITH ME?
B-BMP

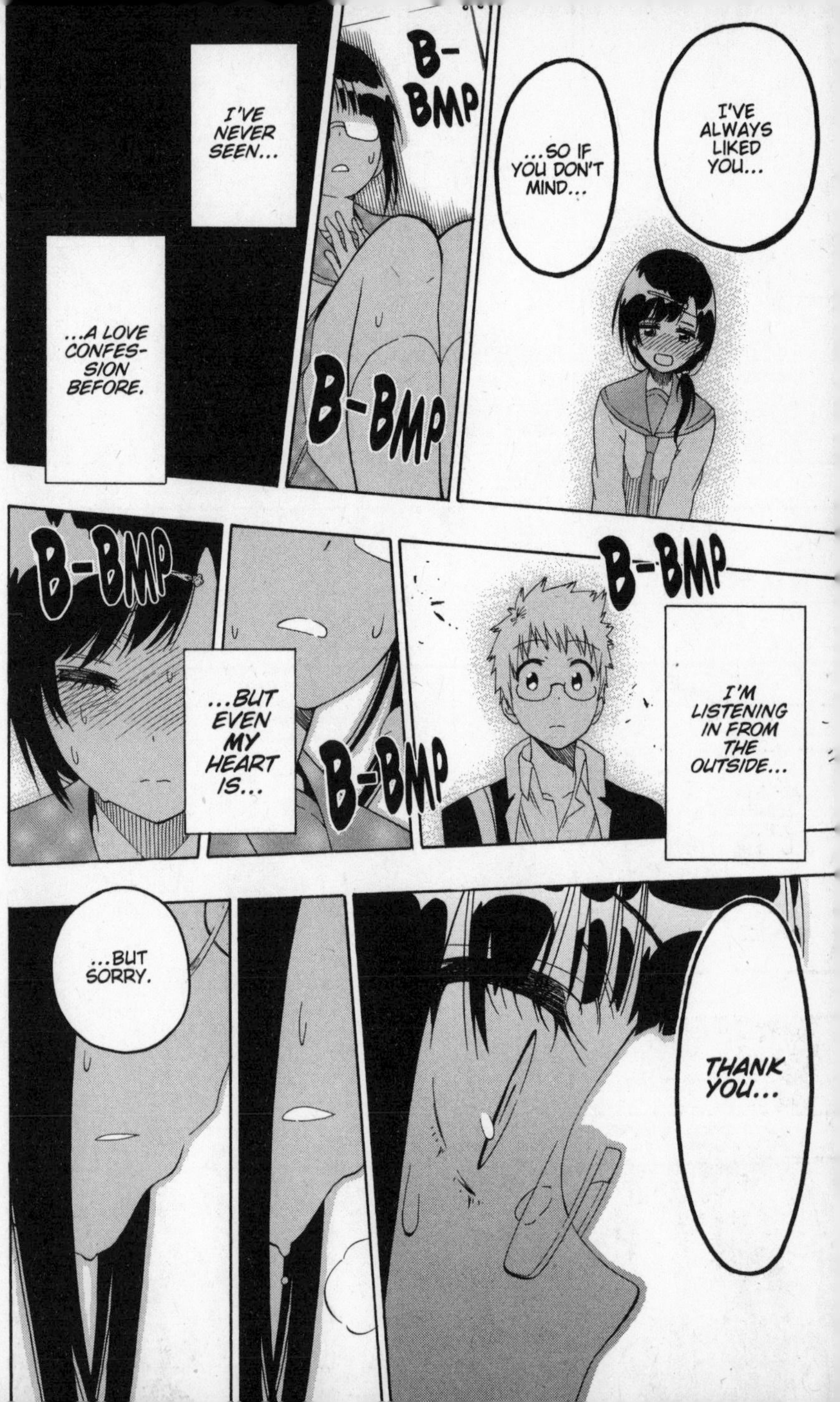
I'VE ALWAYS LIKED YOU...
...SO IF YOU DON'T MIND...
B-BMP
B-BMP
I'VE NEVER SEEN...
...A LOVE CONFES-SION BEFORE.
B-BMP
I'M LISTENING IN FROM THE OUTSIDE...
B-BMP
...BUT EVEN MY HEART IS...
B-BMP
THANK YOU...
...BUT SORRY.

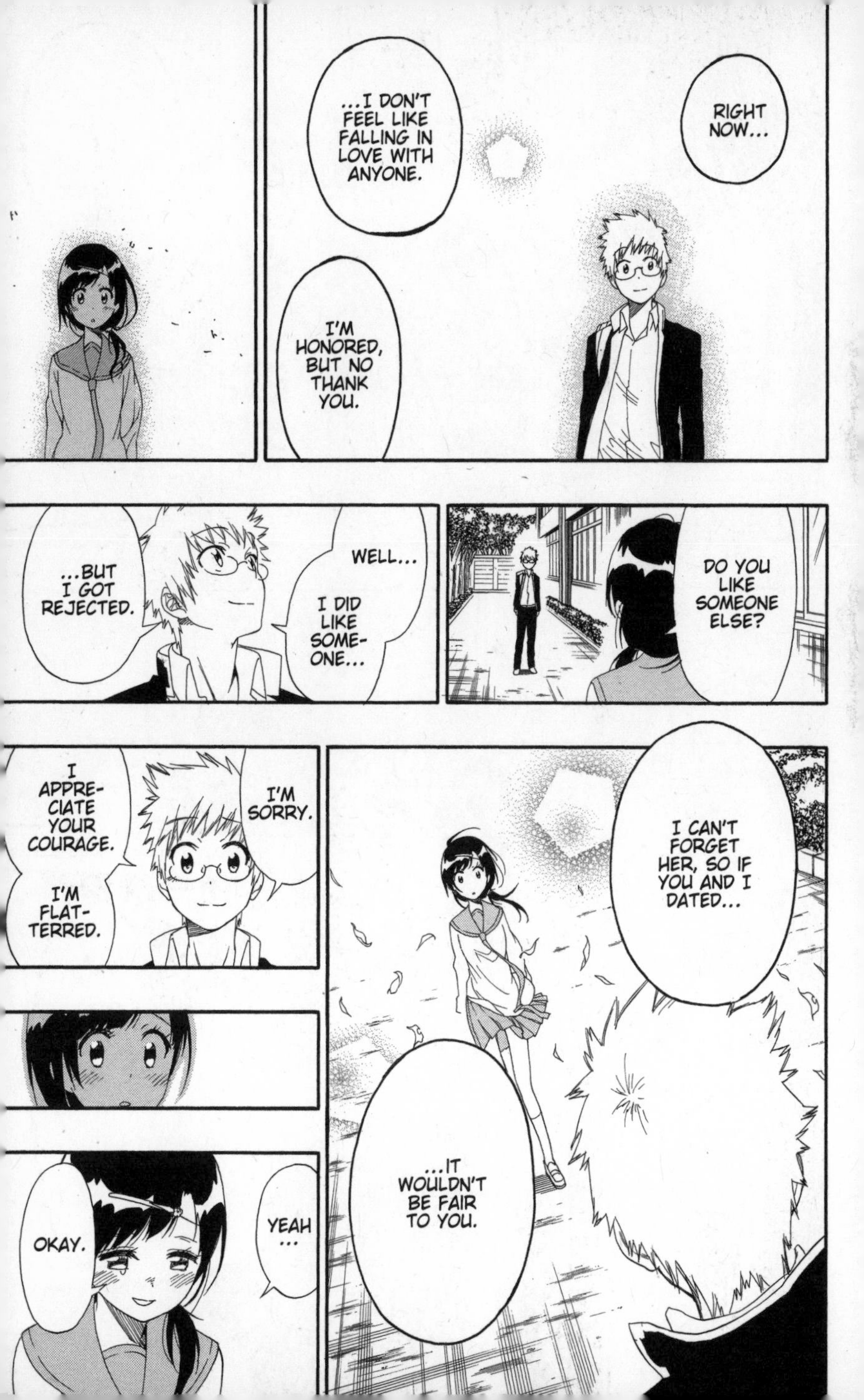
RIGHT NOW...
...I DON'T FEEL LIKE FALLING IN LOVE WITH ANYONE.
I'M HONORED, BUT NO THANK YOU.
DO YOU LIKE SOMEONE ELSE?
WELL...
I DID LIKE SOME-ONE...
...BUT I GOT REJECTED.
I CAN'T FORGET HER, SO IF YOU AND I DATED...
...IT WOULDN'T BE FAIR TO YOU.
I'M SORRY.
I APPRE-CIATE YOUR COURAGE.
I'M FLAT-TERRED.
YEAH...
OKAY.

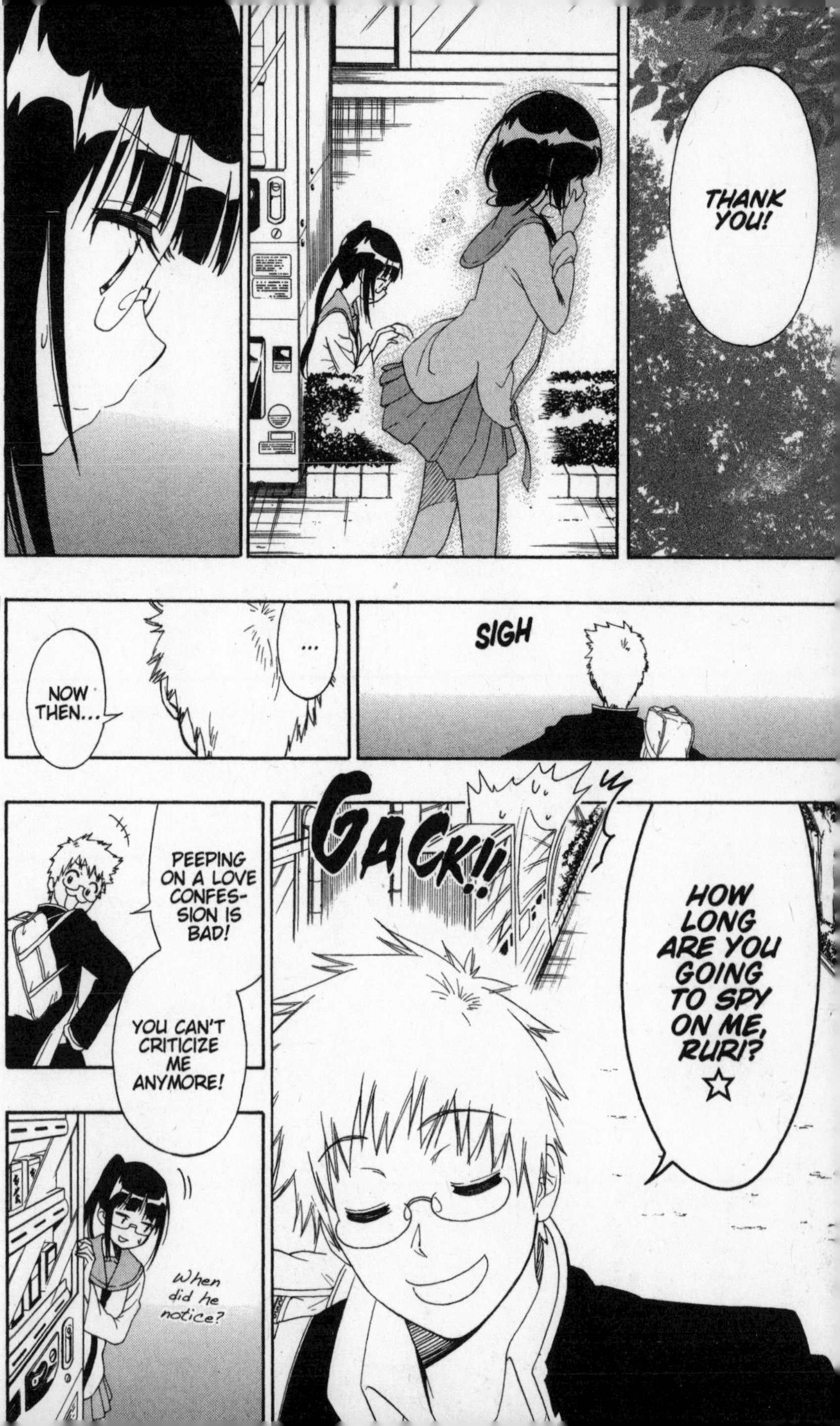
THANK YOU!
SIGH
...
NOW THEN...
HOW LONG ARE YOU GOING TO SPY ON ME, RURI? ☆
GACK!!
PEEPING ON A LOVE CONFESSION IS BAD!
YOU CAN'T CRITICIZE ME ANYMORE!
When did he notice?

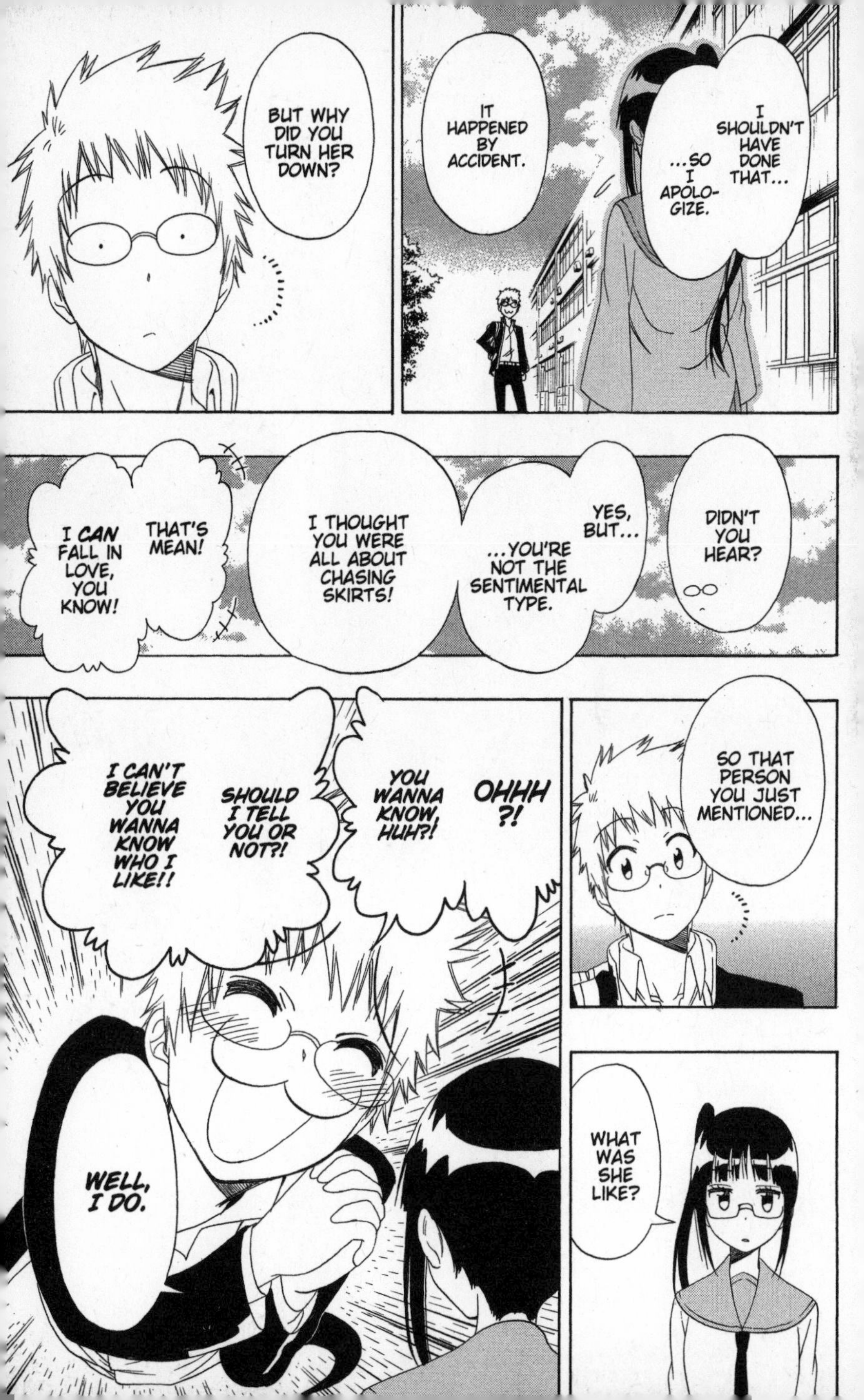
I SHOULDN'T HAVE DONE THAT...
...SO I APOLOGIZE.
IT HAPPENED BY ACCIDENT.
BUT WHY DID YOU TURN HER DOWN?
DIDN'T YOU HEAR?
YES, BUT...
...YOU'RE NOT THE SENTIMENTAL TYPE.
I THOUGHT YOU WERE ALL ABOUT CHASING SKIRTS!
THAT'S MEAN!
I *CAN* FALL IN LOVE, YOU KNOW!
SO THAT PERSON YOU JUST MENTIONED...
WHAT WAS SHE LIKE?
OHHH ?!
YOU WANNA KNOW, HUH?!
SHOULD I TELL YOU OR NOT?!
I CAN'T BELIEVE YOU WANNA KNOW WHO I LIKE!!
WELL, I DO.

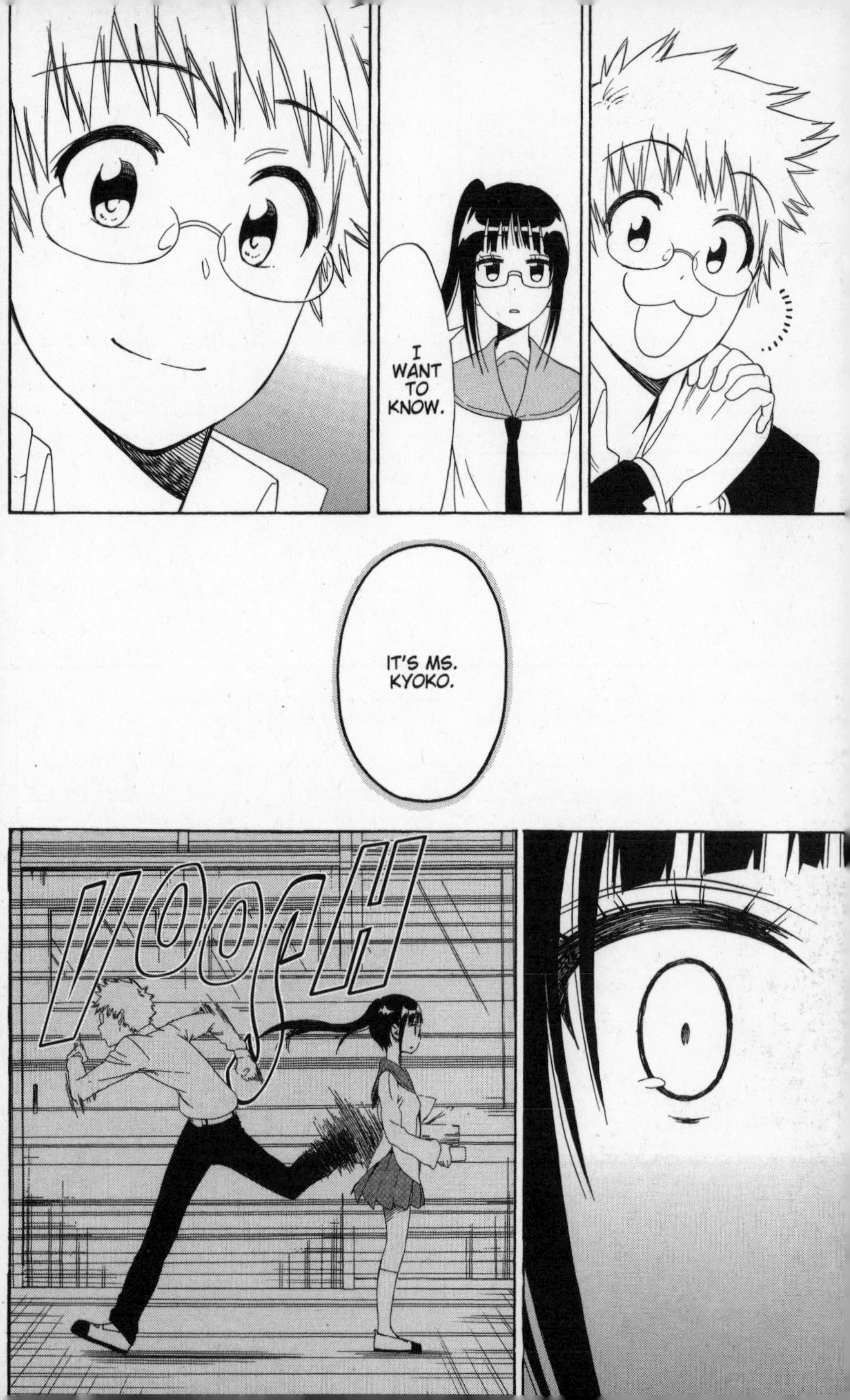
I WANT TO KNOW.
IT'S MS. KYOKO.
VOOSH

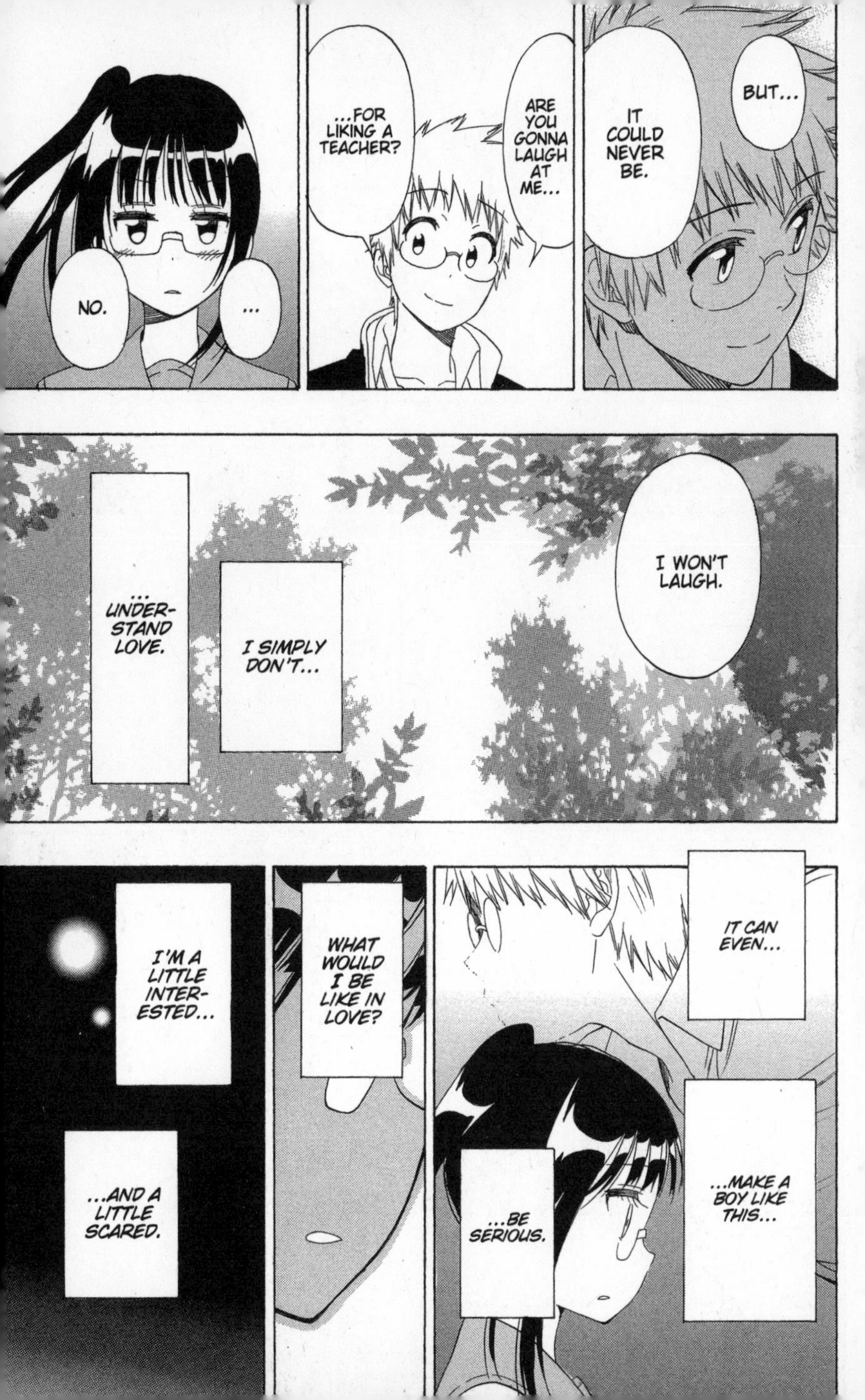
BUT...
IT COULD NEVER BE.
ARE YOU GONNA LAUGH AT ME...
...FOR LIKING A TEACHER?
...
NO.
I WON'T LAUGH.
I SIMPLY DON'T...
...UNDERSTAND LOVE.
IT CAN EVEN...
...MAKE A BOY LIKE THIS...
...BE SERIOUS.
WHAT WOULD I BE LIKE IN LOVE?
I'M A LITTLE INTERESTED...
...AND A LITTLE SCARED.

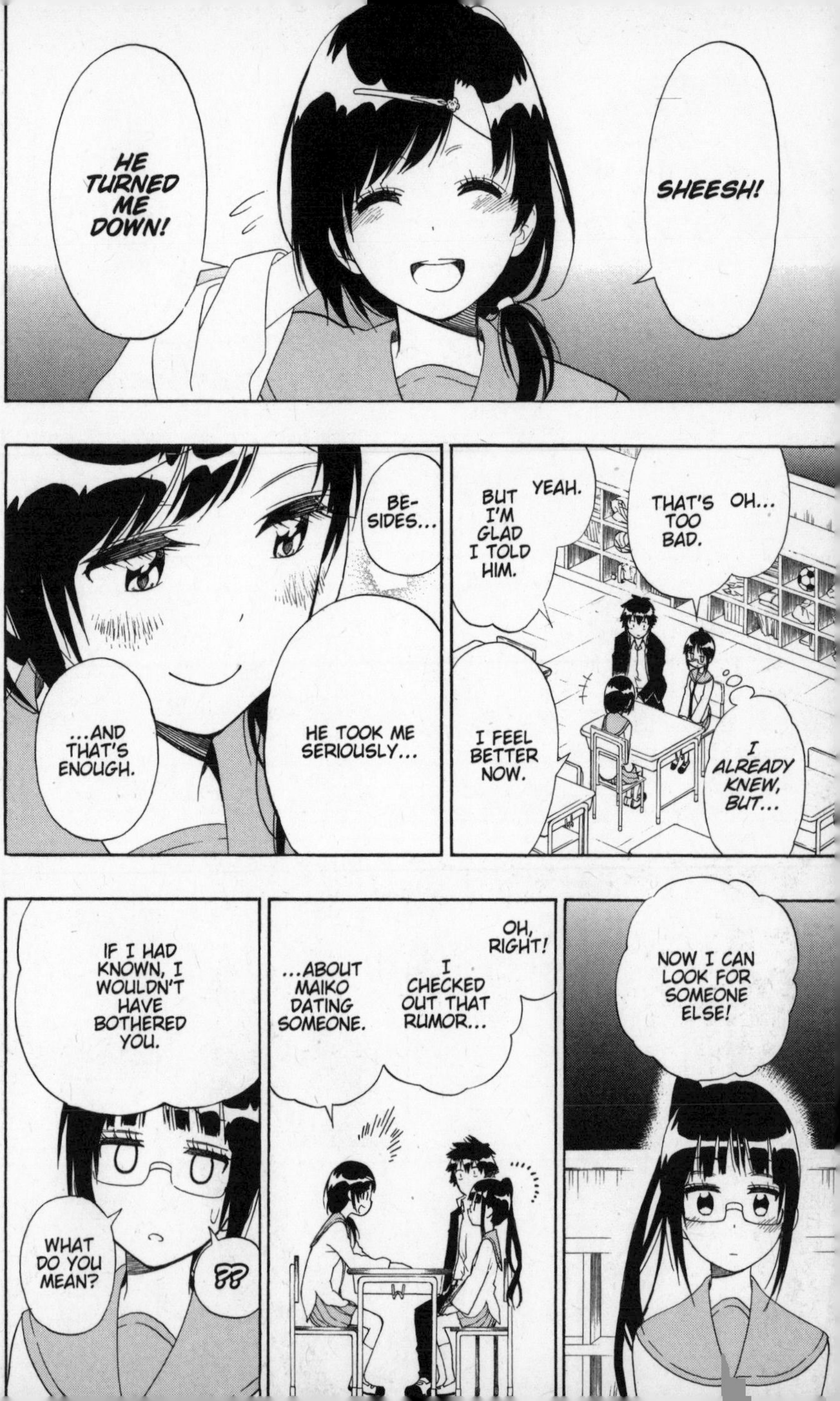
SHEESH!
HE TURNED ME DOWN!
OH... THAT'S TOO BAD.
YEAH. BUT I'M GLAD I TOLD HIM.
I ALREADY KNEW, BUT...
I FEEL BETTER NOW.
BE-SIDES...
HE TOOK ME SERIOUSLY...
...AND THAT'S ENOUGH.
NOW I CAN LOOK FOR SOMEONE ELSE!
OH, RIGHT!
I CHECKED OUT THAT RUMOR...
...ABOUT MAIKO DATING SOMEONE.
IF I HAD KNOWN, I WOULDN'T HAVE BOTHERED YOU.
WHAT DO YOU MEAN?
??

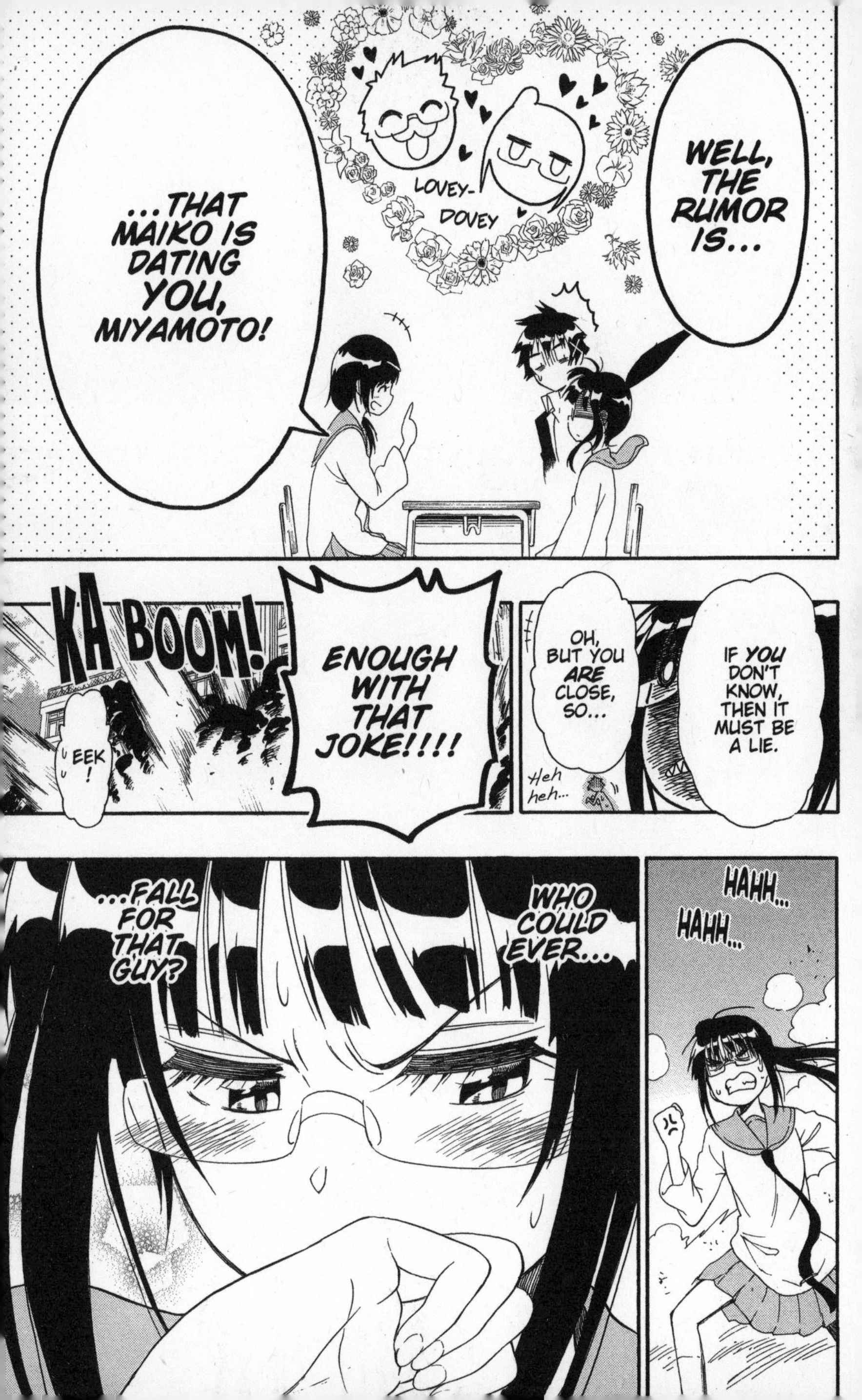
WELL, THE RUMOR IS...
LOVEY-DOVEY
...THAT MAIKO IS DATING YOU, MIYAMOTO!
IF YOU DON'T KNOW, THEN IT MUST BE A LIE.
OH, BUT YOU ARE CLOSE, SO...
Heh heh...
ENOUGH WITH THAT JOKE!!!!
KA BOOM!
EEK!
HAHH... HAHH...
WHO COULD EVER...
...FALL FOR THAT GUY?

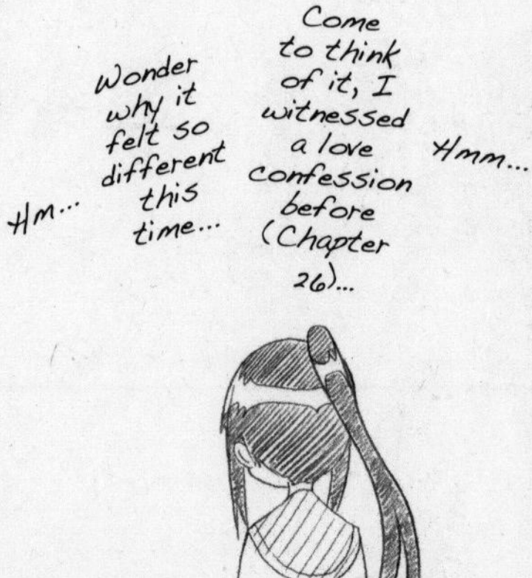

Hmm...
Come to think of it, I witnessed a love confession before (Chapter 26)...
Wonder why it felt so different this time...
Hm...

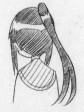

Last Will and Testament

Chapter 142: Animals

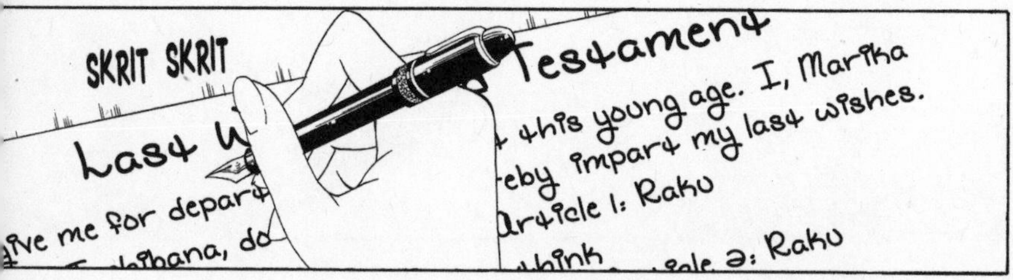
SKRIT SKRIT
Testament
this young age. I, Marika
impart my last wishes.
Last W
give me for depart
Article 1: Raku
Tachibana, do
Article 2: Raku

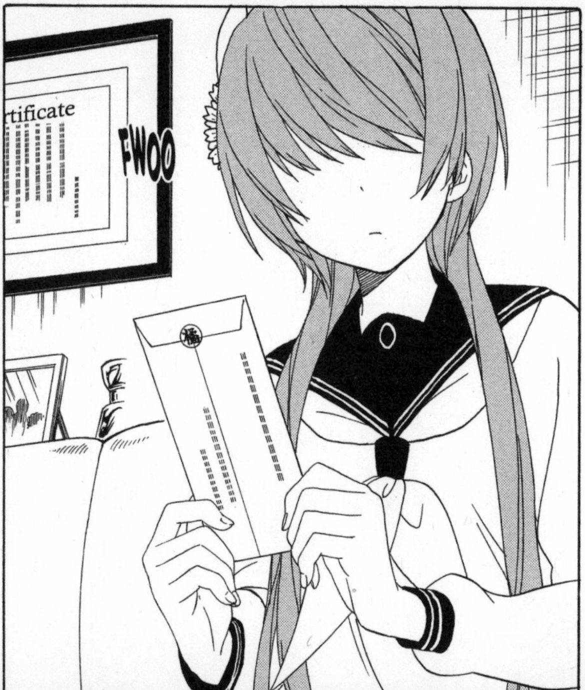
rtificate
FWOO

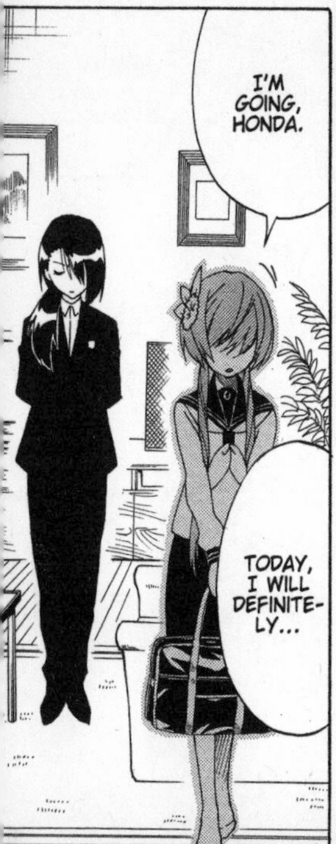
I'M GOING, HONDA.
TODAY, I WILL DEFINITE-LY...

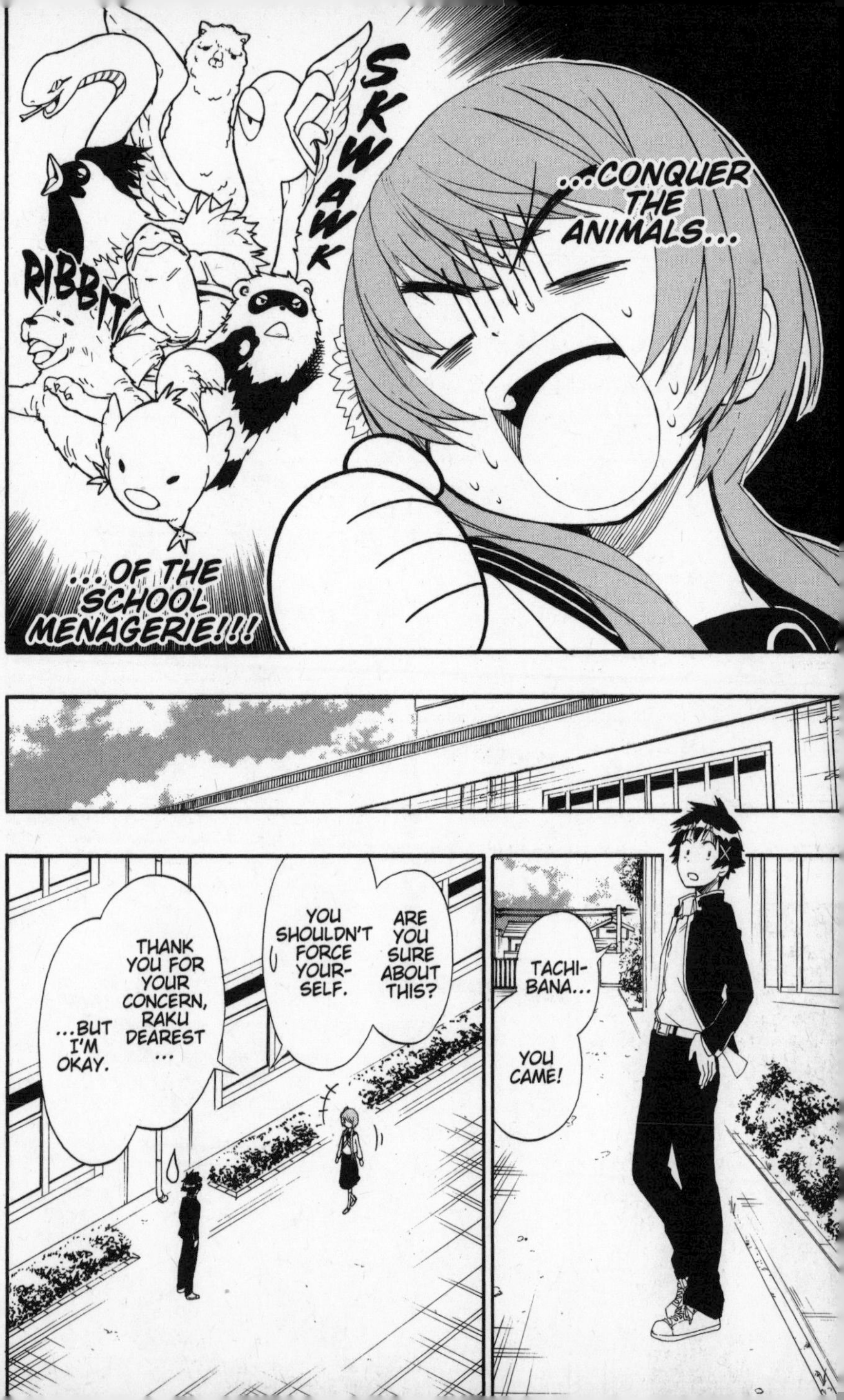
...CONQUER THE ANIMALS...
SKWAWK
RIBBIT
...OF THE SCHOOL MENAGERIE!!!
TACHIBANA...
YOU CAME!
ARE YOU SURE ABOUT THIS?
YOU SHOULDN'T FORCE YOURSELF.
THANK YOU FOR YOUR CONCERN, RAKU DEAREST...
...BUT I'M OKAY.

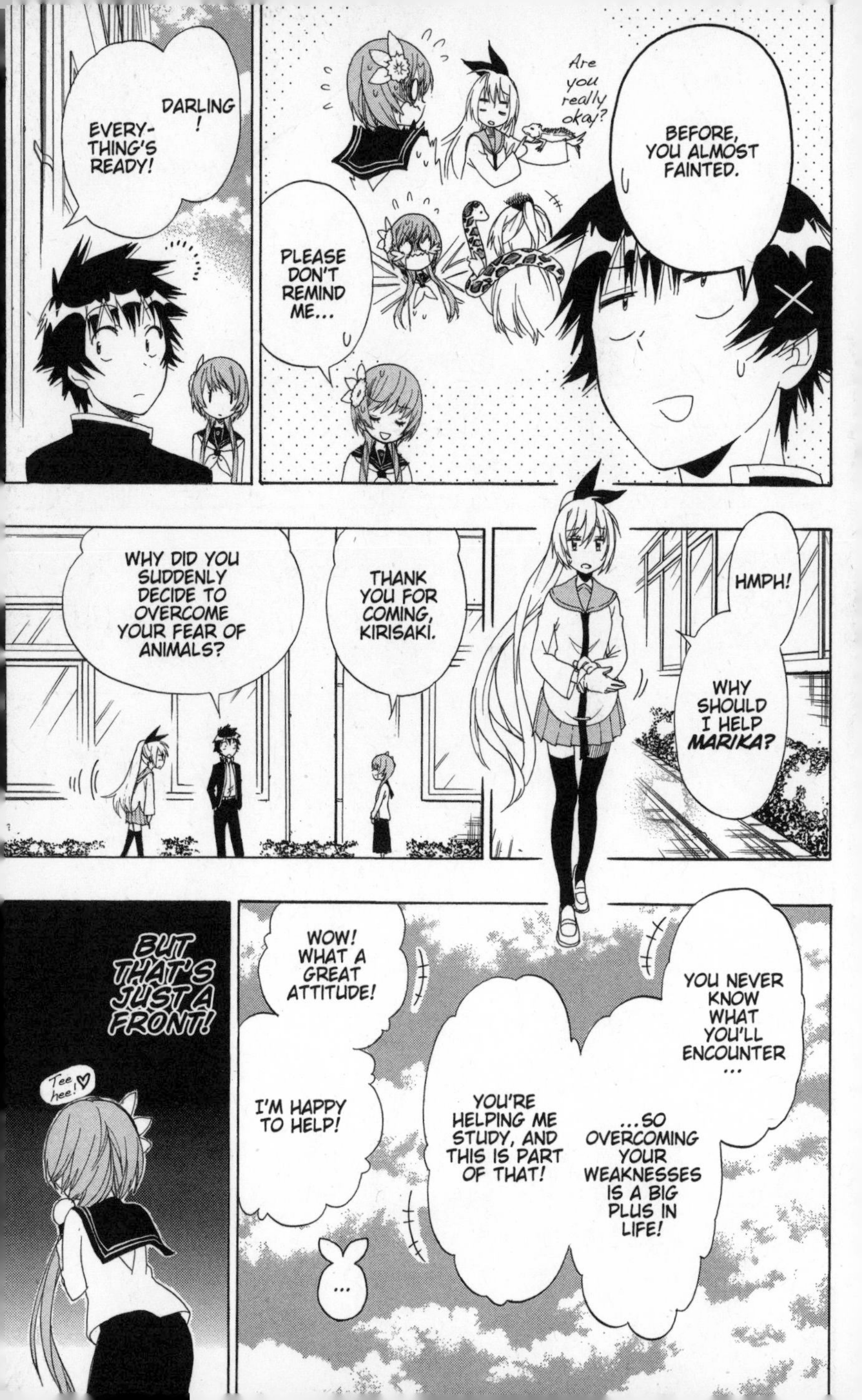
BEFORE, YOU ALMOST FAINTED.
Are you really okay?
PLEASE DON'T REMIND ME...
DARLING!
EVERY-THING'S READY!
HMPH!
WHY SHOULD I HELP *MARIKA*?
THANK YOU FOR COMING, KIRISAKI.
WHY DID YOU SUDDENLY DECIDE TO OVERCOME YOUR FEAR OF ANIMALS?
YOU NEVER KNOW WHAT YOU'LL ENCOUNTER...
...SO OVERCOMING YOUR WEAKNESSES IS A BIG PLUS IN LIFE!
WOW! WHAT A GREAT ATTITUDE!
YOU'RE HELPING ME STUDY, AND THIS IS PART OF THAT!
I'M HAPPY TO HELP!
...
BUT THAT'S JUST A FRONT!
Tee hee!♥

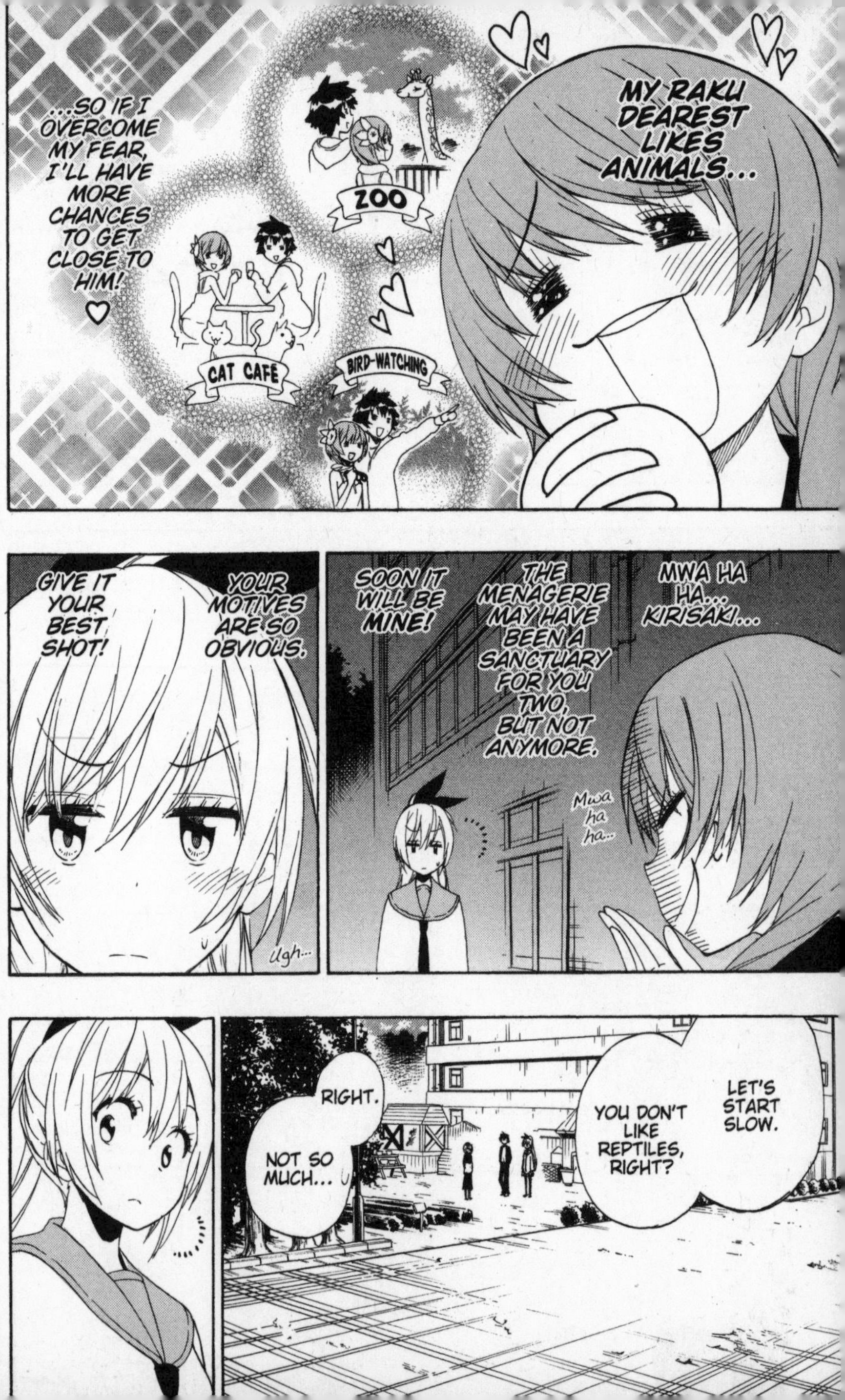
MY RAKU DEAREST LIKES ANIMALS...
ZOO
CAT CAFÉ
BIRD-WATCHING
...SO IF I OVERCOME MY FEAR, I'LL HAVE MORE CHANCES TO GET CLOSE TO HIM! ♡
MWA HA HA... KIRISAKI...
THE MENAGERIE MAY HAVE BEEN A SANCTUARY FOR YOU TWO, BUT NOT ANYMORE.
SOON IT WILL BE MINE!
Mwa ha ha...
YOUR MOTIVES ARE SO OBVIOUS.
GIVE IT YOUR BEST SHOT!
Ugh...
LET'S START SLOW.
YOU DON'T LIKE REPTILES, RIGHT?
RIGHT.
NOT SO MUCH...

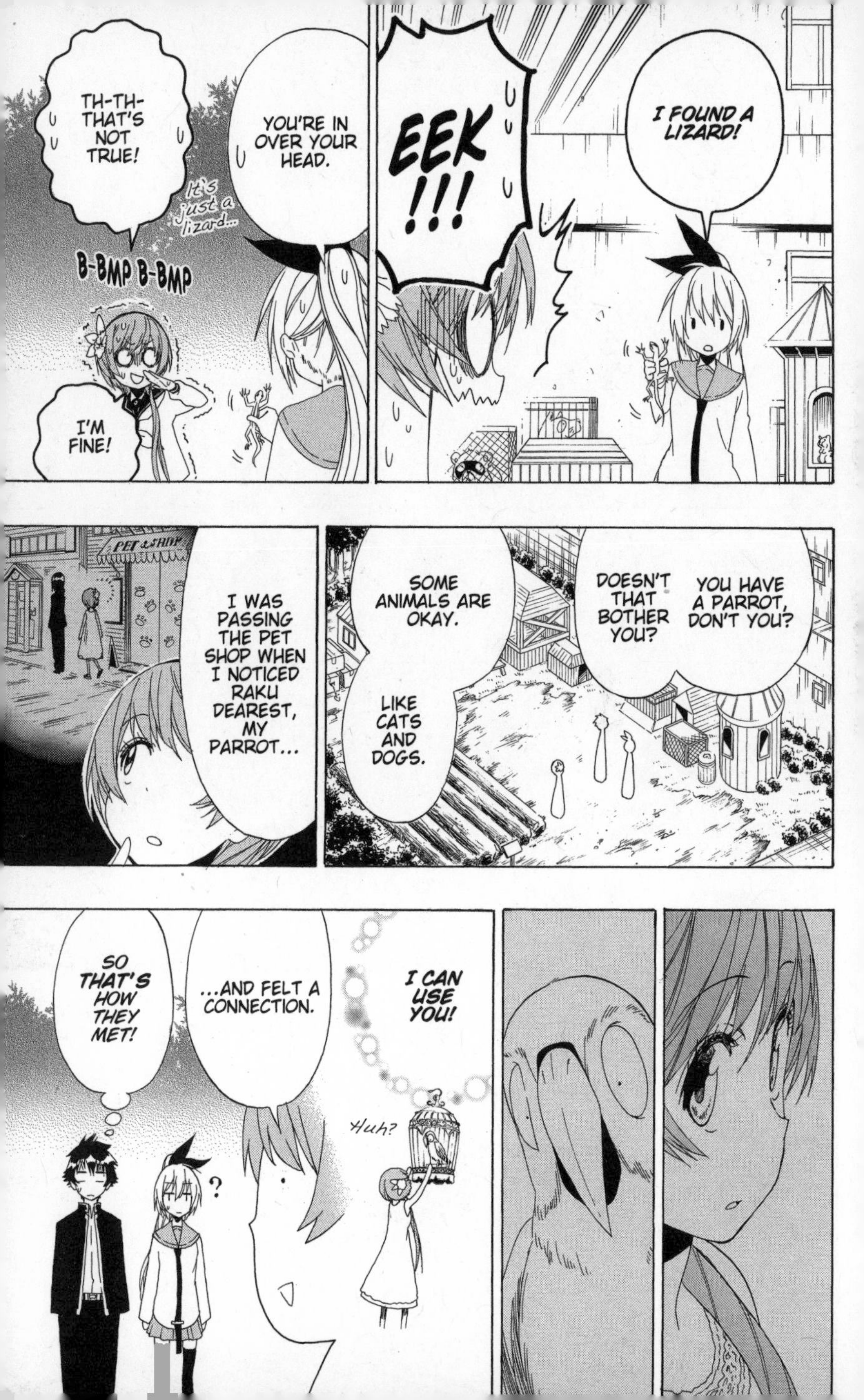
I FOUND A LIZARD!
EEK!!!
YOU'RE IN OVER YOUR HEAD.
TH-TH-THAT'S NOT TRUE!
It's just a lizard...
B-BMP B-BMP
I'M FINE!
YOU HAVE A PARROT, DON'T YOU?
DOESN'T THAT BOTHER YOU?
SOME ANIMALS ARE OKAY.
LIKE CATS AND DOGS.
PET SHOP
I WAS PASSING THE PET SHOP WHEN I NOTICED RAKU DEAREST, MY PARROT...
I CAN USE YOU!
...AND FELT A CONNECTION.
SO THAT'S HOW THEY MET!
Huh?

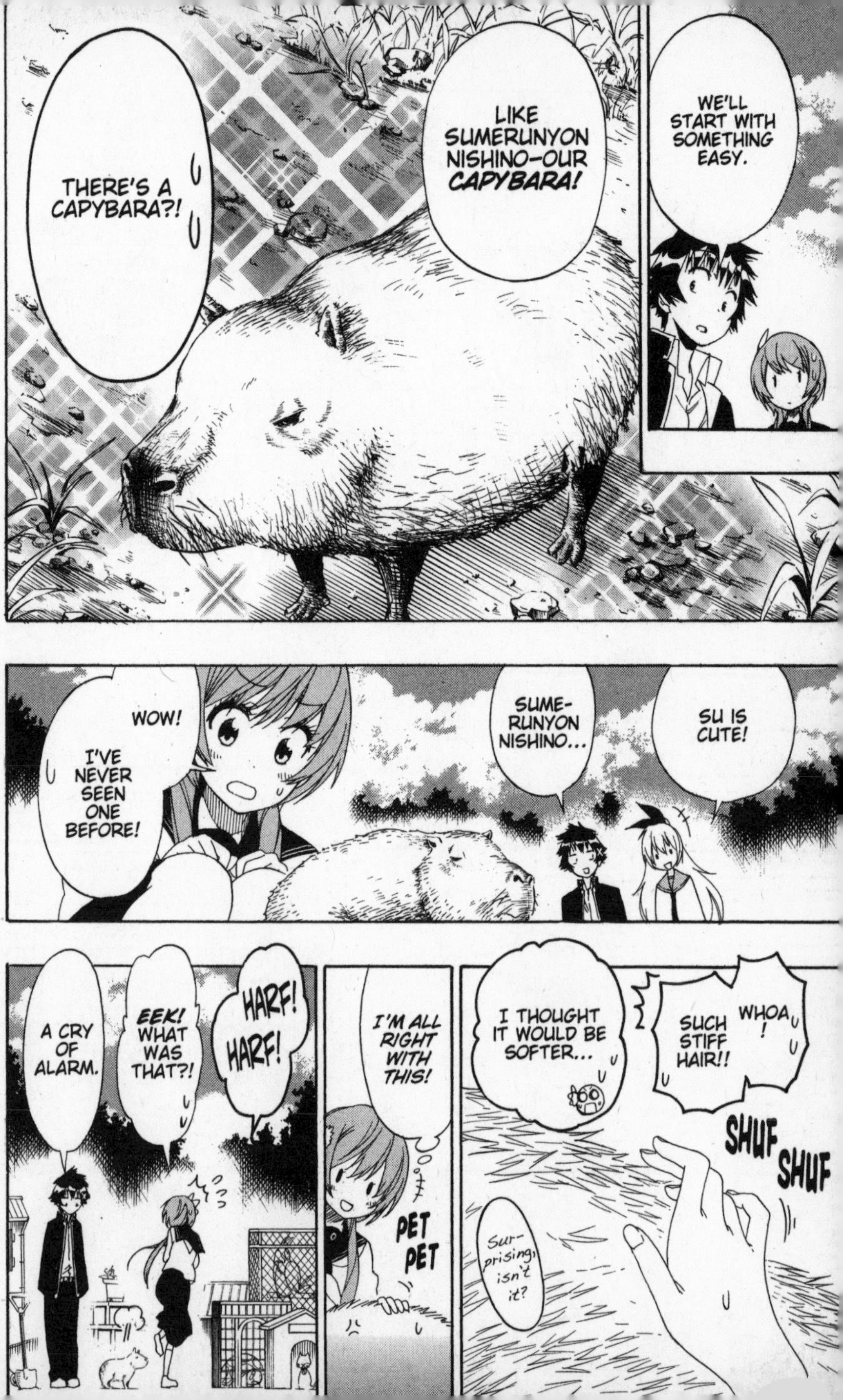
WE'LL START WITH SOMETHING EASY.
LIKE SUMERUNYON NISHINO—OUR CAPYBARA!
THERE'S A CAPYBARA?!
SU IS CUTE!
SUME-RUNYON NISHINO...
WOW!
I'VE NEVER SEEN ONE BEFORE!
WHOA!
SUCH STIFF HAIR!!
SHUF SHUF
I THOUGHT IT WOULD BE SOFTER...
Surprising, isn't it?
I'M ALL RIGHT WITH THIS!
PET PET
HARF! HARF!
EEK! WHAT WAS THAT?!
A CRY OF ALARM.

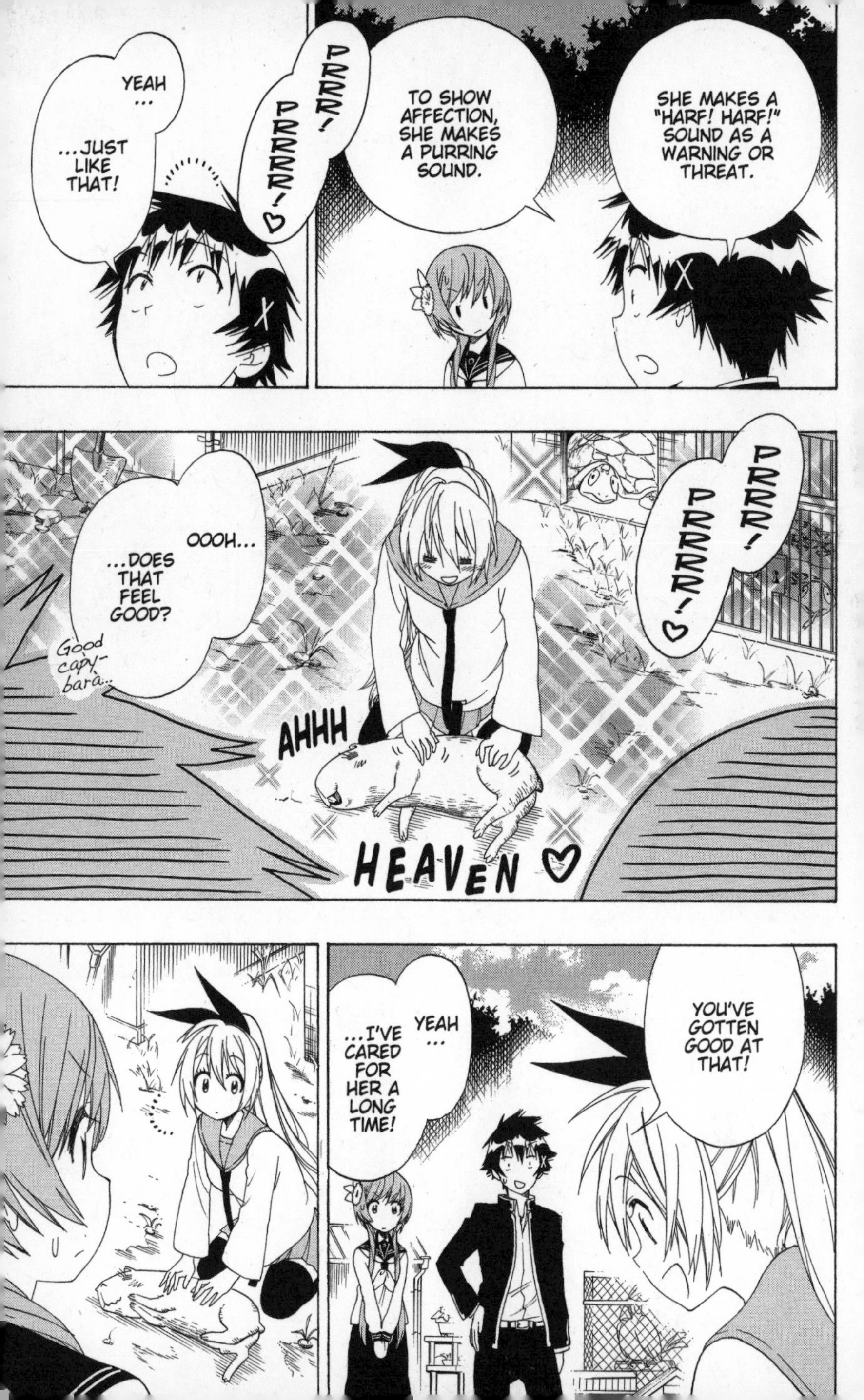
SHE MAKES A "HARF! HARF!" SOUND AS A WARNING OR THREAT.
TO SHOW AFFECTION, SHE MAKES A PURRING SOUND.
PRRR! PRRRR! ♡
YEAH ...
...JUST LIKE THAT!
PRRR! PRRRR! ♡
OOOH...
...DOES THAT FEEL GOOD?
Good capy-bara...
AHHH
HEAVEN ♡
YOU'VE GOTTEN GOOD AT THAT!
YEAH ...
...I'VE CARED FOR HER A LONG TIME!

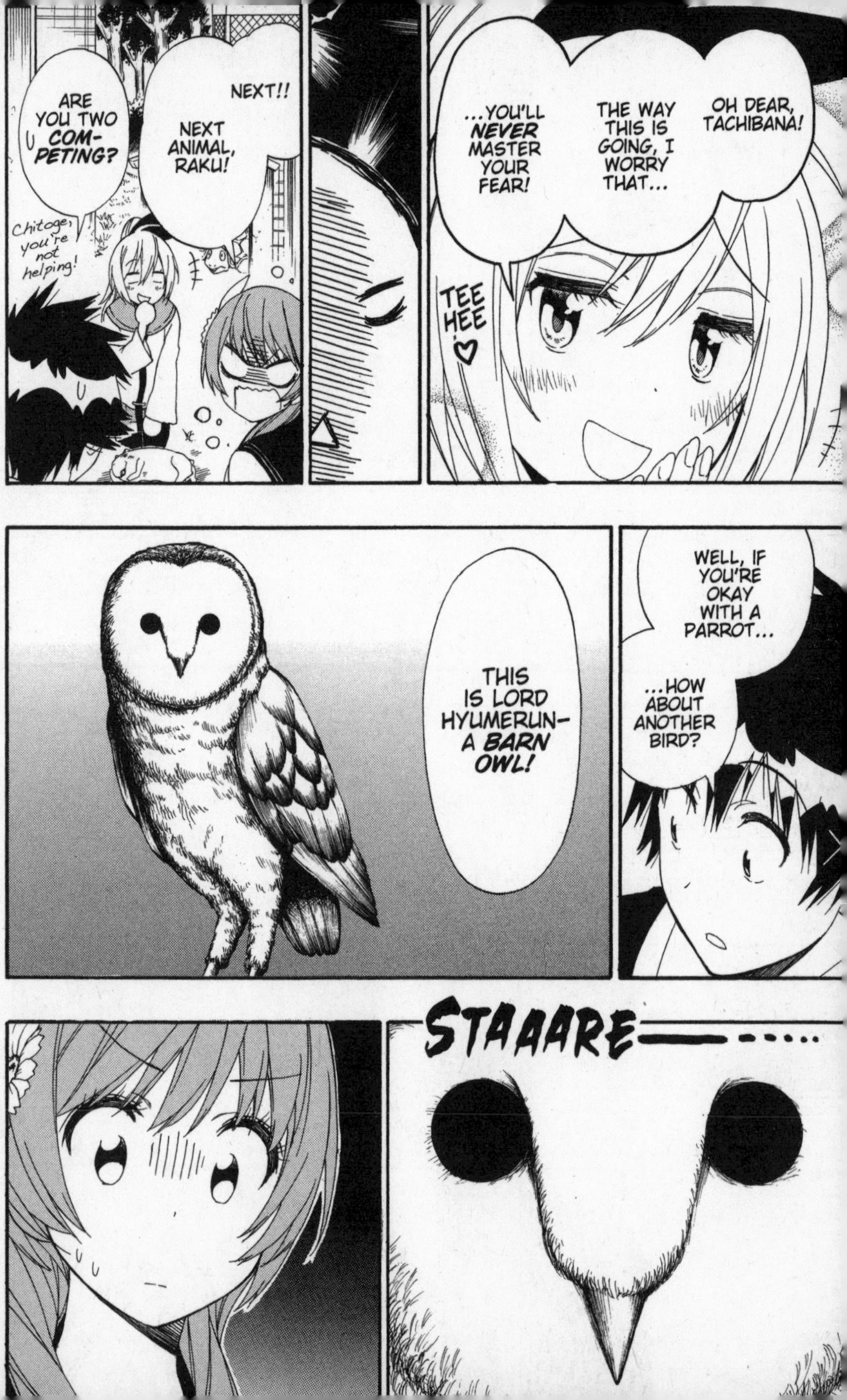
OH DEAR, TACHIBANA!
THE WAY THIS IS GOING, I WORRY THAT...
...YOU'LL NEVER MASTER YOUR FEAR!
TEE HEE ♥
NEXT!!
NEXT ANIMAL, RAKU!
ARE YOU TWO COMPETING?
Chitoge, you're not helping!
WELL, IF YOU'RE OKAY WITH A PARROT...
...HOW ABOUT ANOTHER BIRD?
THIS IS LORD HYUMERUN- A BARN OWL!
STAAARE——-...

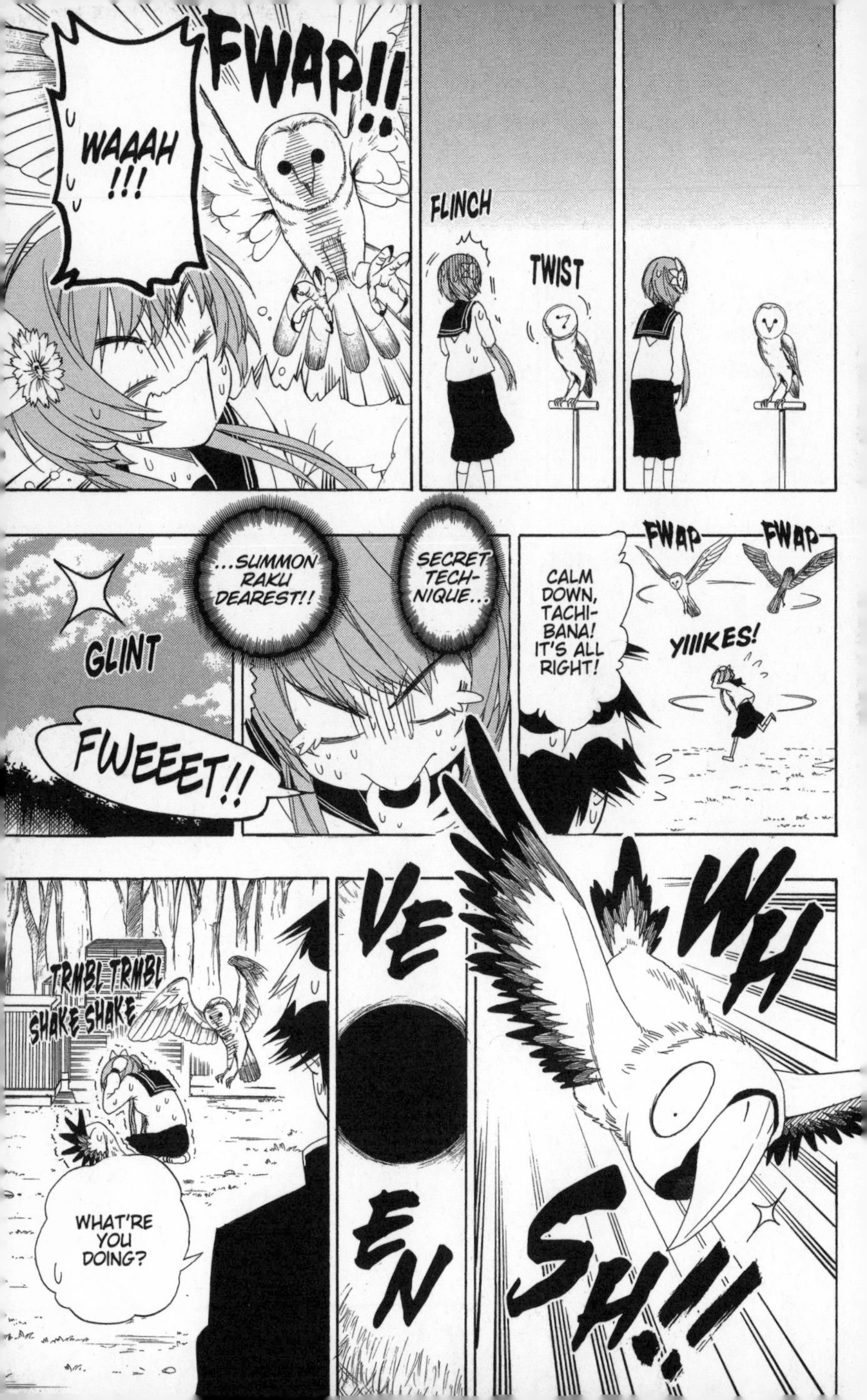
FLINCH
TWIST
WAAAH !!!
FWAP!!
FWAP
FWAP
CALM DOWN, TACHI-BANA! IT'S ALL RIGHT!
YIIIKES!
SECRET TECH-NIQUE...
...SUMMON RAKU DEAREST!!
GLINT
FWEEET!!
WH
SH!!
VE
EN
TRMBL TRMBL
SHAKE SHAKE
WHAT'RE YOU DOING?

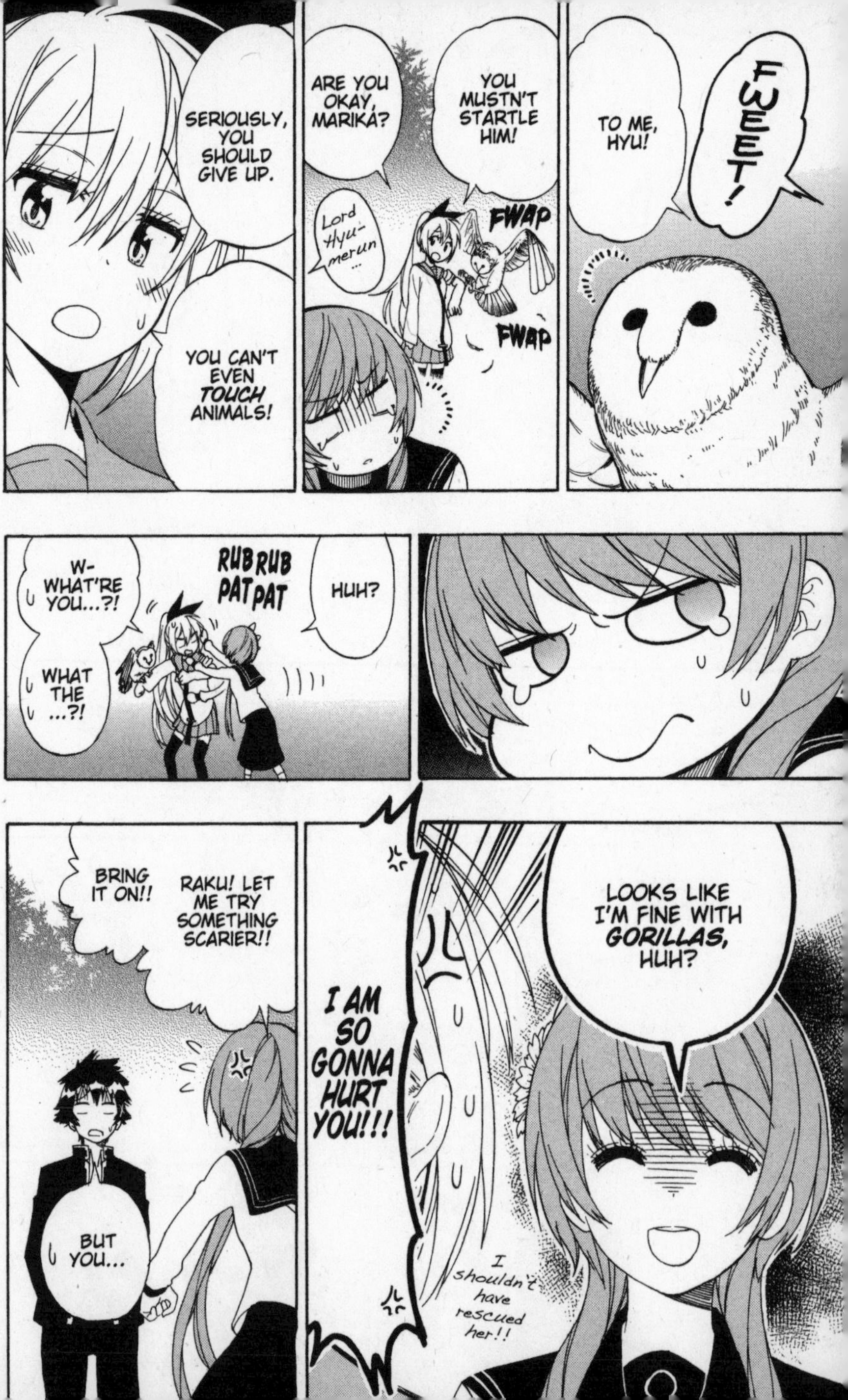

FWEET!
TO ME, HYU!
YOU MUSTN'T STARTLE HIM!
ARE YOU OKAY, MARIKA?
FWAP
Lord Hyu-merun...
FWAP
SERIOUSLY, YOU SHOULD GIVE UP.
YOU CAN'T EVEN TOUCH ANIMALS!
HUH?
RUB RUB PAT PAT
W-WHAT'RE YOU...?!
WHAT THE...?!
LOOKS LIKE I'M FINE WITH GORILLAS, HUH?
I AM SO GONNA HURT YOU!!!
I shouldn't have rescued her!!
RAKU! LET ME TRY SOMETHING SCARIER!!
BRING IT ON!!
BUT YOU...

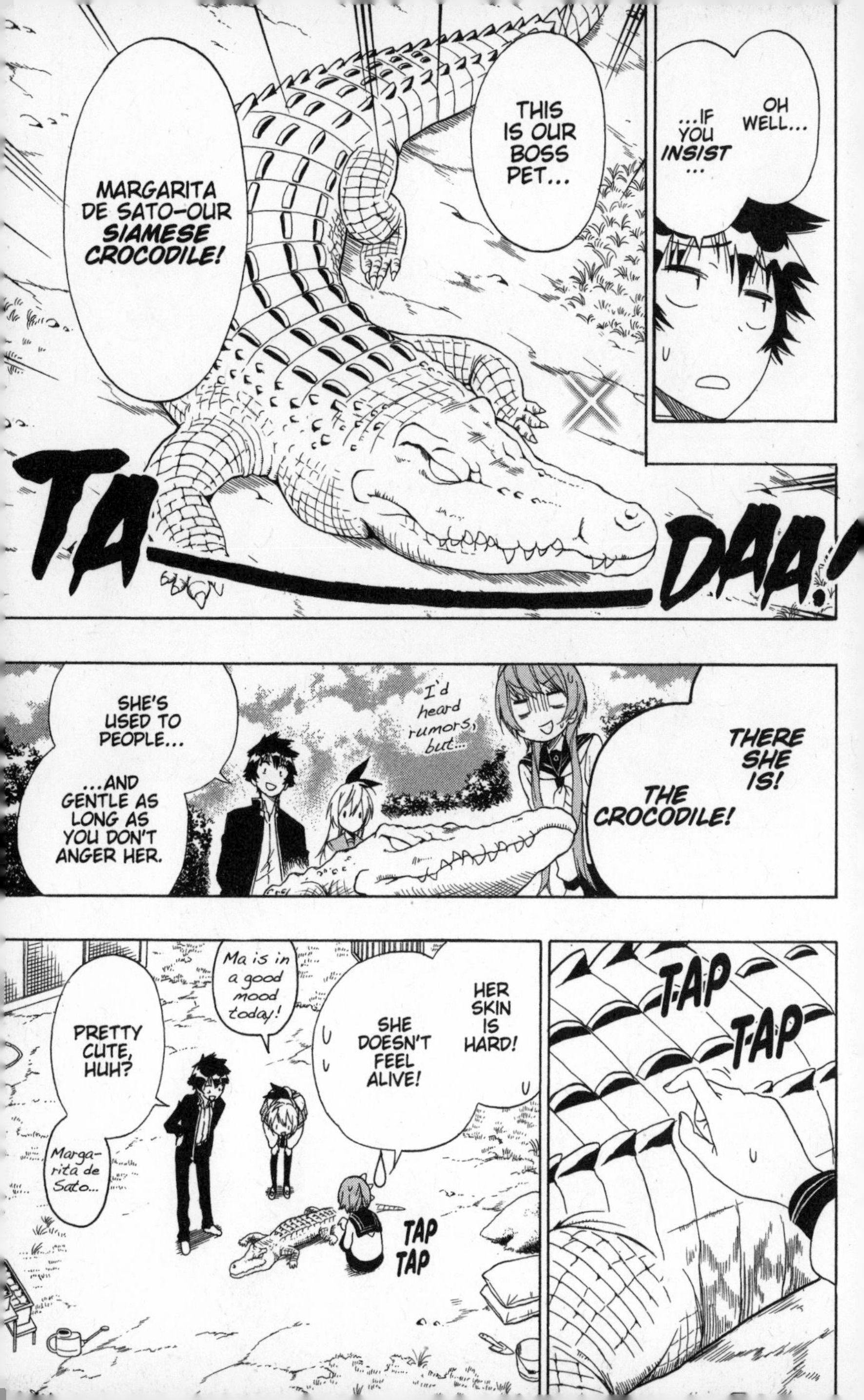
OH WELL...
...IF YOU INSIST...
THIS IS OUR BOSS PET...
MARGARITA DE SATO—OUR SIAMESE CROCODILE!
TA—DAA!
THERE SHE IS!
THE CROCODILE!
I'd heard rumors, but...
SHE'S USED TO PEOPLE...
...AND GENTLE AS LONG AS YOU DON'T ANGER HER.
TAP TAP
HER SKIN IS HARD!
SHE DOESN'T FEEL ALIVE!
TAP TAP
Ma is in a good mood today!
PRETTY CUTE, HUH?
Marga-rita de Sato...

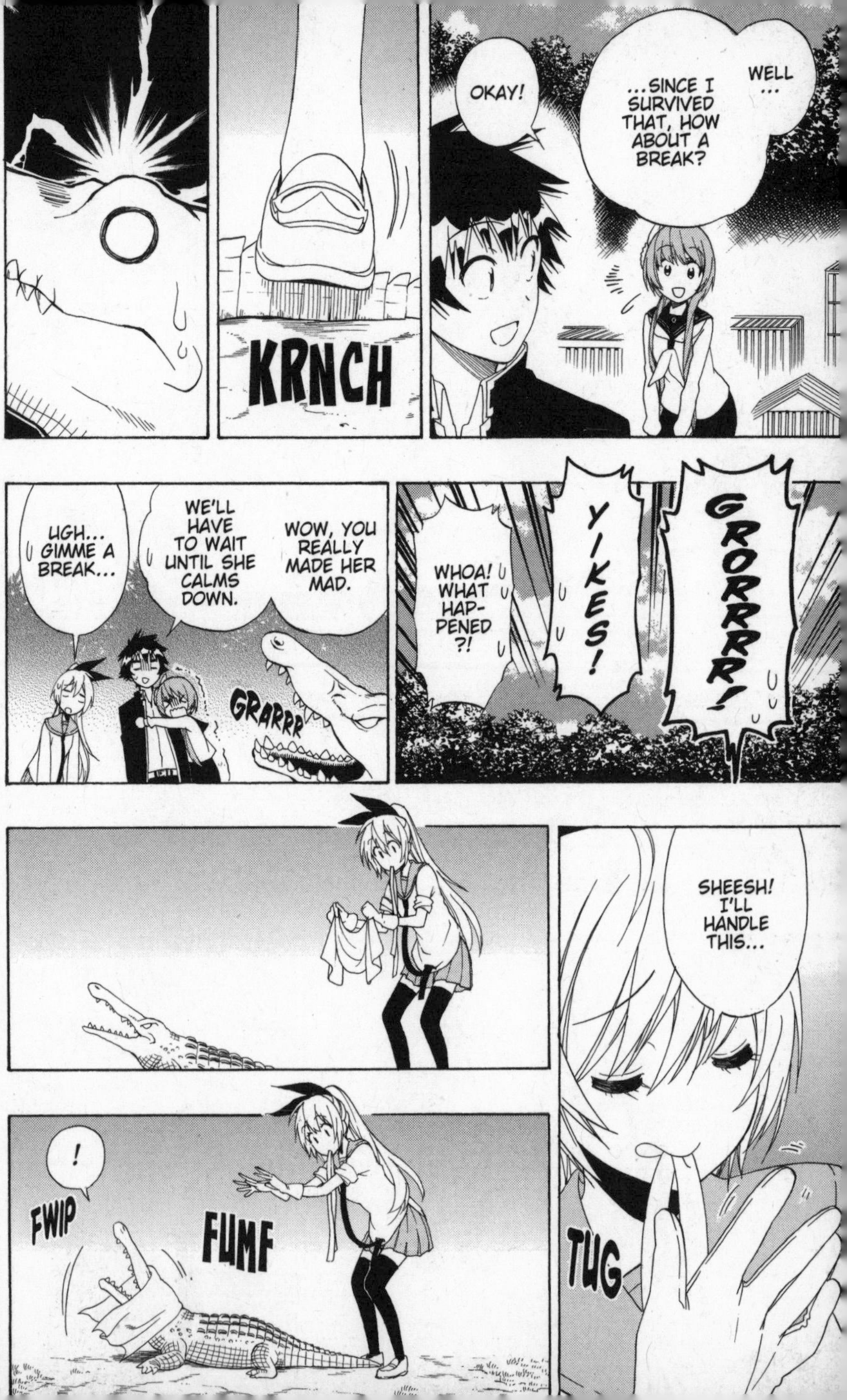
WELL...
...SINCE I SURVIVED THAT, HOW ABOUT A BREAK?
OKAY!
KRNCH
GRORRRR!
YIKES!
WHOA! WHAT HAP-PENED?!
WOW, YOU REALLY MADE HER MAD.
WE'LL HAVE TO WAIT UNTIL SHE CALMS DOWN.
UGH... GIMME A BREAK...
GRARRR
SHEESH! I'LL HANDLE THIS...
TUG
!
FWIP
FUMF

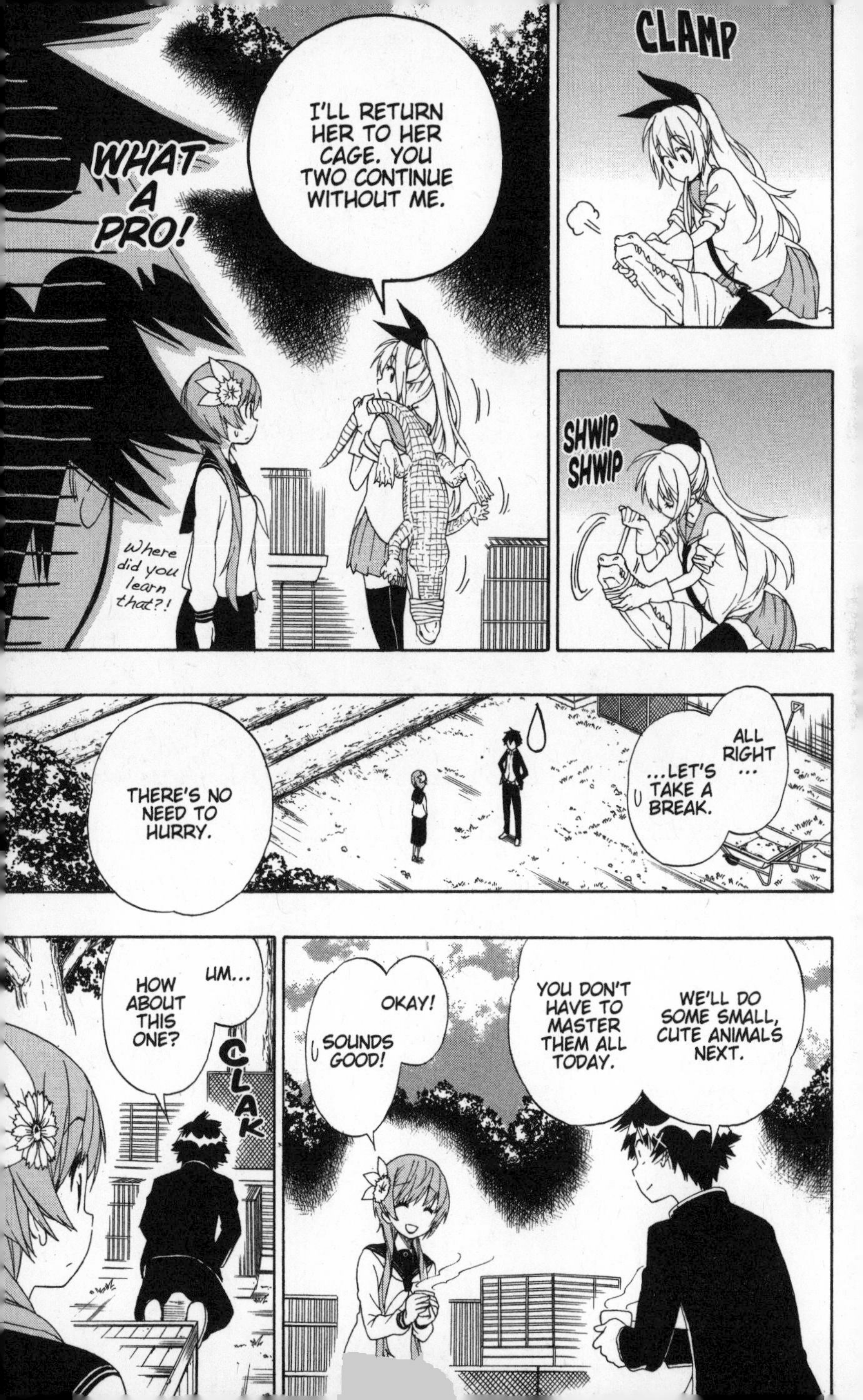
CLAMP
SHWIP SHWIP
I'LL RETURN HER TO HER CAGE. YOU TWO CONTINUE WITHOUT ME.
WHAT A PRO!
Where did you learn that?!
ALL RIGHT... ...LET'S TAKE A BREAK.
THERE'S NO NEED TO HURRY.
WE'LL DO SOME SMALL, CUTE ANIMALS NEXT.
YOU DON'T HAVE TO MASTER THEM ALL TODAY.
OKAY! SOUNDS GOOD!
UM... HOW ABOUT THIS ONE?
CLAK

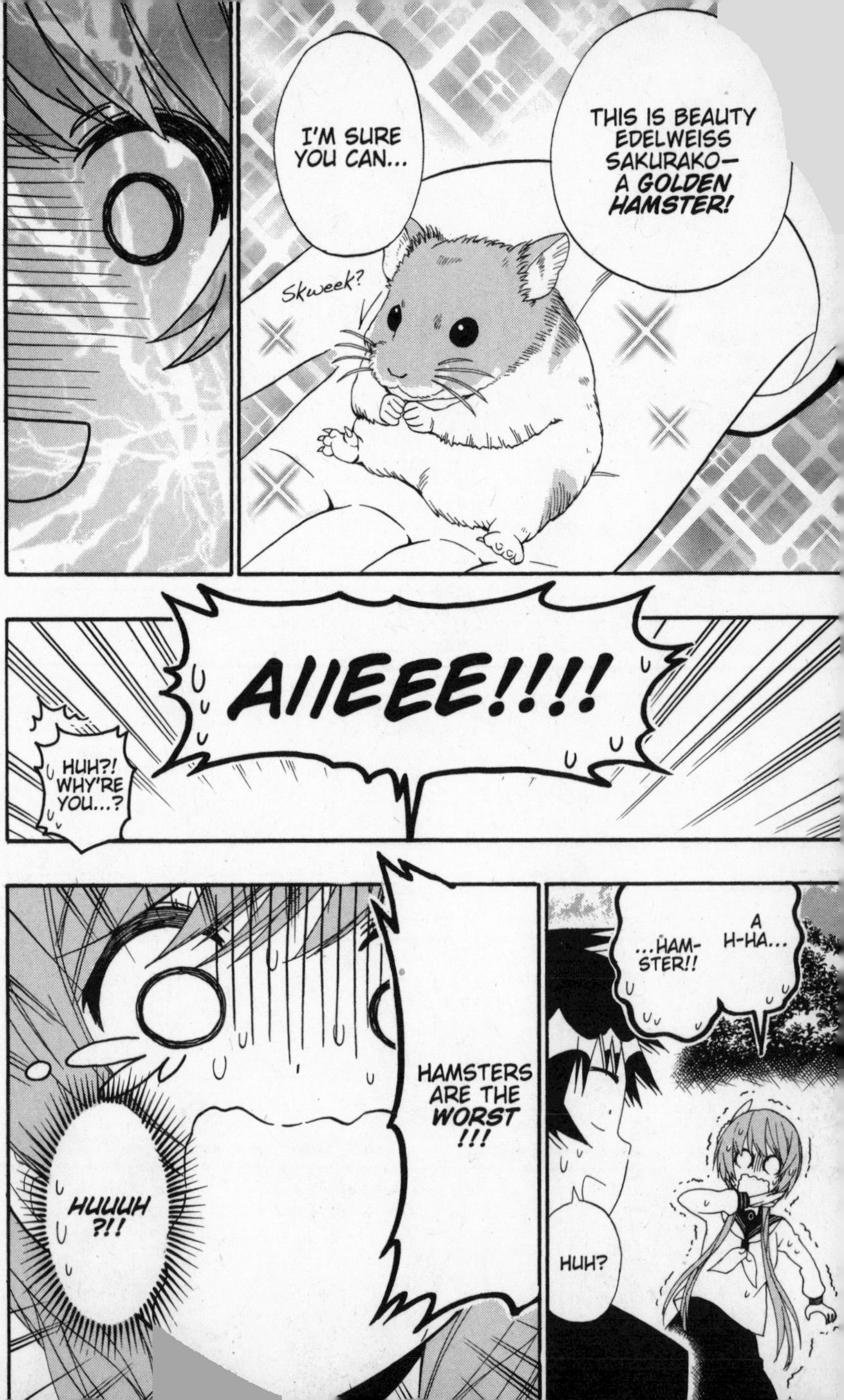
THIS IS BEAUTY EDELWEISS SAKURAKO— A GOLDEN HAMSTER!
I'M SURE YOU CAN...
Skweek?
AIIEEE!!!!
HUH?! WHY'RE YOU...?
A H-HA...
...HAM-STER!!
HUH?
HAMSTERS ARE THE WORST!!!
HUUUH?!!

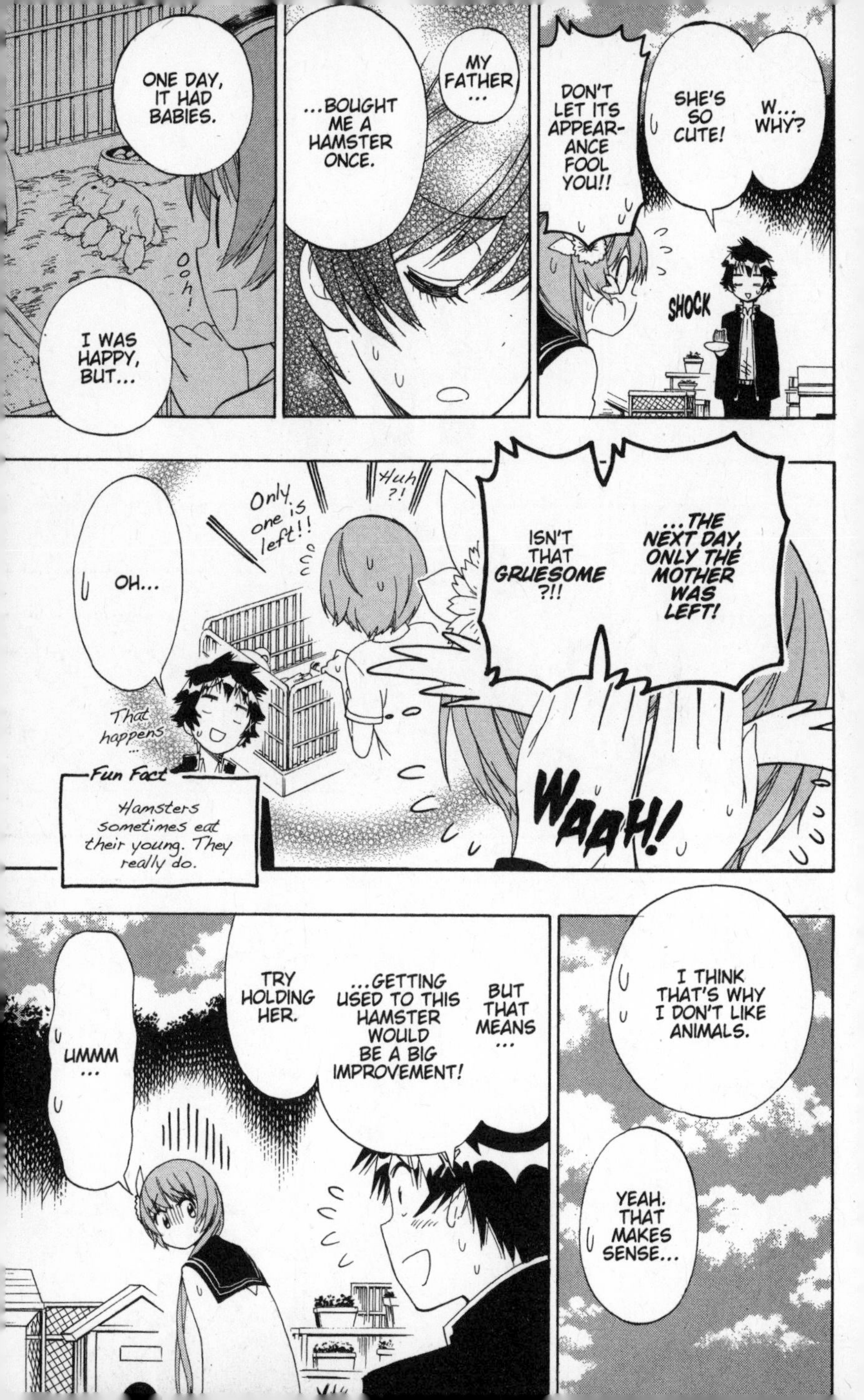
W... WHY?
SHE'S SO CUTE!
DON'T LET ITS APPEARANCE FOOL YOU!!
SHOCK
MY FATHER...
...BOUGHT ME A HAMSTER ONCE.
ONE DAY, IT HAD BABIES.
Ooh!
I WAS HAPPY, BUT...
...THE NEXT DAY, ONLY THE MOTHER WAS LEFT!
ISN'T THAT GRUESOME?!!
WAAH!
Huh?!
Only one is left!!
OH...
That happens...
Fun Fact
Hamsters sometimes eat their young. They really do.
I THINK THAT'S WHY I DON'T LIKE ANIMALS.
YEAH. THAT MAKES SENSE...
BUT THAT MEANS...
...GETTING USED TO THIS HAMSTER WOULD BE A BIG IMPROVEMENT!
TRY HOLDING HER.
UMMM...

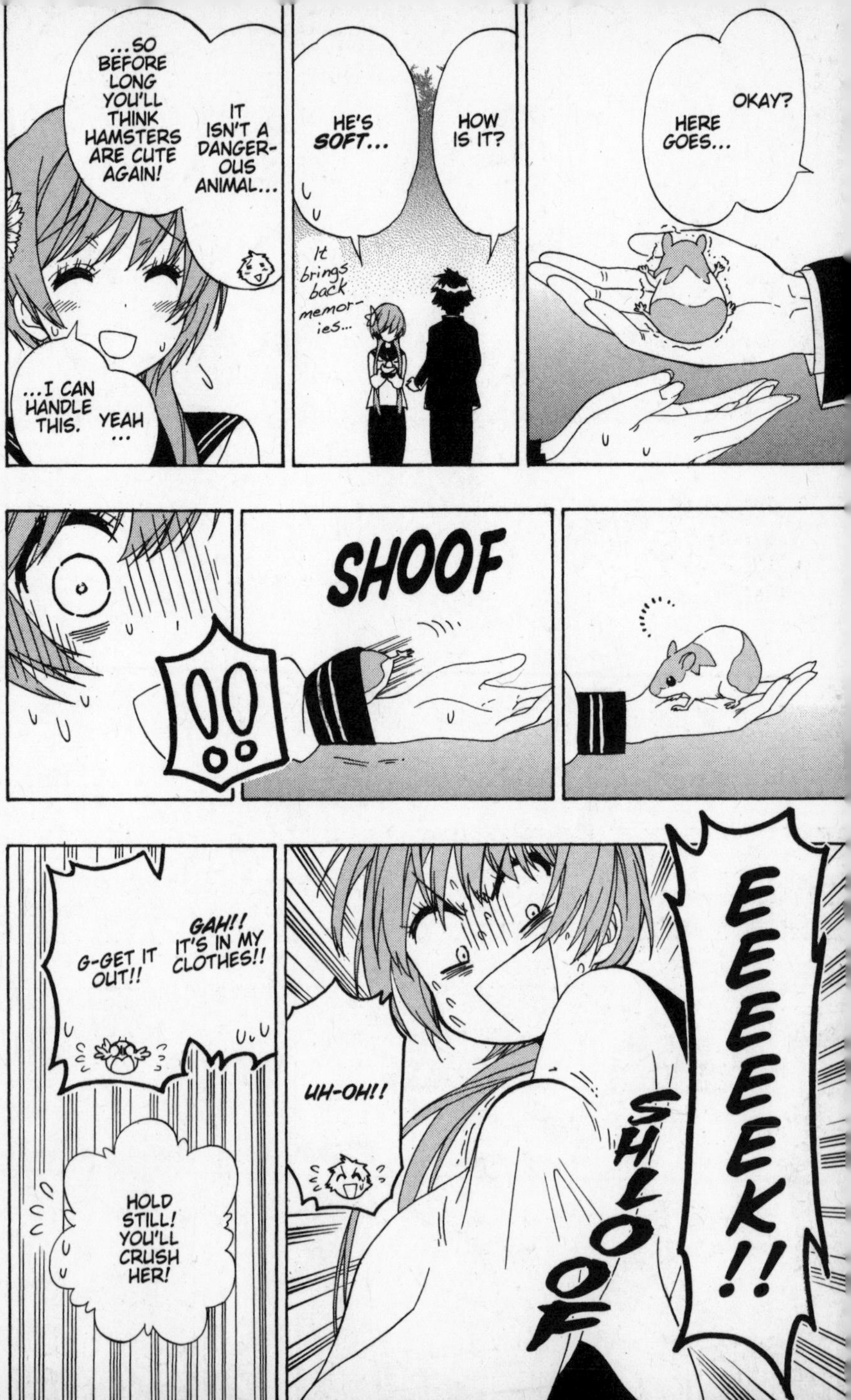
OKAY? HERE GOES...
HOW IS IT?
HE'S SOFT...
It brings back memories...
IT ISN'T A DANGEROUS ANIMAL...
...SO BEFORE LONG YOU'LL THINK HAMSTERS ARE CUTE AGAIN!
...I CAN HANDLE THIS. YEAH...
SHOOF
!!
EEEEEEK!!
SHLOOF
UH-OH!!
GAH!! IT'S IN MY CLOTHES!!
G-GET IT OUT!!
HOLD STILL! YOU'LL CRUSH HER!

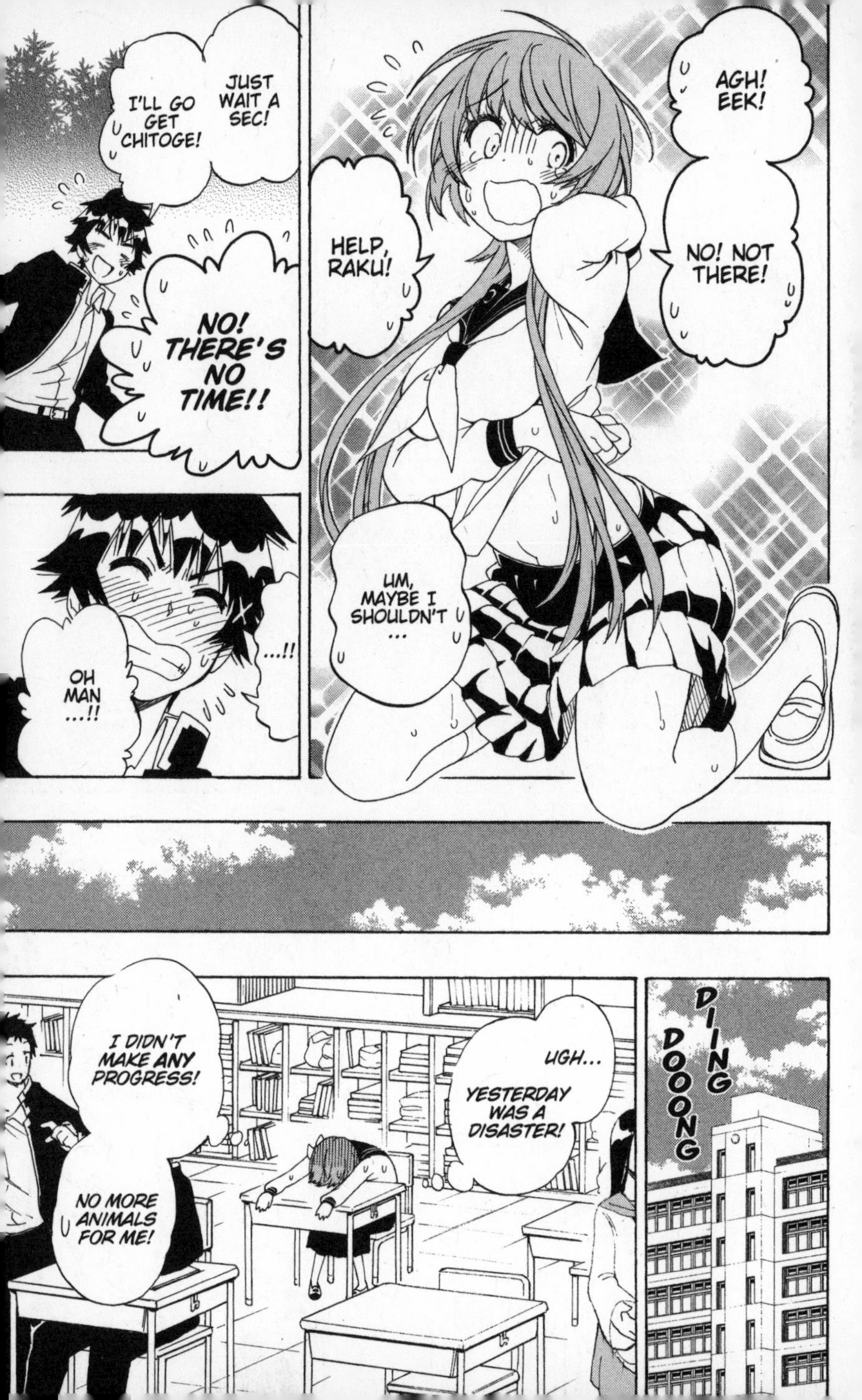
AGH! EEK!
NO! NOT THERE!
HELP, RAKU!
UM, MAYBE I SHOULDN'T ...
JUST WAIT A SEC!
I'LL GO GET CHITOGE!
NO! THERE'S NO TIME!!
...!!
OH MAN ...!!
DIIING DOOONG
UGH...
YESTERDAY WAS A DISASTER!
I DIDN'T MAKE ANY PROGRESS!
NO MORE ANIMALS FOR ME!

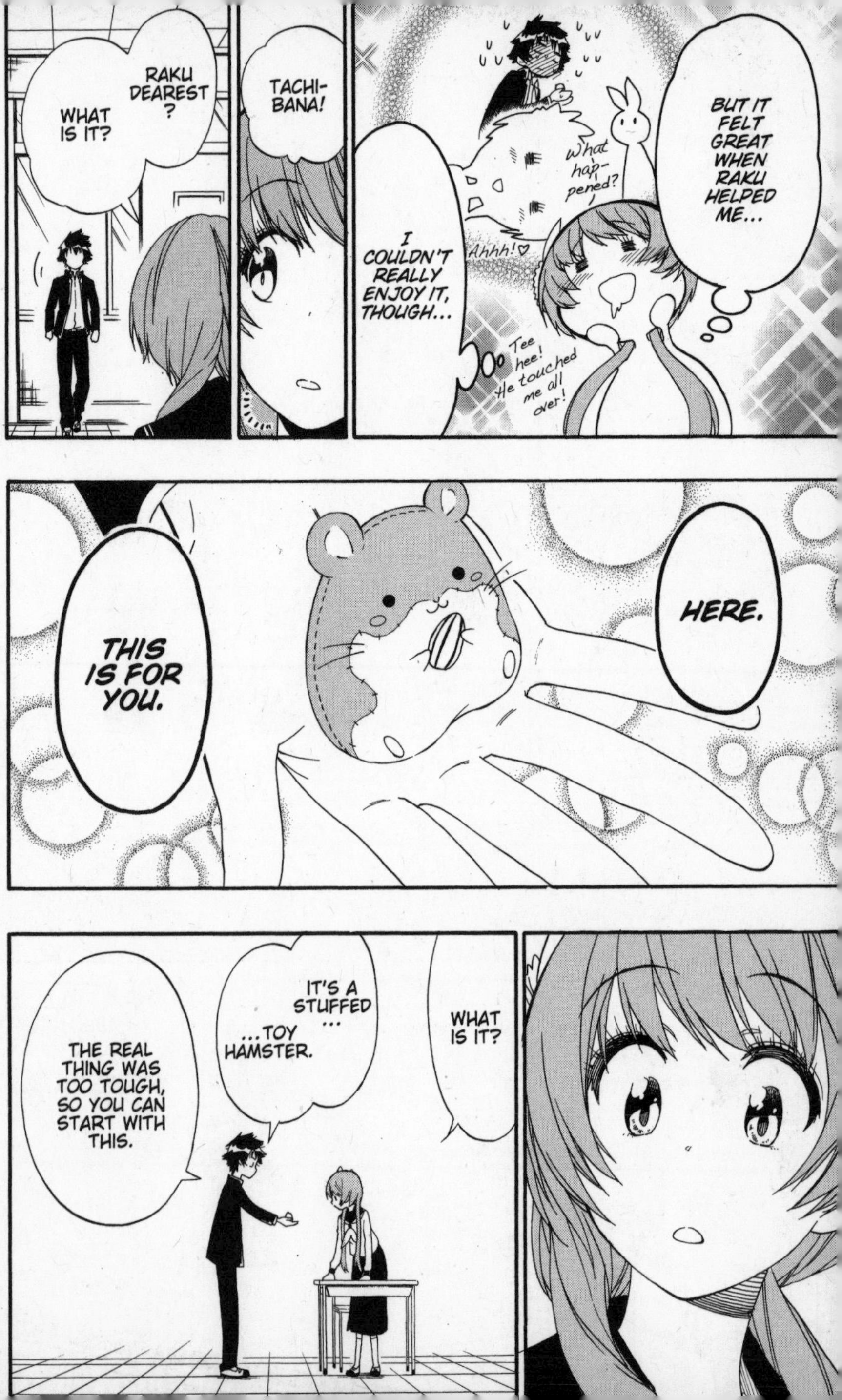
BUT IT FELT GREAT WHEN RAKU HELPED ME...
What hap-pened?
Ahhh!♡
I COULDN'T REALLY ENJOY IT, THOUGH...
Tee hee! He touched me all over!
TACHI-BANA!
RAKU DEAREST?
WHAT IS IT?
HERE.
THIS IS FOR YOU.
WHAT IS IT?
IT'S A STUFFED... ...TOY HAMSTER.
THE REAL THING WAS TOO TOUGH, SO YOU CAN START WITH THIS.

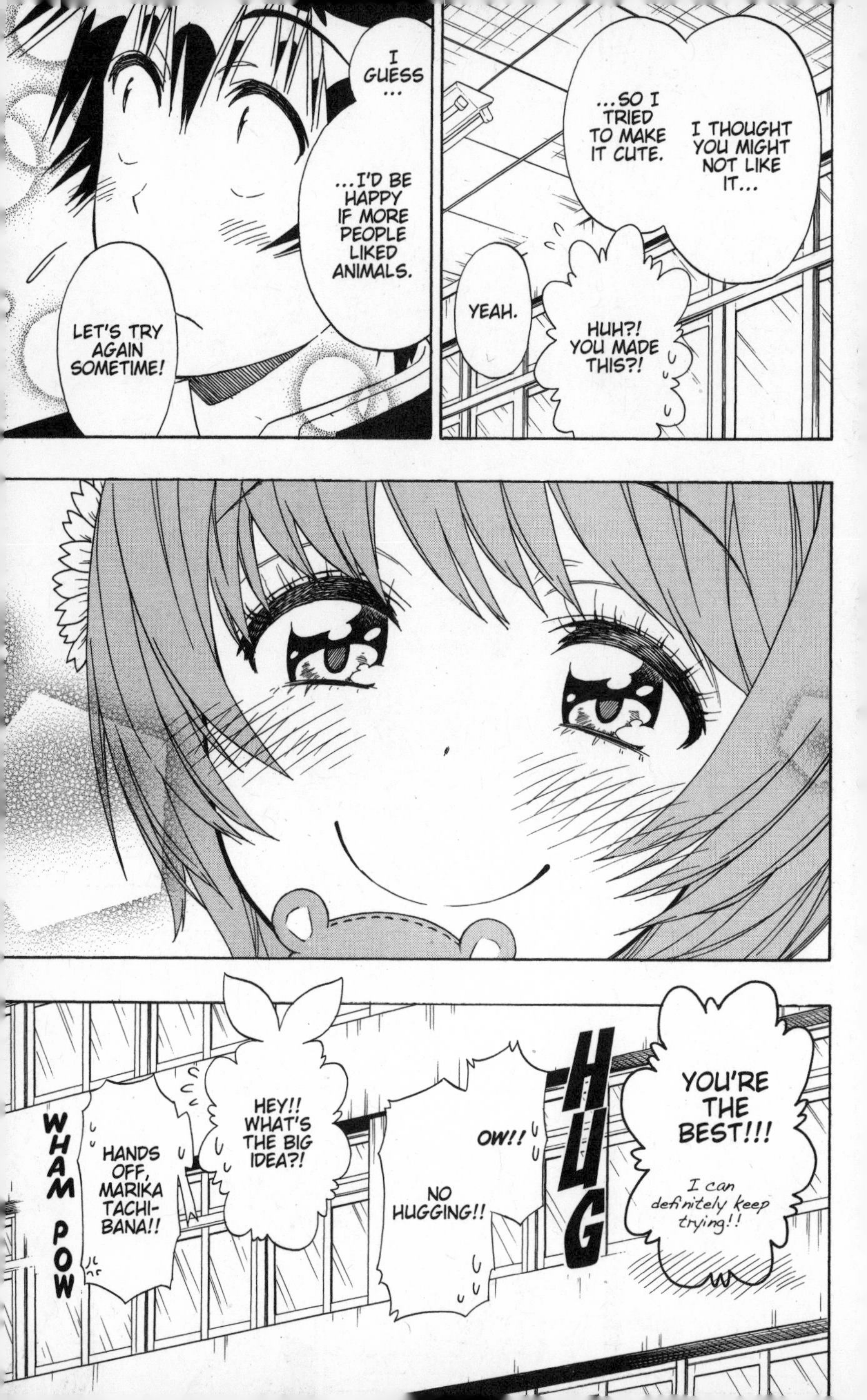
I THOUGHT YOU MIGHT NOT LIKE IT...
...SO I TRIED TO MAKE IT CUTE.
HUH?! YOU MADE THIS?!
YEAH.
I GUESS...
...I'D BE HAPPY IF MORE PEOPLE LIKED ANIMALS.
LET'S TRY AGAIN SOMETIME!
YOU'RE THE BEST!!!
I can definitely keep trying!!
HUG
OW!!
NO HUGGING!!
HEY!! WHAT'S THE BIG IDEA?!
HANDS OFF, MARIKA TACHIBANA!!
WHAM POW

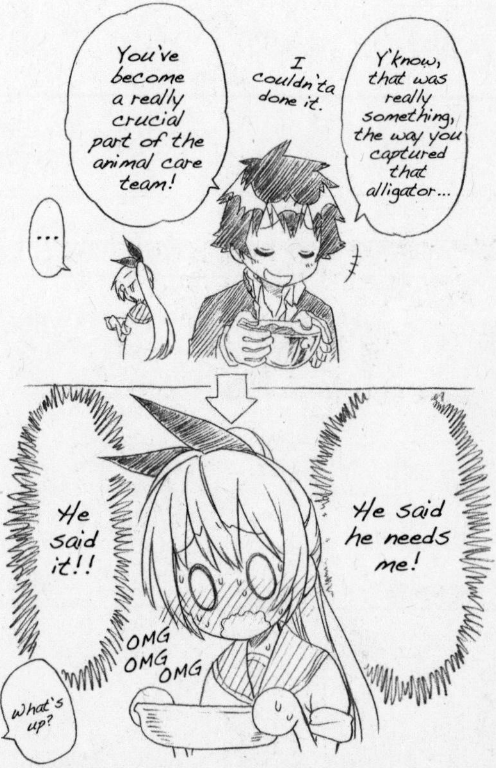
Y'know, that was really something, the way you captured that alligator...
I couldn'ta done it.
You've become a really crucial part of the animal care team!
...
He said he needs me!
He said it!!
OMG OMG OMG
What's up?

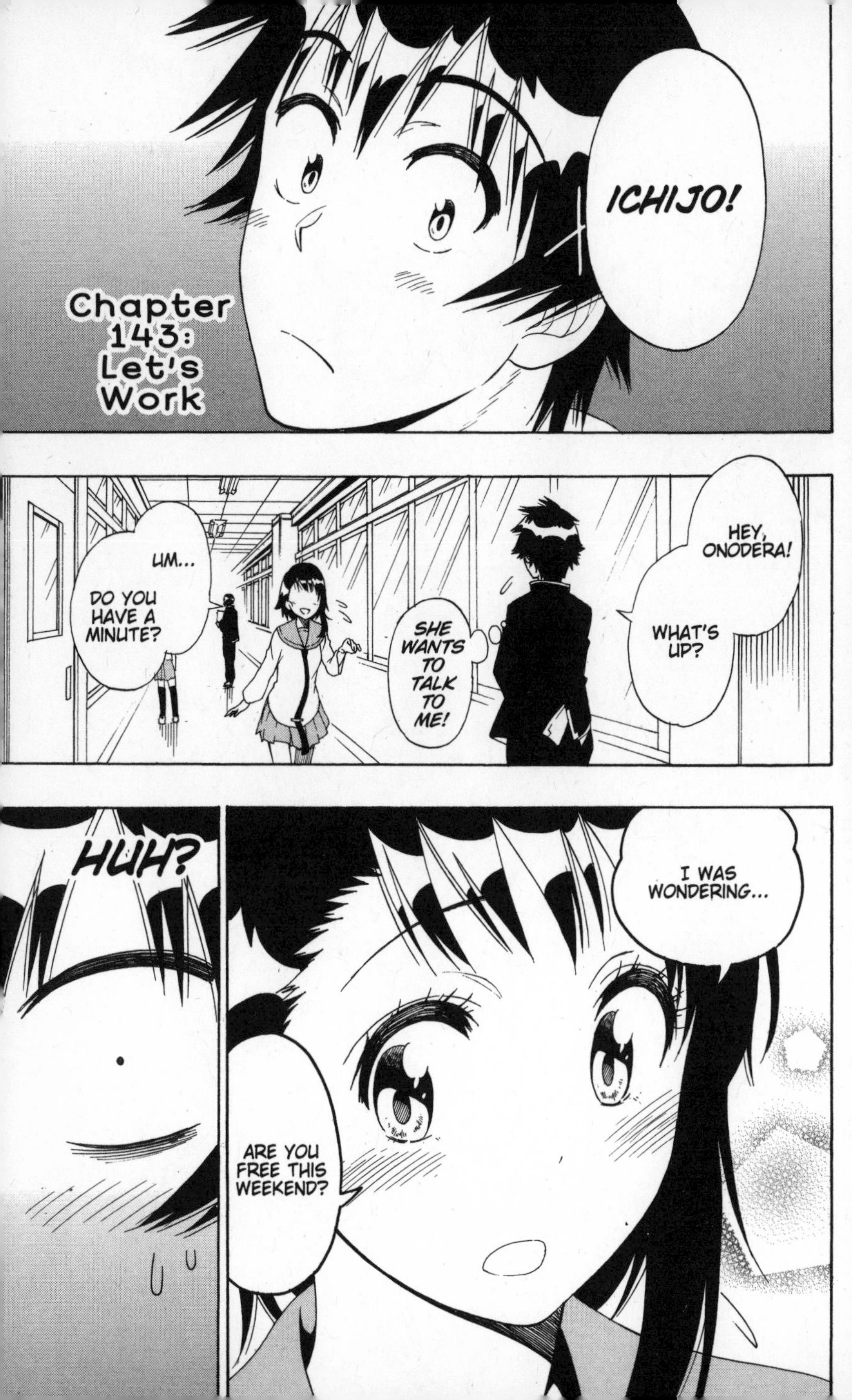
ICHIJO!
Chapter 143: Let's Work
HEY, ONODERA!
WHAT'S UP?
SHE WANTS TO TALK TO ME!
UM...
DO YOU HAVE A MINUTE?
I WAS WONDERING...
ARE YOU FREE THIS WEEKEND?
HUH?

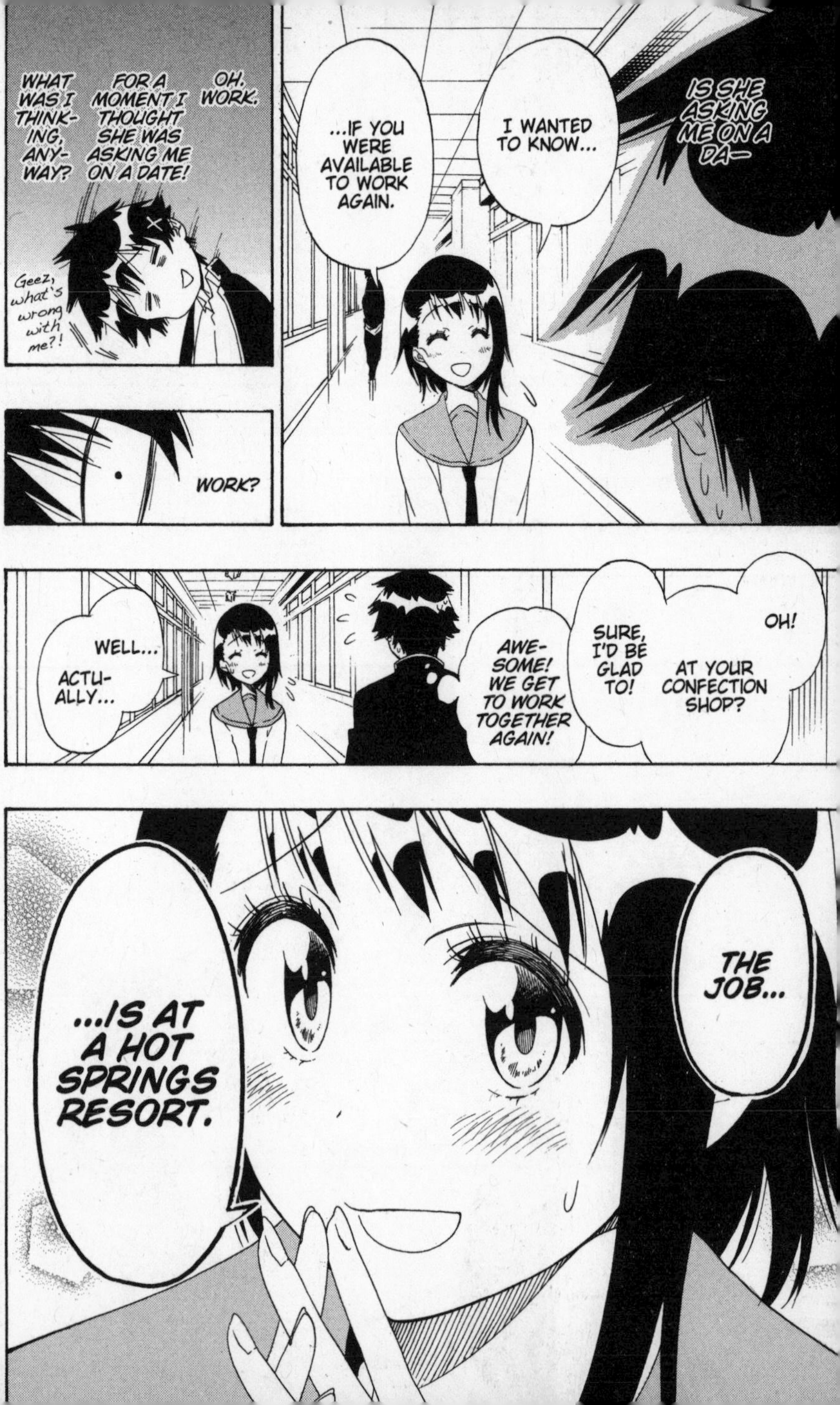
IS SHE ASKING ME ON A DA—
I WANTED TO KNOW...
...IF YOU WERE AVAILABLE TO WORK AGAIN.
OH. WORK.
FOR A MOMENT I THOUGHT SHE WAS ASKING ME ON A DATE!
WHAT WAS I THINKING, ANYWAY?
Geez, what's wrong with me?!
WORK?
OH!
AT YOUR CONFECTION SHOP?
SURE, I'D BE GLAD TO!
AWESOME! WE GET TO WORK TOGETHER AGAIN!
WELL...
ACTUALLY...
THE JOB...
...IS AT A HOT SPRINGS RESORT.

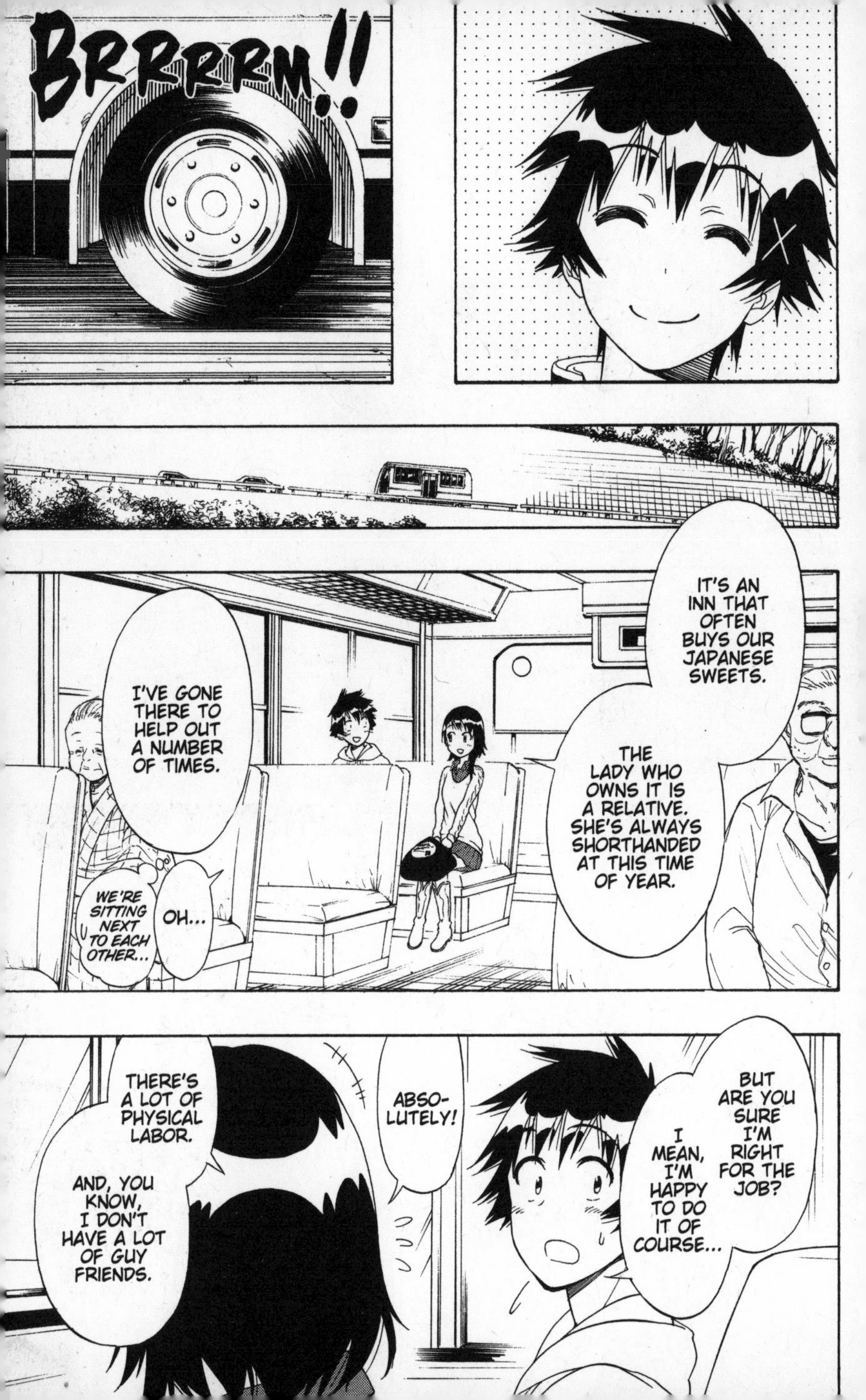
BRRRRM!!
IT'S AN INN THAT OFTEN BUYS OUR JAPANESE SWEETS.
THE LADY WHO OWNS IT IS A RELATIVE. SHE'S ALWAYS SHORTHANDED AT THIS TIME OF YEAR.
I'VE GONE THERE TO HELP OUT A NUMBER OF TIMES.
OH...
WE'RE SITTING NEXT TO EACH OTHER...
BUT ARE YOU SURE I'M RIGHT FOR THE JOB?
I MEAN, I'M HAPPY TO DO IT OF COURSE...
ABSOLUTELY!
THERE'S A LOT OF PHYSICAL LABOR.
AND, YOU KNOW, I DON'T HAVE A LOT OF GUY FRIENDS.

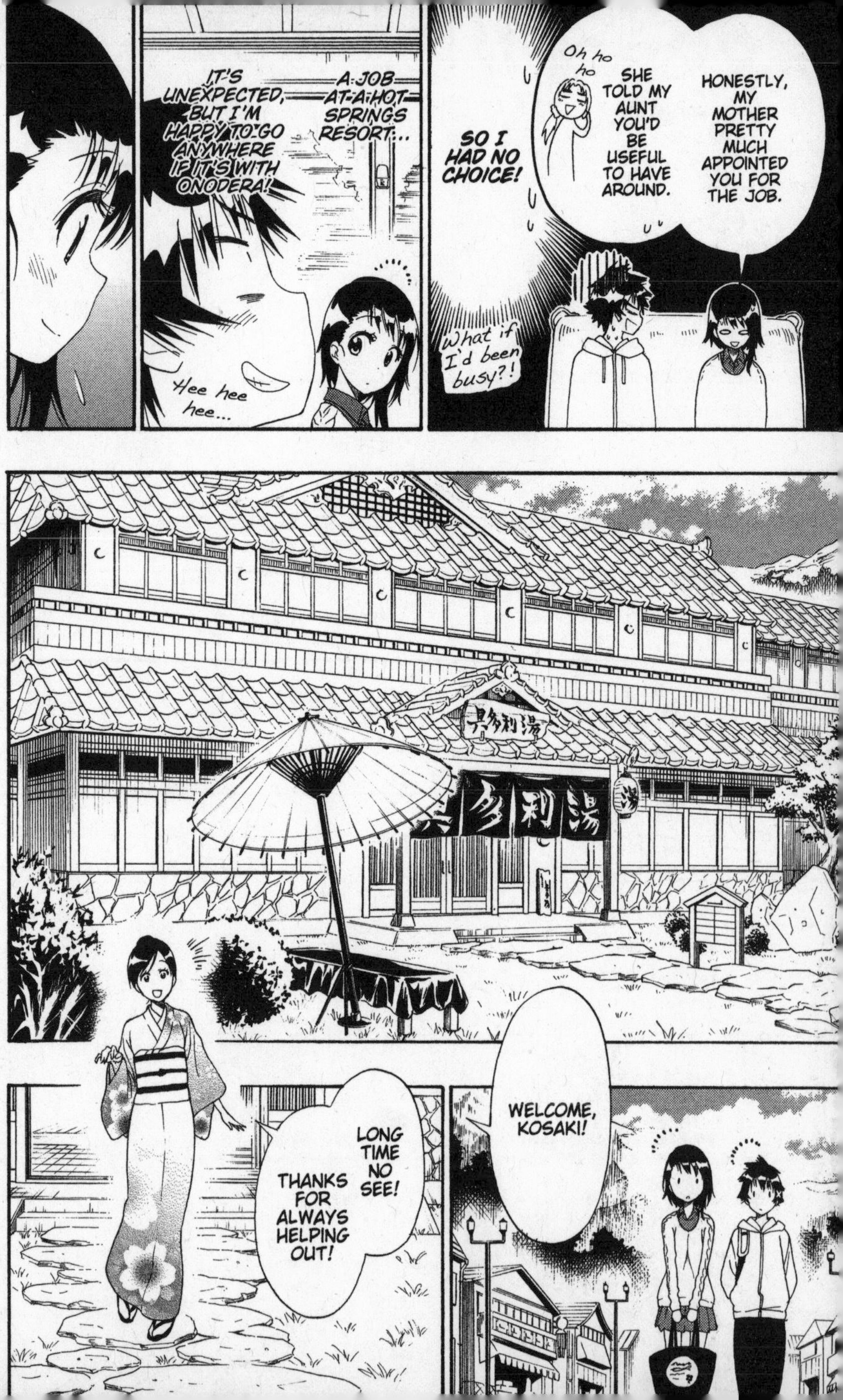
HONESTLY, MY MOTHER PRETTY MUCH APPOINTED YOU FOR THE JOB.
SHE TOLD MY AUNT YOU'D BE USEFUL TO HAVE AROUND.
Oh ho ho
SO I HAD NO CHOICE!
What if I'd been busy?!
A JOB AT A HOT SPRINGS RESORT...
IT'S UNEXPECTED, BUT I'M HAPPY TO GO ANYWHERE IF IT'S WITH ONODERA!
Hee hee hee...
WELCOME, KOSAKI!
LONG TIME NO SEE!
THANKS FOR ALWAYS HELPING OUT!

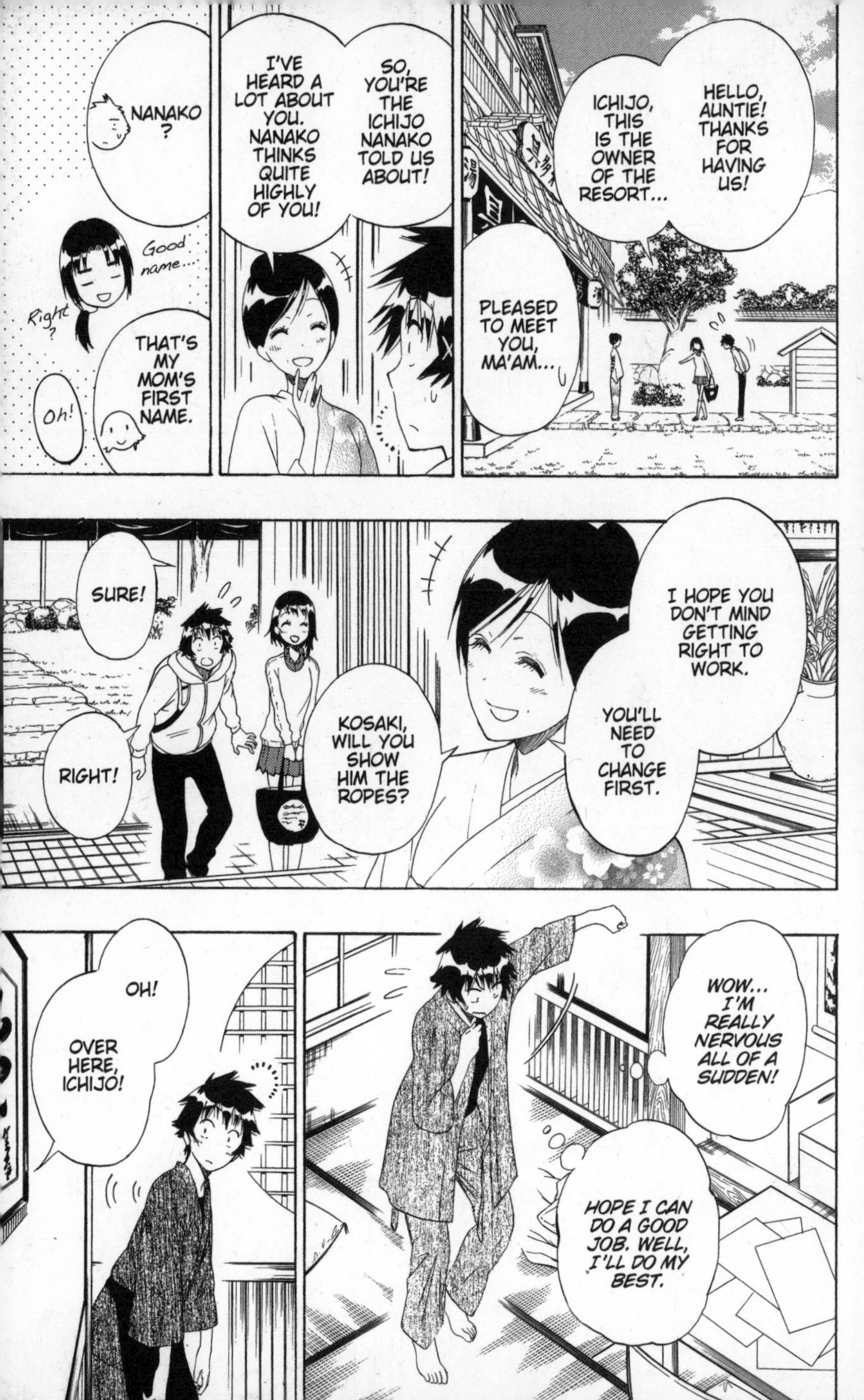
HELLO, AUNTIE! THANKS FOR HAVING US!
ICHIJO, THIS IS THE OWNER OF THE RESORT...
PLEASED TO MEET YOU, MA'AM...
SO, YOU'RE THE ICHIJO NANAKO TOLD US ABOUT!
I'VE HEARD A LOT ABOUT YOU. NANAKO THINKS QUITE HIGHLY OF YOU!
NANAKO?
THAT'S MY MOM'S FIRST NAME.
Oh!
Good name...
Right?
I HOPE YOU DON'T MIND GETTING RIGHT TO WORK.
YOU'LL NEED TO CHANGE FIRST.
KOSAKI, WILL YOU SHOW HIM THE ROPES?
SURE!
RIGHT!
WOW... I'M REALLY NERVOUS ALL OF A SUDDEN!
HOPE I CAN DO A GOOD JOB. WELL, I'LL DO MY BEST.
OH!
OVER HERE, ICHIJO!

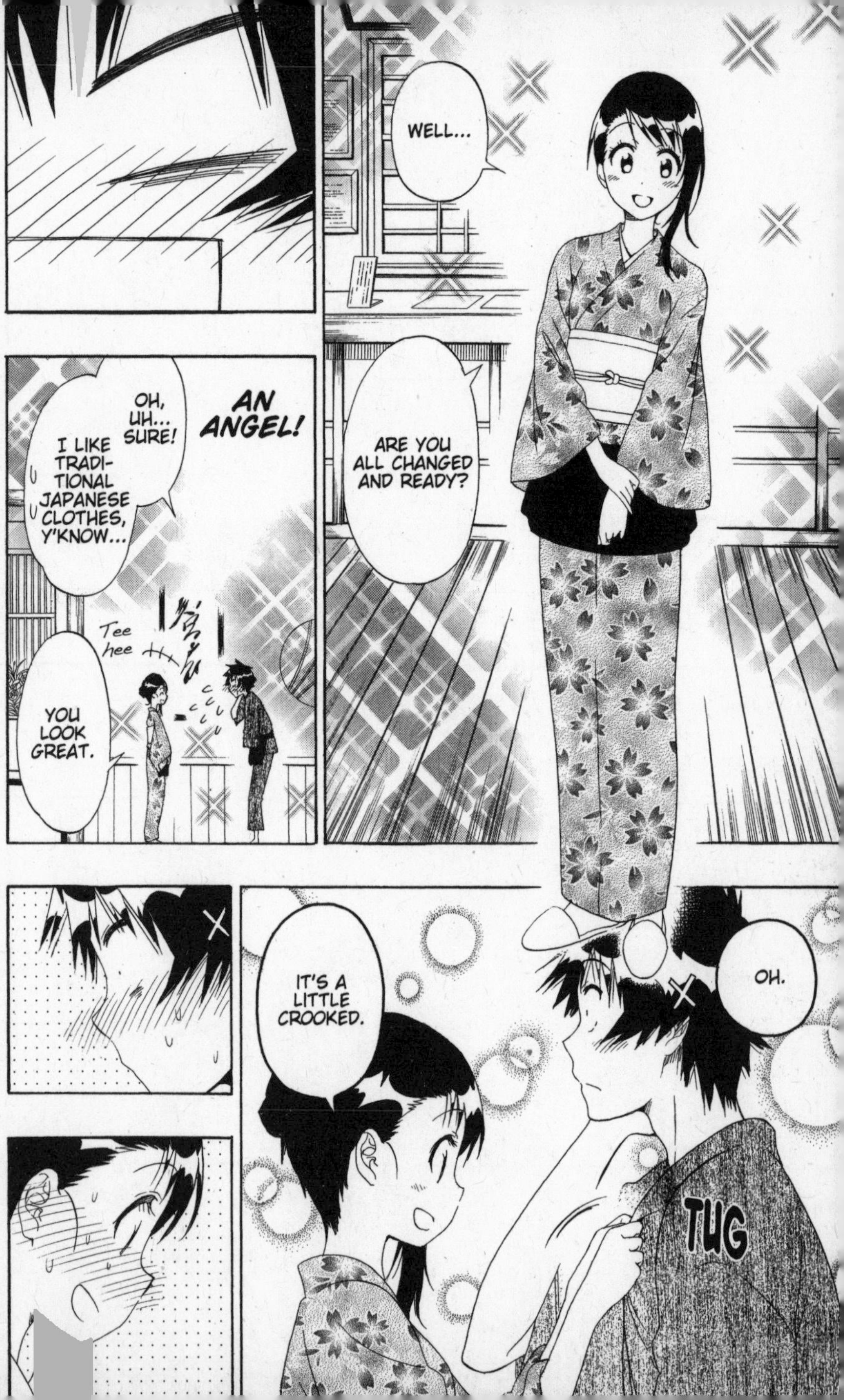
WELL...
ARE YOU ALL CHANGED AND READY?
AN ANGEL!
OH, UH... SURE!
I LIKE TRADI-TIONAL JAPANESE CLOTHES, Y'KNOW...
Tee hee
YOU LOOK GREAT.
OH.
IT'S A LITTLE CROOKED.
TUG

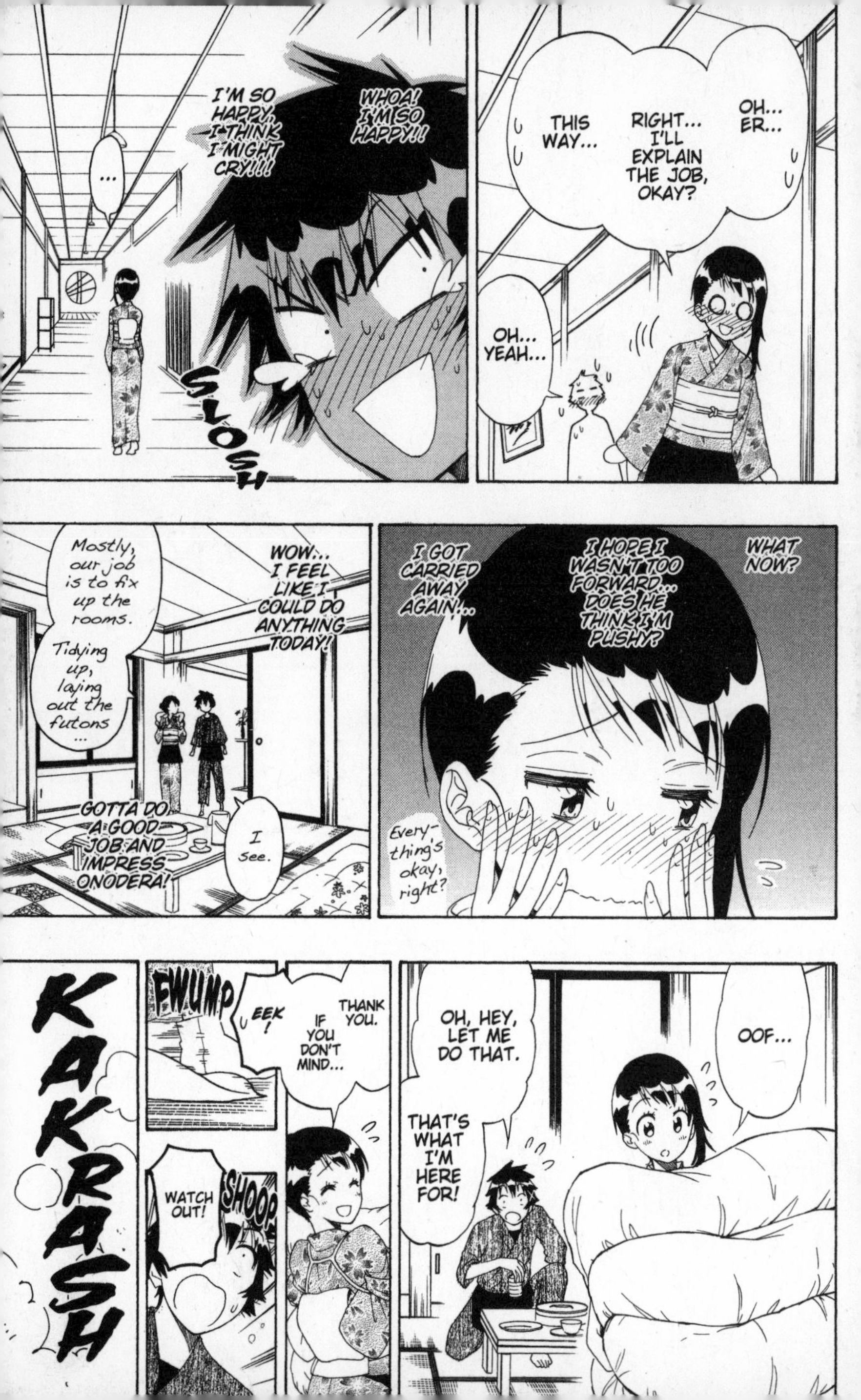

OH... ER...
RIGHT... I'LL EXPLAIN THE JOB, OKAY?
THIS WAY...
OH... YEAH...
WHOA! I'M SO HAPPY!!
I'M SO HAPPY, I THINK I MIGHT CRY!!!
SLOSH
...
WHAT NOW?
I HOPE I WASN'T TOO FORWARD... DOES HE THINK I'M PUSHY?
I GOT CARRIED AWAY AGAIN...
Every-thing's okay, right?
WOW... I FEEL LIKE I COULD DO ANYTHING TODAY!
Mostly, our job is to fix up the rooms.
Tidying up, laying out the futons...
GOTTA DO A GOOD JOB AND IMPRESS ONODERA!
I see.
OOF...
OH, HEY, LET ME DO THAT.
THAT'S WHAT I'M HERE FOR!
THANK YOU.
IF YOU DON'T MIND...
EEK!
FWUMP
SHOOP
WATCH OUT!
KAKRASH

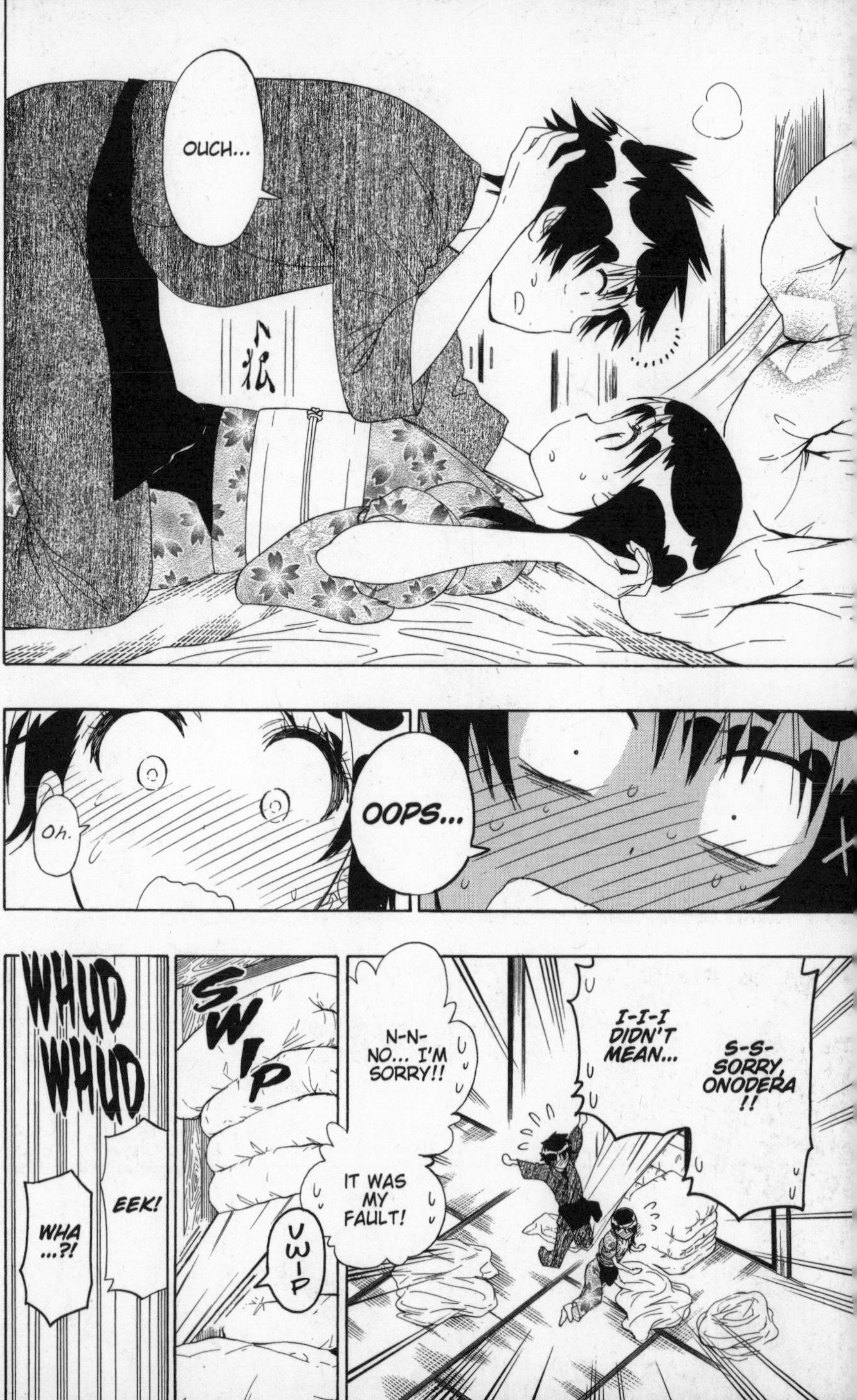
OUCH...
OOPS...
Oh.
S-S-SORRY, ONODERA!!
I-I-I DIDN'T MEAN...
N-N-NO... I'M SORRY!!
IT WAS MY FAULT!
UWIP
SWIP
WHUD WHUD
EEK!
WHA...?!

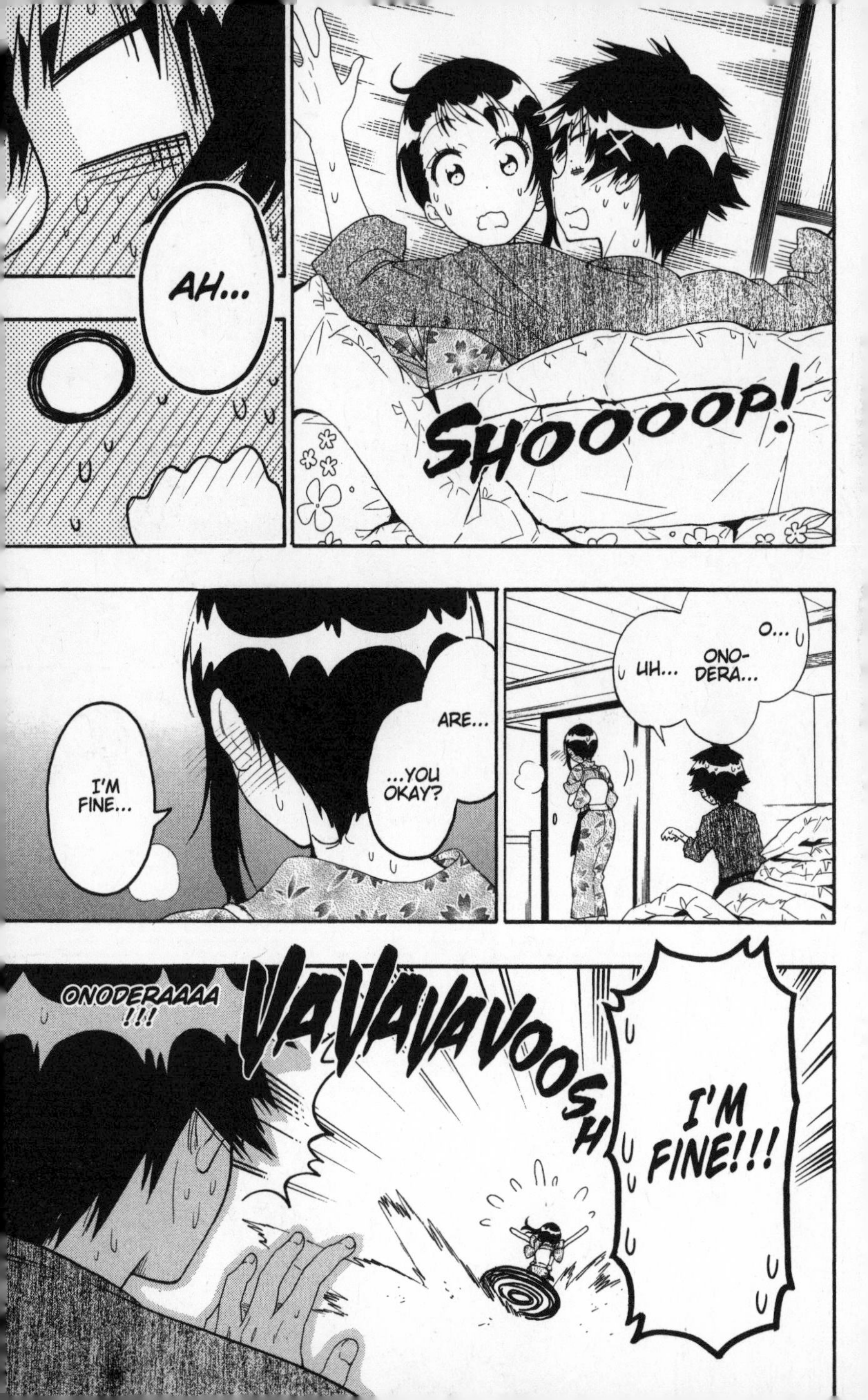
SHOOOOP!
AH...
O... ONO-DERA... UH...
ARE... ...YOU OKAY?
I'M FINE...
I'M FINE!!!
VAVAVAVOOSH
ONODERAAAA!!!

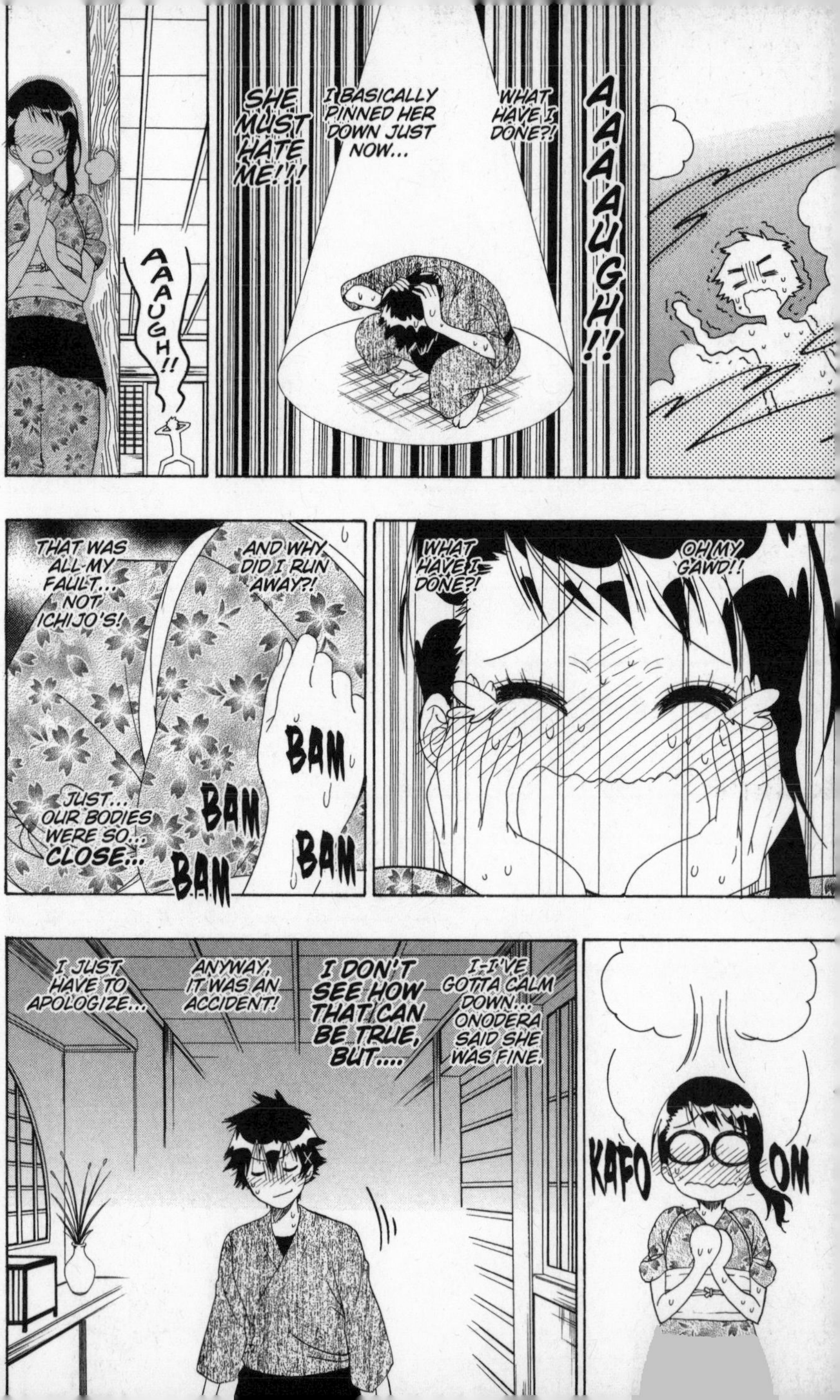
AAAAAUGH!!
WHAT HAVE I DONE?!
I BASICALLY PINNED HER DOWN JUST NOW...
SHE MUST HATE ME!!!
AAAUGH!!
OH MY GAWD!!
WHAT HAVE I DONE?!
AND WHY DID I RUN AWAY?!
THAT WAS ALL MY FAULT... NOT ICHIJO'S!
BAM
BAM
BAM
BAM
JUST... OUR BODIES WERE SO... CLOSE...
KAFOOM
I-I'VE GOTTA CALM DOWN... ONODERA SAID SHE WAS FINE.
I DON'T SEE HOW THAT CAN BE TRUE, BUT....
ANYWAY, IT WAS AN ACCIDENT!
I JUST HAVE TO APOLOGIZE...

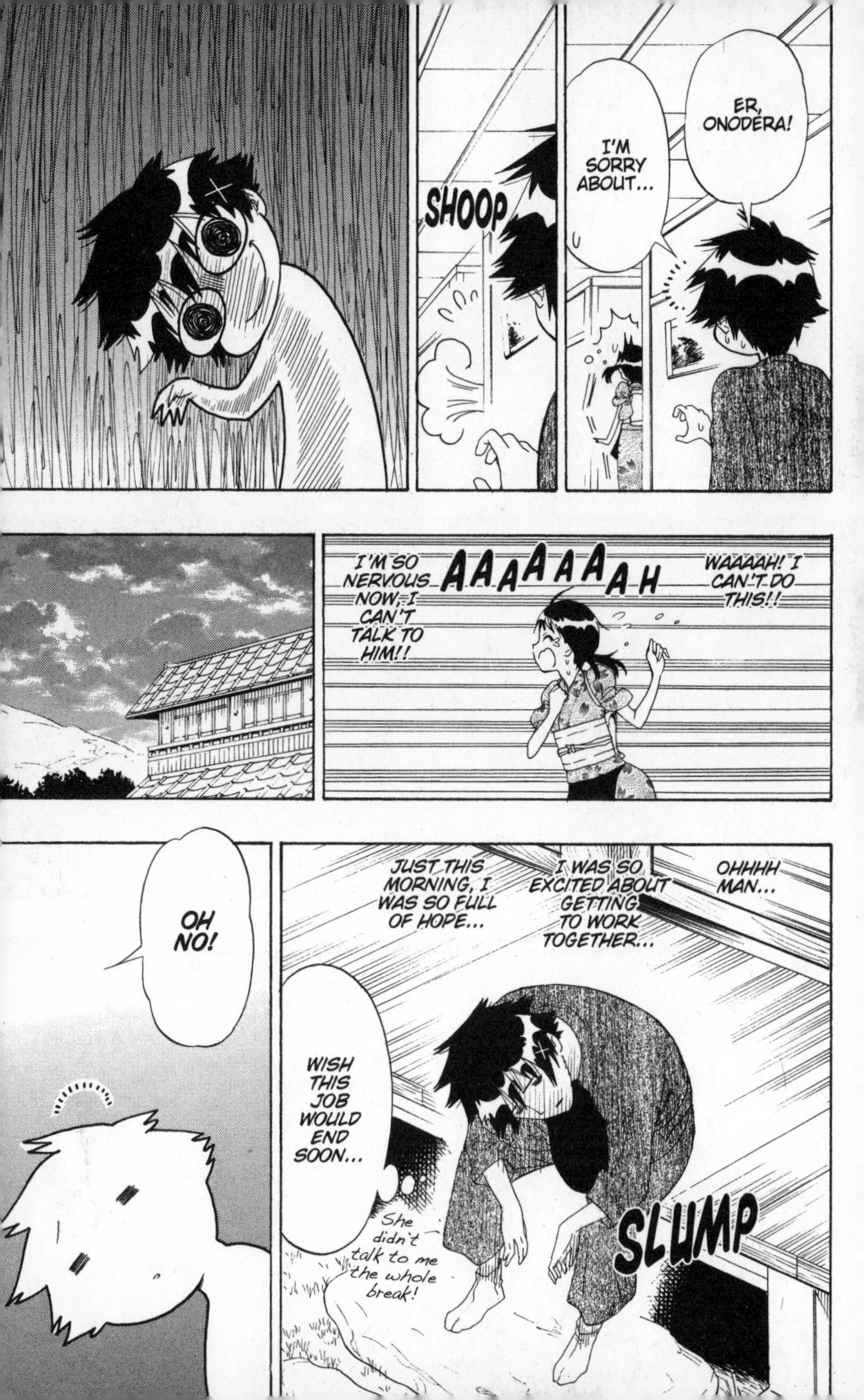
ER, ONODERA!
I'M SORRY ABOUT...
SHOOP
WAAAAH! I CAN'T DO THIS!!
AAAAAAAH
I'M SO NERVOUS NOW, I CAN'T TALK TO HIM!!
OHHHH MAN...
I WAS SO EXCITED ABOUT GETTING TO WORK TOGETHER...
JUST THIS MORNING, I WAS SO FULL OF HOPE...
SLUMP
WISH THIS JOB WOULD END SOON...
She didn't talk to me the whole break!
OH NO!

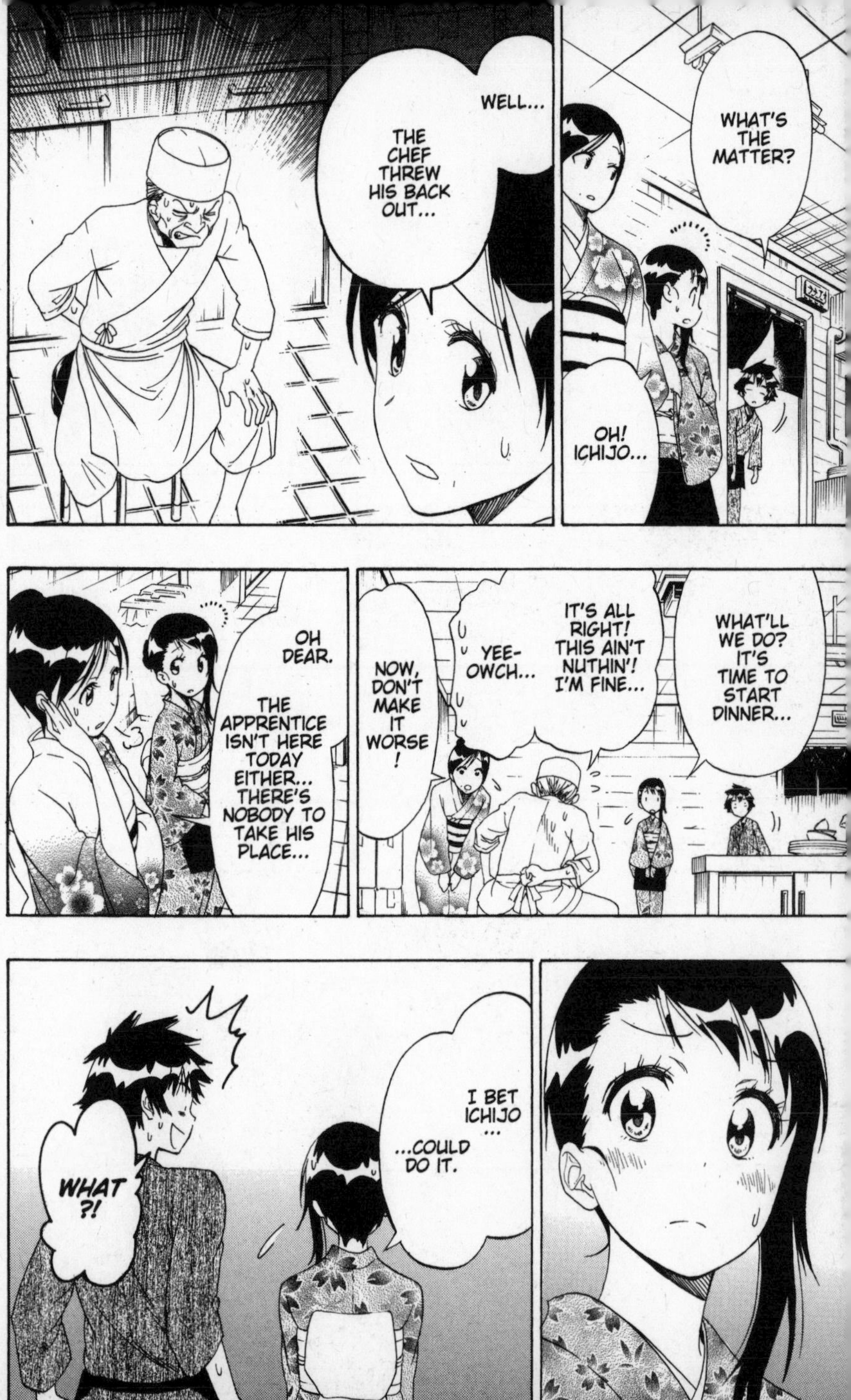
WHAT'S THE MATTER?
OH! ICHIJO...
WELL...
THE CHEF THREW HIS BACK OUT...
WHAT'LL WE DO? IT'S TIME TO START DINNER...
IT'S ALL RIGHT! THIS AIN'T NUTHIN'! I'M FINE...
YEE-OWCH...
NOW, DON'T MAKE IT WORSE!
OH DEAR.
THE APPRENTICE ISN'T HERE TODAY EITHER... THERE'S NOBODY TO TAKE HIS PLACE...
I BET ICHIJO...
...COULD DO IT.
WHAT?!

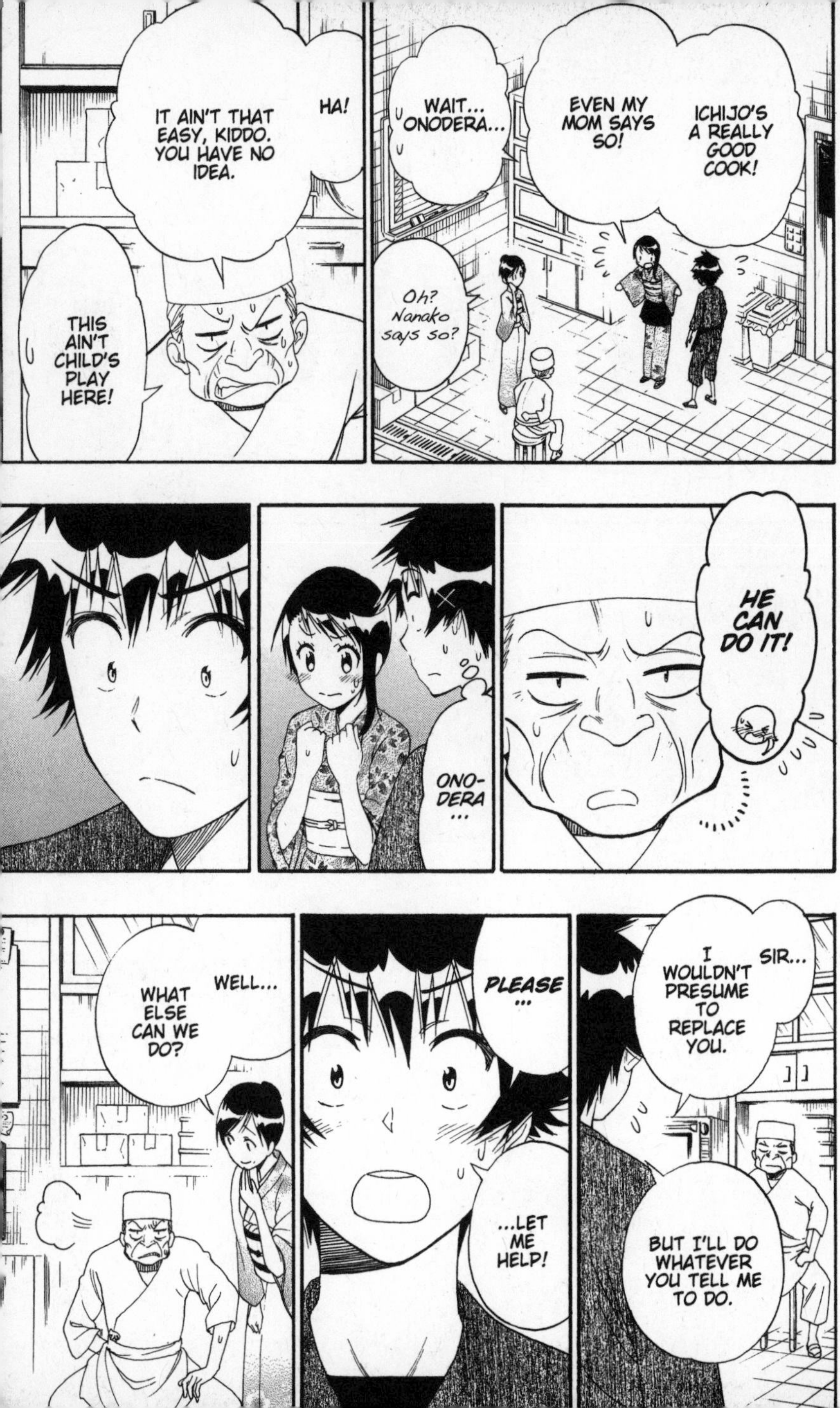
ICHIJO'S A REALLY GOOD COOK!
EVEN MY MOM SAYS SO!
WAIT... ONODERA...
Oh? Nanako says so?
HA!
IT AIN'T THAT EASY, KIDDO. YOU HAVE NO IDEA.
THIS AIN'T CHILD'S PLAY HERE!
HE CAN DO IT!
ONO-DERA...
SIR...
I WOULDN'T PRESUME TO REPLACE YOU.
BUT I'LL DO WHATEVER YOU TELL ME TO DO.
PLEASE...
...LET ME HELP!
WELL...
WHAT ELSE CAN WE DO?

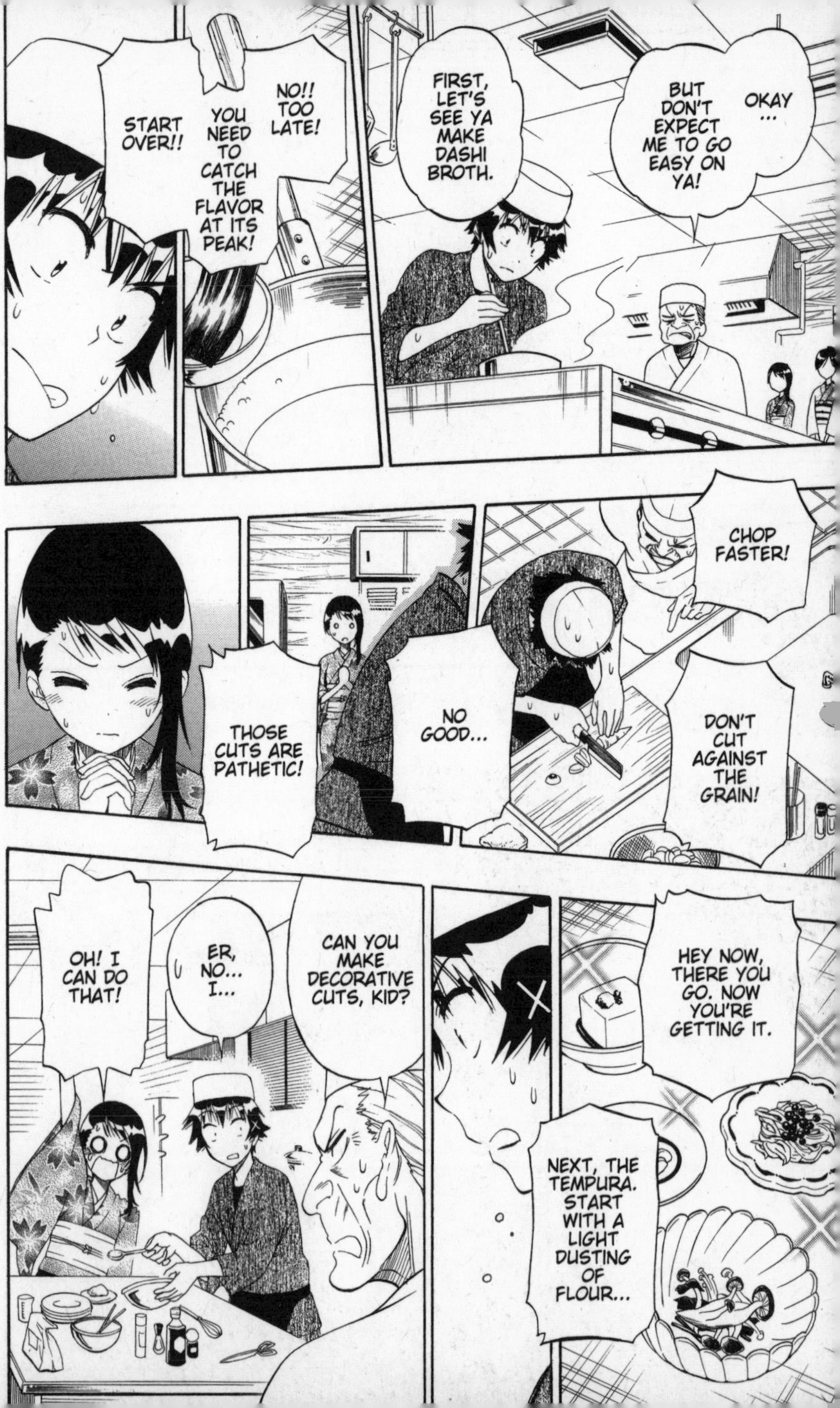
OKAY...
BUT DON'T EXPECT ME TO GO EASY ON YA!
FIRST, LET'S SEE YA MAKE DASHI BROTH.
NO!! TOO LATE!
YOU NEED TO CATCH THE FLAVOR AT ITS PEAK!
START OVER!!
CHOP FASTER!
DON'T CUT AGAINST THE GRAIN!
NO GOOD...
THOSE CUTS ARE PATHETIC!
HEY NOW, THERE YOU GO. NOW YOU'RE GETTING IT.
NEXT, THE TEMPURA. START WITH A LIGHT DUSTING OF FLOUR...
CAN YOU MAKE DECORATIVE CUTS, KID?
ER, NO... I...
OH! I CAN DO THAT!

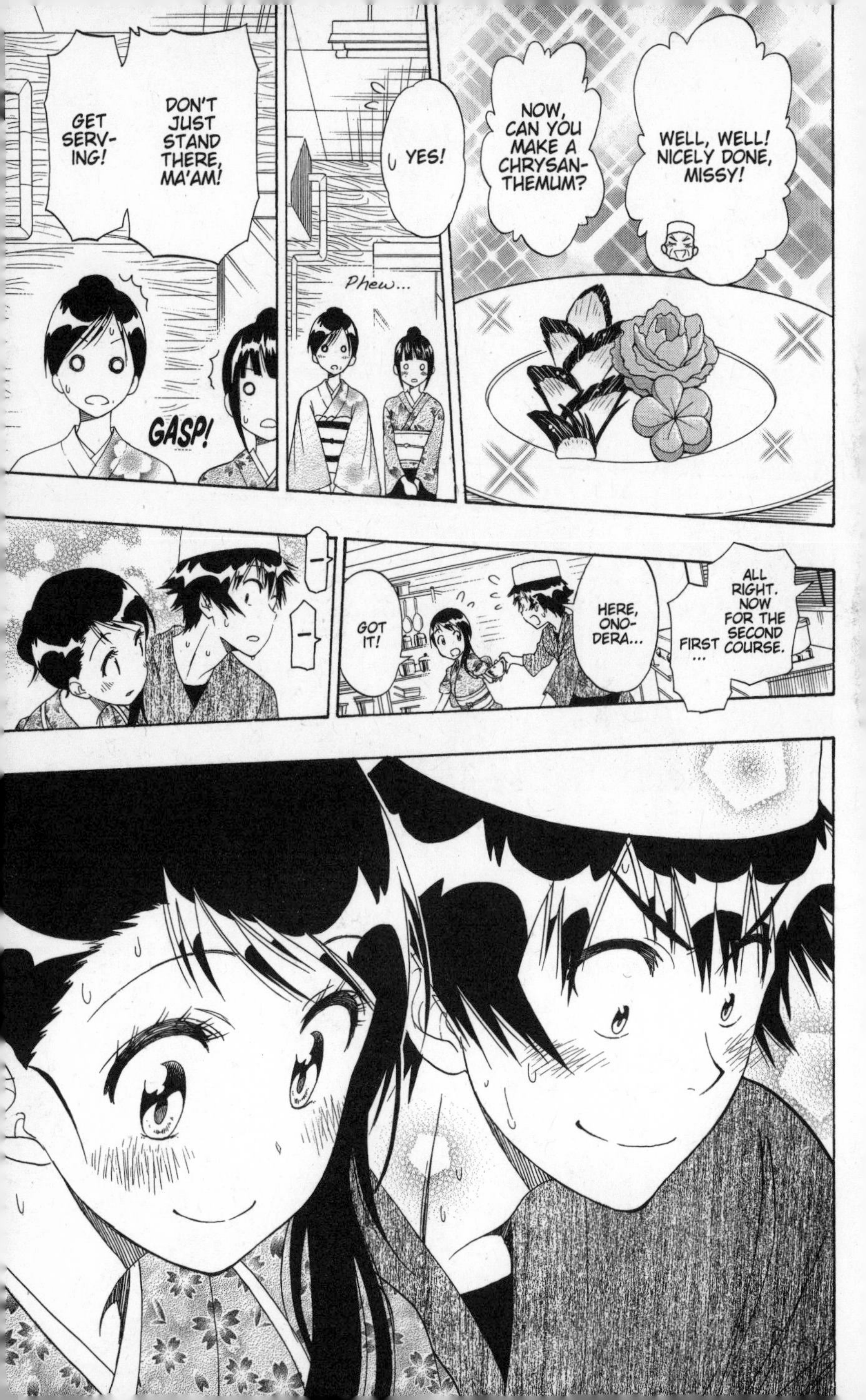

WELL, WELL! NICELY DONE, MISSY!
NOW, CAN YOU MAKE A CHRYSAN-THEMUM?
YES!
Phew...
DON'T JUST STAND THERE, MA'AM!
GET SERV-ING!
GASP!
ALL RIGHT. NOW FOR THE SECOND COURSE.
FIRST...
HERE, ONO-DERA...
GOT IT!

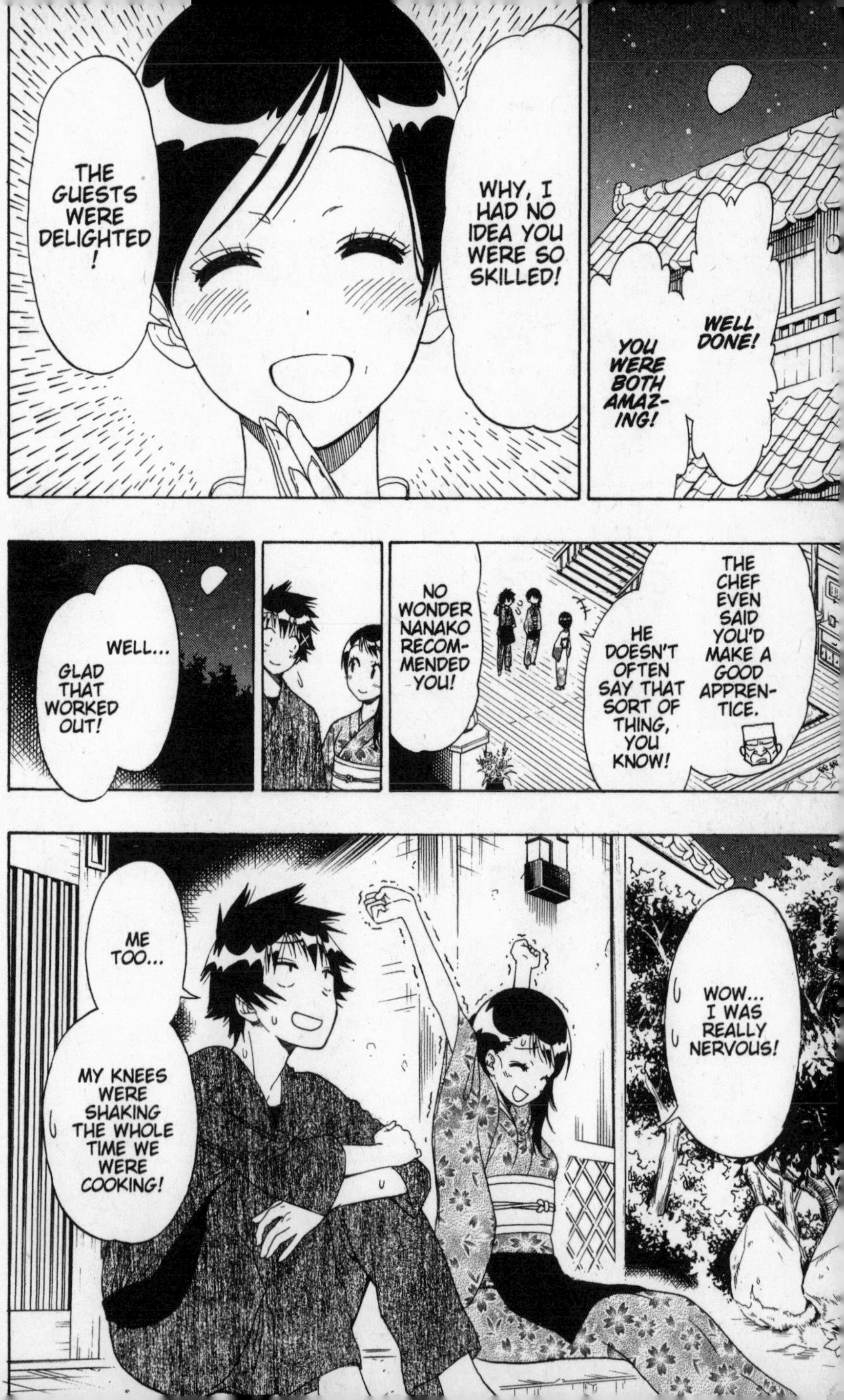
WELL DONE!
YOU WERE BOTH AMAZ-ING!
WHY, I HAD NO IDEA YOU WERE SO SKILLED!
THE GUESTS WERE DELIGHTED!
THE CHEF EVEN SAID YOU'D MAKE A GOOD APPREN-TICE.
HE DOESN'T OFTEN SAY THAT SORT OF THING, YOU KNOW!
NO WONDER NANAKO RECOM-MENDED YOU!
WELL... GLAD THAT WORKED OUT!
WOW... I WAS REALLY NERVOUS!
ME TOO...
MY KNEES WERE SHAKING THE WHOLE TIME WE WERE COOKING!

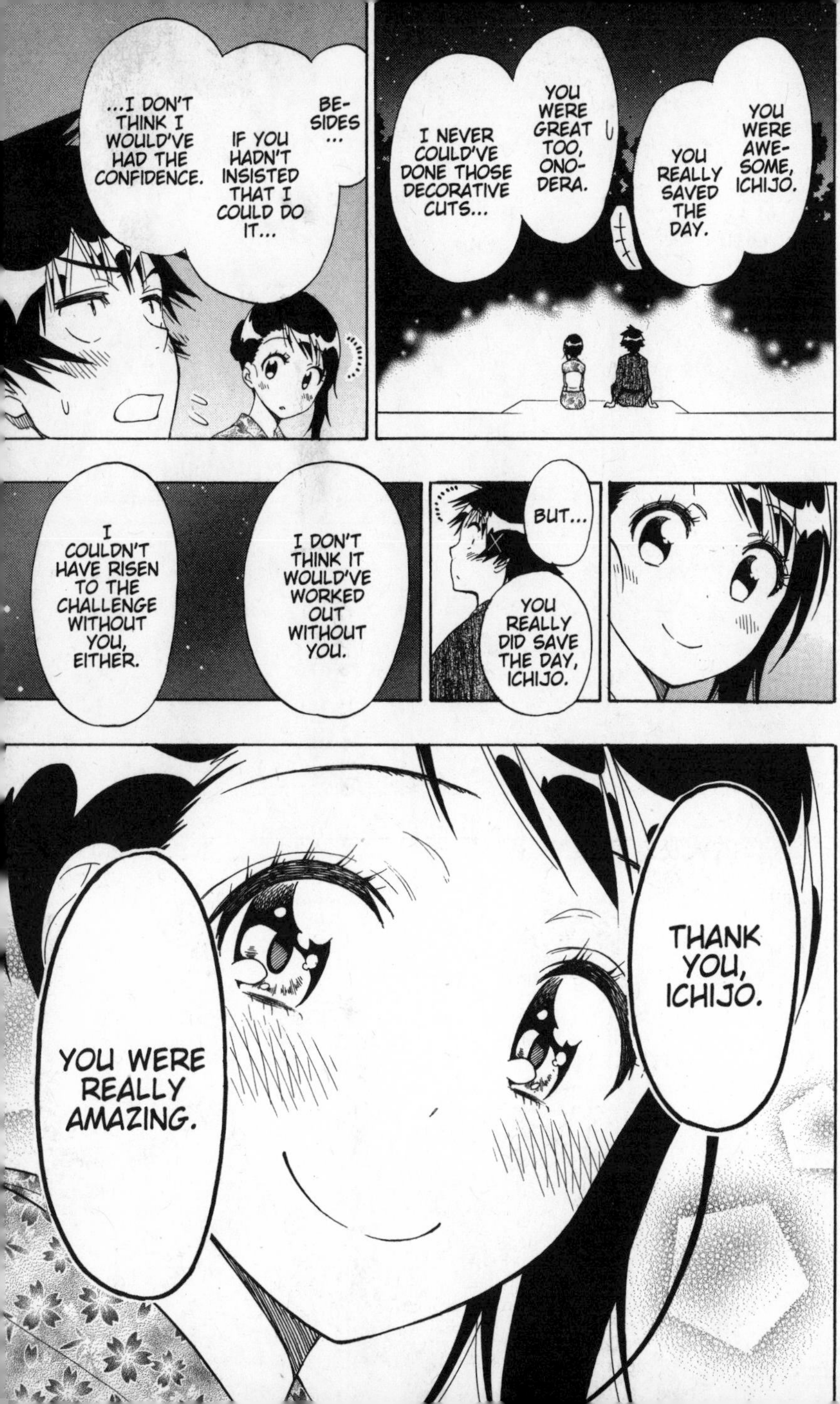
YOU WERE AWE-SOME, ICHIJO.
YOU REALLY SAVED THE DAY.
YOU WERE GREAT TOO, ONO-DERA.
I NEVER COULD'VE DONE THOSE DECORATIVE CUTS...
BE-SIDES...
IF YOU HADN'T INSISTED THAT I COULD DO IT...
...I DON'T THINK I WOULD'VE HAD THE CONFIDENCE.
BUT...
YOU REALLY DID SAVE THE DAY, ICHIJO.
I DON'T THINK IT WOULD'VE WORKED OUT WITHOUT YOU.
I COULDN'T HAVE RISEN TO THE CHALLENGE WITHOUT YOU, EITHER.
THANK YOU, ICHIJO.
YOU WERE REALLY AMAZING.

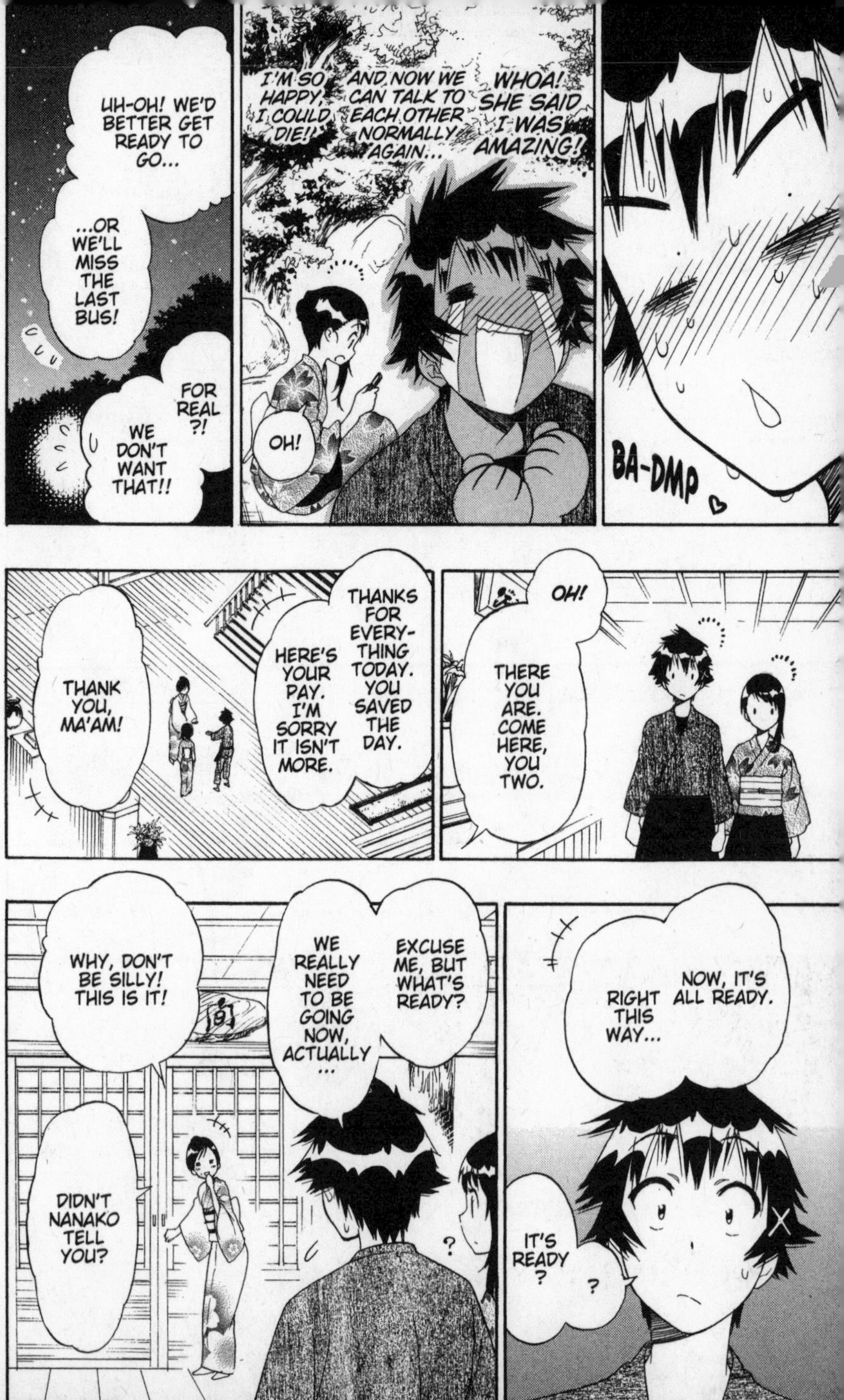
BA-DMP
WHOA! SHE SAID I WAS AMAZING!
AND NOW WE CAN TALK TO EACH OTHER NORMALLY AGAIN...
I'M SO HAPPY, I COULD DIE!!
OH!
UH-OH! WE'D BETTER GET READY TO GO...
...OR WE'LL MISS THE LAST BUS!
FOR REAL?!
WE DON'T WANT THAT!!
OH!
THERE YOU ARE. COME HERE, YOU TWO.
THANKS FOR EVERYTHING TODAY. YOU SAVED THE DAY.
HERE'S YOUR PAY. I'M SORRY IT ISN'T MORE.
THANK YOU, MA'AM!
NOW, IT'S ALL READY.
RIGHT THIS WAY...
IT'S READY?
EXCUSE ME, BUT WHAT'S READY?
WE REALLY NEED TO BE GOING NOW, ACTUALLY...
WHY, DON'T BE SILLY! THIS IS IT!
DIDN'T NANAKO TELL YOU?

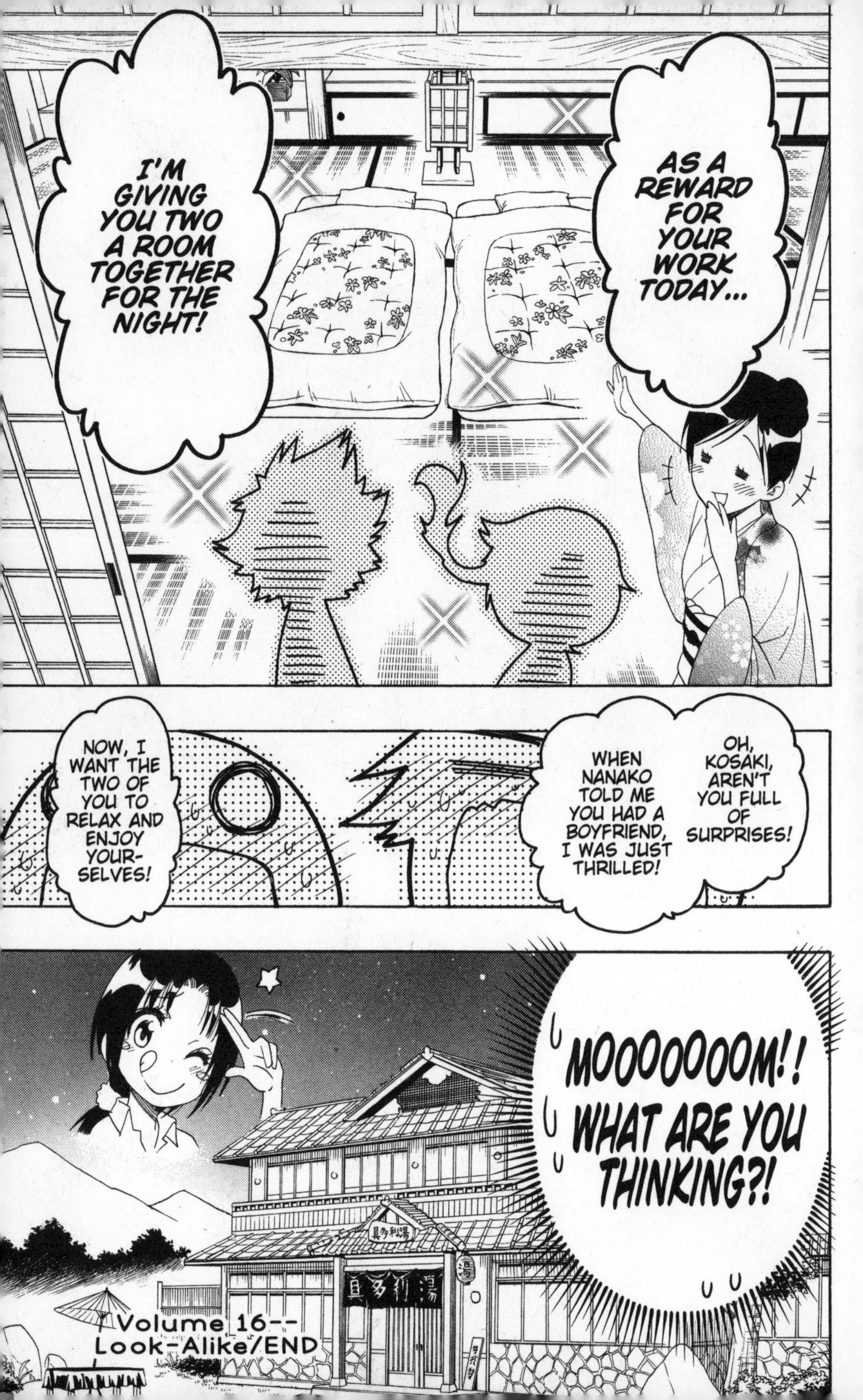
AS A REWARD FOR YOUR WORK TODAY...
I'M GIVING YOU TWO A ROOM TOGETHER FOR THE NIGHT!
OH, KOSAKI, AREN'T YOU FULL OF SURPRISES!
WHEN NANAKO TOLD ME YOU HAD A BOYFRIEND, I WAS JUST THRILLED!
NOW, I WANT THE TWO OF YOU TO RELAX AND ENJOY YOUR-SELVES!
MOOOOOOOM!! WHAT ARE YOU THINKING?!
具多利湯
Volume 16--Look-Alike/END

BONUS COMIC!!

☆That's How Haru Is...☆

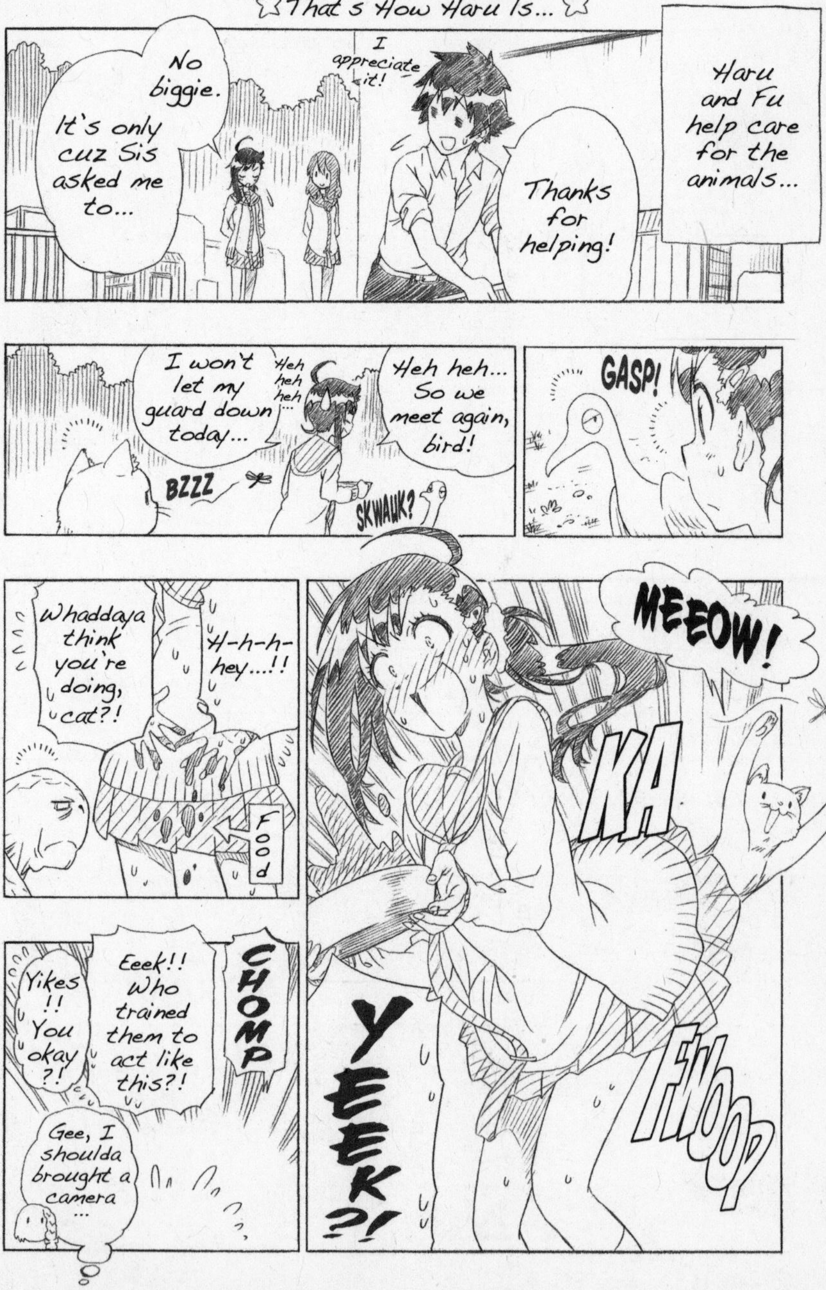

Haru and Fu help care for the animals...
Thanks for helping!
I appreciate it!
No biggie.
It's only cuz Sis asked me to...
GASP!
Heh heh... So we meet again, bird!
Heh heh heh...
I won't let my guard down today...
BZZZ
SKWAUK?
MEEOW!
KA
FWOOP
YEEEK?!
H-h-h-hey...!!
Whaddaya think you're doing, cat?!
Food
CHOMP
Eeek!! Who trained them to act like this?!
Yikes!! You okay?!
Gee, I shoulda brought a camera...

BONUS COMIC!!

☆ That's How Yui Is... ☆

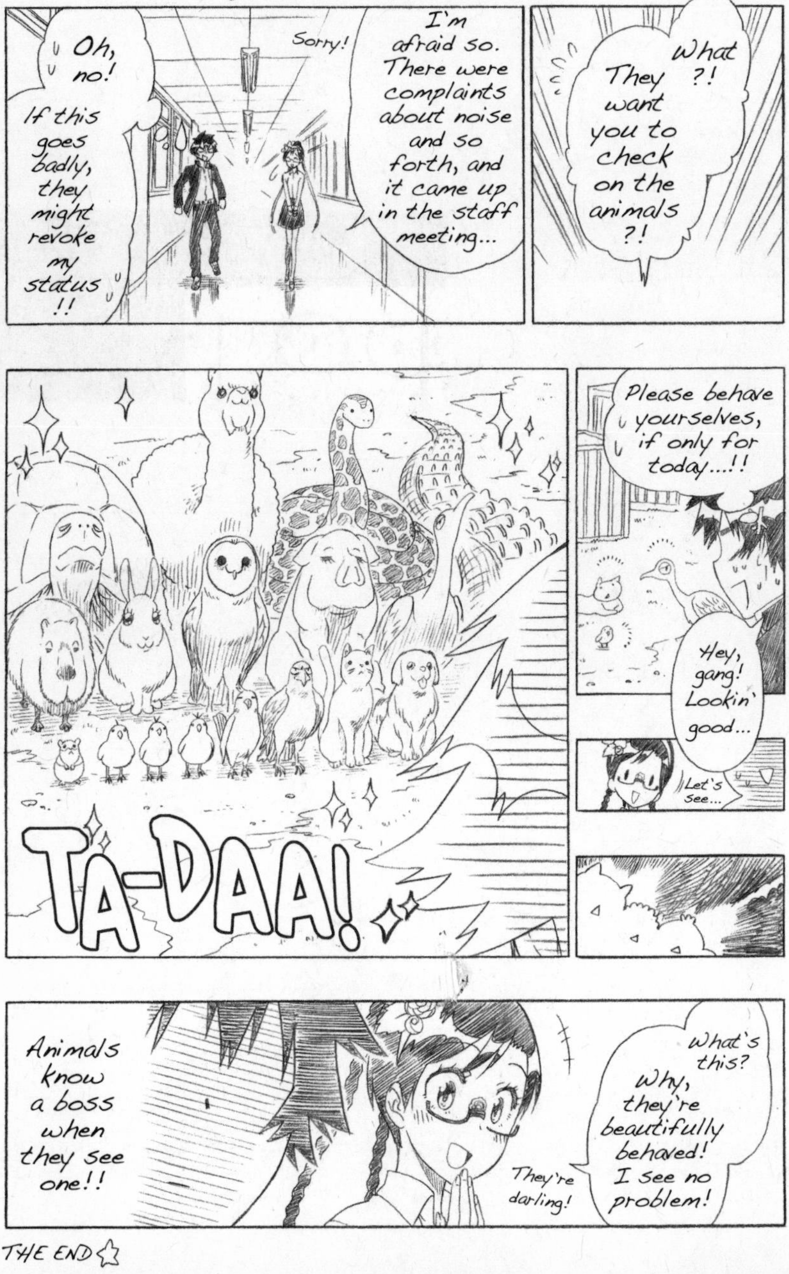
What?! They want you to check on the animals?!
I'm afraid so. There were complaints about noise and so forth, and it came up in the staff meeting...
Sorry!
Oh, no! If this goes badly, they might revoke my status!!
Please behave yourselves, if only for today....!!
Hey, gang! Lookin' good...
Let's see...
TA-DAA!
What's this? Why, they're beautifully behaved! I see no problem!
They're darling!
Animals know a boss when they see one!!

THE END ☆

You're Reading the
WRONG WAY!

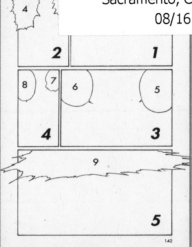

NISEKOI reads from right to left, starting in the upper-right corner. Japanese is read from right to left, meaning that action, sound effects, and word-balloon order are completely reversed from English order.